COMMUNICATION SKILLS FOR OSCES

RACHEL WAMBOLDT (MBBS BScN)
and NIAMH LOUGHRAN (MRes)
Norwich Medical School, University of East Anglia

Scion

© **Scion Publishing Ltd, 2017**

First published 2017

All rights reserved. No part of this book may be reproduced or transmitted, in any form or by any means, without permission.

A CIP catalogue record for this book is available from the British Library.

ISBN 9781907904998

Scion Publishing Limited

The Old Hayloft, Vantage Business Park, Bloxham Road, Banbury OX16 9UX, UK

www.scionpublishing.com

Important Note from the Publisher

The information contained within this book was obtained by Scion Publishing Ltd from sources believed by us to be reliable. However, while every effort has been made to ensure its accuracy, no responsibility for loss or injury whatsoever occasioned to any person acting or refraining from action as a result of information contained herein can be accepted by the authors or publishers.

Readers are reminded that medicine is a constantly evolving science and while the authors and publishers have ensured that all dosages, applications and practices are based on current indications, there may be specific practices which differ between communities. You should always follow the guidelines laid down by the manufacturers of specific products and the relevant authorities in the country in which you are practising.

Although every effort has been made to ensure that all owners of copyright material have been acknowledged in this publication, we would be pleased to acknowledge in subsequent reprints or editions any omissions brought to our attention.

Registered names, trademarks, etc. used in this book, even when not marked as such, are not to be considered unprotected by law.

Illustrations by Graeme Chambers

Typeset by Phoenix Photosetting, Chatham, Kent, UK

Printed in the UK

Contents

List of contributors vi
Preface vii
About the authors viii
Abbreviations ix

Section 1: Introduction to communication skills

1 How to use this book and get the most out of role play 1
2 The importance of communication skills in healthcare 4
3 Application of the Calgary–Cambridge Model 7
4 General approach to information gathering 10
5 Information giving and shared decision making 17

Section 2: System-focused communication

6 Perfecting the systems review 23
7 Psychiatry 27
8 Neurology 55
9 Orthopaedics and rheumatology 69
10 Ophthalmology 83
11 Cardiovascular medicine 91
12 Respiratory medicine 105
13 Ears, nose and throat 116
14 Gastroenterology and hepatology 128
15 Nephrology and urology 147
16 Obstetrics and gynaecology 162
17 Dermatology 185
18 Endocrinology 194

Section 3: Special situations in communication

19 Older people's medicine 205
20 Paediatrics 220
21 Taking a drug history 231
22 The consultation through an interpreter 241
23 Safeguarding vulnerable adults and children 245
24 Breaking bad news 255
25 Communicating error and conflict resolution 262
26 Communicating risk 271
27 Consenting for a procedure 278
28 Talking to colleagues 285

References 292
Index 293

List of contributors

Many thanks to our incredible contributors

Liban Ahmed
Neurology
Norwich Medical School

Dr Sabrina Ahmed
Dermatology
Mid Essex Hospital
King's College London
Medical School

Dr Shafi Balal
Ophthalmology
North Central Thames
Foundation School
Barts and the London
School of Medicine

Dr Florence Beckett
Consenting a procedure
North-east Thames
Foundation School
Norwich Medical School

Joseph Beecham
Older people's medicine
Norwich Medical School

Dr Georgina Clark
Paediatrics
East Anglia Foundation School
Norwich Medical School

Dr Rhianna Davies
*Consultation through
an interpreter*
Addenbrooke's Hospital,
Cambridge University Trust
Imperial College London
Medical School

Dr Stuart Foster
Perfecting the systems review
North-east Thames
Foundation School
Leicester Medical School

Bruno Gnaneswaran
Neurology
Norwich Medical School

James Gooding
*Orthopaedics and
rheumatology*
Norwich Medical School

Clare Hannah
*Orthopaedics and
rheumatology*
Norwich Medical School

Dr Srikirti Kodali
*Gastroenterology and
hepatology*
Addenbrooke's Hospital,
Cambridge University Trust
Barts and the London School
of Medicine

Ryan Love
Endocrinology
Norwich Medical School

Joe Pang
Taking a drug history
Norwich Medical School

Dr Michael Parker
*Communicating error and
conflict resolution*
East Anglia Foundation School
Norwich Medical School

Dr Louise Patterson
Talking with colleagues
East Anglia Foundation School
Norwich Medical School

James Platt
Taking a drug history
Norwich Medical School

Dr Helen Porte
Paediatrics
Royal Manchester
Children's Hospital
University of Cambridge
Medical School

Dr Alina Sanda Gomez
Nephrology and urology
East Anglia Foundation School
Norwich Medical School

Rupert Smith
Ear, nose and throat
Norwich Medical School

Vinitha Soudarajan
*Psychiatry, substance misuse
and motivational interviewing*
Norwich Medical School

Dr Oscar Swift
*Gastroenterology and
hepatology*
Core Medical Trainee
Cambridge University
Hospitals NHS Foundation
Trust

Tom Syer
Endocrinology
Norwich Medical School

Daniah Thomas
*Psychiatry, substance misuse
and motivational interviewing*
Cardiff University School
of Medicine

Harriet Tuite-Dalton
Older people's medicine
Norwich Medical School

Dr Adam Walton
Safeguarding
East Anglia Foundation School
Southampton Medical School

Dr Ben Warner
Nephrology and urology
CMT East Anglia
Norwich Medical School

Dr Gemma Williams
Obstetrics and gynaecology
North East Thames
Foundation School
University College London
Medical School

Preface

Communication skills are the cornerstone of being a good doctor. Medical schools have now recognized that the ability to communicate effectively with patients is one of the most important skills that a student learns in medical school. Not only are medical schools providing more opportunities to learn these skills in a safe and judgment-free setting (usually in small groups with actors) but they are now testing these skills in the OSCE setting.

The aim of this book is to provide a practical and clinical approach to communicating with patients. It is written *by* medical students and junior doctors *for* medical students and junior doctors. *Communication Skills for OSCEs* will focus on preparing you for the examination setting but in doing so, will provide the building blocks for good communication skills throughout your career. It is unique in that it takes the focus away from the theoretical aspects of communication and makes communication skills more simple and accessible.

We hope that this book serves as an excellent resource for your OSCE revision and preparation for history taking on the wards. Please take the time to read the introductory section as it will provide a good base for your future learning. We also encourage you to practise, practise, practise. It is the best way to improve this valuable skill.

Rachel Wamboldt and Niamh Loughran
November 2016

About the authors

DR RACHEL WAMBOLDT

Dr Rachel Wamboldt is a graduate, with course distinction, from Norwich Medical School at the University of East Anglia. She hails from Windsor, Ontario, Canada where she trained as a registered nurse at the University of Windsor and obtained her bachelor of science in nursing degree with a minor in psychology. Upon graduation she was honoured as class Valedictorian. Dr Wamboldt worked for two years as an emergency room nurse in rural Manitoba, Canada, primarily with Aboriginal communities, prior to starting medical school. It was here that she continued to develop her passion for medicine and learnt the importance of effective patient communication. Whilst at Norwich Medical School she founded the UEA Cardiology Society, helped establish the British Undergraduate Cardiology Association (BUCA) and became involved in academic writing. She hopes to continue her career in Canada as an internist.

NIAMH LOUGHRAN (MRES)

Niamh Loughran is a final-year medical student in Norwich Medical School at the University of East Anglia. Originally from Armagh, Northern Ireland, Niamh has always prided herself on her academic performance, achieving the top A-level results in her secondary school, and was awarded the All-Ireland Bursary for outstanding academic achievement. During her intercalated year, Niamh completed a masters in clinical science at the University of East Anglia, during which time she carried out research into haematological malignancies and became a published author. Whilst at medical school, Niamh was on the founding committee for the UEA Cardiology Society and has been an active member of Norwich Medics Rugby Football Club ladies' team. In the future Niamh aims to follow a career in specialty medicine.

Abbreviations

6CIT	six-item cognitive impairment test	FTU	fingertip unit
A&E	Accident and Emergency (department)	FY1	foundation year 1 doctor
		GBM	glomerular basement membrane
ABTS	Abbreviated Mental Test Score	GCA	giant cell arteritis
ACE	angiotensin-converting enzyme	GCS	Glasgow Coma Scale
AD	Alzheimer's disease	GH	growth hormone
ADH	antidiuretic hormone	GI	gastrointestinal
ADLs	activities of daily living	GP	General Practitioner
AF	atrial fibrillation	GPCOG	General Practitioner Assessment of Cognition
AKI	acute kidney injury		
AMTS	Abbreviated Mental Test Score	GTN	glyceryl trinitrate
ANA	antinuclear antibody	GU	genito-urinary
ANCA	anti-neutrophil cytoplasmic antibody	HIV	human immunodeficiency virus
APD	automated peritoneal dialysis	HPV	human papillomavirus
AS	ankylosing spondylitis	IBD	inflammatory bowel disease
BMD	bone mineral density	IBS	irritable bowel syndrome
BP	blood pressure	ICE	ideas, concerns and expectations
BPH	benign prostatic hyperplasia	ICP	intracranial pressure
BPPV	benign positional paroxysmal vertigo	IHD	ischaemic heart disease
BRVO	branch retinal vein occlusion	IM	intramuscular
CAPD	continuous ambulatory peritoneal dialysis	IMB	intermenstrual bleeding
		IMCA	Independent Mental Capacity Advocate
CBT	cognitive behavioural therapy		
CLD	chronic liver disease	IOP	intraocular pressure
CN	cranial nerve	ITU	intensive therapy unit
CNS	central nervous system	IUD	intrauterine device
COC	combined oral contraception	IUS	intrauterine system
COCP	combined oral contraceptive pill	IV	intravenous
COPD	chronic obstructive pulmonary disease	KUB	kidneys, ureters and bladder
		LACS	lacunar stroke syndrome
CPR	cardiopulmonary resuscitation	LBD	Lewy body dementia
CRS	chronic rhinosinusitis	LH	luteinizing hormone
CST	communication skills training	LOC	loss of consciousness
CT	computerized tomography	LPA	Lasting Power of Attorney
DI	diabetes insipidus	LUTS	lower urinary tract symptoms
DM	diabetes mellitus	LVH	left ventricular hypertrophy
DMARD	disease-modifying antirheumatic drug	MCP	metacarpal phalangeal joint
		MDI	metered dose inhaler
DNAR	do not attempt resuscitation	MDT	multidisciplinary team
DOB	date of birth	MEN	multiple endocrine neoplasia
DVLA	Driver and Vehicle Licensing Agency	MI	myocardial infarction
DVT	deep vein thrombosis	MMR	measles, mumps and rubella
ECG	electrocardiogram	MMSE	Mini-Mental State Examination
ECT	electroconvulsive therapy	MSK	musculoskeletal
ENT	ear, nose and throat	NAI	non-accidental injury
EPO	Emergency Protection Order	NBM	nil by mouth
FSH	follicle-stimulating hormone	NSAID	non-steroidal anti-inflammatory drug
FTD	fronto-temporal dementia	OCD	obsessive–compulsive disorder

OD	(in prescribing) omni die (daily)	**SLE**	systemic lupus erythematosus
ON	(in prescribing) omni nocte (at night)	**SOB**	shortness of breath
OPM	older people's medicine	**SOL**	space-occupying lesion
OSCE	objective structured clinical examination	**SSRI**	selective serotonin reuptake inhibitor
OTC	over-the-counter	**STI**	sexually transmitted infection
PACS	partial anterior circulation stroke	**SUNCT**	short-acting unilateral neuralgiform headache with conjunctival injection and tearing
PCB	post-coital bleeding		
PCOS	polycystic ovarian syndrome		
PD	Parkinson's disease	**TACS**	total anterior circulation stroke
PID	pelvic inflammatory disease	**TCA**	tricyclic antidepressants
PMB	post-menopausal bleeding	**TCC**	transitional cell carcinoma
PMR	polymyalgia rheumatica	**TDS**	ter die sumendus ([to be taken] three times a day)
PMS	premenstrual syndrome		
PO	per os (by mouth)	**TFT**	thyroid function test
POCS	posterior circulation stroke	**TIA**	transient ischaemic attack
PR	per rectum	**TORCH**	toxoplasmosis, other, rubella, cytomegalovirus and herpes
PRN	(in prescribing) pro re nata (as required)		
		TRUS	trans-rectal ultrasound
PSA	prostate-specific antigen	**TTH**	tension type headache
PSP	progressive supranuclear palsy	**TURBT**	transurethral resection of bladder tumour
PVD	peripheral vascular disease		
QDS	quarter die sumendus ([to be taken] four times a day)	**TURP**	transurethral resection of the prostate
RA	rheumatoid arthritis	**U&E**	urea and electrolytes
RAS	renal artery stenosis	**UC**	ulcerative colitis
RAV	recognizing, acknowledging, validating	**USS**	ultrasound scan
SBAR	Situation, Background, Assessment, Recommendation	**UTI**	urinary tract infection
		UV	ultraviolet
SIRS	systemic inflammatory response syndrome	**VTE**	venous thromboembolism
		VUJ	vesiculo-ureteric junction

1

How to use this book and get the most out of role play

NIAMH LOUGHRAN

1.1 How to use this book

OSCE-style examinations are now the most commonly used method of testing medical students' knowledge and ability to interact with patients. OSCE stations usually last between 5 and 15 minutes and range from demonstrating the correct venipuncture procedure to the emergency management of an acute asthma attack.

The aim of this book is to help you pass your consultation skills stations in your OSCEs and to give you advice which you can carry with you throughout your careers. Consultation skills stations are extremely common and important. They usually have the following structure:

- Outside your station you will be given a scenario. You will usually have around 1–2 minutes to read the scenario and begin to formulate a plan in your head.
- Once you enter the station you will be met by an actor (or more than one) who will be playing the role of the patient. There will also be an examiner present.
- After entering the station you should immediately address the 'patient' and begin your consultation.

> **OSCE TIP:** Approach each OSCE scenario, whether practising or during the exams, as if it is real life. The more involved you get with the consultation process, the more success you will have in these stations.

Section 1 of this book (*Chapters 1–5*) gives you an overview of the structure which you need to employ when carrying out different styles of consultations.

Section 2 (*Chapters 6–18*) will then take you through the main systems in the body and show you how to take a focused system-specific history. In addition to this we also provide you with information on some of the major topics within each system to help you when it comes to 'giving information'.

Section 3 (*Chapters 19–28*) will look at specific scenarios such as 'breaking bad news', 'dealing with an angry patient', and so on. These can come up in OSCEs and are also situations which you will have to deal with when working as a doctor.

At the end of each chapter we have provided you with some 'practice scenarios'. The purpose of these is to give you the opportunity to employ the skills you have learnt from the associated chapter in an actual consultation. Get together with a small group of your peers with one of you being the patient, one being the examiner and one carrying out the consultation.

1.1.1 Mark schemes

To further help you with this we have created some sample mark schemes. These can be found by clicking on the Resources tab at www.scionpublishing.com/CommsOSCEs. Use these when practising the scenarios to make sure you are covering everything. It may also be helpful to use the 'Summary of Key Points' within each chapter to make sure you're keeping on track.

1.2 How to get the most out of role play

Communication skills are often learnt at medical school through simulation learning, which commonly occurs through role play.

Role play involves practising real-life situations which you may encounter when working as a doctor, giving you the opportunity to gain insight into how you might cope when communicating with patients in these situations. It is an extremely advantageous and effective way of practising your communication skills, as it gives you the chance to face some of the most difficult consultation situations in a safe environment.

Typically when carrying these out in medical school you will be with a small group of your peers under the supervision of an experienced tutor. The 'patient' in these situations will be a skilled actor.

Within these sessions each of you will take turns at being the 'doctor', and real-life situations will be constructed with the actor taking on the persona of a particular patient. Effective role playing during these times will provide you with the opportunity to augment the skills you will read about in this book and have been taught in the lecture theatre.

One vital aspect of communication skills is the non-verbal cues elicited from patients. These include the patient's body language or tone of voice, eye contact or lack of. These are things which we and others can tell you to look out for, but in a role play situation you will be able to actively identify these cues and you will be able to explore how they might affect a consultation. You may even be able to observe how the patient's body language can change as your communication with them improves.

Not only will you be able to practise essential communication skills, but you will also be able to obtain constructive feedback from the tutor, actor and your peers. This provides you with the chance to continue to develop your skills and to adopt different, more effective strategies.

As mentioned, role play offers a safe environment to practise your skills. If at any point you don't know how to deal with a development in the consultation or you simply can't think of where to go next with it, you are free to stop the consultation and ask advice from the tutor and your peers, without feeling embarrassed. It provides you with opportunities to try multiple different techniques to see which strategies work best and so enables you to efficiently learn how to manage certain situations.

Role play can sometimes be seen as a stressful and unnatural situation for some people. However, by being put 'on the spot' as you are when you are required to act out a scenario with the actor, you will be able to develop some effective strategies to deal with the different stressors you encounter. You will then be able to employ these methods in your communication skills, whether in an OSCE-style situation or real life.

One essential aspect of ensuring you get the most out of these sessions is to actively participate. These are stressful situations, and it is tempting to not volunteer and to simply observe how others do it. Although it is important to observe your peers and learn from what they did well and didn't do well, you won't truly know how you will cope with these situations or how you will perform under pressure unless you go for it.

Once you have taken part in a role play scenario, the next important step is to reflect on this interaction and on what feedback you were given. Reflection is a key aspect of getting the most out of the experience; remember to reflect on what went well, as well as what didn't go well. It will do no good to dwell on areas where you believe you made a mistake, although these are important to acknowledge. Remember to think back on areas where you felt you handled or explained something very well. Consider why you think this went so well; what was it that you did? Can you incorporate this into future consultations?

These exercises will help you to identify your strengths and weaknesses. After these sessions you should leave with a greater sense of self-awareness. You now know the areas you perhaps need to do more work on, but you also know where your strengths lie, so be confident in these areas!

1.2.1 Tips for how to get the most out of role play

- Actively participate – don't just sit on the fence!
- Treat it as though it is a real-life situation – tune in to your emotions and the 'patient's' emotions.
- Take on the feedback from those observing you – incorporate this into future consultations.
- Give constructive feedback to your peers and ask them to give you some in return. You can only get better by learning where you are going wrong.
- Reflect on what went well and what didn't – be aware of your strengths and weaknesses.
- Learn from observing your peers – you may pick up some excellent techniques.

REMEMBER

These exercises are not just for timetabled sessions but also for when you're practising for your OSCEs. It is important to get together with a small group of your peers and construct your own consultation scenarios. By doing this you can incorporate all the points outlined above and continue to develop your communication skills. To get the most out of this, ensure you make it like an OSCE station with a timer in place and use the example scenarios at the end of each of the chapters in this book as though they are OSCE scenarios. By practising your communication skills in the ways outlined above you will appear more competent and organized in your OSCE stations.

Use the practice scenarios at the end of each chapter and the sample mark schemes online (at www.scionpublishing.com/CommsOSCEs) to help you with this.

2

The importance of communication skills in healthcare

NIAMH LOUGHRAN

2.1 The journey of communication skills

Communication in healthcare was once governed by a paternalistic attitude in healthcare professionals, whereby it was assumed that the doctor, nurse or other healthcare professional knew best. Decisions would be made on behalf of patients without informing them or discussing their own thoughts and feelings with regard to their own health needs. Indeed, patients weren't really seen as people in their own right, but rather as the 'symptoms' they were presenting with, and the doctor's only job was to make a correct diagnosis and initiate the treatment they thought best.

Fortunately the world of communication in healthcare has now changed. There has been a shift in the balance of power away from medical paternalism, towards a collaborative partnership between the doctor and patient. It has become increasingly recognized that healthcare is underpinned by effective communication and that doctor–patient communication is vital in providing top-quality clinical practice.

Nowadays, rather than the doctor being seen as the only expert in the room, the patient is seen as the expert when it comes to their own health. After all, they are the ones in the best position to tell the healthcare professional about their health complaints and their reasons for seeking help.

2.2 Communication skills as a core clinical skill

Aims of communication skills training (CST):
- To recognize the importance of communication skills as an essential clinical procedure;
- To enable students and professionals to communicate effectively and empathetically with patients;
- To give students confidence in their consultations with patients, by providing them with the ability to utilize appropriate communication skills in specific medical situations.

The practice of communication skills is now acknowledged as a core clinical skill, in the same way as practical procedures such as cannulation and system examinations. In fact, when consultations are viewed as a healthcare procedure, they are the most commonly performed procedure you will carry out in your medical vocation, with doctors conducting as many as 150000 consultations in a typical career.

An appropriate, effective medical consultation can point the way towards the correct diagnosis much more than medical investigations, as it is during the consultation that the exact problems for which the patient is seeking help become clear and where most diagnostic decisions come from. As a result of the growing knowledge of the importance of communication skills, communication skills training (CST) is now an established part of the curriculum in medical schools all over the country.

Research in this area has shown the efficacy of this component of the curriculum, with Hargie stating that, "there is overwhelming evidence that, when used in a systematic, coordinated and informed fashion, CST is indeed an effective training medium".[1] CST gives students and healthcare professionals alike the opportunity to turn medical theory into practice, and demonstrate that how we communicate is just as important as what we say.

The ultimate goal of CST is to develop students' practical skills in communication to enable them to communicate effectively and empathetically with patients.

2.3 Why communication skills are so important

We've been talking a great deal about how important communication skills are, and how they are central to effective clinical practice, but you might be asking, why is this? How do we know it is worth placing so much emphasis on communication skills in our training? Well, we now know that effective communication has been found to improve patient satisfaction, recall, understanding, adherence and overall outcomes of care.

A specific example of this was seen from research from the 1970s, which found that when patients were offered specific information about the level of pain which they may experience and procedures which they may undergo prior to and during an operation, this resulted in the patients suffering less post-operative pain and having a faster recovery time than those who were not given such information.

Indeed, research has shown the presence of a strongly positive relationship between healthcare teams' communication skills and patients' capabilities to follow through with their treatment regimens, improve their self-management of chronic conditions and adopt preventative health behaviours.

All of these improved outcomes can be put down to the simplest of factors in communication, such as the doctor listening more attentively to the patients' concerns, identifying exactly what pieces of information they wish to know and having that information provided to them at an appropriate rate and level.

People are living longer and so the average age of the population is increasing. As a result of this it is now a very common situation for patients to present to their doctor with a number of co-morbidities, rather than just the one problem. In these situations it is best to put your pen down, move away from your computer screen and listen to the patient, and make decisions on where to go next together with the patient.

How you talk to patients and how you elicit a history from them can influence the patients' overall experience of healthcare. How a consultation is conducted can impact on the amount of information the patient discloses to you; you could take a very focused physical history and as a result end up neglecting to ask the patient about any social or psychological problems which they may have, which could be the root of their physical symptoms, and because of this the treatment you recommend or prescribe to them may not be appropriate to their healthcare needs. This can affect their subsequent compliance with the advice and treatment you have recommended and affect their compliance with any future treatments.

> **Aims of effective communication skills in healthcare:**
> - Building of a partnership between physicians and patients
> - Improving patient and physician satisfaction
> - Improving overall health outcomes of patients
> - Encouraging and giving confidence to patients in self-management
> - Improving patients' knowledge and understanding of their health
> - Better relationships within the healthcare team.

Not every patient whom you encounter in your consultation room, on the ward or in the A&E department will be expert in seeking healthcare advice. They may find it difficult in locating the correct services, in understanding a lot of written and verbal medical information and in following self-care instructions which have been given to them. This can lead to a number of adverse outcomes, all of which can be avoided with improved communication to the patient, at a level appropriate to them.

Effective communication skills not only result in improved outcomes for patients, but also they can enable practitioners to be more efficient in their day-to-day practice, easing levels of frustration and increasing the satisfaction in their work. It has been noted that there is a direct association between the level of satisfaction clinicians experience and their ability to build a rapport with patients.

The breakdown of communication, whether between doctors and patients or between healthcare professionals, is recognized as a key factor in the occurrence of adverse clinical events and poor patient outcomes. Effective communication within the healthcare team increases the quality of working relationships and job satisfaction. Most importantly, patient safety is improved by having all members of the team knowing exactly what is happening with regard to their patients' care.

The take-home message

One point to always consider is this: "extensive research has shown that no matter how knowledgeable a clinician might be, if he or she is not able to have good communication with the patient, he or she may be of no help."[2]

3

Application of the Calgary–Cambridge Model

RACHEL WAMBOLDT

Effective communication between the doctor and the patient is the key to a successful therapeutic relationship. Communication is a core skill in medicine that is used to establish an accurate diagnosis, provide patient-centred information and to establish a caring relationship with patients.

The Calgary–Cambridge Model is an internationally accepted model for communicating with patients based on over 40 years of evidence-based research. Using a structure such as the Calgary–Cambridge Model is helpful to maintain control over the consultation. Models are also helpful to fall back on in the case of a difficult consultation. There are four main sections of the Calgary–Cambridge Model which help to sequence the consultation. Running alongside the main sections are tasks related to 'building the relationship' and 'structuring the consultation' (*Fig. 3.1*).

Providing structure

Initiating the session
Preparation
Establishing rapport
Identifying reason for consultation

Gathering information
Uses the biopsychosocial perspective
Establishes the patient's perspective
Determines background information (PMHx,
Medications, Family Hx, Social Hx)

Physical examination

Explanation and planning
Provides the correct type and amount of
information
Aids with recall and understanding
Reaches a shared understanding
Shared decision making

Closing the session
Ensures appropriate point of closure
Sets plan of care

**Building the
relationship**
Appropriate non-verbal
communication
Develops rapport
Involves the patient

Figure 3.1 The Calgary–Cambridge Model. Reproduced with permission from Drs J.D. Silverman, S.M. Kurtz and J. Draper[3, 4, 5].

The Calgary–Cambridge Model can be divided into two subsections; interviewing the patient and explanation and planning. This is a useful division for those in the earlier years of medicine preparing for an OSCE, as these two models are often tested independently of one another. As students enter the later years of medicine and their careers, it is expected that the two models are combined, in order to complete the entirety of the therapeutic consultation. For the purpose of this book, we will discuss these two divisions on their own. In the following two chapters, these subsections will be explored in more detail. This chapter will focus specifically on tools that help to build a good therapeutic relationship and for providing structure to the consultation.

3.1   Key process elements to any consultation

The following key elements should be employed throughout the entire consultation. In the OSCE scenario, they are often key marks for process and they help to establish a good rapport with the patient.

3.1.1   Building the relationship

- Try to ask **open questions** as much as possible. **Closed questions** should only be used to fill in the gaps or to move through a large number of questions quickly (like in the systems review).
  - Open question: *'Can you tell me a bit more about the pain you have been experiencing?'*
  - Closed question: *'Have you been experiencing any shortness of breath?'*
- Use concise questions and avoid jargon. For example, ask if the patient has high cholesterol rather than dyslipidaemia.
- **Listen** attentively. Allow the patient adequate time to complete statements, leaving thinking time before and after. Try listening to not only what they are saying but the meaning behind what they are saying.
  - Nodding along with the patient, reflective facial expressions and eye contact let the patient know that you are concerned and that they have your full attention.
  - Paraphrasing what the patient has said is a good way to show active listening: *'So what you are saying is that the pain is preventing you from getting a good night's sleep.'*
- Encourage the patient's response through the use of verbal and non-verbal communication. This includes silence, repetition, paraphrasing and interpretation.
- Humour can sometimes be used in the consultation but choose your audience. Humour can sometimes be misinterpreted as the doctor being patronizing or derogatory, if used inappropriately.
- Use **empathy** to communicate to the patient that you understand and appreciate the difficulty that they are experiencing.
  - *'I understand that this must be a difficult time for you.'*
  - *'It must be difficult working, with your back hurting you so much.'*
- **Normalizing** is an excellent way to show empathy and understanding, if used correctly. It can reduce feelings of sadness, hopelessness and isolation. It is also a more gentle way of asking difficult or sensitive questions.
  - *'Many people who have had a stroke experience periods of low mood or sadness. Have you ever had these feelings?'*
  - *'Sometimes when people experience depression they have thoughts of harming themselves. Have you ever felt this way?'*
- Pick up on verbal and non-verbal cues such as facial expressions, tone of voice and body language. This can get you OSCE points for **Recognizing, Acknowledging and Validating (RAV).**
  - *'You look as though you are disappointed in yourself.'*
  - *'It sounds to me like you have had a rough time the last couple of months.'*

- ○ Often these statements can be left open without a question; they allow the patient to reflect on their emotions and to verbalize how they might be feeling.
- Clarify any statements that are unclear or require amplification.
- **Share your thoughts** with the patient and explain the **rationale** for the questions you may be asking.
  - ○ *'I'm thinking that the symptoms that you are experiencing might be related to your heart failure. Do you mind if I ask you a bit more about it?'*
  - ○ *'Sometimes people with diabetes experience a change in the sensation of their feet. Have you ever noticed any injuries to your feet which you did not feel at the time that they occurred?'*
- Act **sensitively** when asking questions that might be embarrassing or difficult to talk about (for example, sexual and mental health histories).
  - ○ Acknowledge that the subject may be difficult for them to talk about and describe why it is important to ask them.
  - ○ *'I need to ask you some personal questions about your erectile dysfunction. I know that this may be embarrassing to talk about but it's really important so that I can help determine what might be causing it.'*

3.1.2 Structuring the consultation

- **Signposting** involves alerting the patient to what lies ahead in the consultation. It can also be used to prepare them for difficult questions.
  - ○ *'I need to ask you a couple of personal questions about your sexual health.'*
  - ○ *'I would like to ask you a few questions about your general health.'*
- **Agenda setting** is often neglected in student OSCEs but can be very valuable for structuring the consultation. It is very similar to signposting, which involves telling the patient what you would like to discuss next, but sets a more global tone for the consultation. Both of these tools help you remain in control of the consultation and prevent aimless wandering by both yourself and the patient.
  - ○ *'What I would like to do is ask you some specific questions about what you have told me today and then I would like to get a bit more information about your health in general.'*
  - ○ *'Today I would like to talk to you about your heart attack, what might have caused it, what further tests we need to do and the options for your treatment. Are there any other questions that you would like answered today?'*
- **Summarize periodically**. This will let the patient know that you have understood what they have said and help you to gather your thoughts. Patients may also choose to add information that they might have forgotten initially.
- Explaining your **thought process** is a great way to be patient-centred. It can also be mixed with signposting to provide more structure to the consultation.
  - ○ *'From what you have described, it sounds like you may be experiencing symptoms of asthma. I would like to ask you a few more specific questions about your symptoms to make sure that there isn't anything else going on.'*

3.2 Summary

- Using a model helps to structure the consultation and ensures that you cover all of the relevant areas.
- 'Building the Relationship' and 'Structuring the Consultation' run in parallel to the main sequence of a Calgary–Cambridge consultation. Both are marked heavily in OSCEs.
  - ○ Building the relationship depends on the use of active listening, empathy and a non-judgmental approach. Verbal and non-verbal tools can be used to make patients feel more at ease.
  - ○ The structure and sequence marks can be achieved by using tools such as agenda setting, summarizing and signposting.

4

General approach to information gathering

RACHEL WAMBOLDT

> **OSCE TIPS:**
> - Make certain that you have read the scenario thoroughly, taking note of the type of station; information gathering vs. giving.
> - You do not need to enter the station as soon as you are notified to do so. Take a breath and collect your thoughts before entering. This is called 'housekeeping'.
> - When you enter the station, walk in slowly but confidently. Make eye contact with the patient and smile. First impressions are key.

4.1 Interviewing the patient

1) Initiating the session and establishing rapport
- Greet the patient in a friendly manner.
- Introduce yourself, your role and the reason for the interview.
  - *'My name is Sam Jones and I am a 4th year medical student from Norwich Medical School. I understand that you have come in to talk to me today because you have been feeling tired.'*
- Ask for the patient's name and, if appropriate, their date of birth/age.
  - Asking their date of birth is sometimes seen as a bit awkward and is more relevant for procedures or examinations. During an OSCE history taking station, it is often more useful to simply ask how old they are.
- Body language and tone of voice are key in the early stages of the interview. If you show the patient that you respect them and are interested, they are more likely to help you out later in the consultation.

2) Identifying the reason(s) for the consultation
- Start by **identifying** the main issue(s) that the patient would like to discuss.
  - *'What has brought you in to the surgery today?'*
  - *'What can I help you with today?'*

> **Golden Minute.** Allow time for the patient to make their opening statement without interrupting them. Give them a few seconds of silence after their initial statement as they may want to just gather their thoughts before continuing. Silence is very important when discussing a sensitive or difficult issue.

- Use non-verbal communication such as nodding, reflective facial expressions (mirror the patient's facial expression) and good eye contact to show the patient that you are interested in what they have to say.
- Verbal communication such as *'uh-huh'*, *'yes'* and *'I see'*, encourages the patient to continue telling their story.

- **Clarify** elements of their opening statement by asking both open and closed questions.
  - *'You mentioned that your knee has been bothering you. Can you tell me a bit more about that?'*
  - *'Can you clarify what you mean by a funny turn?'*
- **Summarize** the patient's concern (key OSCE marks) and **screen** for any other problems.
  - *'You have come in today because you have found yourself more tired lately and you have been having increasing difficulty keeping up with your housework. You also mentioned that your joints have been increasingly stiff, especially in the morning. Is there anything else that has been worrying you?'*
- Ensure that you have established **a sequence of events.**
- Negotiate the agenda.
  - *'Thank you very much for that information. I would like to start by asking you some specific questions about the reason you have come in today and then I would like to ask about your general health and wellbeing. Is that all right?'*

3) Gathering information

At this stage in the consultation, you want to gather as much information as possible about the reason for their attendance.

SOCRATES is often used to ask patients about their pain symptoms but it can be adapted to most symptoms. It is therefore a great basis for questioning about each symptom.

- **Site**
- **Onset**: establish a timeline for the symptom including when it started, the mode of onset, progression, duration and frequency.
  - *'When did you first start noticing the flutters in your chest? Have they increased in frequency over time or have they stayed about the same?'*
- **Character**: this is the patient's description of the symptom. It is useful as an open question at the start.
  - *'You mentioned earlier that you have been more short of breath. Can you tell me more about that?'*
  - *'How would you describe the pain that you are having?'*
- **Radiation**: not relevant unless related to pain.
- **Associated symptoms**: based on their presenting symptoms, you want to ask system-specific questions to identify presenting symptoms that may have been missed. Please refer to *Section 2* of this book for a breakdown of each system.
- **Timing**:
  - *'Is there a certain time of day that is worse than others?'*
- **Exacerbating and relieving factors**:
  - *'Is there anything that makes your shortness of breath worse?'*
  - *'Is there anything that makes your shortness of breath better?'*
- **Severity**: how much is the patient bothered by the symptom or how is it affecting their daily life?
  - *'Is there anything that your shortness of breath is preventing you from doing? Is it keeping you awake at night? How far can you walk before you feel short of breath?'*
- **Complete a systems review**. This is a technique used in medicine to enquire about specific symptoms in other organ systems that may not have been uncovered in the initial stages of information gathering. Focus on symptoms that relate directly to the patient's

problem. Running through an entire checklist is tiring to both you and the patient and in an OSCE shows a lack of comprehension. See *Chapter 5* on how to do a systems review.

4) Understanding the patient's perspective

Ideas, concerns and expectations (ICE) are important elements of the consultation. In the realm of information gathering, ICE can help to clarify the reason for attendance, which can sometimes be different from what was expressed in the initial information gathering section, and may reveal clues to establish the right diagnosis.

Eliciting the patient's ICE is also useful for the negotiation of the management plan. Any shared decision needs to balance the values, concerns and preferences of the patient with those of the doctor, which come in the form of evidence-based guidelines and relevant ethical / legal principles. You should always refer back to their ICE as you explain why you are suggesting the diagnosis and management options because it lets them know that you have taken these into consideration.

- Enquire about the patient's ideas or beliefs about what might be causing their symptoms.
    - *'Do you have any idea about what might have caused this?'*
    - *'I have some thoughts about what might be causing these symptoms but I would like to know if you have any ideas.'* or ... *'I would like to know what you think is going on.'*
- Ask the patient what concerns them the most about their symptoms.
    - *'What has concerned you most about these symptoms?'*
    - *'What is it about this symptom that is worrying you the most?'*
- Establish what the patient is expecting to gain from the consultation.
    - *'Is there anything in particular that you are hoping to get out of your visit today?'*
- Ask the patient how this problem has affected their life.

In the OSCE, the answers to some of these questions may have arisen in the Golden Minute or with your initial information gathering. To ensure that you get the marks, you should try to acknowledge that they may have already answered the question but **screen** for any other issues.

- *'You mentioned earlier that you think your tiredness is because you are working more hours at your job. Have you had any other ideas about what might be causing this?'*
- *'You said that you were worried that the pain could get worse over time. Is there anything else about the pain that is worrying you?'*

5) Exploring the patient's background

Before exploring the patient's background, it is a good idea to signpost and let them know that you would like to ask them some routine questions about their general health and wellbeing. This is an example of signposting.

Past medical and surgical history

- **Major or chronic illnesses**
    - *'Do you have any conditions that you see your doctor for regularly?'*
    - *'Have you ever had to stay in hospital?'* If so, ask when and why, any complications or follow-up.
    - Ask specifically about diabetes and hypertension, as patients often normalize these conditions and therefore forget about them.
    - Ask about organ system related risk factors. For example, if they have atrial fibrillation, ask if they have ever had a heart attack or if there is any history of thyroid disease.
    - *'Have you ever had any serious infections?'*
    - *'Have you had any serious injuries or any trauma to your head?'*

- **Psychiatric history**
  - *'Have you ever seen a counsellor or taken medication for a mental health concern?'*
  - If the answer to the above question is yes, you should gather more information. See *Chapter 7* on Psychiatry.
- **Previous surgeries or procedures**
  - *'Have you had any surgeries?'* If so, ask when, where, why and if there were any associated complications.
  - *'Have you ever had any special investigations, for example a CT scan or MRI?'* If so, ask what it was for and what the result was.
- **Childhood illnesses**
  - *'Did you have any serious illnesses as a child?'*
  - *'Were you ever hospitalized as a child?'*
- **Obstetrics and gynaecology**
  - At a minimum, all women of child-bearing age should be asked when their last menstrual period was.
  - For any obstetrical or gynaecological complaint, a complete menstrual, obstetrical and sexual history should be taken; see *Chapter 16* for more detail.
- **Health promotion history**
  - Immunizations: *'Have you had your routine immunizations?'* If relevant, you may want to inquire about travel and associated vaccinations.
  - Screening: has the patient undergone age-appropriate screening – newborn screening, cervical smear, mammogram, faecal occult blood test?

Medication history

See *Chapter 21* for how to take a proper drug history.
- *'Do you have any allergies?'*
- Prescribed medication: ask for their dose and frequency.
  - *'Do you know why you are taking this medication?'*
  - *'Do you take this medication regularly? On average, how many days per week do you forget to take your medication? Why do you forget to take your medications?'*
  - *'Have you been experiencing any side-effects from your medication?'*
- *'Do you take any over-the-counter medication?'*
- *'Do you take any vitamins or supplements?'*

Family history

- Determine the health and presence of illness in the immediate family. Family history is a risk factor for several diseases and therefore important to screen for.
- In certain patient populations, for example children and child-bearing families, you may also want to screen for hereditary diseases and family traits.
  - Drawing a pedigree diagram might be helpful for organizing the information.
- Some illnesses that run in a family may be the result of a shared environment (e.g. smoking, drinking, mental illness, infectious diseases).

Social history

The social history is important for the development of the doctor–patient therapeutic relationship but is also helpful for establishing risk factors for disease. The social history plays a role in the patient's ability to recover from illness, which then contributes to the number of days that they spend in hospital and the number of visits that they make to the GP.
- **Occupation**: *'Are you currently working? What do you do? Are you currently looking for work? Tell me about your job. What other jobs have you done during your life?'*
  - If relevant, you may also want to ask about workplace exposures that may contribute to disease (e.g. noise, chemicals, dust, overuse injuries, stress).

- ○ If the patient has spent some time in the military, you want to know about where they spent their time, length of time, any physical trauma / injuries, any mental harm (depression, post-traumatic stress disorder, substance abuse) and any exposures.
- **Marital status**
- **Social support**
  - ○ *'Who do you currently live with at home?'*
  - ○ *'Who do you rely on most for support?'*
  - ○ *'How is your relationship with your husband? children? parents?'*
  - ○ *'Does your family have any social services involvement?'*
  - ○ In practice, be prepared for these sorts of questions to open up difficult home life situations. Refer to *Chapter 23* on safeguarding for tips on how to discuss cases of abuse or neglect.
- **Education**: enquire about the highest level of completed education. This is not relevant in most consultations but there are some cases where it might be relevant, for example in a psychiatric history.
  - ○ *'Where did you go to secondary school? Did you complete your GCSEs?'*
  - ○ *'Did you complete any post-secondary education?'*
- **Functional status**
  - ○ Assess the patient's ability to perform their activities of daily living (ADLs) and independent activities of daily living (IADLs); see *Chapter 19*.
- **Tobacco**
  - ○ *'Do you currently smoke cigarettes? Have you ever smoked?'*
  - ○ *'What type of tobacco do you use (smoking, filtered vs. unfiltered, cigar, chewed)? How many cigarettes do you smoke on an average day? Have you always smoked that many cigarettes?'*
  - ○ *'How old were you when you started smoking?'*
  - ○ *'Have you ever thought about giving it up?'*
- **Alcohol**
  - ○ *'Do you drink alcohol? On average, how many days per week do you drink alcohol? In an average sitting, how much do you drink?'*
    - – Never ask a patient how many units they drink. Most patients believe that a pint of beer is the equivalent of 1 unit when in reality it is 2–3.
    - – Ask what type of alcoholic beverages they drink and how much, in order to quantify that number of units yourself.
  - ○ For someone who drinks more than the recommended units of alcohol, use the CAGE substance abuse screening tool.
    - – **C** Have you ever felt you should **cut down** on your drinking?
    - – **A** Have people **annoyed** you by criticizing your drinking?
    - – **G** Have you ever felt bad or **guilty** about your drinking?
    - – **E** Have you ever had a drink first thing in the morning to steady your nerves or to get rid of a hangover (**eye-opener**)?

  If the patient has two positive answers, you should question the patient further about their drinking and its implications. Please refer to *Chapter 7: Psychiatry* for more information about how to do this.
- **Illegal drug use**
  - ○ *'Do you use any illegal drugs or substances? What type of drugs do you use? How often do you use this substance? How long have you been using this substance? How do you administer the drug (snorted, smoked, injected, etc)?'*
  - ○ The CAGE score can also be easily adapted to help question people about their addictive behaviours related to illegal substances.

- It is also important to screen for risky behaviour. Establish how they are taking the drug, what material they are using to prepare it, whether they are sharing needles, when they were last tested for hepatitis or human immunodeficiency virus (HIV) and enquire about whether they are using protection during sexual activities.

- **Diet**

The easiest way to assess someone's diet is to conduct a 24-hour recall.
- *'Tell me what you had to eat yesterday starting at breakfast.'*
- *'Does this represent a typical day for you? How is it different?'*
- *'Have you ever tried going on a diet? What was successful? What wasn't successful and why not?'*

- **Exercise**

Use the mnemonic **'WORK IT'.**

W   In the last **week**, how many times did you engage in moderate exercise for at least 10 minutes?

O   What types of activities do you **o**rdinarily like to do?

R   On days that you do moderate activity, how long do you do it for (**r**outine)?

K   In the last 3 months, has the exercise that you have done this week been more, less or the same as normal (**k**eeping trends)?

I   Do you wish you could exercise more (**i**ntent)?

T   Why do you want to be more physically active? What is getting in the way (**t**rue motivation)?

- **Travel**
- *'Have you been travelling recently?'*
- *'Did you have to travel on any long-haul flights or drives?'*
- It is also important to establish risk factors for infectious disease. Ask what they did on their holiday, how their meals were prepared, if they had unprotected sex or experienced any symptoms / injuries whilst travelling.

- **Spirituality / religious beliefs**
- *'Do you hold any strong religious or spiritual beliefs?'*
- *'How do you cope with illness or bad news?'*

6) Closing the consultation

- **Summarize** the key elements of the consultation.
- Screen for anything that may have been left out.
- Share with the patient your current thoughts about what they have come in to discuss.
  - *'From everything you have told me it sounds like...'.* Relate this back to things that they have told you in the consultation.
- You should end the consultation with a plan. In an OSCE information gathering station it could be as easy as, *'I would like to discuss this further with the doctor and then she will come in to talk to you about the plan going forward.'*
- Alternatively, inform the patient that you would like to perform a physical examination, explaining specifically what you would like to assess, and ask their permission to proceed.
- Always close by thanking the patient.

Summary of key OSCE process marks:

Initiating the session: give a clear introduction of who you are, your role and the purpose of the consultation. Confirm that you have the right patient.

Identify the reason for the consultation: ask an open question followed by a Golden Minute of active listening. Summarize what the patient has said and then negotiate an agenda for the consultation.

Gather information.

Understand the patient's perspective using ICE.

Past medical history: major or chronic illnesses, psychiatric illness, previous surgeries or procedures, childhood illnesses, obstetrics and gynaecology history, health promotion.

Medication history: current medications, allergies, over-the-counter medications and supplements.

Family history.

Social history: occupation, marital status, social support, education, functional status, tobacco, alcohol, illicit drug use, diet, exercise, travel history, spirituality.

Closing the consultation: summarize, screen, establish a plan of care and thank the patient.

5

Information giving and shared decision making

NIAMH LOUGHRAN

Information Giving and Shared Decision Making: Keys to Success

- Provide the correct type and amount of information.
- Aid accurate recall and understanding.
- Offer explanations that are related to the patient's perspective.
- Employ an interactive approach throughout to ensure a shared understanding of the problem.
- Involve the patient to the extent they wish to be involved in the planning of their treatment.
- Build a relationship with the patient so that they feel supported.

This takes the consultation a step further from information gathering. The process of information giving and shared decision making is a tricky one, and one in which every person develops their own style. In this chapter we outline some of the essential points to cover when carrying out these types of consultations and give you a framework on which to base your consultation. Throughout this chapter we will be adopting the Calgary–Cambridge Model, which was outlined in *Chapter 3*, and using the same communication principles as those used in information gathering.

5.1 The process of information giving

The following points outline some important stages within this type of consultation.

OSCE TIP: Don't spend too much time gathering information. Remember that your time is limited and the most important aspect of this station is providing the necessary information. Always make sure you read the scenario carefully as in some cases it may state: *'Do not take a history'*; however, you may still find it useful to find out a little about what's been going on in order to build rapport with the patient and to structure your consultation afterwards. Remember in real life to always take a history beforehand.

---

1) Initiating the session

- Establish initial rapport with the patient: introduce yourself, ask their name and their age.
- Identify reason(s) for the consultation, e.g.:
  - Doctor: *'I understand that you have come in because you would like to know a little more about your recent diagnosis.'*
  - Patient: *'Yes that's correct.'*

2) Gathering information

- Explore the patient's problems; take a brief history from them about what's been going on that's led them to this point.
- Start by asking an open question, e.g.:
  - Doctor: *'Can you tell me a little about what's been happening up until this point?'*
  - Patient: *'Well, I've been feeling very tired recently and I haven't been able to go to work, so I came to the doctor who took some bloods...'*
- Attempt to gain an understanding of the patient's perspective by asking about their ideas, concerns and expectations (ICE). It is important to include the patient's unique viewpoint when discussing the plan for further management. For example:
  - Patient: *'I really want to be able to go back to work.'*
  - Doctor: *'I completely understand that and hopefully by finding the right treatment option for you we'll be able to get you back to work.'*
- Ensure you incorporate your other consultation skills throughout this, for example by looking out for any non-verbal cues and clarifying unclear statements.

3) Setting the agenda

- Before you begin bombarding the patient with information, take time to set an agenda. This will help you to structure your consultation and ensure you cover everything you want to.
- Ask the patient if there are any specific topics they would like to cover in the consultation, e.g.:
  - Doctor: *'Is there anything in particular you would like to talk about today? Just so I make sure I'm giving you the information you want.'* or *'Are there any specific questions that you would like to have answered today?'*
  - Patient: *'Yes, I want to know what my treatment options are and what would be best for me.'*
- Once you've addressed the patient's agenda it's important to set your own. State the things you would like to cover, if they have not already been said by the patient. There may be some vital information, such as side-effects of medication, that you need to make the patient aware of. For example:
  - Doctor: *'So we will go through each potential treatment option for you and discuss the benefits and side-effects of each. I would also like to discuss the need for your long-term follow-up care. Does this sound OK to you?'*
  - Patient: *'Yes that sounds good.'*
- Ensure the patient agrees with the agenda.
- Within this part of the consultation the patient may raise some concerns they have which they wish to be addressed. Clarify and acknowledge these concerns and incorporate them into your explanations; in other words address their ICE.

4) Assessing the patient's starting point

- Once you have clarified the agenda for the consultation it is then important to ask the patient how much they know on the topic already. An example may be *'Do you know much about...?'* or *'What can you tell me about...?'*
  - Patient: *'I haven't got a clue what it all means.'*
- This allows you to form a rough idea in your head of whether they have a good idea about the topic at hand or if perhaps they have come across some misleading information, which you will then be able to clarify.
- It is also helpful to address how much information the patient would like. We don't want to overload them with specific details which are not relevant to them and won't help in giving them peace of mind.

○ Simply ask something along the lines of: *'How much information would you like?'* Clarify this by stating: *'Would you like me to go into a lot of detail or for today would you just like an overview?'*

○ Patient: *'I only want to know as much as I need to, I don't need all the details.'*

> **OSCE TIP**: At this stage, if they have not already mentioned anything, it is a good point to ask if they have any particular ideas, concerns or expectations.

After these stages you will then be ready to begin giving the necessary and appropriate information to the patient. Important techniques to adopt when it comes to giving information include:

- **Organize your explanations using a logical sequence** and relate the information back to the patient's **ideas, concerns and expectations (ICE).**
  - ○ The aim of this is to make the information easier for the patient to remember and understand.
  - ○ Following your agenda helps to keep you on the right track.
  - ○ Doctor: *'So first of all let's talk about what treatment options there are.'*
- **Chunk and check**
  - ○ Organize the information into easily digestible chunks so as not to bombard the patient with a lot of different information all at once.
  - ○ After each 'chunk' of information, check the patient's understanding, by asking something along the lines of: *'Does that all make sense?' 'How does all that sound to you?'* or *'Do you have any questions about what we've just talked about?'*
  - ○ Patient: *'Yes, I'm not sure what you meant about…'*
  - ○ Use the patient's response as a guide for how to proceed.
- **Signpost**
  - ○ Use signposting throughout as it makes your consultation more organized; it also informs the patient that you are moving on to discuss a new section of information.
  - ○ For example: *'Now we're going to move on to talk about changes you can make to your lifestyle.'*
- **Repetition and summary**
  - ○ It's helpful to reinforce important points throughout the discussion.
  - ○ It's also good to get into the habit of briefly summarizing after every 'chunk' of information and providing a general summary at the end; this also allows the patient to clarify anything they are unsure about.
  - ○ Doctor: *'I know that I've given you a lot of information. If it's OK with you, I'd just like to summarize what we've covered so far…'*
- **Use succinct and easily understood language**
  - ○ Avoid jargon and complicated medical terminology as this may confuse the patient and will result in you having to spend time explaining the terminology.
- **Use visual methods of giving information**
  - ○ Sometimes when explaining conditions it's helpful for the patient and for you to draw a simplified diagram explaining the process.
  - ○ You can also use this method to write down difficult words such as medication names for the patient.
  - ○ This gives the patient a reference for when they are explaining it back to you or to others.
- **Check patient's understanding**
  - ○ As mentioned before, always check the patient understands everything throughout.
  - ○ Sometimes it is helpful to have the patient explain back in their own words what you have just told them. This gives you the opportunity to see that you have explained everything to them appropriately.

○   For example: *'Just to check that I've explained that to you OK, could you repeat back to me in your own words what you've understood from this?'*

5) Closing the consultation

Once you feel you have given all the information the patient wanted and anything additional which you wanted to cover, you can then move to the end of the consultation.

- **Invite further questions (screen)**
  - ○   Encourage the patient to ask questions throughout.
  - ○   Importantly at the end, screen for any further questions they have.
  - ○   *'Is there anything else you would like to ask me?' 'Is there anything I haven't covered that you're concerned about?'*
- **Close the session:**
  - ○   Summarize the session briefly.
  - ○   Invite further questions.
  - ○   Offer the patient helpful information leaflets.
  - ○   Provide them with a resource for answering future questions that they may have.

5.2   **The process of a shared decision consultation**

Shared decision making is another essential communication skill. It can be seen as an exchange of views between the healthcare professional and patient. Your role in this scenario is to enhance patients' understanding of the decision making process and involve them, to the extent they wish to be involved, in order to come to the correct decision for them. It is important to remember that not all patients wish to be involved in making a decision; however, this is not something which you can just assume and so you must explore each individual patient's wishes.

Some essential features in a shared decision consultation:

- It involves both the healthcare professional and the patient.
- The healthcare professional and patient work together to come to a consensus about the preferred option.

1) Initiating the session

- Introduce yourself, confirm patient's name and date of birth.
- Obtain the purpose for the patient's visit, or confirm reason they are there, e.g. *'So I understand you are here to discuss your treatment options.'*

2) Gathering information

- As with information giving, you may find it useful to obtain a short history from the patient about what has led them to this point.
- This may also be a good stage to elicit any ideas, concerns or expectations the patient may have, which you can then take into consideration when presenting them with their options.

3) Giving information

- You may find that although we have separated these two processes into two sections, they are often intertwined in the same consultation.
- The patient may present with a particular problem, aspects of which they will require some information on before they are able to go on to make an informed decision.
- This may not be the case in all 'shared decision' consultations; remember to treat each one you encounter as an individual case and conduct the consultation by taking the lead from the patient.

> **EXAMPLE:** A patient may present with poorly controlled diabetes. From taking a brief history you elicit that they are not aware of the complications that you are trying to prevent by maintaining normal blood glucose. This prompts you to give information on the importance of this, stating what complications they are at risk of, before then discussing what treatment options are available to them.

4) Involving the patient

- Throughout the consultation, whilst you are outlining different options available to the patient, encourage them to contribute their ideas and thoughts.
- Encourage the patient to state whether they think the options explained may or may not be suitable for them.
- It may become apparent, when you are offering your opinion, that the patient is not happy with this; this will give you the opportunity to explore why the patient feels this way and take these reasons into account when discussing alternative options.
- Whilst giving the options, incorporate any ideas, concerns or expectations previously mentioned by the patient in order to tailor the consultation to them as an individual.
- Ensuring that the patient is involved and happy with the plan of care helps to improve concordance and satisfaction, e.g.:
  - Doctor: *'So what do you think about what we've discussed so far?'*
  - Patient: *'Well, you're saying that I don't have enough insulin in my body and that I might need regular injections but I hate needles!'*
  - Doctor: *'I know it's a scary thought but we might be able to start you out on some tablets and see how they go. Unfortunately if these don't work we'll have to come back to the insulin injections.'*

5) Exploring the options

- Elicit the patient's preferences and goals of treatment so the most appropriate options are discussed.
- **Discuss options**:
  - Signpost what you are going to tell them about the options.
  - Remember that 'doing nothing' is always an option but even within this there are opportunities for symptom control and improving wellbeing.
  - Treatment options should be given in accordance to the patient's unique case.
  - Some examples include:
    - investigations that the patient may have to go through to confirm their diagnosis
    - treatment options available including conservative, medication or surgery
    - it may also be appropriate in some cases to discuss preventative measures that the patient can take. This includes primary, secondary and tertiary prevention strategies.
- Present a topic to the patient, and then go into some detail on this, for example: the steps involved, how it will work, advantages and disadvantages to it, including important side-effects the patient should be aware of.
- **Summarize** after you have discussed each option.
- **Example**: Doctor: *'One tablet which can be used is called metformin. This will help to improve your blood sugar. Some side-effects of metformin include feeling sick, vomiting and diarrhoea.'*

6) Sharing your own thoughts and opinions

- Whether you are in a consultation with a patient about deciding on investigations or planning treatment, you as the healthcare professional should share your thoughts. This should make the patient feel as though they are not on their own in making the decision

and may lead to them being more satisfied with the advice being offered and the final decision.
- Always provide a rationale for your opinion.

If the patient declines an option, which you firmly believe is the correct one, you must share this opinion with the patient, giving a clear rationale as to why you feel this way.

- Patient: *'I really don't want to take any tablets or injections. Can't I just eat healthily and do more exercise?'*
- Doctor: *'Eating healthily and keeping fit are really important and we need you to do these but unfortunately these measures alone don't seem to be working for you and you need a bit of extra help at lowering your blood sugar. I really believe if we leave you without any treatment your control will only get worse and this can have really serious effects on your health.'*

7) Negotiating a mutually acceptable plan
- Once you have presented the patient with the information / options as appropriate and you have expressed your own preference regarding the options at hand, you should determine the patient's preferences.
- Obtain the patient's views and concerns about possible treatments.
- Take the patient's lifestyle, cultural beliefs and background into consideration.
- Doctor: *'Now that we've discussed everything and you understand it all, are you happy to begin taking metformin? Or do you have any other questions?'*
- Patient: *'No, I think you've answered everything and it seems as though I really need to start metformin.'*

8) Closing the session
Check with the patient that their concerns have been addressed and they are happy with the plan.

- Invite any further questions and advise who to contact if they have any more questions or concerns.
- Offer an information leaflet if available.
- Thank the patient.

> **OSCE TIP**: An important question to ask is whether or not the patient has a support system; for example, *'Do you have anyone at home that you can talk to about this?'*

> **Summary of key OSCE marks:**
> Explore management options with patient: fully explore each option, discussing the pros, cons and alternatives.
> State your own preference and explain your reasons behind it.
> Acknowledge the patient's ICE by giving them options suited to their unique clinical situation. Consider the physical, social, financial and psychological implications of each decision.
> Involve the patient in the decision making: firstly ascertain how involved they wish to be, and if appropriate encourage them to make decisions by evaluating each choice they have.
> Negotiate a mutually acceptable plan, ensuring you check the final decision.

6

Perfecting the systems review

STUART FOSTER AND RACHEL WAMBOLDT

Systems Review: Keys to Success

- The systems review should be incorporated into every consultation.
- Ideally it should follow the history of the presenting complaint.
- Be sure to signpost to the patient that you will be asking a set of closed questions.
- To keep organized, work from head to toe.
- If the patient confirms that they have one of the symptoms, then it should be explored in more detail.
- Important issues that are not relevant to the current presentation can be addressed at a follow-up visit.

6.1 Overview of the systems review

6.1.1 What is a systems review?

A systems review is a brief and fairly crude tool to gather more information during a medical history. It is very important as it allows the clinician to briefly assess for other symptoms which have yet to emerge during the main focus of the consultation.

6.1.2 Why is it useful?

The systems review is a very useful tool when you are having difficulty consolidating the patient's history. It not only gives you more time to collate the information you have already obtained, but may provide you with new knowledge that could prove to be the 'missing piece in the puzzle' with regard to the formulation of a differential diagnosis and management plan.

It gives the patient an opportunity to mention anything else that *they* think could be relevant. It also allows *you*, the clinician, time to decide whether this new information is related and/or important with respect to this consultation.

Some of the information you can obtain from a systems review may influence your management plan. For example, if a patient presenting with pain tells you that they are chronically a bit short of breath and wheezy, you may want to avoid giving them NSAID analgesia as they may have (undiagnosed) asthma. Similarly, a patient presenting with new atrial fibrillation (AF) who mentions that he sometimes gets blood in his urine probably should not be started on anticoagulation until this is further explored.

Other information may influence and allow you to expand your differential diagnosis. For instance, a patient presenting with cough and weight loss who tells you during the systems review that they also have noticed that their right eyelid is a bit droopy, should lead you to think about Horner's syndrome secondary to a Pancoast tumour of the lung.

6.1.3   How to introduce the systems review to the patient

The systems review should be completed after your history of the presenting complaint. As this section is done quickly using closed questions, it is important to prepare the patient. If the patient is inadequately prepared, they may see this as an opportunity to discuss symptoms that they have experienced in the past. This may not be relevant to the current consultation. You might want to say, for example, *'I just need to ask you a few more quick questions about symptoms that you might be experiencing.'*

Generally, most relevant information will be from the same sort of time scale as that of the presenting complaint itself. For instance, urinary frequency and urgency in an elderly gentleman for the last three years is unlikely to be relevant when he presents with a five-hour history of central chest pain. Therefore, it can be useful to ask the patient to think if they have had *'any of the following symptoms over the last three months'.*

A good way to structure the systems review is to work from head to toe. Choose three important symptoms from each system and ask the patient if they have had any of them. Then move on to the next body area, until completed. Exclude the system / body part that was the focus of the main history as this has already been done.

Remember that the systems review must be concise, especially in an OSCE station that also involves an examination. In these situations, it is helpful to inform the patient that they can just answer these questions with a 'yes' or 'no'. Additionally, if you are already confident that you have formulated a reasonable differential diagnosis, in the interest of time, you should limit your systems review to cover just the 'main' systems, i.e. the ones which tend to cause the most common and serious pathologies, namely the heart, lungs and gastrointestinal tract. If, however, you are not yet confident in your differential diagnosis, you may find it helpful to carry out a full and thorough systems review, as you can gain more information this way.

> **OSCE TIP**: In an OSCE station, they generally will not try to trick you with irrelevant symptoms. If a patient tells you that they are experiencing a symptom, it is probably relevant to the case and should be explored.

If the patient reports that they have experienced one of the symptoms you ask them about, this needs to be briefly explored. To not do so may appear to the patient that you're not actually listening to what they are saying, and to the examiner that you don't appreciate that this information could be relevant. However, time is very tight in an examination scenario, so you should not spend too long in exploring this symptom further (no more than half a minute). You should ask the patient how long they have had the symptom for, and if they have had previous episodes in the past. Recent recurrence of a chronic problem may be of little relevance to their presenting complaint.

If a symptom sounds suspicious or worrying, for example a smoker with occasional haemoptysis, you need to show to the examiner that you appreciate the importance of this finding, without jeopardizing your history by dwelling on it for too long. In the context of an OSCE station, you should tell the patient that you are concerned about what they have told you, e.g. *'We really need to explore as soon as possible why you have been coughing up blood'.* You then need to balance this with a comment about a lack of time in the current consultation, but with a good and appropriate 'safety net' and follow-up plan – *'I'm afraid that we are a bit short of time at the moment and I really want to explore this issue properly. I'd like you to come back and see me tomorrow, and of course if you are very concerned in the meantime you should go to A&E'.* In a real consultation the most appropriate thing to do may be to explore any worrying symptom fully, without delay and the potential loss to follow-up.

6.2 Key symptoms of a systems review

An example of how to do a quick systems review is shown in *Fig. 6.1*. Remember that if the patient has had any of the symptoms that you have enquired about, a more thorough review should be done to find out more about it and to screen for any other system-related symptoms.

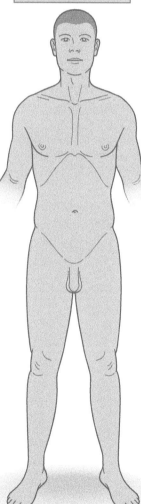

Psychological
- Depression: mood, loss of interest, change in appetite, change in sleep, hopelessness
- Anxiety
- Suicidal ideation, self-harm or harm to others
- Elevated mood and psychosis (delusions, hallucinations, increased energy)

Abdomen
- Appetite
- Abdominal pain, indigestion, bloating
- Nausea and vomiting (haematemesis)
- Change in bowel habit; diarrhoea or constipation
- Blood or mucus in stool
- Jaundice

Urinary tract/reproductive
- **Urinary**
  - Storage: frequency, urgency, incontinence, retention
  - Voiding: hesitancy, incomplete voiding, dribbling
  - Others: dysuria, haematuria
- **Reproductive**
  - *Men:*
  - Erectile dysfunction
  - Penile discharge
  - *Women:*
  - Last known menstrual period, cycle length
  - Menstrual irregularities (menorrhagia, inter-menstrual bleeding, post-coital bleeding, menopausal symptoms, post-menopausal bleeding)
  - Pain (dyspareunia, dysmenorrhoea)
  - Pregnancy: are they or could they be pregnant? If they are pregnant, a thorough obstetrics and gynaecological history should be conducted
  - Vaginal discharge

Constitutional
- Weight loss/gain, fevers, night sweats

Head
- **Neurology**
  - General: headaches, seizures, neck stiffness, memory loss or tremors
  - Motor deficits: weakness, muscle wasting, coordination
  - Sensory deficits: numbness, tingling or pain to the limbs
- **Visual disturbance:** change in acuity, blurred vision, floaters or photophobia, redness, pain
- **Ears, nose and throat**
  - Ear: hearing loss, discharge, tinnitus, pain, vertigo/dizziness
  - Nose: bleeding, congestion, rhinorrhoea
  - Throat: pain, difficulty swallowing, masses

Heart
- Chest pain, palpitations, dyspnoea
- Orthopnoea
- Syncope/dizziness
- Exercise intolerance
- Peripheral oedema

Lungs
- Dyspnoea, cough, wheeze
- Haemoptysis
- Sputum production
- Exercise intolerance

Arms and legs
- Neurological symptoms: weakness, numbness or tingling
- Vascular symptoms: pain, pallor, numbness/tingling, ulcers/wounds
- Orthopaedic and rheumatology: pain, swelling, stiffness, locking, instability, concerns with ambulation

Skin
- Rashes, ulcers, bruising, pruritus

Figure 6.1 *Example of a quick systems review.*

6.3 **Quick systems review example**

'Thank you very much for the information that you have given me so far. I would just like to ask you about a few more symptoms in case we missed anything. You can simply answer yes or no.

- *Have you experienced any weight loss? Have you been feverish or had any night sweats?*
- *Have you had any headaches or changes in your vision?*
- *How has your mood been lately?*
- *Have you suffered from chest pain, shortness of breath or palpitations?*
- *Have you had any abdominal pain, nausea or vomiting? Have you noticed any recent changes in your bowel movements? When was your last bowel movement?*
- *Do you have any trouble passing water?*
- **For women,** *when was your last period? Is there any chance that you could be pregnant?*
- *Do you suffer from numbness, tingling or weakness in your arms or legs?*
- *Have you noticed any skin changes? Do you have any ulcers or wounds?*

Thank you again. I would now like to ask you some questions about your general health.'

> **Summary of key points (GET YOUR MARKS):**
>
> **The systems review can be incredibly useful if done well:** it can help you with your differential diagnosis and management plan, and in answering any questions that your examiner asks you at the end.
>
> **It is crucial to keep it concise:** practise taking a systems review, including introducing it and any additional questions, in less than 90 seconds.
>
> **Work through each relevant part of the body** from head to toe, with three core symptoms for each body area.
>
> **Don't forget to clearly acknowledge and 'safety net' with a follow-up plan,** any symptom that needs further exploration.

7

Psychiatry

VINITHA SOUNDARAJAN, DANIAH THOMAS AND NIAMH LOUGHRAN

> **Psychiatry: Keys to Success**
>
> The psychiatric consultation can be one of the most difficult to conduct. The patients are often in a vulnerable position and the interviewer may find it difficult to balance the appropriate amount of sensitivity and support. The psychiatric consultation is seen as daunting by students due to its complexity and multiple components. The most important thing you can do as an interviewer is to ask open-ended questions and allow the patient time to talk and reflect. The psychiatric interview should not be a tick-box exercise, as the patient will pick up on this.
>
> Developing rapport early is pivotal. As with any history, patients find it easier to talk about the medical aspects of their illness first (e.g. sleep, mood, appetite) before feeling comfortable enough to speak about their personal and social history. Some things might even be too sensitive to discuss in your first meeting with the patient. Let the patient guide the consultation.

Red flags for a mental health problem:

- Changes in a person's behaviour/mood in multiple areas of their life and normal functioning.
- If they have recently undergone a major or complicated life event, e.g. death of loved one.
- If the person's mood/actions pose a risk to their own health or that of others.
- In adolescents/children: unexplained onset of persistent/disruptive changes in their mood or behaviour.
- Hallucinations, delusions or poor self-care.
- Expressed suicidality with a plan.

7.1 Mental health history

1) Introduce yourself and your role on the healthcare team

2) Ensure consent and confidentiality

3) Confirm the patient's name and DOB/age

4) Take a history of the presenting complaint

'What can we do for you today?' or *'How are you feeling today?'*

> **The Golden Minute:** this refers to the first minute of the consultation. Allow the patient to tell you in their own words about what has brought them to see you. Once the patient has finished telling you about what their problem is, you can expand on what they've said by taking a full psychiatric history. You can also use the opportunity to clarify any details that they have already told you.

Take a detailed history of each presenting symptom. Ask about **chronology** (when did it start, which came first if there is more than one), **progression** (how have the symptoms changed over time, is there any fluctuation), **severity, associated symptoms, associated life events, and any precipitating, aggravating or relieving factors**. It is also important to explore **the impact their symptoms are having on their daily life** – are they able to go to work, do things around the house, or are their symptoms stopping them from doing these things?

> **Key Knowledge:** When taking the history of presenting complaint, remember to do a symptom screen. If the patient does not mention any of these in their history, you must ask specifically about them. Keep this as brief as possible, asking about the main symptoms.

- **Depression**: low mood; lack of energy; anhedonia (an inability to enjoy things that they usually enjoy); early morning waking; reduced appetite.
  - *'How has your mood been recently?'*
  - *'Do you still enjoy doing the same things that you used to?'*
  - *'Have you noticed a change in your sleeping pattern? If you wake up early, are you able to go back to sleep, or do you lie awake?'*
  - *'Has your appetite changed recently? Are you eating less than you usually would? Are you feeling less hungry, or is there a different reason?'*
- **Psychosis**: hallucinations; delusions. Acknowledge that the patient may find these experiences difficult to talk about, and try to normalize the question:
  - *'I want to ask you about something that some people may experience, but find it difficult to talk about. These are questions that we ask everyone.'*
  - *'Do you ever see or hear things that other people might not be able to see or hear?'*
- **Anxiety**: worry; panic; palpitations; chest tightness; shortness of breath.
  - *'Talk me through a normal day. Is there anything that makes you feel worried or anxious?'*
  - *'Do you worry about little things most days?'*
- **Insight**: the conscious ability to recognize their symptoms as dysfunctional; insight is an important distinguishing factor for severe mental illness.
  - *'Do you think that there is something wrong?'*
  - *'Do you think that you might benefit from treatment? Is there anything about treatment that worries you?'*

See relevant sections for more in-depth histories of each condition.

5) Systems review

A systems review is always important in order to rule out any concerning physical symptoms that the patient might be experiencing, which could be due to an underlying illness. Below is an example of a brief systems review from *Chapter 6*. Obviously you will have to base your systems review on each individual patient, as some of the below questions / symptoms may have already come up in the consultation. Use the following as a guide:

- *Have you experienced any recent changes in your weight? Have you been feverish or had any night sweats?*

- *Have you had any headaches or changes in your vision?*
- *How has your mood been lately?*
- *Have you suffered from chest pain, shortness of breath or palpitations?*
- *Have you had any abdominal pain, nausea or vomiting? Have you noticed any recent changes in your bowel movements? When was your last bowel movement?*
- *Do you have any trouble passing water?*
- **For women,** *when was your last period? Is there any chance that you could be pregnant?*
- *Do you suffer from numbness, tingling or weakness in your arms or legs?*
- *Have you noticed any skin changes? Do you have any ulcers or wounds?*

6) ICE

This is a crucial part of the history, as establishing the patient's health beliefs and main concerns can help to build a good rapport with them.
- Ideas – *'What do you think is making you feel this way?'*
- Concerns – *'Is there anything in particular that is causing you concern?'*
- Expectations – *'What help are you expecting with these problems? Do you have any thoughts on what I can do to help you?'*

7) Past psychiatric history

- Ask about previous episodes of the current presenting complaint.
- Ask about any previous psychiatric diagnoses, and whether they received any treatment.
- Establish whether they have previously been admitted and managed as an inpatient. Clarify whether they have been seen in a day hospital or in an outpatient community setting.
  - Find out whether any previous admissions or treatment were carried out under the Mental Health Act.

Always ask about suicide ideation, previous suicide attempts and self-harm.

> **OSCE TIP:** Any time you are conducting a psychiatric consultation, you **must** ask about suicidal ideation and self-harm. In real life it is always safe to ask.

This can be a difficult question to ask someone, as it is a sensitive issue. One way of asking is to normalize the question, for example: *'Sometimes when people are feeling very low, they have thoughts about wanting to end their life or hurting themselves. Have you ever had any thoughts like that?'* (see *Section 6.2.6*).

8) Past medical history

Always ask about any past or current illnesses, as they may have implications on the treatment you are able to offer a patient, or may be relevant to the presentation. Specifically ask about head injuries, epilepsy and endocrine disorders (hypothyroidism and depression; hyperthyroidism and anxiety).

9) Medication history

The patient's medication history is also important – ask for the names and doses of current medications, and of any psychiatric medications they may have taken in the past. Also ask if they've experienced side-effects from any medications, particularly any psychiatric ones, as this may also have treatment implications. For example levodopa, used in the treatment of Parkinson's disease, can cause psychosis.

It may also be important to ask whether the patient has suddenly stopped taking any medication recently, as this could cause psychiatric effects.

10) Family history

Ask if there is a family history of mental illness, particularly affecting their parents or siblings. Family dynamic and their relationship with family members are also important to ask about.

11) Social history

The social history includes their living arrangements (with whom, state of housing, heating, living conditions), their level of social support (family, friends, social contacts), their financial circumstances, and whether they have any children.

You should also ask the patient about their history of substance use:

- **Tobacco** – calculate their pack years.
- **Alcohol** – the CAGE questionnaire is a useful screening tool for alcohol dependence. Calculate the number of units they consume daily, and the type of alcohol that they drink.
- **Illicit drugs** – have they ever used recreational drugs? Record the names, route of administration, the frequency of use, and the length of time they've been using.
- **Caffeine** – high doses of caffeine can cause unexplained panic attacks, so this is important to consider in some cases.
- Look out for signs of harmful use or dependence.

12) Personal history

- **Birth and development, including pregnancy**
    - Did they have a pre-term or traumatic birth (including forceps delivery)?
        - *'When your mother was pregnant with you, are you aware of any difficulties that occurred during the pregnancy or the birth?'*
    - Did they achieve their developmental milestones?
        - *'Did you start to walk and talk at the right times, as far as you're aware?'*

- **Early childhood experiences**
    - What are their memories of early childhood? Are they happy ones?
        - *'Tell me about your childhood. What are your earliest memories?'*
        - *'Would you say that you had a happy childhood?'*
    - Did they have any traumatic experiences? (sexual, psychological or physical abuse). Acknowledge that these questions are sensitive, and remember to signpost appropriately.
        - *'Some people have bad experiences during childhood that can be difficult to talk about. Did you have any bad experiences, such as abuse?'*
    - Were they a sickly child?
        - *'Were you ill a lot as a child? Did you miss a lot of school through illness?'*
    - What was their family dynamic like? (parents together, planned pregnancy, siblings and step-siblings)
        - *'Were your parents married when you were born? Are your parents together now? Do you have any brothers or sisters, or step-siblings?'*
        - *'What was it like growing up with your family? How did you all get on?'*

- **Education**
    - *'Did you enjoy school? If not, why?'*
    - *'Did you get along with the other children at school?'*
    - *'Did you get along with your teachers?'*
    - *'Were you bullied at school?'*
    - *'Were you often in trouble at school? What sort of things did you get into trouble for?'*
    - *'Did you finish school? What qualifications did you leave school with?'*

- **Occupational record**
  - *'Are you currently working?'*
  - *'Can you tell me where you've worked, in order?'*
  - *'Did you enjoy your jobs? If not, why?'*
  - *'Why did you leave your previous jobs?'*
  - *'Did you get along with your boss and colleagues? How would you describe your relationship with them?'*

- **Psychosexual history**
  - What is their sexual orientation?
    - *'How would you describe your sexuality?'*
    - *'How old were you when you had your first relationship?'*
  - How many relationships have they had? How long were they together for? What were the reasons for the breakdown of their relationship (if applicable)?
    - *'Could you tell me about the major relationships you've been in? How long were you together for? Why did the relationship end?'*
    - *'Are you currently in a relationship?'*
  - Do they have any children from their current or previous relationships? Where do their children live? How would they describe their relationship with their children and with their child's other parent?
    - *'Do you have any children? Can you tell me about your relationship with your children? How would you describe your relationship with your child's father/mother?'*
  - If the patient is female, remember to ask about stillbirths and miscarriages.

If you find these questions difficult to ask, signposting can be a very useful tool to warn the patient that some of the questions may be sensitive and that they may need to talk about some difficult things.

13) Forensic history

Ask about any previous convictions, particularly for violent crimes. Have they ever been in prison? If yes, what sentence did they receive? Do they currently have any outstanding charges or convictions?

- *'Have you ever been in trouble with the police?'*
- *'Do you have a criminal record?'*
- *'Have you ever been charged with or convicted of anything? If so, what offence, and what sentence did you receive?'*

14) Premorbid personality

Premorbid personality refers to what the patient was like before the onset of mental illness. It may be useful to get a family member or friend to give you a collateral history, in order to confirm what the patient is telling you.

- *'How would you describe yourself?'*
- *'How would others describe you? Would they describe you differently now to how they would before?'*

15) Closing the consultation

Concisely summarize what the patient has told you, giving them the opportunity to correct you or to add anything else. Provide an opportunity for them to ask you any questions that they may have. Thank the patient for speaking to you.

> **Summary of key points (GET YOUR MARKS):**
>
> **Establish rapport** (clear introduction of who you are, what your role is and why you are there).
>
> **History of presenting complaint:** key symptoms to screen for are low or high mood, lack of energy, appetite, loss of interest, early morning waking, anxiety, delusions, hallucinations, suicidal ideation.
>
> **Systems review:** rule out differentials (see *Chapter 6*).
>
> **ICE.**
>
> **Psychiatric history:** ask about similar symptoms in the past, previous psychiatric diagnoses, treatments and always ask about SUICIDAL IDEATION.
>
> **Past medical history:** any acute or chronic disease can have implications on a patient's mental wellbeing. Ask specifically about a history of head injuries, epilepsy and thyroid disease.
>
> **Medication history:** current medication, allergies, over-the-counter medications and supplements.
>
> **Family history:** first-degree relative with mental illness. It is also helpful to ascertain the patient's relationship with people in their family.
>
> **Social history:** disease impact on occupation and activities of daily living. History of smoking, alcohol intake, recreational drug use and caffeine. Dietary and exercise history if time permits.
>
> **Forensic history:** ask about previous convictions and time spent in prison.
>
> **Premorbid personality:** what they were like before the onset of their mental illness.
>
> **Closing the consultation:** let the Calgary–Cambridge Model be your guide. Remember your key skills such as summarizing and screening. Always leave the patient with a plan of care, even if it is that you need to speak with your colleagues. Thank the patient.

7.2 Focused information gathering

7.2.1 Depression

The core symptoms of depression:

> **Key Knowledge: Mood vs. Affect**
>
> **Mood:** subjective, person's own description of how they feel.
>
> **Affect:** objective description of apparent emotion conveyed by person's non-verbal behaviour, or reaction to the external environment.

Low mood, anhedonia (lack of enjoyment) and low energy are the key symptoms that aid in the diagnosis of depression. For diagnosis, at least one of these symptoms must be present for most days, for **at least 2 weeks**.

- **Mood**
  - *'How would you describe your mood?'*
  - *'How long have you felt this way?'*
  - *'Does it vary throughout the day? Is it worse at any time of day, e.g. first thing in the morning? Is your mood low every day?'*
  - *'Does anything help improve your mood? Does anything make it worse?'*
- **Anhedonia**
  - *'Do you still enjoy the things that you would normally like to do?'* e.g. hobbies, work, laughing at a funny movie.

- **Lack of energy**
  - *'How are your energy levels?'*
  - *'Do you feel more tired than usual?'*
- **Biological symptoms**
  - **Sleep:** *'How is your sleep? Has your sleeping pattern changed? When do you sleep? How long do you sleep? Do you wake up in the night? When do you wake in the morning? How do you feel on waking? Do you sleep much during the day?'*
  - **Appetite:** *'How has your appetite been?'*
  - **Weight loss:** *'Have you noticed any weight change?'*
  - **GI symptoms:** *'Have you noticed any change in bowel habits? Stomach aches? Indigestion?'*
  - **Libido:** *'Any change to your interest in sex?'*
- **Cognitive symptoms**
  - **Guilt:** *'Do you feel guilty about anything?'*
  - **Tearfulness:** *'Is there anything that makes you cry? Have you been tearful recently?'*
  - **Worthlessness:** *'How do you see yourself compared to others?'*
  - **Self-esteem:** *'How do you feel about yourself?'*
  - **Poor memory:** *'Do you have any problems with your memory?'*
  - **Poor concentration:** *'Do you have any problems with concentration? For example, can you watch a TV programme all the way through?'*
  - **Agitation:** *'Have you been feeling angry or irritable? What makes you feel this way?'*
- **Past psychiatric history**
  - *'Have you experienced low mood before?'*
  - *'Have you been diagnosed with depression previously?'*
  - *'Have you had any other mental health problems in the past?'* It is important to elicit past history of self-harm, suicide attempt(s)
  - *'When was your first contact with mental health services?'*
  - *'Have you had any treatment for a mental health problem?'* e.g. medication, psychological therapy, electroconvulsive therapy
  - *'Have you ever been admitted to the hospital for a mental health issue?'*
- **Remember to screen for:**
  - **Bipolar affective disorder**: if a patient with undiagnosed bipolar disorder is commenced on antidepressants, this can precipitate a manic episode. It is therefore important to screen for suggestive symptoms, in order to confirm the correct diagnosis.
    - *'Have you experienced any times where you've felt quite the opposite, for example on top of the world, inexplicably happy?'*
  - **Psychotic symptoms**: patients with severe depression can experience psychotic symptoms. People with psychotic depression usually experience symptoms in line with themes about depression, such as worthlessness.
    - *'Have you ever heard or seen anything that other people say isn't there? Do you hear voices telling you what to do or how to behave?'*
    - *'Do you hold any strong beliefs?'*
    - *'Do you feel like there is anyone out to get you?'*
  - **Alcohol misuse**: a useful tool for doing this is the CAGE questionnaire (see *Section 6.2.7*).

7.2.2 Anxiety

These are the areas you specifically need to ask about when taking a history from a patient with anxiety:

- *'Is there anything in particular that you're worried about/that is making you anxious?'*
- *'How long has this been going on for?'*

- Panic attacks
  - *'Have you ever had a panic attack? Could you describe it to me?'*
  - *'Have you ever felt like you couldn't breathe/your heart was racing and you were going to collapse?'*
  - *'How long does this last for?'*
  - *'Does anything make it stop?'*
  - *'Does anything in particular make this happen? Does it happen unexpectedly?'*
- Physical symptoms of anxiety
  - *'Do you ever feel your heart beating abnormally fast or pounding?'*
  - *'Do you ever have chest pain?'*
  - *'Have you been feeling restless or on edge recently?'*
  - *'Have you been finding it more difficult to concentrate recently?'*
  - *'Do you find yourself lying awake at night worrying?'*
  - *'Do you ever have any stomach pain or loose motions?'*

OSCE TIP: ALWAYS screen for depression and substance misuse in patients who are presenting with anxiety.

- Screen for depression:
  - *'Has your mood been lower than usual recently? If so, for how long?'*
  - *'Do you still enjoy doing things in your spare time?'*
  - *'Do you feel that you have less energy than you usually do?'*
  - *'Have you been having any feeling of helplessness/hopelessness/guilt?'*
  - *'Sometimes when people feel low, or anxious, they have thoughts about hurting themselves, or feel that they don't want to live any more. Have you had any thoughts like this?'*
- Potential stressors:
  - *'Is there anything about your current state of affairs that is worrying you?'*
  - *'Are you having any problems at work or at home that are worrying you?'*
  - *'Do you drink alcohol? How many units a week do you normally drink?'*
  - *'Do you use, or have you ever used recreational drugs?'*

OSCE TIP: If you find it difficult to ask people how much they drink or if they use recreational drugs, it can be helpful to normalize the questions first, i.e. *'This is something that I ask everyone who comes to see me…'*

7.2.3   Psychosis

Key Knowledge: Schizophrenia vs. Psychosis

Schizophrenia: a mental illness characterized by psychotic symptoms and other associated clinical features.

Psychosis: a group of illnesses that share certain symptoms (hallucinations, delusions, thought disorders), characterized by loss of connection with reality and lack of insight.

Hallucinations and delusions can be very real experiences for patients, and can cause significant distress. It is therefore important to approach history taking in a sensitive, non-judgmental manner. Symptoms of schizophrenia can be separated into positive and negative symptoms. Below are a few examples of questions to elicit details about each symptom subset.

- *'Could you tell me about how you have been feeling recently?'*
- *'Your friends/family have mentioned that you have been quite stressed out and haven't been sleeping or eating properly for the past few weeks. It might be helpful to figure out*

what's going on. I was also wondering if I could ask you a few questions to get a clearer picture of what's been going on?'

Positive symptoms

Delusions: a delusion is a fixed, false belief despite evidence of the contrary, which is not in keeping with the individual's cultural or religious norms. Patients with schizophrenia commonly experience paranoid or persecutory delusions. Below are a few examples of questions to elicit different types of delusions.

- **Persecutory / paranoid**: *'Do you feel that you are in danger? Do you feel as though someone is out to get you? Is there anything that you're worried about?'*
- **Delusions of perception**: abnormal significance attributed to a normal sensory perception (e.g. patient sees a traffic light turn from red to green, and interprets that as someone trying to kill them).
  - *'Do you feel that you see things in the same way as other people?'*
- **Passivity / somatic control**: fixed, false belief that an outside force has control over the patient's emotions, actions and bodily sensations. This is also known as **delusions of control**.
  - *'Do you ever feel as though you don't have control over your feelings or actions?'*
- **Grandeur**: patient believes that they have extra-special powers or abilities, seen more commonly in mania.
  - *'Do you have any special powers? Is there anything special about yourself that makes you different from others?'*
- **Thought**: *'Do you ever feel as though you don't have control over your own thoughts? Could you tell me a bit more about this?'*
  - **Thought insertion**: thoughts are placed in patient's mind by external force
    - *'Do you feel that your thoughts are your own? Do you feel as though someone is placing thoughts in your head?'*
  - **Thought withdrawal**: thoughts are removed from patient's mind by external force
    - *'Do you ever feel as though your thoughts have been taken out of your mind?'*
  - Thought broadcasting: patient's thoughts can be accessed by others
    - *'Can other people tell what you're thinking?'*
- **Conviction**: *'Is there a chance that you might be wrong about these things?'*

Hallucinations: a hallucination is a perception in the absence of a stimulus. They can take several forms, but auditory hallucinations are the commonest type in schizophrenia.

Auditory hallucinations can be:
- **Second person**: voice speaks directly to patient
- **Third person**: voice(s) talk about the patient
- **Running commentary**: voice(s) comments on patient's actions
- **Thought echo**: patient hears their thoughts as, or shortly after, they are formed.

It is important to also explore the content of hallucinations, duration and frequency, precipitating factors, impact on patient's life and the degree of insight. For example:
- *'Have you ever heard voices around you even though nobody was around?'*
- *'Do you hear things that other people around you don't seem to hear?'*
  - *'Where do these voices come from?'*
  - *'How many voices are there?'*
  - *'Do they talk to you or about you?'*
  - *'Do they comment on everything you do?'*
  - *'Do they tell you to do things?'*
  - *'What do they say? Can you give me an example?'*
- *'Have you noticed these voices start speaking while you're doing something in particular?'*

- *'Have these voices affected your daily life in any way?'*
- *'Could you share with me your ideas on why you hear these voices?'*

> **Mnemonic: PACT**
>
> **First-rank symptoms**: Schneider's first rank symptoms of schizophrenia can be easily remembered using **PACT**:
> - **Delusions of Perception**
> - **Auditory** hallucinations (3rd person or commentary)
> - **Somatic Control** (passivity of affect, volition and impulse)
> - **Thought**: insertion, withdrawal, broadcasting.

Negative symptoms
- **Asocial**: social withdrawal
- **Avolition**: lack of motivation
- **Anhedonia**: inability to gain pleasure from normally enjoyable activities
- **Anergy**: low energy levels.

Patients may also exhibit affective flattening, apathy, alogia and attentional impairment, which may be better observed than elicited with questions. Questions to ask might include:
- *'Do you still spend time with your friends or family? Can you tell me why you prefer not to spend time with them?'*
- *'How are your energy levels?'*
- *'Do you still feel motivated to go to work or school or to take part in hobbies?'*
- *'Do you still find pleasure in doing things that you normally enjoy?'*

Other symptoms
- Mood: patients may feel depressed, irritable or angry.
- Physical: patients may experience sleep disturbance, appetite loss, somatic complaints (e.g. abdominal pain), loss of energy, as mentioned above.

Risk assessment
Approximately 10% of patients with schizophrenia commit suicide. This is likely to be a result of command hallucinations, or depressive symptoms. Command hallucinations, which are voices that direct the patient to carry out a certain action, can also result in harm to others.
- *'Have you ever thought about hurting yourself or someone else?'*

Assessment of insight
Assessment of insight allows you to estimate the patient's compliance with treatment.
- *'Do you think there is anything unusual going on?'*
- *'Do you think you need any help for what you are going through?'*

You may find it particularly difficult to communicate with a psychotic patient, perhaps because they are out of touch with reality, or paranoid of your intentions. If a patient finds it difficult to trust your motives, the following can be a helpful phrase to reaffirm their faith in your role as a medical professional:
- *'I am a doctor. My only intentions are to provide any help possible to get you back on track. I can see how this situation has made things very difficult for you. So we share the same aim of wanting you to feel better.'*

7.2.4 Bipolar disorder

> **OSCE TIP**: You can assess pressure of speech and disorders of thought (flight of ideas, knight's move thinking, etc.) whilst taking the history.

These are the specific areas you need to focus on when taking a history from someone presenting with acute mania:
- *'How would you describe your mood?'*
- *'Has your mood changed in any way recently?'*
- *'Have you been behaving differently to how you usually would?'*
- *'Do you feel like you have a lot more energy compared to people around you?'*
- *'Are you sleeping less than you usually do, but without being more tired?'*
- *'Are you doing more things in a day than you would normally do?'*
- *'Are you able to concentrate on what you're doing during the day?'*
- *'How would you describe yourself compared to other people? Would you say that you're different?'*

> **OSCE TIP**: Taking a thorough history from a manic patient can be very difficult, as they may go off on a tangent and their train of thought may be very difficult to follow. In an OSCE, it is crucial that you take control of the situation in a polite but firm way, and redirect the patient back to the line of questioning to ensure that you take a full history.

- *'Have you had any new ideas or interests lately?'*
- *'Can you do anything that other people can't do? Do you have any special abilities?'*
- *'Have you had any experiences recently that you can't explain, like seeing or hearing things that aren't there?'*
- *'Has anyone told you that you're behaving differently to how you usually do?'*
- *'Has anything like this ever happened to you before?'*
- *'Has your mood ever been very low? Does this alternate with how you're feeling now?'*

Remember to ask about family history of bipolar disorder and about substance misuse.

> **OSCE TIP**: When asking about depressive episodes, remember to screen for risk of suicide and self-harm.

7.2.5 Obsessive–compulsive disorder (OCD)

When taking a history from someone with OCD, these are the areas you need to focus on:
- **Obsessive thoughts**
  - *'Can you tell me about your thoughts?'*
  - *'Do you ever have thoughts that you don't want, or that make you upset?'*
  - *'Do you keep having the thoughts even if you try to get rid of them?'*
  - *'Do these thoughts disrupt your day?'*
  - *'Are the thoughts repetitive?'*
  - *'What do you do when you get these thoughts? Do you try to resist them?'*
  - *'Can you give me any specific examples of the thoughts you're having?'*
  - *'Do you ever feel worried about being dirty/contaminated, even after washing?'*
  - *'Do you ever have thoughts about doing bad things that you don't want to do, like hurting people?'*

> **OSCE TIP**: Watch the patient's body language – they may display signs of distress at not being able to carry out their compulsions, or they may look worried or on edge.

- **Compulsive actions**
  - *'Do you ever have to perform any sort of ritual?'*
  - *'Do you have to touch, tap, or count things a number of times?'*
  - *'What happens if you don't do these things?'*
- **Symptoms of depression and anxiety**
  - *Screen for the symptoms of depression and anxiety.*
  - *Remember to assess risk of suicide/self-harm.*

> **OSCE TIP**: The patient usually has good insight into the condition, and recognizes that the thoughts are not delusions, and are products of their own mind.

7.2.6 Suicide risk assessment

The goal of a suicide risk assessment is to determine the risk of death by suicide, based on the patient's current mental state. Key aspects of this assessment include a thorough history and mental state examination, with specific focus on suicide risk factors. An effective way of obtaining history from a patient who has attempted suicide is by dividing the history into three components:

1. Before the attempt
2. During the attempt
3. After the attempt

This systematic approach is a sure-fire method of obtaining key information. It will also make it easier to summarize your history at the end of an OSCE station, and report on the estimated level of risk.

Before the attempt

Life events before suicide attempt: it is important to assess the patient's state of mind, and events leading up to the attempt. Exploring this aspect of the history will identify any key risk factors, such as a relationship breakdown, loss of job, ongoing depression, etc. It is also important to elicit the patient's ideas on what triggered their suicide attempt.

- *'It seems as if things have been quite rough for you. Can you tell me about what's been going on in your life recently?'*
- *'Can you please tell me how you were feeling the day before the attempt?'*
- *'Can you explain why you decided to end your life?'*

Plan for suicide attempt: a planned suicide attempt, with efforts to avoid being discovered poses a higher level of immediate suicide risk. Therefore, it is vital to elicit this in the history.

- *'How long have you been planning to end your life?'*
- *'Can you explain why you acted on your thoughts on this occasion?'*
- *'Did you write a suicide note? What other plans did you make?'*
- *'Did you make any attempts to avoid being discovered?'*

During the attempt

It is vital to identify key features of the attempt: method, place and time, intentions, and concomitant alcohol/drug consumption.

- *'Could you talk me through what happened during the attempt?'*
- *'How did you attempt to end your life? When and where did this happen?'*
- *'Describe what happened and what your thoughts were during the attempt?'*
- If a medication overdose was taken, what was it?
- *'Did you take any drugs or alcohol before or during it?'*
- *'What were you expecting to happen when you took those pills?'* (amend as appropriate)
- *'Did you make any attempts to avoid being discovered?'*

After the attempt

This section allows gathering of information about what stopped the patient from successfully carrying out the suicide attempt. It can also provide an insight into the patient's current state of mind, and their retrospective thoughts on the suicide attempt. Many patients may convey feelings of guilt and embarrassment related to the attempt. Therefore, it is vital to show empathy and provide reassurance.

- *'Could you walk me through what happened after this?'*
- *'Do you know what stopped you from going through with it?'*
- *'How were you found?'*
- *'How do you feel about it now?'*
- *'What are your concerns at the moment?'*
  - *'Do you feel that your reasons to live outweigh your reasons to die?'*
  - *'Do you think you could get access to (pills, weapon, poisons, etc.) if you needed to?'*
  - *'How long have you been feeling this way for?'*

Future risk assessment

- *'As you feel now, do you think you're likely to try something like this again?'*
- *'Do you intend to try something like this again?'*
- *'How do you feel about the future?'*
- *'Do you have a support network around you? Do you live alone?'*
- *'Do you feel like you need help to deal with this?'*
- *'What made you stop/seek help?'*

Relevant past history

- Past attempts of suicide or self-harm
- Does the patient currently self-harm?
- Psychiatric history
- Family history of psychiatric conditions, suicide or self-harm
- Past medical history: chronic illnesses, chronic pain, other medical illnesses that may have had a major impact on patient's wellbeing

Social situation

- Employment
- Isolation
- Relationship status
- Support network

Protective factors

- Religious/cultural background
- Family

> **OSCE TIP:** Remember to screen for depression and psychosis when doing a suicide risk assessment, as the suicide attempt may be the presenting feature in some cases.

7.2.7 Substance misuse

When carrying out a consultation with someone who is suffering with substance misuse it is important to adopt an **empathetic, non-judgmental approach** throughout.

Alcohol

When taking an alcohol history, it is important to distinguish between **alcohol dependence** and **alcohol misuse**. Many people misuse alcohol, but not all are dependent.

> **Key Knowledge: Signs of dependence**
> - Withdrawals e.g. tremor, sweating, mood changes, hallucinations, delirium tremens
> - Cravings
> - Drinking despite negative consequences
> - Tolerance
> - Primacy – where they put drinking before other activities e.g. seeing family, eating

Taking an alcohol history:

An 'alcohol history' can take on many forms such as screening for alcohol abuse in a new patient, ascertaining severity of abuse by taking a thorough alcohol history or approaching the subject of cutting down/stopping drinking.

Check why they are here. They may not have come to see you to explicitly to talk about their drinking:

- *'Why have you come to see me today?'* or *'Can I double check why you are here today?'*

Assess their current drinking behaviour. Ask specifically about alcohol intake in the last 24 hours and the last 7 days:

- *'How much have you had to drink in the previous 24 hours?'*
- *'How much would you drink in one week?'*

You may also want to ask about a typical day for them:

- *'Can you take me through a typical day for you? What do you do?'*

If the scenario is pointing you in the direction of screening someone for alcohol abuse, a very useful tool is the **CAGE questionnaire**:

- Have you ever thought about **Cutting down** on your drinking?
- Have you ever got **Annoyed** with someone for criticizing your drinking?
- Have you ever felt **Guilty** about your drinking?
- Do you ever need to have an **Eye-opener** in the mornings? i.e. do you need to have a drink first thing in the morning to stop withdrawal symptoms?

Other questions you need to ask to get an idea about their drinking:

- *'What types of alcohol do you drink?'* **Narrowing of repertoire**: as people become more dependent on alcohol, the range of beverages they drink declines so that they may only drink one or two types of alcohol.
- *'Do you find that you have to drink more to get drunk?'* Investigating their tolerance.
- *'Where would you typically drink? In the pub? At home?'*
- *'Do you drink alone or with others?'*
- *'Have you had any treatment for alcohol misuse in the past?'*

ALWAYS ASK ABOUT WITHDRAWAL SYMPTOMS! (See below)

A useful way of remembering all these questions is: **TWiRP CHER:**

- **Tolerance**: *'Do you feel like you have to drink more to get drunk/the same effect as before?'*
- **Withdrawal symptoms**: *'When you stop drinking do you experience shaking, sweating, feeling sick? Have you ever had an unusual experience where you've heard a voice when no-one was around? or seen things which aren't really there?'*
- **Repertoire**: *'Where do you drink? At home/in the pub? Alone/with friends? Is this always the same? When do you drink? Throughout the day? Early morning? What do you drink? Do you always drink the same thing?'*
- **Primacy**: *'Is drinking a major part of your life? Do you put it before other things?'*
- **Control/compulsion**: *'Do you find you have reduced control over how much you drink? Do you ever feel like you need a drink?'*

- **Harm**: *'How has your drinking affected your work / relationships / health? Do you continue drinking despite the harm it has caused?'*
- **Eye opener**: *'Do you have a drink first thing in the morning to avoid withdrawal symptoms?'*
- **Rapid reinstatement / relapse**: *'Have you ever tried to cut down before? If so, what happened?'*

Drug misuse

In this history you need to ask about **each individual substance**.

'What drugs do you take?' For each type of drug you should ask:
- *'How much do you take each time?'*
- *'How often do you use?'*
- Try to elicit a pattern of usage: *'Are there any particular times you use?'*
- *'When was the last time you used?'*
- *'How do you take it? Do you inject? Do you smoke?'*

Other questions:
- *'Do you take any prescribed medication?'*
- *'Do you drink alcohol?'* Ask about quantity, frequency and pattern of use (see above)

Assessment of risk:
- **Overdose risk**: *'Have you ever overdosed before? Have you ever come close to overdosing?'*
- **Polydrug and alcohol misuse**: you will have elicited this from history of what drugs they are currently taking and whether they are drinking alcohol or not.
- **Unsafe injecting practices**: *'Where do you get your needles to inject? Do you use clean needles? Do you share needles with others?'*
- **Unsafe sexual practices**: *'Are you sexually active? Do you use condoms? How many sexual partners have you had in the last 3 months?'*

Topics which you need to cover in both types of consultation:

Depression screen
- Ask about mood, sleep, appetite and concentration.
- Risks of self-harm or harm to others: *'Have you ever had thoughts of harming yourself?'* *'Have you ever had thoughts of harming others?'*

Assessment of social functioning
- Ask about partners, family and if they have any support
- Housing, education, employment
- Benefits and financial problems
- Enquire about any risks to dependent children:
  - Ask about their children, their ages and the level of contact they have with them.
  - Does their drinking / drug-taking affect their ability to look after their children?
  - It may be helpful to ask about everyday things such as: *'Does your drinking have an effect on your child's daily routine, such as getting to school on time?'*
  - Do they store their alcohol / drugs safely, out of reach from the children?

Local child protection procedures should be followed if there is risk of significant harm to children.

Assessment of physical and psychological health
- Past medical history, including psychiatric history.
- Current or past infection with blood-borne viruses – *'Have you ever suffered from hepatitis B or C? Have you been diagnosed with HIV?'*

- For women specifically you may want to ask about cervical screening and pregnancy history.
- It is also important to ask about their sexual health: *'Have you ever had a sexually transmitted infection? Are you currently using contraception?'*
- Ask if they are taking any other prescribed or non-prescribed medication.

Forensic history
- *'Have you ever been arrested? Have you ever been in prison?'*

Cessation advice
It may be worthwhile to find out whether they are interested in trying to stop drinking or using drugs. One way to approach this is to ask *'Do you think you are drinking too much? Would you like to try and reduce the amount you are drinking? Would you like to eventually stop taking drugs?'*

You can also ask them *'Why do you want to cut down/stop, what is motivating you? What do you think will get better if you were to stop?'* It is important to incorporate ICE in this section; if, for example, they want to be able to go back to work you could say *'The desire you have to want to quit could be the first step in getting you back to work'.*

Support available
- Groups and charities, e.g. Alcoholics Anonymous
- Refer them to the community alcohol team
- Ask them whether they have support from their family and friends.

7.2.8 Eating disorders

When a child or adult presents with a possible eating disorder it is important to take a thorough history of the development of the disorder and the patient's ideas.

Firstly discover exactly what they mean by 'weight loss':
- *'How much weight have you lost over the period of time?'*
- *'What are your thoughts about this weight loss? Did you want to lose weight?'*
- *'What's your normal pattern of eating, do you eat three meals a day or do you snack a lot?';* *'Talk me through what you ate yesterday.'*

> **Key Knowledge:**
> **SCOFF questionnaire**: screens for eating disorders
> - Do you make yourself **sick** because you feel uncomfortably full?
> - Do you worry that you have lost **control** over how much you eat?
> - Have you recently lost more than **one stone** in a 3-month period?
> - Do you believe yourself to be **fat** when others say you are too thin?
> - Would you say **food** dominates your life?
>
> Two or more positive answers indicate a likely case of anorexia or bulimia.

IMPORTANT QUESTION: *'What do you think about your weight and appearance; are you happy with your weight?'* This is important as it allows you to gain an idea of how the patient views their body image.

Rule out any organic cause for the weight loss (infective, metabolic, endocrine):
- *'Have you had any diarrhoea or vomiting recently?'*
- *'Have you been abroad recently?'*
- *'Do you have regular periods?'* Ascertain if they have amenorrhoea.

Explore psychological factors: consider all relationships in the patient's life; one person may have affected the child greatly.
- *'How is your relationship with your family?'*
- *'How is school, do you enjoy it?' 'Do you have any problems at school?'*
- *'Are there family arguments at dinnertime?'*

Go through the **symptoms of eating disorders** systematically to see if they have any related symptoms:
- Ask questions about preoccupation with food, hoarding, cooking excessively for others, binging, self-induced vomiting, laxative use, etc.
- It may be helpful to speak to another family member about these signs as well.

It is also important to ask about **family history of eating disorders or anything similar.**

7.2.9 Motivational interviewing

This is a special style of consultation whereby you are aiming to engage with the intrinsic motivation within the patient in order to facilitate a change in their behaviour.

Important strategies to use in motivational interviewing:

OARS
- **O**pen-ended questions
- **A**ffirmations
- **R**eflective listening
- **S**ummary statements

Ask open-ended questions:
- *'What brings you here today?'*
- *'What do you think about the possibility of stopping your drinking?'*
- *'Tell me about the last time you had a drink.'*
- *'What has your drug use been like this past week?'*

Affirm: this shows that you are acknowledging the difficulties the patient has been going through: *'I appreciate how hard it must have been for you to come and speak to me today. You've taken a big step.'*

Listen reflectively: this is a way of checking that you understood what the patient meant:
- Patient: *'When I wake up from a night of heavy drinking I feel so terrible, I can't focus, sometimes I can barely get out of bed.'*
- Doctor: *'It messes with your head so that you can't think straight or concentrate.'*
- Patient: *'Yes and sometimes...'*

Summarize
This is important in any type of consultation, and particularly here. It helps to reinforce what the patient has told you, demonstrates that you have been listening to them, and prepares for the consultation to progress. It also highlights if you have missed out anything important that the patient may have told you or if you have misunderstood the patient.
- *'This is what I have understood from what you have told me so far. Let me know if I have missed anything...'*

Incorporate the ability to **elicit self-motivational statements**. This is the fundamental component of motivational interviewing. Rather than simply helping the patient to identify the problem and encouraging ways to solve it, you have to help the patient realize how their life might be better and allow them to choose ways to achieve this. It is important that the patient persuades themselves to make the change, not you. A sign that the patient's resistance to making a change is diminishing is the self-motivational statement, e.g. *'I've got to do something about this before it gets worse.'*

DEARS

Five principles of motivational interviewing, **DEARS**:

- **D**evelop **D**iscrepancy
- **E**xpress **E**mpathy
- **A**mplify **A**mbivalence
- **R**oll with **R**esistance
- **S**upport **S**elf-efficacy

Develop Discrepancy

- By developing discrepancy you can help the patient realize that their current behaviour is not taking them towards their desired goals.
  - *'How do you think your life would be different if you stopped drinking?'*
  - *'Where do you see yourself in 5 years' time if you continue to use drugs? Is that where you want to be?'*

Express Empathy

- If the patient believes that you truly understand where they are coming from, they will be more likely to share their thoughts and experiences with you.
  - *'That must have been so hard for you.'*

Amplify Ambivalence

- Ambivalence to or uncertainty about "change" is normal; however, by helping the patient to verbalize their uncertainties, you can then help them to work through it.
  - *'What was your life like before you started taking drugs? What's scaring you the most about changing?'*

Roll with Resistance

- Resistance is always to be expected when it comes to preparing to make a big change.
- It's important to not force the patient into making a change, instead try to clarify and understand what they're feeling.
- Encourage them to come up with their own solutions.
  - *'It's OK if you're not ready to quit, it's completely your choice.'*
  - *'What do you want to do? Where do you want to go from here?'*

Supporting Self-efficacy:

- For change to be possible, the person has to believe that they are capable of making the change.
- Help and encourage them to believe that change is possible and attainable.
  - *'You've made some great progress. How do you feel?'*
  - *'You've got a strong action plan to make these changes possible and you've put a lot of thought into your goals.'*

The 5 **R**s for someone struggling to change their behaviour:

- **Relevance to patient**: make it personal to them, incorporate patient's ICE.
- **Risks of behaviour**: go through what risks a continuation of their behaviour pose. This could be anything ranging from health risks to social risks.
- **Rewards of changing**: state what benefits there are to changing.
- **Roadblocks**: what is stopping them from changing?
- **Repetition**: each time you see the patient, try to incorporate some sort of motivational intervention. Reassure unsuccessful patients that they can do it.

Key principles for motivational interviewing
- Throughout the consultation it is important that you engage with the patient, be empathetic and really try to understand their perspective.
- Constantly guide the patient to focus on a target area – find out what is most important to them at that time.
- Draw out their own ideas and reasons for change.
- Constantly summarize and reflect throughout.
- Ask key questions to determine their readiness for action planning.

7.3 Information giving and shared decision making

The following section is a quick overview of what you might tell the patient during an information giving or shared decision making station. Use this section as a guide to what information might be relevant for the patient. Be sure to always assess the patient's starting point. Drawings and the use of models are very helpful for patients and often count for one or more marks. If you don't have anything to draw, writing long words for patients can also be helpful.

Review *Chapter 5* to get the most OSCE points possible.

7.3.1 Schizophrenia

What is it? A problem of the mind that affects your thoughts, emotions and behaviour.

What happens? You can experience unusual symptoms such as:
- **Hallucinations**: this is when you hear, see, or less commonly smell, feel or taste something that isn't necessarily there. The commonest is hearing voices when there is nobody around. These experiences can seem very real and can cause a lot of distress.
- **Delusions**: when you believe something and are completely sure of it, even though it may not be true. It's as though you see things in a different way to others. You may feel that your thoughts are being controlled in some way.
- **Other symptoms**:
  - You may find it harder to concentrate, for example to finish a book or watch TV, or keep up with your studies.
  - You may feel sad, and lose interest in things you used to enjoy doing.
  - You might not bother to get up or go out of the house.
  - You may feel uncomfortable in social situations, or with being around people.

How common is it? Schizophrenia is common; it affects around 1 in 100 people over the course of their life.

What causes it? There is not one specific cause. It is likely a result of a combination of several things, which is different for different people. These include genetics, brain damage, drugs such as amphetamines or heavy cannabis use, alcohol, stress, difficult childhood.

What's the outlook? If you take 5 people with schizophrenia:
- 1 will improve within the first five years of when they started having symptoms.
- 3 will improve, but will have times when the symptoms get worse again.
- 1 will experience distressing symptoms for a long period.

How is it treated?
Therapy: examples include cognitive behavioural therapy (CBT), counselling, family therapy. This helps to concentrate on problems you find most distressing, and how they can be dealt with.

Medication: the group of medicines used to treat schizophrenia are called antipsychotics. They reduce the effects of the symptoms on your daily life and can help you function better.

7.3.2 Anxiety

What is it? When you are anxious you feel fearful and tense. In addition you may have one or more unpleasant physical symptoms. We all experience anxiety at some point during our lives, which is normal, and it can be beneficial in some cases – for example, you might work harder for an exam if you're a bit anxious about it. It is when anxiety becomes excessive or inappropriate that it becomes a problem, and is thought of more as an illness. For example, anxiety is thought of as abnormal if it persists after a stressful situation, if it occurs when there is no stressful situation, or if you feel much more anxious than you should for a particular situation.

Anxiety can manifest itself in a number of different ways: physical symptoms include chest pain, breathlessness, diarrhoea, vomiting and headaches. It also causes people to feel agitated, tense, or like something awful is going to happen to them. It most commonly causes exhaustion, insomnia, irritability and worry.

Who gets it? Everyone will experience anxiety at some point during their lives, but it is when this anxiety becomes excessive and impacts on your day-to-day life that it becomes a problem. There are many factors that can contribute to anxiety disorder, such as having close relatives who suffer with anxiety, being made redundant at work, having an anxious or worry-prone personality, having financial problems, or the breakdown of a relationship.

Although these factors can contribute to developing anxiety, it may not occur in people who may have some of these factors, and can also affect people who don't have any of these factors.

What can be done about it? There are a number of options available for the treatment of anxiety.
- **Medication**
  - Antidepressants are normally used for depression, but they can be helpful in anxiety even if you don't have depression. Selective serotonin reuptake inhibitors (SSRIs) are the ones usually used in anxiety, and help to reduce the anxiety symptoms you may be experiencing. It's important to bear in mind that antidepressants will not work immediately, and can take a couple of weeks to help your symptoms, so you should try to keep taking them for at least 4 weeks to see if they will help.
- **Cognitive behavioural therapy (CBT)**
  - CBT is a mixture of both cognitive and behavioural therapy. Cognitive therapy uses the idea that particular thinking patterns can contribute to or trigger some health problems, such as anxiety. Behavioural therapy focuses on how we behave, and how we can change our behaviour to try to deal with feelings of anxiety. For example, an unhelpful behaviour in anxiety is to avoid situations that make you anxious, and behavioural therapy can help to change this behaviour and help you overcome your anxiety.
- Self-help books and classes can also be very helpful for some people who suffer from anxiety.

7.3.3 Bipolar disorder and mania

What is it? Bipolar disorder is a condition where you have periods of depression and periods of 'highs' (mania). It used to be called manic depression, and involves long periods, usually several weeks each, of either depression or mania. The first episode you experience can be either mania or depression, and you can be diagnosed with bipolar disorder after experiencing at least one episode of mania with either a second episode of mania, or an episode of depression, either before or after the mania.

Mania is an altered mental state, where someone experiences an unusually high or irritable mood. It is often seen as part of bipolar disorder, where a person's mood may fluctuate between elation and depression. It usually lasts at least a week, often much longer, and it may develop suddenly, or come on gradually over weeks. Mania is associated with many symptoms, and most people with mania will have three or four of the following:

- Grand ideas about your self-importance, and grand new ideas and plans
- Increased energy – there is less need for sleep, and everything is done in a rush
- Restlessness – difficulty in sitting still
- Anxiety
- More talkative and speaking faster than usual
- Flight of ideas – thoughts may be racing and train of thought may be difficult for others to follow
- Easily distracted
- Irritation or agitation, particularly with people who don't understand or agree with the grand plans and ideas
- Disinhibition and spontaneity, which may lead to risky behaviours such as excessive drinking or taking drugs, or to excessive spending, making rash decisions about jobs and relationships, and being less inhibited about sexual behaviours.

If the mania is severe you may be able to hear voices or see things that other people cannot (hallucinations), or believe things that are untrue (delusion). These false beliefs are usually related to the grand ideas, such as believing they are a very important person or a celebrity.

A person with mania may not realize that they are high. It is usually picked up by friends and family as their behaviour changes and becomes more bizarre. It may also be noticed due to the rash decisions that are made, such as quitting a job unexpectedly. Family members may notice a person becoming more irritable, overactive and talkative and behaving differently – they may do embarrassing things in public or spend money excessively. The person with mania may describe feeling more alert, driven and sociable, with higher self-esteem.

What causes it? Many factors can lead to the development of bipolar disorder. It can be caused by changes in the concentrations of certain chemicals in the body, such as serotonin. Genes also have a part to play in the disorder, as your risk of developing it is much higher if you have a parent or sibling who is affected, especially if you have an affected identical twin. Stressful life events may trigger the first manic episode, but do not cause mania or bipolar disorder.

Who gets it? The lifetime risk of developing bipolar disorder is 1–3%. It most commonly begins in late teenage years or early adulthood, but can start at any age. It affects males and females equally, and in the UK, the risk is higher in black and other minority ethnic groups.

What can be done about it? If mania is not treated, it can cause significant damage to relationships, health, career and finances. People who have experienced an episode of mania often regret their behaviour once they have recovered from the high.

Acute mania can be treated with antipsychotics such as olanzapine. If a person is diagnosed with bipolar disorder, they can be given prophylactic treatment with a mood stabilizer such as lithium. This aims to prevent any manic or depressive episodes, stopping their mood from fluctuating.

7.3.4 Obsessive–compulsive disorder

What is it? Obsessive–compulsive disorder (OCD) is a mental health condition that involves obsessive thoughts and compulsive actions as a result of the obsessive thoughts. The thoughts are typically recurring and the actions tend to be repetitive. A common example is having obsessive thoughts about being contaminated with germs, and having to wash your hands multiple times a day. However, obsessional thoughts can be about anything. Sometimes they may make you feel repulsed, and may cause anxiety, and you may try to ignore these thoughts. As a response to the thoughts, you may feel that you must do something, such as washing your hands, to deal with the thoughts you are having.

The thoughts are often unwanted, and you may recognize that they are irrational, but still feel the need to carry out the compulsive act. These obsessional thoughts and actions can be very distressing, and cause a lot of anxiety for the person who is experiencing them. It may be very difficult to resist thinking and carrying out these thoughts and actions, and you may not like doing the action but it normally helps to relieve some of your distress and anxiety.

Who gets it? OCD affects up to 3% of people, and is most commonly diagnosed in young adults. It affects males and females equally, but is more common in people who have relatives with OCD than in people who don't.

What can be done about it? There is more than one treatment option available for OCD. Options include CBT and antidepressant medication, usually an SSRI (see notes above). CBT is thought to be the most effective treatment for OCD, and helps you understand that the thoughts you are having will not cause you harm, and that you don't have to carry out the compulsive action to stop the thoughts or to stop bad things from happening. CBT and SSRIs can be used separately or together, depending on how they may work for you.

It is important to realize that your symptoms may not completely resolve with treatment, but it may help to improve the symptoms and reduce the anxiety and other symptoms that you may have as a result of the OCD.

7.3.5 Depression

What is it? Is it common? It is normal to feel fed up, miserable or sad at times, with or without an obvious reason. Normally these feelings last only for a few weeks and don't interfere much with our daily lives. We are able to cope.

Depression is when you experience low mood or other key symptoms, which don't go away after a few weeks. They carry on for months and interfere with life, causing distress.

Who gets depressed? Depression is very common and can affect anyone. About 2 in 3 adults have depression at some point in their life. The same person can get more than one episode of depression at various times in their life. Women are more likely to be depressed than men. Particularly common times are after childbirth and during menopause.

What causes it?
- The exact cause is not known.
- Some people are more prone due to their genetics; thus it can be passed on through families.
- Things that happen in our lives: it is normal to feel depressed after a distressing event such as losing someone, losing a job or a divorce. After a while you come to terms with what happened. But you may get stuck in a depressed mood, which doesn't seem to lift.
- Circumstances: if you are alone, have no friends around, are stressed, have other worries or are physically run down you are more likely to become depressed.

- Physical illness: life-threatening illnesses like cancer and heart disease, long-term / painful illnesses like arthritis, hormonal problems like an underactive thyroid.
- Alcohol and drugs.

How can we tell if you are depressed?

- Many people can recognize when they are depressed, based on how they are feeling and how it is affecting their day-to-day life. But some people may not realize this. They may know they are not right and are not functioning well, but don't know why. Some people may also put their symptoms down to a physical illness.
- We suspect depression based on how you describe your feelings, thoughts and behaviour. We also ask about some physical problems that can occur with depression.
- In terms of feelings, a depressed person feels persistent sadness or low mood. This may be with or without weepiness. Feelings of worthlessness and excessive guilt are also common. They also experience marked loss of interest or pleasure in activities, even ones they normally enjoy. You might even feel quite irritable and agitated.
- Thoughts: your thoughts may become quite pessimistic. Sometimes these thoughts can progress into thoughts and even plans of self-harm or suicide. This could be accompanied by despairing thoughts such as *'Life is not worth living,'* or *'I don't care if I wake up tomorrow.'*
- Physical problems: when someone is depressed they may feel less hungry, and lose weight. Rarely, depression can make people comfort eat so they gain weight. In the same way, sleep can be affected in opposite ways. Most of the time, someone who is depressed lacks sleep. They tend to wake up earlier than usual in the morning, but can also find it difficult to get off to sleep. Sometimes, depression can make a person sleep more than they would usually sleep. You might also find that you have poor concentration or indecisiveness. Simple tasks can suddenly seem difficult. When someone is depressed they can also feel very tired and lack energy. Also with depression it is common to develop headaches, palpitations, chest pains and general aches.
- In terms of officially diagnosing depression, we look for a certain number of symptoms. The combination of your symptoms and the extent to which they affect your life gives us a clue to whether you have mild, moderate or severe depression. We also do some blood and urine tests make sure that your symptoms aren't due to medication side-effect, alcohol or drug misuse, or an underactive thyroid or pituitary gland.

What can we do about it?

- **Non-medicine**
  - Guided self-help: education, exercise advice.
  - Talking treatments:
    - CBT: focuses on changing your habits of thinking to better cope with your situation.
    - Counselling: talking about your feelings and what is going on in your life with a counsellor.
    - Couples therapy: if depression is connected with relationships.
    - Support groups and group therapy: sharing experience with others who have had similar experiences can be very safe and helpful. But sometimes it can bring up bad memories from the past and make you feel worse for a while. Or it can put a strain on a close relationship. If you are concerned that these problems are arising, talk about it with your doctor or therapist. Unfortunately talking treatments are still in short supply and you might have to wait several months for it.
- **Medicine**
  - If depression is severe or goes on for a long time, your doctor may suggest a course of antidepressants. These are not tranquilizers, but they can help you feel less anxious and more relaxed.
  - These tablets can help cope with depression and relieve the symptoms you experience.

- They work by altering levels of certain chemicals in your brain. This has been shown to have an uplifting effect on your mood.
- If you start taking them, you probably won't feel any effect for two to four weeks. You may notice that you start to sleep better and feel less anxious after a few days.

More information giving on treatment:
- Antidepressants are tablets used to treat depression or prevent it recurring.
- How do they work? They are thought to work by increasing levels of certain chemicals in the brain. These chemicals can improve mood and emotion, although this process isn't fully understood.
- While antidepressants can treat the symptoms they don't always address the cause. This is why they're usually used in combination with therapy to treat more severe depression.
- How effective are they? Most people benefit to some degree, but it depends on the individual. They're the most effective known treatment in relieving symptoms quickly, particularly in severe depression.
- Doses and duration: usually taken as a tablet at the lowest dose possible that can improve your symptoms. Usually need to be taken without missing a dose for 2–4 weeks before you see a marked improvement. It's important not to stop them if you get some mild side-effects early on, as these will wear off quickly. I will tell you more about these in a little while. Treatment usually lasts six months at least, but may go on for two years.
- Side-effects: have a range of different side-effects depending on which tablet you take.

How to live with depression
- Helping yourself:
  - Don't keep it to yourself – talk to someone close to you. You may need to do it more than once.
  - Do something: get outdoors for some exercise, listen to music.
  - Keep active.
  - Eat well: try to eat regularly even if you don't feel like eating.
  - Beware of alcohol: try not to drown your sorrows with a drink. Alcohol may take the edge off at first but it actually makes depression worse, and can lead to physical health problems.
  - Beware of drugs. These can make your symptoms worse, especially thoughts of guilt and helplessness.
  - Sleep: give your body a chance to rest and give your mind a break.

7.3.6 Lithium

What is it? It is a mood stabilizer used to treat a number of mood disorders such as mania, hypomania and depression. It helps to maintain your mood at a stable level and reduce the intensity and frequency of mood swings. It works by affecting the amount of certain chemical substances in your brain which are known to control mood.

Lithium is a long-term treatment; it is prescribed for a minimum of six months and can be used lifelong.

Before you start to take lithium:
There are certain conditions that if you have, you cannot take lithium. It is important to tell your doctor if you have any of the following:
- Pregnant, trying to get pregnant or are breast-feeding
- Hypothyroidism
- Heart condition or kidney condition
- Epilepsy or psoriasis
- Addison's disease

Always tell your doctor if you are taking any other medications (including herbal or OTC).

How to take lithium:
- Lithium can only be started by a specialist doctor in the hospital.
- Before you start taking lithium you will have to have certain tests, e.g. blood tests looking at your kidney and thyroid function, BP, weight, ECG.
- Following this you will have to have regular blood tests to make sure the dose you are prescribed is adjusted to suit you; these are known as 'lithium level' blood tests.
- These are because the amount of lithium in your blood has to be just right; too little and it will not work sufficiently, too much and it may cause you harm.
- You will need these tests quite frequently at the start of your treatment, but less often once your lithium level has stabilized.
- Take lithium exactly as your doctor tells you to and try to take it at the same time each day.
- If you forgot to take a dose, take it as soon as you remember (unless it is nearly time for your next dose, in which case just leave out the missed dose). Do not take two doses together!

It's important to remember that lithium can take several weeks to become effective and for you to start feeling the benefits but you should continue to take your prescribed dose every day.

Contraindications to lithium:
- Always check with your doctor before you take any other medications along with lithium, as they may increase the lithium level in your blood.
- NSAIDs (painkillers e.g. ibuprofen) are particularly important to avoid.
- Other medications: ACE inhibitors, diuretics, SSRIs.

Whilst taking lithium:
- If you get an infection where you are sweating profusely or have vomiting / diarrhoea speak to your doctor, as this could affect your lithium levels.
- Ensure you drink lots of fluids.
- Only drink alcohol in moderation.
- **DO NOT STOP TAKING LITHIUM ABRUPTLY**. This can cause severe problems.

How often will these tests be done?
- Blood tests for lithium level (12 hours post-dose): check levels after 5 days and 5 days after changes
- Further blood tests to check lithium level/U&Es at least every 3 months, TFTs every 6–12 months and calcium and creatinine every 12 months.

What main side-effects can you experience?
- Upset stomach – especially when you first start taking it
- Fine shake (tremor) of your hands
- Passing more urine and feeling thirsty
- Weight gain
- A metallic taste in your mouth
- Ankle swelling

If you experience the following side-effects you should let your doctor know as soon as possible: **blurred vision, vomiting, diarrhoea, muscle weakness or jerking, drowsiness / lack of coordination**. These could mean you have too much lithium in your blood.

7.3.7 Clozapine

What is it? Clozapine is a type of antipsychotic medicine commonly used to treat schizophrenia. Antipsychotic medicines act on the balance of chemical substances within your brain and help to stop you experiencing unwanted symptoms such as hallucinations.

Clozapine is often helpful when other antipsychotics have not worked.

Conditions you should tell your doctor about if you are thinking of starting clozapine:
- If you are pregnant or breast-feeding
- Any heart, liver, kidney or prostate problems
- Any breathing problems
- If you have had any bowel surgery or suffer from bowel problems
- Any of these conditions: epilepsy, depression, glaucoma or myasthenia gravis
- Medicines which may interfere with it include other antipsychotics, epilepsy drugs, anaesthetics.

Whilst taking clozapine:
- It's important to remember that it can take up to 8 weeks to start working.
- DO NOT SUDDENLY STOP TAKING IT. If you want to stop, speak to your doctor.
- If you forget a dose, take the missed dose as soon as possible, but do not double dose.
- If you miss more than two days, seek help from your doctor or pharmacist straight away.

What monitoring will be done while taking clozapine?
You will have to have the following tests if taking clozapine:
- Blood tests: done weekly for first 18 weeks, 2-weekly for 1 year, then monthly. We are checking for the number of white blood cells, as clozapine can cause them to drop. This will help us to decide whether it's safe to continue prescribing clozapine.
- Tracing of your heart, which is called an ECG.
- Blood pressure.
- Weight and waist circumference.

What are the side-effects?
Not everyone taking the medicine will get side-effects, and most of them will go away eventually. However, some side-effects can be serious. These include dry mouth or too much spit, weight gain, blurred vision, constipation, feeling sleepy, tired or dizzy, headaches or sweating.

Safety netting for agranulocytosis
While clozapine can be very effective, it can occasionally reduce to worrying levels the number of white blood cells, which fight off infection in your body. This can increase your risk of developing serious infections and lead to certain symptoms. Because of this, it is important for you to see your doctor, or go to the hospital immediately if you experience any of these symptoms while taking clozapine:
- Fever, high temperature or sore throat
- Rashes
- Fits or blackouts.

Is there anything I can't do with clozapine?
Alcohol, caffeine and smoking can affect the levels of clozapine. So we recommend you don't drink alcohol while taking clozapine. It is also important that you don't make any big changes in the amount of caffeine that you drink. It is also important to inform your doctor if you smoke, or have quit smoking so that your clozapine levels can be adjusted accordingly.

Sleepiness is a common side-effect with clozapine, particularly in the first few weeks. We recommend that you avoid using heavy machinery or driving during this time.

We don't know yet whether clozapine is safe to use during pregnancy or breast-feeding, so it is important to tell your doctor if you are pregnant, or trying to get pregnant, so that this can be taken into account.

7.3.8 Electroconvulsive therapy (ECT)

What is ECT? ECT stands for electroconvulsive therapy. It sounds pretty scary but it is a painless, quick procedure that can be very effective for certain patients with severe mental health issues. It is most commonly used for severe depression, and sometimes used to treat severe mania after several different medications have not been effective, if the side-effects of your medications are too severe or if your life is in danger (e.g. if you are not eating or drinking).

How does it work? It involves sending an electric current through your brain. This triggers a fit, which aims to relieve your symptoms. It usually works quickly, but often the effects don't last long so you are likely to need repeat sessions. You will be assessed after each treatment to see if another one is needed. It is also important to consider other types of treatment in the period following ECT so that you can have the best recovery possible.
- ECT is done under general anaesthetic in a hospital or clinic. This means you will be asleep throughout the entire procedure.
- The doctor will also use muscle relaxants. This means that your muscles will only twitch very slightly, as opposed to full-blown movements, as are seen with normal fits.
- ECT can be given unilaterally or bilaterally:
  ○ Unilateral: an electrode is placed on one temple.
  ○ Bilateral: an electrode is placed on each temple. This is usually used as it is more effective. Unilateral ECT may be used if you have unpleasant side-effects to bilateral ECT or if unilateral ECT has worked well for you in the past.

What are the side-effects?
Immediately after, you may feel very groggy and sleep for a while. Other side-effects include confusion, headache, feeling sick, muscle aches or loss of appetite.

Longer-lasting side-effects can include difficulty concentrating, short-term memory loss (gradually fades over time) or difficulty learning new information.

7.4 Practice scenarios

1. You have been asked to see Callum Evans, a 21-year-old male, who was brought to A&E by his girlfriend. She tells you that he has been acting 'strangely' for the last few days, telling everyone he's been promoted at work and is 'basically the head of the company', when in fact he was sacked last week. He has also been hyperactive, staying up late working on new ideas about how he's going to 'expand his company worldwide' and barely sleeping. He has also been more sexually demanding of late. Callum is very restless and over-excited, with an increased rate of speech, and is easily distracted by his own ideas and other things in the room whilst you are talking to him.

   A. Take a history from this patient, with the aim of establishing a working diagnosis.

   B. Following resolution of this acute episode, you are asked to speak to Callum regarding the treatment options for his condition (bipolar disorder). Discuss the available options, including their side-effects, and what monitoring, if any, needs to be done whilst Callum is on the treatment.

2. Maryam Kharoushi, a 51-year-old lady, comes to see you at your GP practice. She tells you that every time she goes to the shopping centre on a Saturday afternoon, she gets terrible

chest pains and finds it difficult to breathe, and she feels very light-headed. This doesn't happen at any other time, and she's now too nervous to go back to the shopping centre, in case the same thing happens again.

A. Take a full history from Maryam, ensuring you cover all the important and relevant points in the history.

B. Maryam wants to have treatment to help with her symptoms, but doesn't like the idea of taking tablets. Talk her through the treatment options available to her, with the aim of finding the option that is both appropriate and acceptable to her.

3. A mother brings her 15-year-old son, Ethan Thompson, to see you. She is concerned about his "strange behaviour" recently. She reports that he has taken to switching the lights on and off a number of times whenever he leaves a room, and has started washing his hands noticeably more often. He also seems to be more preoccupied with cleaning the kitchen counters and surfaces where food is being prepared.

A. Take a full history from Ethan in order to establish what could be going on.

B. Ethan's mother is very upset by the diagnosis, and is worried about what treatment will involve. Discuss the available options with both Ethan and his mother.

4. Sabine Morneau, a 35-year-old woman, complains of feeling tired and low. She has recently been fired from her job as a software company manager due to missing too many days of work. Take a thorough history in the next 10 minutes, and summarize the information gathered. (TIP: depression screen)

5. Lisa Knowles, a 21-year-old female, has taken an overdose of paracetamol. She has been treated in the emergency room and is now stable in terms of her physical health. You have been called by the A&E registrar to assess her suicide risk and psychological status.

6. Lucy Johnson brings her 62-year-old grandmother, Myrtle, to your GP practice because she is complaining that the neighbours are spying on her through the letterbox. Talk to the grandmother in the next 10 minutes to elicit a thorough history.

7. Alvin de la Cruz has started taking lithium for bipolar disorder. He would like to find out more about this medication.

8

Neurology

BRUNO GNANESWARAN AND LIBAN AHMED

The Neurology System: Keys to Success

The clinical history is crucial in establishing a diagnosis, particularly in neurology. The development of a diagnosis in neurology requires a basic understanding of neurological diseases and answering two questions: firstly, *'Where is the lesion?'* and secondly, *'What is causing that lesion?'* It is essential to discern the onset, time course, frequency and recovery (if any) of the presenting complaint. Discriminant questions can also be effective when producing a mental differential diagnosis. For example, if a patient presents with paraesthesia it will be useful to discriminate between a 'glove and stocking' and dermatomal distribution.

Eliciting the impact that a neurological disease has on a patient is important in order to address the concerns of patients and manage the complications and psychosocial impact a neurological condition may have. In some cases it is important to take a collateral history in circumstances where the patient's recall may be unreliable due to pathology.

Red flags in neurology:

- Confusion or loss of consciousness
- Slurred speech
- Change in vision
- Loss of bladder / bowel control
- Headaches:
  - thunderclap headache
  - associated with changes in posture / vomiting
  - early morning headaches
  - associated with visual disturbance or jaw claudication

8.1 Information gathering

1) Introduce yourself and your role on the healthcare team

2) Ensure consent and confidentiality

3) Confirm the patient's name and DOB; ask about occupation

It is sometimes helpful to ask the patient about their occupation early in the consultation. Asking about what the patient does for work along with a follow-up question such as *'What does that involve?'* or *'Do you enjoy your job?'* can establish rapport early and may provide some context later in the consultation when you are asking about limitations.

4) History of presenting complaint
'What has brought you into the emergency department/clinic/office today?'

> **Allow for the Golden Minute:** establish when they started having the symptoms, the frequency, duration, progression, severity, relieving and exacerbating factors. See below under the appropriate section for example questions.

8.1.1 Headache

This is essentially a pain history, so the basic principles of **SOCRATES** can help explore pain and give us a more detailed picture.
- **Site**: *Where is the pain?*
- **Onset**: *When did it start? How long did it take to reach its utmost severity?*
- **Character**: *How would you describe the pain? (throbbing, dull, sharp, etc.)*
- **Radiation**: *Does the pain go anywhere else?*
- **Associated features**: Nausea, vomiting, visual changes, altered movements, fever, or other neurological symptoms
- **Timing**: *Is it continuous, fluctuating, progressive or improving? Does it have a diurnal variation?*
- **Exacerbating or relieving factors**: *What affects the pain? What makes it worse/better? Posture, activity, light, smells?*
- **Severity**: *How bad is the pain? How would you rate it out of 10?*

These features will be explored further:

Site
- *'Can you tell me where the pain is exactly?'*
- *'Could you point to where the pain is?'*

Firstly, establish whether the headache is unilateral; this would suggest a diagnosis of migraine, which is the most common differential for unilateral headaches. In bilateral headaches, the top differential should be tension-type headaches (TTH). A TTH is commonly described as a band around the forehead. Occipital headaches could again indicate TTH, as could cervicogenic headaches, which are headaches caused by a pathology within the neck. If the patient points to anterior aspect of the ears, consider temporomandibular joint dysfunction. Cluster headaches, another type of focal headache, are unilateral but around the eye. Trigeminal neuralgia, another differential for headache, has a course that is specific to either the 2nd or 3rd branch of trigeminal nerve, so it occurs over the maxillary (cheek) or mandibular (jaw) area, respectively. An example of diffuse non-specific headache is giant cell arteritis.

Onset
- *'Why are you consulting now?'*
- *'When did it/they first start? Has this ever happened before?'*
- *'How fast did it peak?'*

If it peaks in...
- Seconds → thunderclap headache, short-acting unilateral neuralgiform headache with conjunctival injection and tearing (SUNCT)

- ○ Subarachnoid haemorrhage should be considered first but we must ask about other acute precipitants (i.e. what the patient was doing at the time of onset).
  - ○ Remember exercise, coughing and sex can all precipitate a sudden onset headache too.
- Minutes → cluster headaches
- Hours → migraine, TTH

> **Red flag:**
> Early morning headaches are a bad sign. Think raised ICP.

Character

- *'Could you describe the pain?'*

Use an open-ended question and make sure not to give patient adjectives to choose from, to receive an independent answer.

Migraine headaches are usually described as throbbing or pulsating. TTH are usually described as pressing, tightening or band-like pain. Cluster headaches are usually described as sharp orbital pain. Intracranial pressure headaches are usually dull – but may have small peaks due to things that can increase in intracranial pressure transiently. It is useful to create your own mnemonics to help remember things; for things that exacerbate intracranial pressure here is an example mnemonic 'Lion Cubs Breathe Super Slowly':

- **Lion** is for Lying down
- **Cubs** is for Coughing
- **Breathe** is for Bending forwards
- **Super** is for Straining
- **Slowly** is for Sneezing.

Radiation

- *'Does it move?'*

If the pain is felt across the face in a sharp, shooting, stabbing manner, intermittently and usually on one side of the face, this is indicative of trigeminal neuralgia. It can be triggered by light touch or cold winds.

Associated symptoms

- *'As well as the headache, are there any other symptoms bothering you?'*
- *'During the headache, how do you generally feel?'*

Remember again to use open-ended questions before systematically going through some of the symptoms.

During a migraine there can be symptoms of photophobia and phonophobia. Patients also tend to report gastrointestinal symptoms, such as nausea and vomiting, so it is worth exploring these symptoms further. In women, it might be worth asking about menstrual migraines, which occur within a day or two of menstruating.

It is imperative to ask about the presence of autonomic features – conjunctival injection (a fancy way of saying red eye), facial sweating and tearing. If present, it is important to determine if they are on the same side (ipsilateral) to the location of a unilateral headache.

In TTH – remember the location can be occipital so there may be related neck pain.

In order to rule out raised intracranial pressure, eliminate other associated symptoms such as depressed level of consciousness and nausea and vomiting. In conjunction with this, look for focal neurological deficits in your history taking. Headaches with signs of raised intracranial pressure and focal neurological deficits could be the result of a space-occupying lesion such as a tumour.

A 3-step screening system for focal neurological deficits is:
1) *'Have you noticed any problems with your limbs?'*
2) *'Have you had any problems with your vision?'*
3) *'Have you had any problems with your speech?'*

If there is an associated fever, consider infection such as meningitis, encephalitis or a brain abscess. An easy mnemonic for meningitis is **MISS** – **M**eningeal symptoms, **I**ntracranial pressure raised, **S**eptic signs and **S**pinal signs. In terms of information gathering, meningeal symptom questions might be *'Have you or your family noticed a change in your behaviour?'* *'Have you become sensitive to light?' 'Can you move your neck?'*. With these questions you are trying to determine the presence of the meningism triad (headache, photophobia and neck stiffness).

For giant cell arteritis, ask screening questions for the following symptoms: polymyalgia rheumatica, malaise, jaw claudication, fever, and amaurosis fugax.

To summarize, when asking about associated symptoms make sure to ask about:
- vision
- autonomic symptoms
- fever
- nausea and vomiting
- photophobia / phonophobia.

Timing
- *'How long do they last?'*
- *'Do your headaches change at all?'*
- *'How do you feel between attacks?'*
- *'Has this happened before?'*

Migraines last between 4 and 72 hours. TTH last between 30 minutes and 1 week. Cluster headaches last hours. SUNCT lasts seconds. Paroxysmal hemicranias last minutes.

Exacerbating and relieving factors
- *'What happened before the headache?'* – this is screening for precipitating factors.
- *'Do you think anything triggered your headache / have you noticed any triggers?'*
- *'Is there anything that makes the headache worse?'*
- *'Is there anything that makes your headache better?'*

Severity
- *'How does it affect your daily routine?'*

TTH headaches do not usually interfere with general activities. Migraines tend to be classified as moderate to severe, as they interfere with daily activity. If the patient describes this as their worst headaches, you should immediately think of a thunderclap headache which is normally described as 'first and worst'.

Other factors to consider:
- Age – children harder to differentiate migraine and TTH.
- Sex – males are more likely to have cluster headaches.
- Neurological symptoms review – loss of consciousness or confusion, visual problems, altered movements, sensory symptoms, balance issues, seizures, weakness, speech / language / memory issues.

In an OSCE situation it is unlikely to be a serious headache for communication skills but you still need to screen for red flags. You should also be aware of these red flag symptoms and diagnoses for SimMan stations and written examinations:

- Associated with neurological signs and symptoms
- New headache in those aged >50
- Symptoms of raised ICP
- Vomiting.

8.1.2 Loss of consciousness

There are numerous causes to think of when a patient presents to you with loss of consciousness (LOC). Diagnoses will not be purely neurological. Cardiac, metabolic and psychiatric causes can all lead to LOC. A careful and thorough history is essential in managing such patients as a clinician will rarely have witnessed the episode. *Table 8.1* outlines the possible diagnoses if a patient presents with LOC.

Table 8.1 Possible diagnoses in LOC

System	Diagnoses
Neurological	• Seizure disorder • Stroke / TIA
Cardiac	• Structural cardiac or cardiopulmonary disease • Arrhythmias • Vasovagal syncope / neurally mediated syncope • Orthostatic hypotension
Metabolic	• Hypoxia • Hypoglycaemia • Hyperventilation
Psychiatric	• Somatization disorder • Panic attack

Ruling out syncope

Note: A description of events must be sought from an independent witness in order to accurately diagnose and manage a patient.

By using the 5 Ps you can differentiate whether the loss of consciousness was due to a cardiac dysfunction or was neurological.

Base your questioning on the 5 Ps to rule out cardiac causes of syncope: **P**recipitants, **P**rodrome, **P**alpitations, **P**osition, **P**ost-event phenomena.

Precipitants
- *'What were you doing before you lost consciousness?'*
- *'Was it a warm or crowded place? Were you in emotional distress, fearful or in pain?'*
- *'Were you coughing, going to the loo or laughing?'*
- *'Had you been standing for a long period of time?'*

A 'yes' to any of the last three questions could suggest vasovagal, situational or orthostatic hypotension syncope, respectively.

Prodrome
- *'Did you feel light-headed or dizzy?'*
- *'Were you sweaty or nauseous, or did you have abdominal pain?'*
- *'Did you experience any chest pain or shortness of breath?'*

Palpitations

Refer to *Chapter 11* on how to enquire about palpitations.

- *'Did you feel like your heart was racing?'*

Position

- *'Did you move suddenly from lying or sitting to a standing position?'*

Post-event phenomena

- *'How did you feel after losing consciousness?'*
- *'How quickly did you recover?'*
- *'Can you remember the event?'*
- *'Did you not feel like yourself? If so, how long did this feeling last?'*

8.1.3 Epilepsy

If cardiac syncope is an unlikely diagnosis, it needs to be established whether the loss of consciousness was a seizure. A witness is imperative and video evidence is desirable. Epilepsy can take many forms and not all types of epilepsy produce loss of consciousness. Certain features will point towards a seizure rather than any other causes of LOC. It is useful to break down the features of a seizure in the following manner:

1. Pre-seizure
2. During seizure
3. Post-seizure

Pre-seizure

- *'Did you feel a warning before you lost consciousness, such as a strange feeling, taste or smell?'*
- *'Did you have a sense of déjà vu?'*
    - These symptoms can indicate an aura and are suggestive of seizure activity.

During seizure

- *'Were you awake or asleep during the attack?'*
- *'How long did you lose consciousness for?'*
    - Minutes for seizure, seconds for syncope
- *'Were you lying down or standing?'*
    - If attack occurred whilst lying down, it is suggestive of a seizure.
- *'What were your limbs doing when you lost consciousness? Did you go stiff?'*
    - A tonic phase followed by rhythmic jerking of limbs (clonic) is suggestive of epilepsy.
- *'Did you lose continence during the seizure?'*
    - Although this more commonly occurs in seizures, it is still non-specific.
- *'Did you bite your tongue or notice you had injured the side of your tongue when you regained consciousness?'*
- *'Did you appear pale or blue during the attack?'*

Post-seizure

- *'How did you feel after the attack?'*
- *'Did you have a period of confusion or drowsiness after the attack?'*
- *'Can you remember what happened immediately before the attack?'*
    - Retrograde amnesia is suggestive of a seizure.

Prolonged confusion and amnesia are described as the post-ictal state in epilepsy.

It is also useful to enquire about past medical chronic conditions that can confuse the picture:

- Heart disease

- Diabetes
- Parkinson's disease
- Alcohol dependency or illicit drug use
- Family history of sudden cardiac death
- Drug history – antihypertensives that can cause orthostatic hypotension.

Remember: if cerebral perfusion is delayed following a vasovagal syncope, secondary anoxic seizures can occur, mimicking epilepsy-like movement.

8.1.4 Movement disorders

The term 'movement disorders' mostly applies to pathology arising from the basal ganglia. This gives rise to abnormal movements which cannot be attributed to sensory loss, weakness, spasticity or obvious cerebellar ataxia.

Movement disorders fall into two main categories:
1. **Hypokinesia** – characterized by slowness or absence of movement. This includes rigid akinetic disorders such Parkinson's disease (PD).
2. **Hyperkinesia** – characterized by involuntary, excess abnormal movement that are not controllable. Also known as dyskinesia.

Hypokinesia

The goal here is to elicit features of PD, the most common hypokinetic movement disorder, to establish a diagnosis. The diagnosis of PD is clinical and although PD is the most common akinetic-rigid disorder, there are other causes that need to be ruled out if the clinical diagnosis is unclear.

> MNEMONIC: **TRAP**
>
> **TRAP** can help you remember the key diagnostic features of PD:
>
> **T**remor
>
> **R**igidity
>
> **A**kinesia
>
> **P**ostural instability

Tremor: there are three types of tremor: resting tremor, postural tremor and intentional tremor. Typically, in PD, a resting tremor is present and the characteristic 'pin-rolling' tremor may be present.
- *'When did you notice a tremor? Is there a tremor present in another part of your body?'*
- *'Is the tremor present at rest or does it go away when you raise your arms?'*
- *'Is the tremor worse when you are emotionally stressed?'*

Rigidity: this can be detected on clinical examination when there is resistance to passive manipulation of a limb. The characteristic 'cog-wheel' rigidity may be present whereby the rigidity is broken up. Differentiate rigidity and spasticity.
- *'Can you feel your muscles become rigid if someone moves your arms or is shaking your hand?'*

Akinesia: this can represent a variety of symptoms and can be the most disabling for patients. It represents bradykinesia, hypokinesia and general poverty of spontaneous and automatic or associated movement.
- *'Have you noticed difficulty in initiating movement such as walking?'*
- *'Have you noticed you've become slower than other people your own age?'*

- 'Are you moving with very small steps and shuffling?'
- 'Have you noticed that you don't swing your arms when walking?'
- 'Have you or a close relative noticed that your facial expressions have changed?'
- 'Do you "freeze" when walking and become rooted to the spot? Especially when passing through doorways or when attempting to turn?'
- 'Have you noticed your handwriting changing?'
- 'Has your speech changed?'

Differential diagnosis of akinetic-rigid syndromes: PD (most common), progressive supranuclear palsy (PSP), multisystem atrophy, corticobasal degeneration, drug-induced parkinsonism, Wilson's disease.

Postural instability: as the disease progresses, patients will experience a tendency to fall due to postural instability.
- 'Do you have a tendency to fall?'
- 'Do you feel unstable when sitting up or standing?'
- 'Do you find it difficult to keep upright?'

It is important to note that in PD, the condition most commonly starts on one side of the body, typically in an arm, and remains asymmetric. The same holds true when the opposite side becomes affected.

Non-motor symptoms

Commonly, patients with PD will also experience a host of non-motor symptoms that can often be disabling. These include: dementia, depression, disturbed sleep, autonomic disturbances and anosmia.
- 'Have you had trouble with your memory?'
- 'How has your mood been recently?'
- 'Do you have any trouble with your sleep?'
- 'Are you having any trouble with your waterworks? Do you feel dizzy when standing up from sitting or lying? Do you feel constipated?'
- 'How is your sense of smell?'
- 'Do you have difficulty swallowing? Do you tend to drool?'

Hyperkinesia

> **Key Knowledge: Definitions**
>
> **Tremor**: a rhythmic sinusoidal involuntary movement of the muscles.
>
> **Chorea**: characterized by rapid, irregular, jerky movements.
>
> **Myoclonus**: brief, shock-like muscular contractions. Normally irregular and asymmetrical.
>
> **Tics**: characterized by brief stereotyped involuntary muscle contractions.
>
> **Dystonia**: a sustained spasm of muscle contractions causing increased tone and distorting the body into characteristic postures for prolonged periods of time.

Many diseases of the nervous system can manifest as abnormal involuntary movement – dyskinesias. These can be broadly categorized into five categories:
1. Tremor
2. Chorea
3. Myoclonus
4. Tics
5. Torsion dystonia

These categories are not distinguishable diseases but rather they are clinically identifiable single symptoms or symptom-complex with a variety of causes.

Tremor
- *'When do you notice a tremor?'*
- *'Is it present at rest?'*
- *'Does it only occur when you move your arms out in front of you and maintain them there? Does it occur when you are doing any type of movement?'*

Differential diagnosis: essential tremor, PD, physiological, drug-induced (antipsychotics, TCAs, amphetamines, pseudoephedrine) or drug withdrawal, cerebellar (intention tremor), psychogenic (anxiety), metabolic (hypoglycaemia, hyperthyroidism, hypocalcaemia, hepatic encephalopathy).

Chorea
- *'Do you experience random muscle jerks?'*
- *'Is your walking interrupted by the involuntary movements of your limbs?'*
- *'Has your grip been affected?'*

Differential diagnosis: Huntington's disease, Wilson's disease, infectious / post-infectious, autoimmune disorder (SLE) or familial syndromes.

Myoclonus
- *'Do you experience brief jerking movements that occur in the same muscles?'*

Differential diagnosis: partial seizure, basal ganglia disorders (Lewy body dementia, Huntington's disease, PD, PSP), metabolic (hypercapnia, hypoglycaemia, hypocalcaemia, hyponatraemia, liver failure, uraemia), Creutzfeldt–Jakob disease, viral encephalopathy.

Tics
- *'Can you control the muscle contractions through will?'*
- *'Does trying to control them make you anxious and increase inner mounting tension?'*
- *'Does it involve blinking, sniffing, lip smacking or pouting or shrugging?'*

Differential diagnosis: Tourette syndrome, OCD, partial seizure, Huntington's disease, Wilson's disease, medications (typical antipsychotics), psychogenic.

Dystonia
- *'Do you experience sustained spasms?'*
- *'Do parts of your body, such as your neck, back or arm remain in an unnatural position?'*

Differential diagnosis: Torticollis, medications (metoclopramide, antipsychotics), Wilson's disease.

Other movement disorders
Restless legs syndrome
Symptoms usually begin or worsen during periods of rest or inactivity, including lying down or sitting. The symptoms are exacerbated or only present in the evening or at night.
- *'Do you have the urge to move your legs?'*
- *'Is that accompanied by an uncomfortable or unpleasant sensation in your legs?'*
- *'When do your symptoms normally begin or worsen?'*
- *'Are your symptoms partially or totally relieved by movement?'*

8.1.5 ## Stroke

A stroke is a debilitating cerebrovascular event producing long-term sequelae. It can be difficult obtaining a history from a patient suffering from a stroke, as their consciousness or speech could be impaired. The nature of the anatomy of the cerebral vasculature gives rise to a set of symptoms or stroke syndromes that aids the clinician in diagnosis, management and prognosis. The Oxfordshire Community Stroke Project is the classification commonly used. The mnemonic FAST is widely used, especially as a marketing tool, for those suffering from a stroke to seek medical help.

> Mnemonic: **FAST**
>
> **F**acial weakness
>
> **A**rm weakness
>
> **S**peech problems
>
> **T**ime to call 999

Total anterior circulation stroke (TACS) is a stroke containing a combination of all three clinical elements:

- New cerebral dysfunction (e.g. dysphasia)
- Homonymous hemianopia
- Ipsilateral motor and/or sensory deficit in at least two areas (arm, leg or face).
  - 'Have you noticed your arm or leg feeling weak?'
  - 'Have you noticed your arm or leg feeling numb or experienced pins and needles in them?'
  - 'Have you noticed one half of your face drooping?'
  - 'How is your vision? Do you find yourself walking into furniture?'
  - 'Are you able to see on one side of your visual field?'
  - 'Has your speech changed suddenly?'

Partial anterior circulation stroke (PACS) is a stroke with only two components of a TACS.

Posterior circulation stroke (POCS) is a stroke that consists of any of the following: cranial nerve palsy with contralateral motor and/or sensory deficit, bilateral motor or sensory deficit, disordered eye movement, cerebellar dysfunction or isolated homonymous hemianopia.

- 'Do you experience double vision?'
- 'Do you feel dizzy? As if the room is spinning?'
- 'Do you have difficulty speaking? Do you understand what you want to say but the words do not come out correctly?'
- 'Do you feel unsteady on your feet?'
- 'Do you feel nauseous? Are you vomiting?'

Lacunar stroke (LACS) is a pure motor or sensory stroke.

- 'Do you feel more clumsy than usual?'

Space-occupying lesion

There are four types of symptoms that space-occupying lesions can present with:

1. Focal neurological deficits
   - 'Are you experiencing weakness on one side of your body?'
   - 'Are you experiencing numbness or tingling on one side of your body?'
   - 'Are you experiencing double vision?'
   - 'Is one of your eyelids drooping?'
2. Raised intracranial pressure (covered elsewhere in this chapter)
3. Epileptic seizures (covered elsewhere in this chapter)
4. Endocrine disturbances (see *Chapter 18*).

Cognitive and behavioural changes only occur in a small number of patients but are well recognized.

8.1.6 Loss of sensation

Sensory loss can mean loss of touch, joint position, pain or temperature sense. The axons in the posterior column carry information about the sensory modalities of vibration, joint position, touch and two-point discrimination in the corticospinal tracts. They then cross in the brainstem at their 2nd order synapses before heading to the thalamus. In comparison the spinothalamic tracts carry pain and temperature which cross within the spinal cord then ascend up the spinal cord. Sensory loss can be the only symptom of worrying diseases like Guillain–Barré syndrome or multiple sclerosis.

It's important to use non-jargon descriptions here:
- Burning, tingling, pins and needles are all examples of paraesthesias – abnormal sensations that should never happen.
  - Burning and tearing are types of thalamic pain – this occurs when the spinothalamic tracts are affected.
- If a usually non-painful stimulus causes an unpleasant sensation this is a dysaesthesia.
- Heaviness, weakness and numbness are terms that may be used to describe a loss of sensation.

It's important to understand the tracts because of the distribution of sensory problems. If there is a cord hemisection problem, there is a contralateral loss of pain and temperature but in the case of ipsilateral loss of corticospinal tract (vibration, light touch, proprioception (joint sense)). This type of lesion is called a Brown-Séquard lesion.

A few important questions to ask in an OSCE station:
- *'Where exactly is the abnormal sensation?'* (LOCATION is very important; getting the patient to point on their own body is useful)
  - Furthermore it's important to clarify if the sensation is worse in the arms vs. the legs, or felt more proximally vs. distally.
  - *'Is the abnormal sensation worse in your arms or legs?'*
  - *'Is the weakness moving towards your body or out towards your toes and/or fingers?'*
- *'Is the feeling the same on both sides?'* (establishing a pattern is necessary)
  - A glove and stocking distribution is indicative of a peripheral neuropathy.
- *'How quickly have these symptoms developed?'*
  - Conditions like Guillain–Barré syndrome, infections or toxic substances have an acute onset.
  - Conditions like diabetes mellitus (DM), other hereditary and metabolic polyneuropathies have a longer time span, often years.
    - *'Have you recently been ill?'*
    - *'What kind of work is involved in your current job?'*
    - *'How have the symptoms changed over time?'*
  - Carpal tunnel syndrome tends to be worse at night.
  - If the patient complains of worsening symptoms like a progressive weakness, think Guillain–Barré syndrome.
    - *'Have you noticed a change in the way you walk?'*
  - In neuropathic disorders, the gait may be 'high stepping' and 'stamping' as the patient is not aware of where their foot is in relation to the ground.
- Lifestyle questions are going to be very important at this stage. Ask about alcohol consumption and illicit drug abuse.
- Medications such as dapsone, used to treat leprosy, famously causes a central polyneuropathy. Isoniazid and hydralazine both interfere with pyroxidine metabolism and can cause polyneuropathy.

- Are there any other symptoms? (screening, especially for other neurological symptoms is important)

Don't forget to summarize, signpost and screen; simple marks to help you in structure but also allows the patient to give extra information.

5) Neurological systems review

- *'Have you had any visual problems?'*
- *'Have you had seizures?'*
- *'Have you noticed any odd movements?'*
- *'Have you lost consciousness recently?'*
- *'Do you suffer with headaches?'*
- *'Have you noticed any weakness problems?'*
- *'Have you had any issues with sensation?'*
- *'How is your balance?'*
- *'Have you had recent memory or planning troubles?'*

In addition to the above questions, a thorough system review should be conducted to help develop the differential diagnosis.

6) Past medical history

- *'Are there any conditions you regularly see the doctor for?'*
- *'Have you ever had a surgical procedure in the past?'*
- *'Have you ever been diagnosed with diabetes?'*
- *'Do you have a history of atrial fibrillation or hypertension?'*
- Ask about any previous infections, trauma or seizures.

7) Drug history

It is important to take a thorough drug history as certain drugs can cross the blood–brain barrier and cause neurological symptoms. Antipsychotics and anti-emetics are a perfect example of drug-induced neurological conditions.

8) Family history

- It is important to focus on first-degree relatives – siblings, offspring and parents.
  - *'Has anyone in your family had similar symptoms?'*
  - *'Is there anyone in your family who's ever had a stroke, Parkinson's disease, Charcot–Marie–Tooth, multiple sclerosis, Huntington's disease?'*
  - *'What medical conditions run in the family?'*
  - *'Does your mother / father / sister / brother have any medical problems?'*

9) Social history

- Remember to signpost to social history questions as they can be personal; however, they can be used as a good way to develop rapport with the patient.
  - Enquire about smoking and alcohol status, past and present.
  - *'Have you ever used recreational drugs?'*
  - *'What are your stress levels at work and home like?'*
  - *'Do you have any pets?'*

10) Closing the consultation

Always use your basic communication skills according to the Calgary–Cambridge Model. Remember to summarize and be sure to screen in order to ensure that the patient has had the opportunity to express anything else they feel is relevant.

Always close by thanking the patient and informing them of the next step in their plan of care.

- *'Thank you so much for all of the information that you have given me. I am now going to quickly speak with my colleagues and then I will be back to discuss the plan with you.'*
- *'Thank you for all that information. The next step is to do a few blood tests and an ECG so that we can come up with a plan. Do you have any questions?'*

Summary of key points (GET YOUR MARKS):

Establish rapport (clear introduction of who you are, what your role is and why you are there).

History of presenting complaint: key symptoms to screen for – headaches, seizures, change in vision, change in sensation, motor disturbances and loss of consciousness.

Systems review: rule out differentials by asking about red flags including thunderclap headache, seizures, loss of consciousness, sudden onset of motor or sensory loss, neck stiffness, loss of balance, change in memory.

ICE.

Past medical history: ask about seizure disorders, risk factors for stroke (hypertension, AF, hypercholesterolaemia and smoking).

Medication history: current medications (including inhalers), allergies, OTC medications and supplements. Consider if any of their medications are causing their symptoms.

Family history: first-degree relatives with PD, Huntington's disease, Charcot–Marie–Tooth, multiple sclerosis, heart disease or stroke.

Social history: disease impact on activities of daily living and occupation. Establish a history of asbestos exposure, occupational hazards, smoking or exposure to second-hand smoke, recreational drug use, pets / birds, exercise tolerance, infectious contacts and travel history.

Closing the consultation: use the Calgary–Cambridge Model throughout. Summarize and screen as you go. Develop a plan of care with the patient as your partner in the shared decision making process. Thank the patient.

8.2 Information giving and shared decision making

The following section is a quick overview of what you might tell the patient during an information giving or shared decision making station. Use this section as a guide to what information might be relevant for the patient. Be sure to always assess the patient's starting point. Drawings and the use of models are very helpful for patients and often count for one or more marks. If you don't have anything to draw, writing long words for patients can also be helpful.

Review *Chapter 5* to get the most OSCE points possible.

8.2.1 Migraine

What is it? A migraine is a condition that involves intermittent headaches along with nausea and vomiting, or visual symptoms. The headache is usually described as throbbing or pulsating. It is often unilateral. Classically, people experience an aura, which is an abnormal sensation, which can involve seeing weird things or your vision blurring. It can also involve pins and needles spreading over your body or losing control of your limbs or tongue. When people get these auras they tend to occur about half an hour before a migraine. Sometimes people can have migraines without auras; these are called common migraines. You may have noticed when you have a migraine that you don't like sounds or bright lights; this is common and most people cope by lying down in a dark room. (Intermittently ask the patient to summarize.)

We don't know exactly what causes migraines but it is thought that the headache is due to spasms in the blood vessels of the brain. Genetic links have been found. This could explain why members of your family suffer with them too. In addition, there are various environmental triggers, so people sometimes find it helpful to keep a diary to identify their own triggers. Common triggers are chocolate, hangovers, cheese, hunger, stress, oral contraceptives and exercise.

Who gets it? 1 in 4 women and 1 in 12 men are affected. It usually begins around adolescence and the frequency of attacks can differ from a couple every few years to a few every week.

How is it treated? Different people have different triggers so it's important to track yours to prevent future migraines. One in three people with migraines suffer from auras as well; remember these start and usually finish before the headache. It can be safely treated with painkillers and triptans, and sometimes anti-sickness tablets can help with nausea and sickness.

However, remember if you have any significant limb weakness or headache that seems like the worst headache you've ever had, you should urgently seek medical attention (SAFETY NETTING – this is important in any consultation).

8.3   Practice scenarios

1. Giselle Knowles is a 62-year-old female who was recently admitted after suffering a transient ischaemic attack. After being discharged she has to see her doctor to discuss her recent admission and future management. You are the F1 at the GP practice and you've been told to see this patient. Please take a full history from this patient and discuss what treatment she now needs, including lifestyle measures, medications and her risk of further TIAs / stroke.

2. Robin Sheffield is an 82-year-old man who has been having problems with his memory and balance. A neurologist has confirmed that this patient has PD. He will be started on levodopa and carbidopa. You have been asked by your consultant to see this gentleman to answer any questions he has regarding his diagnosis and explain his treatment to him.

3. Olivia Gonzales is a 23-year-old woman who has been suffering from episodic headaches. Her GP gave her the diagnosis of migraine with aura. As an F1 at the practice you have been asked to explain the diagnosis and the treatments available.

4. Samuel Hewitt, a 23-year-old avid cyclist and snowboarder, has recently been diagnosed with epilepsy (tonic–clonic seizures). He has been started on sodium valproate and is worried because he thinks this will make him drowsy. He is also reluctant to stop driving as he needs to commute to work every day. You have been asked to speak with him and explain his medication to him and answer his questions regarding how this will affect his lifestyle.

5. You have been asked to obtain consent from Mr Roberts with regard to his wife, Janine Barker, who has recently suffered a stroke. It has been 2 hours since the onset of her ischaemic stroke. Inform Mr Roberts about the risks and benefits of thrombolysis and come to a shared agreement.

9

Orthopaedics and rheumatology

CLARE HANNAH AND JAMES GOODING

Orthopaedics and Rheumatology: Keys to Success

When taking a musculoskeletal history there are four important domains that need to be covered:

1. The patient's current symptoms.
2. The evolution of the patient's complaint – is it an acute problem or a chronic condition?
3. Does their problem involve any other systems?
4. How does the problem impact the patient's quality of life?

Patients who suffer from orthopaedic or rheumatological conditions are likely to present with one or a combination of the following symptoms:

- Joint pain
- Stiffness
- Swelling
- Back pain
- Sports injuries/fractures

Red flags in orthopaedics/rheumatology:

- Hot, painful, swollen joint +/– fever
- Morning stiffness >1 hour
- Recent onset of temporal headaches or jaw claudication
- Loss of vision
- Scapular and pelvic girdle pain (polymyalgia rheumatica – PMR)

9.1 Information gathering

1) Introduce yourself and your role on the healthcare team

2) Ensure consent and confidentiality

3) Confirm the patient's name and DOB; ask about occupation

It is sometimes helpful to ask the patient about their occupation early in the consultation. Asking about what the patient does for work along with a follow-up question such as *'What does that involve?'* or *'Do you enjoy your job?'* can establish rapport early and may provide some context later in the consultation when you are asking about limitations.

4) History of presenting complaint

'What has brought you into the emergency department/clinic/office today?"

> **Allow for the Golden Minute:** if a patient presents with one or more of the key symptoms in their Golden Minute (joint pain, swelling, stiffness, back pain, fractures) they should be explored in further detail. Establish when they started having symptoms, the frequency, duration, progression, severity, relieving and exacerbating factors.

9.1.1 Joint pain

SOCRATES is commonly used to assess pain of any type.

The questions do not have to be asked in the exact order and most times the patient will give you the answer to more than one question at a time. If at the end you have asked a question from each section, you can be fairly confident that you have taken a thorough pain history.

Site: *'Can you show me exactly where you felt the pain?'*
        'Do you have the same pain on the other side? Are there other joints affected?'

It is important to determine whether the pain is confined to a single joint or multiple joints. If a single joint is affected this is known as monoarthritis. If 2–4 joints are affected this is oligoarthritis, and more than four joints affected is polyarthritis.

The causes of joint pain are different for a monoarthritis than for polyarthritis.

If a patient presents with a single hot joint you must consider septic arthritis as a diagnosis, as if this is missed it can lead to irreparable joint damage.

Onset: *'How long have you had the pain?'*
        'When did the pain start?'
        'What were you doing when the pain first started?'
        'Has the pain come on quickly or slowly?'
        'Has the pain changed with time?'

It is important to distinguish if the pain has come on suddenly over a course of hours to days, or has come on slowly over a number of months. You should also determine if the patient has been suffering with chronic pain for a number of months, with episodes of acute, more severe pain representing a "flare-up" of the disease.

Character: *'Can you describe to me what the pain feels like?'*

Give the patient enough time to be able to describe what the pain feels like to them. If they are having difficulty you can ask them a few more specific questions:

'Would you describe the pain as aching, burning, stabbing, throbbing?'
- Aching: chronic arthritis
- Stabbing: ruptured tendon
- Burning: neuralgia
- Throbbing: abscess
- Numbness/tingling: nerve compression.

What bothers the patient **MOST**?

- What joint or joints are affected (wrists, fingers, elbows, shoulders, knee, ankles, atlanto-axial joint, back)?
- Is it one or more joints?
- Is it persistent or relapsing?

Radiation: *'Does the pain go anywhere else?'*
              'Does your pain move from joint to joint?'

This question is good for helping differentiate between radicular pain, due to root or nerve entrapment (i.e. sciatica) and referred pain. For example many patients with osteoarthritis of the hip can feel pain in their knee.

Associated symptoms:
- Are there any skin nodes or nodules? *'Have you noticed any rashes, or lumps on your skin?'* (psoriasis / SLE)
- *'Have you experienced any muscle weakness?'*
- *'Has there been any locking of the joint or instability?'*
- *'Have you had any recent fevers?'*
- *'Have you had any recent infections? Is there anyone with diarrhoea in the family?'*
  - Consider reactive arthritis if there are bowel symptoms (diarrhoea, abdominal pain, vomiting) or STIs (dysuria, genital discharge)
- *'Have you had any sore throats?'* (rheumatic fever)
- *'Have you noticed a pain or redness in your eye? Is there any eye pain / red eye / back pain?'* (ankylosing spondylitis – AS)
- Are there any features of inflammatory bowel disease (IBD) (Crohn's, ulcerative colitis)?
  - *'Have you had any diarrhoea, rectal bleed, abdominal pain, vomiting, weight loss, fever?'*

Timing:
- *'When do you get the pain and/or stiffness?'*
- *'Do you notice that your pain is worse at certain parts of the day?'*
  - Morning pain is usually suggestive of inflammatory joint disease.
  - Evening pain or pain following activity suggests degenerative joint disease.
- *'How long does the morning stiffness last?'* (stiffness lasting only a few minutes is usually suggestive of "joint gelling" associated with degenerative disease. Morning stiffness lasting over an hour indicates inflammatory conditions such as PA, AS, PMR).

Exacerbating / relieving factors:
- *'Is there anything that makes the pain worse?'*
- *'Does your pain get worse when you are active or when you are at rest?'*
- *'Is there anything that makes your pain better?'*
- Was there trauma to the joint?
- Did it coincide with starting any medications?
- *'Do you remember injuring the joint?'*
- *'Have you recently started any medication that may coincide with when the joint pain started?'*

Severity scale:
- *'How severe is the pain on a scale of 1–10, with 10 being the worst pain you've ever experienced?'*
- What are the functional consequences? *'How does the pain affect your day-to-day activities (dressing, getting to the bathroom, washing, cooking, cleaning, shopping)?'*

Functional enquiry:

- Always remember that pain is subjective and you cannot judge the severity of someone's pain based on how they look objectively.
- *'Does your pain prevent you from doing anything that you used to be able to do?'*

Systematic review

- Ask particularly about systemic features of illness such as fever, weight loss, rashes. Ask about dry eyes or mouth (Sjögren's syndrome) and Raynaud's.
- Consider symptoms of PMR (aching and stiffness of muscles of neck, shoulders, hips, thighs) or temporal arteritis (headache, scalp tenderness, jaw claudication, visual disturbance).
- Is there any GU or GI disease (Reiter's)?

9.1.2 Stiffness

When a patient describes a joint as 'stiff' they're usually referring to some limitation in their range of movements and therefore the use of the joint. Stiff joints can arise in both inflammatory and non-inflammatory joint conditions and it's important to differentiate between the two through history taking:

- *'**When** do you experience the stiffness in your joints?'*
- *'Is the stiffness present only at certain times of the day?'*
- *'Have you recognized a pattern to when you experience the stiffness?'*
- *'**Where** is the stiffness? Is it in a particular joint or more widespread?'*
- *'How **long** does the stiffness in your joints last?'*
- *'Do you find anything **precipitates** or **relieves** the stiffness?'*
- *'Have you noticed the stiffness getting better or worse over time?'*

Stiffness in any joint, particularly the hands, can interfere with daily activities of living. It's important to find out the extent to which this is affecting a patient:

- *'Do you find your joint stiffness makes it difficult to go about your daily life?'*
- *'Do you find the stiffness in your joints limits the activities you can do?'*
- *'Do you find this stiffness prevents you from doing things you used to be able to do?'*

The main two conditions in orthopaedics and rheumatology that are guilty of causing stiffness are:

- **Rheumatoid arthritis (RA)**. This is an inflammatory arthritis causing a characteristic widespread stiffness first thing in the morning on the patient's waking – early morning stiffness. This joint stiffness improves during the day but the length of time for which it lasts is a useful indicator of disease activity. In this way it can be helpful to ask the patient to compare how long their stiffness lasts now to how long it previously lasted; if these periods are getting shorter it can be suggestive of a reduction in the underlying inflammatory activity. A diurnal variation to the stiffness is possible with a second attack of it at night-time.
- **Osteoarthritis (OA)**. On the opposite side of the scale to RA, the stiffness of OA is usually confined to a few specific joints and there's not one time of day in which it's worse. Instead the patient may complain of it flaring up following a long period of rest such as a lengthy car journey. Typically the attacks of stiffness last for half an hour or less – a shorter period than those of RA.

9.1.3 Joint swelling

- *'Have you noticed any swelling of the joint?'*
- *'When have you noticed that your joints swell up?'*

Swelling can be due to synovitis (inflammation of joint lining), osteophyte formation (new bone formation), or accumulation of fluid within a joint (effusion).

If a patient presents with intermittent joint swelling, it can be a good indicator of an inflammatory disease; however, this is not always the case, as joints can swell up following trauma or in osteoarthritis. Ankle swelling can sometimes be confused with ankle oedema.

9.1.4 Back pain

Back pain is the primary cause of disability in those under 50 years of age. It can present in the acute setting or become a chronic problem. There's an increased risk of the latter in certain social circumstances, iterating the importance of a good social history in someone presenting with back pain. As in assessing pain in any system, **SOCRATES** can be used to aid structured history taking and clinical reasoning:

Site: *'Where exactly in your back have you experienced the pain?'*

The patient will commonly point to whereabouts they have experienced the pain.

Onset: *'What were you doing when the pain first started? Can you think of anything that might have precipitated your back pain?'*

Various activities can trigger an episode of mechanical back pain such as bending or straining, often in association with heavy lifting, whilst certain sporting individuals, such as cricket bowlers, are at an increased risk of spondylolithesis.

Character: *'How would you describe the pain?'*

In some cases, patients may find this question quite difficult; if they're struggling with giving an adequate description it can be useful to suggest some terminology: *'Would you describe the pain as a sharp, stabbing pain, or more of a dull ache?'*

Radiation: *'Is the pain only in one spot or do you find it travels to other parts of your body?'*

In true sciatica the patient will complain of pain spreading down the lower limbs; this is also a problem in spinal stenosis where the pain radiates to the lower limbs and buttocks.

Associations: back pain can be associated with other symptoms that you might not expect to be linked. *'Can you think of any other problems you've experienced recently? Particularly any temperature, night sweats or weight loss?'*

Fever is usually present in infective causes of back pain such as osteomyelitis and discitis, whilst the red flag features queried above can help distinguish a case of malignancy. **Other features suggestive of a diagnosis of malignancy include pain that is relentless, persisting in all positions and at all times including at night.**

Where you suspect a diagnosis of malignancy, it can be useful to ask about any past medical history, particularly of cancer of the breast, lung or prostate. Most patients will tell you about this when asked about any medical problems they've had treatment for in the past. If they don't and you want to double-check, questioning should be done sensitively so as not to unnecessarily worry the patient. This could be in the form of a mini screening question:

- *'Have you ever had any other problems you've visited the doctor for, such as problems with your heart, lungs or any diagnosis of cancer?'*

Cauda equina is a medical emergency requiring urgent MRI. Symptoms include incontinence of the bladder or bowels, loss of sensation of the lower limbs bilaterally, groin and buttocks (*saddle anaesthesia*) or weakness of the lower limbs. All should be specifically asked about:

- *'In some cases, problems with your bladder or bowels, particularly loss of control over either, can relate to back pain. Is this something you've experienced?'*
- Alternatively, *'Have you noticed any numbness or loss of sensation in your lower limbs, buttocks or groin area?'*
- *'Have you noticed any weakness in your lower limbs?'*

Time course: *'Does this pain occur at any particular time of day? Does it change throughout the day?'*

Exacerbating/relieving factors:
- *'Have you found anything that makes the pain better or worse?'*
- *'Do you find the pain is better in certain positions?'*
- *'Do you find the pain gets better at rest?'*

Certain positions such as sitting can become more difficult in sciatica whilst straining motions like coughing can exacerbate the pain.

The pain of spinal stenosis tends to arise with exercise, is exacerbated by extending the spine and eases with lumbar flexion or rest. Where the latter is the main relieving factor, **intermittent claudication** may be on your differential and vascular risk factors should be asked about.

Severity: *'On a scale of 1 to 10, how bad would you say the pain is?'*

9.1.5   Fractures

Fractures are most commonly associated with trauma; however, additional differentials should always be considered.
- Due to injury, stress fracture, or pathological fracture
- Malignancy – primary bone malignancy, haematological malignancy, e.g. multiple myeloma, or secondaries, usually from breast, prostate, lung, thyroid, skin
- Benign bone tumour
- Osteomyelitis
- Metabolic causes.

When taking a history of a fracture you should always explore the events surrounding the injury. This is important in order to assess the degree of trauma, to consider whether it could be a pathological fracture and to determine whether there could be other injuries. Secondly, fractures are painful, therefore a **SOCRATES** approach can be taken. Finally, a thorough screening of systemic features should be conducted, including red flags of weight loss, night pain, fever or night sweats.

5) Systems review

Many rheumatological conditions have an underlying inflammatory basis that can trigger a range of extra-articular features. Enquiring about the below symptoms can help give an insight into the patient's quality of life and help to plan necessary treatment. The presence of certain features can differentiate a non-specific arthritis:

9.1.6   Constitutional symptoms

Anorexia

This can be an important symptom to elicit from the patient as those of an older generation may relate reduced appetite to their age, making them less likely to mention it.
- *'Do you find that you've been eating less than you used to, recently?'*
- *'Have you noticed you're not feeling as hungry as usual?'*

Weight loss

- *'Have you lost any weight recently despite not trying to?'*
- *'Have you noticed your clothes feeling looser or not fitting like they used to?'*

Fever and night sweats

- *'Have you found yourself feeling particularly hot despite your surroundings?'*
- *'Have you had any episodes of feeling feverish recently?'*

Fatigue

This can occur in most of those rheumatological conditions with an underlying inflammatory basis and may be the most disabling feature for some patients. This makes it important to try to gain an insight into its impact on the patient's life and validate it in the process.

- *'Have you found yourself feeling tired despite getting a good night's sleep?'*
- *'Have you noticed you feel tired despite minimal exertion?'*
- *'Have you found yourself feeling too tired to carry out daily activities?'*

9.1.7 Systemic symptoms

Neurological

A range of neurological features can coincide with a diagnosis in rheumatology – particularly lupus. In this way it can be useful to do a quick screen:

- *'Some patients experience problems related to their nervous system when they have some of the symptoms you've been having. Have you noticed any headaches or changes in the sensation of your fingers, toes or limbs?'*
- *'Have you ever experienced a seizure or "fit"?'*
- *'How's your mood been recently? Did you notice any changes in this around the time of your diagnosis?'*

Many conditions in rheumatology are chronic, making the latter an important screening question.

Ophthalmology

A red, painful, dry or infected eye is a common association with several of the rheumatological conditions, making these features important to enquire about:

- *'Have your eyes felt particularly dry or sore recently?'*
- *'When you look in the mirror do your eyes ever look redder than normal?'*

Episodes of anterior uveitis are a known association with ankylosing spondylitis but can occur prior to the diagnosis being made:

- *'Have you experienced particularly painful eyes either recently or in the past? Was there any redness or blurring of the vision at the time?'*

Patients experiencing reactive arthritis may have associated conjunctivitis:

- *'Have your eyes felt particularly sticky or difficult to open in the morning recently?'*

Haematological

Often relating to their chronic aetiology, some of the conditions in rheumatology can cause anaemia that can result in fatigue or dyspnoea. Antiphospholipid syndrome can result in a thrombotic tendency, making this important to ask about:

- *'Have you ever had problems with blood clots in any of your vessels?'*
- *'Have you ever experienced blood clots in your legs or lungs?'*
- For women, *'Have you ever had a miscarriage?'*

Dermatology

Many of the conditions in rheumatology go hand in hand with changes in the skin, making it important to ask if the patient has experienced any problems here:

- *'Have you noticed any changes in the appearance of your skin recently?'*
- *'Have you noticed any rashes or markings that are unusual for you recently?'*
- *'Has anyone commented that your skin looks different recently?'*

In conditions such as psoriatic arthritis, skin disease may present first; following treatment it may no longer be obvious, making it important to enquire about:

- *'Have you ever had any problems with your skin?'*

A range of skin changes are possible in lupus and individuals may find they become more photosensitive or experience a rash in response to sunlight:

- *'Have you noticed that your skin burns more easily in the sun recently?'*
- *'Have you noticed a link between rash development and the sunlight?'*

Cardiovascular

Many of the cardiovascular features that arise in relation to the rheumatological conditions relate to inflammation of the lining of the heart and vessels that can cause palpitations, chest pain or even heart failure. Raynaud's is a further possibility in a variety of rheumatology diagnoses and should be asked about:

- *'Do you ever feel like your heart is racing?'*
- *'Have you noticed any swelling in your legs or ankles?'*
- *'Do you ever notice your fingers changing colour, particularly when it's cold?'*

Respiratory

As some of the conditions discussed can cause anaemia, it is important to ask about any recent dyspnoea the patient might have been experiencing. Additionally, some conditions can be associated with pleural effusions, pulmonary hypertension and interstitial lung disease. These conditions can also trigger dyspnoea as well as a cough which may therefore be worth asking about.

- *'Have you been feeling more out of breath than usual recently?'*
- *'Have you experienced a cough that's unusual for you?'*

Gastrointestinal

Many of the conditions in rheumatology can cause problems with dysphagia and regurgitation of food due to, most commonly, dryness of the oral cavity or muscle weakness. This makes it worth asking about these symptoms and the effect on the patient's quality of life they may be having:

- *'Do you ever have difficulty in swallowing your food? Do you have any idea why this might be?'*
- *'Do you ever find that you bring up undigested food?'*
- *'Do you have difficulty swallowing solids, liquids or both? If both, did you start with having difficulty with solids or liquids?'* If the difficulty swallowing started with liquids and has progressed to solids, this indicates a neurological cause or muscular weakness.

At the opposite end of the GI system it's important to ask about bowel symptoms that might be the missing link in diagnosing enteropathic arthritis from a non-specific joint disease. Enteropathic arthritis involves the combination of inflammatory arthritis and inflammatory bowel disease.

- *'Have you noticed any changes in your bowel habits recently? Particularly any loose stools, the passage of mucus or blood alongside them?'*

Renal

Renal disease can be a big cause of mortality in conditions such as lupus and systemic sclerosis. Specific symptoms are unlikely to be experienced initially so it can be useful to ask questions alluding to an underlying renal issue:

- *'Have you ever been told you have a problem with your kidneys?'*
- *'Do you regularly have your blood pressure checked?'*
- *'Does your doctor regularly ask to check a sample of your urine?'*

Genitourinary

Particularly affected in Sjögren's syndrome, just as the mouth and eyes become dry, the mucous membranes of the vagina can have the same problem and may cause dyspareunia:

- In women, *'Sometimes people with dry eyes and/or mouth also experience dryness down below. Is this something you've experienced recently?'*
- *'Has this caused you any problems such as pain during intercourse?'*

If you're considering a case of reactive arthritis it can be useful to ask about any symptoms suggestive of urethritis that may have been triggered by a sexually transmitted infection (STI):

- *'Have you noticed you've been going to the toilet more often recently?'*
- *'Has going to the toilet been causing you more pain than usual recently?'*
- *'It's possible to develop problems with the joints like what you've experienced after having an infection down below. Have you noticed any features that might suggest an infection of your penis/vagina, such as discharge or pain when you pass urine?'*

If there are any suggestions of a sexually transmitted infection, a full sexual, obstetrical and gynaecological history should be obtained.

6) ICE

Although many people expect to experience some degree of arthritis with age, individuals may have serious worries about requiring surgery and the risk of losing their mobility. Additionally for those with conditions such as lupus or rheumatoid arthritis, the systemic symptoms and the constellation of other problems the patient is warned about can be overwhelming. It's really important therefore to make sure you take the time to enquire about the patient's specific concerns – in an OSCE setting, these simple screening questions can open up an issue the patient has been secretly wanting to share but avoiding; therefore doing so can score you big marks.

7) Past medical history

- *'Have you ever had any problems with your joints in the past?'* i.e. rheumatism, arthritis, gout, infections
- *'Have you ever had any joints aspirated, injected with a steroid or replaced?'*
- *'Have you ever been in a road traffic accident?'*
- *'Have you ever had to see a physiotherapist before?'*
- *'Do you suffer from osteoporosis?'*
- *'Do you have a history of serious medical conditions, such as an autoimmune disorder?'* (SLE, IBD, psoriasis)

8) Medication history

- *'Have you tried taking anything to help treat the pain?'*
- *'Have you ever been on corticosteroids or immunosuppressants?'*
- *'Are there any medications that you take regularly? Did you bring a list of your medications with you?'*
- Ask about anticoagulant medication (haemoarthrosis).

- Has the patient taken any medication that could be a risk factor for gout? (thiazide diuretics, ciclosporin).
- *'Do you have any drug allergies?'*
- Check the patient's compliance with medication.

Always make sure to check if the patient is taking any OTC medication.

9) Family history
- *'Is there a family history of musculoskeletal problems or arthritis?'*
- *'Is there a family history of gout, psoriasis, AS, IBD?'*
- *'Is there a family history of autoimmune disease?'*
- *'Does anyone in your family suffer with osteoporosis?'*

10) Social history
It is important to conduct a social history in orthopaedics and rheumatology:
- **Smoking**: this can make conditions such as rheumatoid arthritis and osteoporosis worse.
    - *'Have you ever smoked cigarettes before? If so, how many? And for how long?'*
- **Alcohol**: as with smoking, excess alcohol intake can worsen conditions such as osteoporosis and gout.
    - *'How often do you drink alcohol?'*
    - *'Have you ever been a particularly heavy alcohol drinker?'*
- **Weight-related problem**: although you can normally get a good idea of the body habitus of a patient from conducting the face-to-face interview, asking about any problems they've previously had with their weight can be important, particularly for orthopaedics. Obesity is a big risk factor for osteoarthritis of particular joints such as the knees, whilst women who've been underweight have an increased risk of developing future osteoporosis.
    - *'Although you look well today, have you ever had any problems with your weight? Have you ever been particularly under- or overweight?'*
    - *'Are you happy with your weight at the moment?'*
    - The last question will hopefully come across to a patient as less judgmental; in this way, if it's obvious to you they do have a problem with their weight, they may discuss this with you without getting too defensive or feeling judged.
- **Occupation**: this is a crucial part of the history in both orthopaedics and rheumatology as the individual's ability to work may be limited by a reduction in mobility or increased fatigue and medical requirements:
    - *'Are you currently working? What does your job involve?'*
    - *'Do you think your injury/condition will prevent you from carrying out your current work?'*
    - *'Are there measures you think you or your employer could put in place for you to continue working with this condition/injury?'*
    - *'Is there anything you'd like us to do with regard to your work?'*
- **Hand dominance**: this question commonly leads on from asking about occupation, particularly if your patient happens to be a painter or writer with a problem relating to the upper limb:
    - *'What hand do you use to write with?'*
- **Social functioning**: as with occupation, some conditions can really affect an individual's quality of life and ability to take care of themselves alone, making it important to gently enquire:
    - *'How do you think the condition is affecting you personally?'*
    - *'Lupus can be quite a debilitating problem. Do you find you're still able to take care of yourself and jobs around the home?'*

> ○ *'Do you ever think you might benefit from some extra help at home?'*
> ○ *'You've mentioned the stiffness in your hands has stopped you doing some things like you used to. Are there any adaptations you think could be made at home that might help with this?'*

11) Closing the consultation

Once you have completed your entire history you should *summarize* the major points and issues before *screening* for any additional concerns. If there are no further issues, discuss the *plan of care* going forward, which in an OSCE might be that you are going to discuss the case with a senior. Close by *thanking* the patient and wishing them well.

> **Summary of key points (GET YOUR MARKS):**
> **Establish rapport** (clear introduction of who you are, what your role is and why you are there).
> **History of presenting complaint:** key symptoms to screen for – joint pain, swelling or redness, reduced range of motion, acute trauma / injury, systemic features, back pain.
> **Systems review:** weight loss, fever, night sweats, shortness of breath, chest pain.
> **ICE.**
> **Past medical history:** previous autoimmune disorders, bleeding disorders, miscarriages, immunodeficiency.
> **Medication history:** current medication, allergies, OTC medications and supplements.
> **Family history:** first-degree relative with rheumatological or autoimmune disorders.
> **Social history:** disease impact on occupation and activities of daily living. History of smoking, alcohol intake, recreational drug use and caffeine. Dietary and exercise history if time permits.
> **Closing the consultation:** let the Calgary–Cambridge Model be your guide. Remember your key skills of summarizing and screening. Always leave the patient with a plan of care, even if it is that you need to speak with your colleagues. Thank the patient.

9.2 Information giving and shared decision making

The following section is a quick overview of what you might tell the patient during an information giving or shared decision making station. Use this section as a guide to what information might be relevant for the patient. Be sure to always assess the patient's starting point. Drawings and the use of models are very helpful for patients and often count for one or more marks. If you don't have anything to draw, writing long words for patients can also be helpful.

Review *Chapter 5* to get the most OSCE points possible.

9.2.1 Rheumatoid arthritis

What is it? Arthritis is when your joints become inflamed (sore, red, swollen). Rheumatoid arthritis (RA) is a type of arthritis which is caused by the body's own immune system attacking its own tissues (we call this an autoimmune condition). In RA, proteins (antibodies) which normally act to protect us against bacteria and viruses instead target the tissue that surrounds each joint. This causes inflammation within the joint and, if left, this inflammation can damage the joint.

Who gets RA? It affects approximately 1 in 100 people. It can develop at any age but usually affects people between 40 and 60 years old. It is more common in women than men.

What symptoms should I look out for?
- Usually people with RA suffer from stiffness in their joints, which is typically worse first thing in the morning or after you've been resting for a while. Your joints are usually painful and can become swollen.
- The joints which are most commonly affected in RA are those in your hands and fingers, wrists, feet, ankles and knees. However, any joint can be affected.
- Other symptoms which can occur in RA include the development of painless lumps (nodules) on your elbows or lower arms; these are harmless. You might develop anaemia, in which case you might feel more tired than usual. Sometimes you might have a fever, weight loss and muscle aches and pains.
- RA is a chronic condition; this means that it is persistent. Typically it comes in waves, with the symptoms flaring up at times and other times when it isn't too bad.

The aim of treatment is to prevent these flare-ups or at least increase the time between the flare-ups. This is because the flare-ups can result in damage to your joints and this is what we want to avoid.

What are the complications? Your risk of some other conditions increases if you have RA; these include:
- Heart problems – angina, heart attack, stroke
- Anaemia
- Infections (within your joints and more systemic)
- Osteoporosis (where your bones become weaker).

What is the treatment? By treating RA we want to prevent joint damage as much as possible. The options are:
- Disease-modifying medicines:
  - Disease-modifying anti-rheumatic drugs (DMARDs). These help to control your symptoms and reduce the damage to your joints. They work by blocking certain chemicals which act to cause the inflammation in your joints.
    - It's usual to be started on these ASAP after your diagnosis. You may even be started on a combination of two. It's important to note that they don't have an immediate effect in reducing your symptoms and can take weeks to become effective, it's just important to stick with them!
    - You will need to have some regular blood tests to check the medicines are working well and to keep an eye on some of your other body systems.
  - Biological medicines:
    - These are considered a step up from DMARDs. They also function to block the chemicals which cause inflammation.
    - These medicines have to be given by an injection and they are expensive. Usually you will be started on these if DMARDs aren't working for you.

What other medicines can I take to help ease pain and stiffness?
- NSAIDs such as ibruprofen. If you are started on these you will also be started on a medicine to help protect your stomach, as these types of tablets can cause ulcers in your stomach.
- Painkillers such as paracetamol or codeine.
- Steroids are commonly prescribed during a flare-up of your RA if NSAIDs are not controlling it. They are usually only given for short periods of time. Sometimes you can get a steroid injection into the affected joint to help ease your symptoms.

What other things can I do?
- Keep as active as possible. A physiotherapist can recommend exercises to help strengthen the muscles around your joints.

- Eat a healthy diet.
- Think about losing weight if you are overweight.
- Do not smoke (this can make symptoms of RA worse).

9.2.2 Methotrexate

This is a type of DMARD (see above) which is commonly prescribed for treatment of RA.

Before taking methotrexate you should inform your doctor if you have any of the following conditions:
- If you are pregnant or are trying to get pregnant.
- If you are breast-feeding.
- If you have a stomach ulcer or any bowel problems.
- If you have any problems with your liver or kidneys.
- If you have a blood disorder.

How you take methotrexate

There are certain rules which you have to follow when you are taking methotrexate:
- You do not take methotrexate every day; instead you take one dose once a week.
- Take the tablets on the same day every week.
- Take the tablets with some water. You can take them before or after food.
- If one week you forget to take your tablets when you are supposed to, then take them as soon as you remember as long as it is within 2 days of when you should have taken them. If it is after 2 days, contact your doctor for advice on what to do. Never take two doses together!
- You will be required to take folic acid tablets while you are on methotrexate. These are to help stop some unwanted side-effects of methotrexate. You will take these on another day (or days) of the week; you must not take your folic acid tablets on the same day you take your methotrexate as it can make the methotrexate work less well.

Other important things to take note of

- Don't take any painkillers such as aspirin or NSAIDs whilst you are on methotrexate, unless these have been prescribed by your doctor.
- Don't take any vitamin preparations which contain folic acid.
- Only drink alcohol in moderation.
- Avoid getting pregnant or fathering a child whilst on methotrexate and for a further 3 months after your treatment has ended.

Side-effects of methotrexate

You are more likely to get an infection whilst taking methotrexate, as it lowers the number of white cells in your blood. Let your doctor know if you start to develop a sore throat or fever.

Common side-effects:
- Nausea / vomiting
- Loss of appetite
- Stomach pain
- Diarrhoea

Serious side-effects:
- Mouth ulcers, unusual bruising
- Severe stomach pain, accompanied by vomiting and dark urine
- Breathlessness, cough, fever
- Severe skin rash

Contact your doctor immediately if you start to experience any of these symptoms.

9.3 **Practice scenarios**

1. Jane Mumford is a 49-year-old lady who over the past few months has been experiencing painful swelling in the joints in her hands. She has recently undergone X-rays of her hands and has also had some blood tests carried out. She is here today to find out what the results of these are. The results have come back suggesting that she has rheumatoid arthritis. Please explain this to her and answer any questions which she may have.

2. Kamal Ahmed is a 25-year-old man who has been having worsening back pain and stiffness over the past year. He has simply taken painkillers for the pain but is now starting to find it unbearable and it is affecting his job as a personal trainer. His GP suspects a diagnosis of ankylosing spondylitis. Your job is to explain to Kamal that this is most likely the diagnosis and answer any questions he may have.

3. Betty White is a 67-year-old lady who's been experiencing a long-term recurring pain in her left knee diagnosed as osteoarthritis. She has previously managed this with over-the-counter pain relief but it has recently begun to interfere with her regular bowel patterns. She has come in today to find out what other options are available to her. Please discuss the treatment options for Betty's osteoarthritic knee and come to a joint decision.

4. Mr Banks is a 47-year-old businessman. As part of his work he attends many dinners and frequent parties, resulting in an indulgent lifestyle. Over the last year, he has experienced several attacks of gout, believed to be a result of this. The GP at the practice that you are currently working with asks you to discuss the option of prophylactic therapy with him and come to a shared decision regarding whether or not he'd like to start this. He is not currently experiencing an attack of gout.

5. You are currently working as part of the surgical team when you are called to see Tess Jones. Mrs Jones is a 62-year-old woman who, when out walking her dog this morning, slipped on some ice and sustained a displaced intra-capsular hip fracture. She has been scheduled for surgery this afternoon but remains nervous about 'requiring an operation at her age'. The consultant has asked if you'll go and discuss with her the practicalities of this surgery and the choice of a total hip replacement versus hemiarthroplasty.

6. Tiki Pham is a 42-year-old woman recently diagnosed with rheumatoid arthritis. She presented with moderate swelling in the MCP joints of both hands but wanted to try some herbal remedies she had read about on the internet before trying medications. She returns 3 months later for a check-up. She explains that her joint disease is worsening and beginning to have an impact on her ability to get ready first thing in the morning. As a result she's become more open to the possibility of starting DMARD therapy. Please discuss the possibility of starting methotrexate with Tiki, including the risks and benefits, and come to a joint decision.

10

Ophthalmology

SHAFI BALAL

Ophthalmology: Keys to Success

Those afflicted with an ailment of the eye are likely to present with one of the following symptoms:
- Red eye
- Visual loss (gradual or sudden)
- Floaters and/or flashing lights
- Irritable eyes
- Diplopia.

Of course there are other complaints which the patient may make you privy to, and they will not come to you with this exact phrasing. It is your job to elicit and extricate what the underlying concern and issues are.

Red flags in ophthalmology:
- Moderate–severe eye pain
- Photophobia
- Marked redness
- Reduced visual acuity
- Foreign body or penetrating eye injury
- Visual field defect
- Sudden onset diplopia/nystagmus

10.1 **Information gathering**

1) Introduce yourself and your role on the healthcare team

2) Ensure consent and confidentiality

3) Confirm the patient's name and DOB; ask about occupation

It is sometimes helpful to ask the patient about their occupation early in the consultation. Asking about what the patient does for work along with a follow-up question such as *'What does that involve?'* or *'Do you enjoy your job?'* can establish rapport early and may provide some context later in the consultation when you are asking about limitations.

4) History of presenting complaint

'What seems to be the issue with your eyes today? What have you noticed wrong with your vision? Why did the optometrist refer you?'

> **Allow for the Golden Minute:** if a patient presents with one or more of these key symptoms in their Golden Minute (red eyes, visual loss, floaters / flashing lights, ptosis, pain or discomfort), each one must be explored in further detail. Establish when they started having the symptoms, the frequency, duration, progression, severity, relieving and exacerbating factors.

If one or more of the five core symptoms are not mentioned in the Golden Minute, you must specifically ask about them, as the patient might not have associated the symptom with the reason that they have presented.

10.1.1 Red eye

Past ocular history
- *'Have you had any recent trauma to the eye?'*
- *'Have you worn or do you wear contact lenses?'* (corneal ulceration, keratitis, abrasion and infection)
- *'Are you long-sighted (hypermetropic)?'* (closed-angle / acute glaucoma)
- *'Have you had recurrent bouts of red eye?'* (uveitis)

Nature of discomfort
- *'Do your eyes itch?'* (allergic), *'Do they feel gritty?'* (infective)
- *'Do you get pain or photophobia when reading?'* (uveitis)
- *'Does it feel like there is something in your eye?'*
  - Suggests corneal involvement if the patient is unable to keep the eye open. Alternatively it can be a sign of dryness or an allergic or viral cause.

Discharge
- Is there a watery (viral conjunctivitis, corneal abrasion), purulent (bacterial conjunctivitis) or mucoid (allergic conjunctivitis) discharge?

Unilateral or bilateral
- *'Has it only affected one eye (infection begins unilaterally; uveitis) or both?'* (allergic conjunctivitis)

Vision
- *'Has your vision been persistently and significantly affected i.e. you cannot do normal daily activities of living?'* Can indicate a serious underlying issue such as orbital cellulitis; does not usually occur in simple conjunctivitis.
- *'Are your eyes sensitive to light?'* (active corneal process or iritis).

Other medical history
- *'Have you had a recent chest infection?'* (viral or bacterial conjunctivitis may be preceded by an upper or lower respiratory tract infection).
- *'Do you suffer from sarcoidosis, inflammatory bowel disease or other conditions requiring steroids / immunosuppressants?'* (uveitis and scleritis are associated with these).
- *'Have you ever been diagnosed with rosacea?'* (blepharitis)

10.1.2 Visual loss (sudden or over minutes / hours)

Onset

- *'Was it very sudden* (arterial emboli) *or recurrent and transient?'* (emboli, migraines, raised ICP, GCA)
- *'Did you have any trauma to the eye?'*

Quality of visual loss

- *'Did you experience a profound loss of vision?'* (arterial)
- *'Blurring?'*
- *'Distorted vision?'* (macular involvement)

Area of visual field affected

- *'Is the vision loss in one or both eyes?'*
  - If the vision loss only affects one eye then you should consider diseases in the visual pathways behind the optic chiasm.
  - Monocular vision loss can be due to ischaemic optic neuropathy, branch retinal vein occlusion (BRVO) or incomplete retinal detachment.
  - In patients with homonymous hemianopia, the patient may only perceive vision loss in the side where the vision is affected.
- *'Was your central vision affected?* (macular) *Just one area or field of your vision?'* (hemianopia)
- *'Did it progress from the periphery towards the centre* (retinal detachment, arterial emboli) *or was it moving from the centre to the periphery* (migraine with aura)?'

Associated ocular symptoms

- *'Did you experience any pain in your eye with the redness?'* (closed angle / acute glaucoma, keratitis or endophthalmitis)
- *'Was there pain predominantly on eye movement?'* (orbital cellulitis, optical neuritis)
- *'Have you had any previous eye surgeries?'* (endophthalmitis)
- You should also take a thorough past medical history, screening specifically for risk factors for vascular disease, including diabetes, hypertension, hypercholesterolaemia, coronary artery disease, previous strokes, renal disease and smoking.

10.1.3 Floaters and/or flashing lights

Floaters

- *'Did they come on suddenly?'* (posterior vitreous detachment; rarely retinal detachment)
- *'Was it sudden AND associated with changes in your vision?'* (vitreous haemorrhage)
- Note: this usually occurs in elderly patients and is very common.

Flashing lights

- *'Were the flashing lights transient or occurring with head and eye movement?'* (posterior vitreous detachment)
- *'Is this a recurrent occurrence lasting a few minutes and/or associated with zigzags or lines?'* (scintillating scotoma or migraine with aura)

Past ocular history

- *'Do you suffer from long- or short-sightedness? Do you wear glasses, bifocals or contact lenses?'* (posterior vitreous detachment, but this group is susceptible to retinal detachment)

Past medical history

- Has the patient suffered from diabetes and/or had eye complications such as retinopathy/ laser treatment? (posterior vitreous detachment)

10.1.4 Irritable eyes

Appearance

- *'Are they worse in a warm or dry atmosphere, especially towards the end of the day?'* (this indicates dry eyes usually seen in older female patients)

Visual loss

- *'Have you experienced any visual loss?'* (this can indicate a significant underlying pathology, such as corneal problems or orbital cellulitis)

Past ocular history

- *'Are you a contact lens wearer?'* (problems with tolerance of lens or an allergic reaction)
- *'Do you use any creams or ointment on your face?'* (allergic reaction or sensitivity)

Past medical history

- *'Have you suffered from disorders such as rheumatoid arthritis or thyroid dysfunction?'* (associated with dry eyes, Sjögren's syndrome)
- *'Do you or a family member suffer from allergic conditions such as hay fever, eczema or asthma?'* (allergic conjunctivitis)

10.1.5 Diplopia

Binocular

- *'Can you see two clear images with both eyes open but only one image when a single eye is open?'*
  - If the patient has binocular diplopia, this suggests a problem with ocular alignment. In contrast, in cases of monocular diplopia the cause is either related to a refractive error or a local pathology.
- *'Does the double vision only occur in one eye?'* (usually cataract)
- *'Is the double vision worse when you are looking at things that are close to you or things that are in the distance?'*
  - When the double vision is worse with objects in the distance, it is more likely to be a sixth nerve palsy. If it is related to objects that are close, the issue is with the medial rectus.

Pain

- *'Are you having any pain?'*
  - When diplopia is associated with pain you need to consider infiltrative diseases (intracranial tumours, metastases), infections and vascular pathologies (GCA, carotid or cerebral aneurysms or cavernous thrombosis)

Position of images

- *'Are both images appearing side by side?'* (6th cranial nerve (CN) palsy)

Intermittent

- *'Does it tend to occur intermittently or only towards the end of the day?'* (myasthenia gravis, thyroid eye disease)

History of trauma

- *'Have you had any recent trauma associated with your double vision?'* (4th CN palsy, orbital fracture)

Other medical history

- Ask about thyroid eye disease, causes of raised intracranial pressure (ICP) and myasthenia gravis.

5) Systems review – see *Chapter 6*

6) ICE

Vision is something that is extremely precious. When somebody's vision is threatened it can be extremely frightening. It is therefore particularly important to address your patient's concerns. Vision is also important for everyday function so even if something seems relatively minor such as a viral conjunctivitis, it can still impact the patient's ability to perform their ADLs.

7) Past medical history

Many conditions in ophthalmology will have medical causes. These should be enquired about; examples are:
- Sarcoidosis (uveitis)
- IBD (uveitis)
- Rheumatoid arthritis (uveitis, scleritis)
- Trauma
- Ocular surgery
- Diabetes (glaucoma, cataracts, thromboembolic events / vessel occlusion)
- Hypertension (retinopathy)
- Atrial fibrillation (thromboembolic events)
- Asthma / chronic obstructive pulmonary disorder (COPD) (beta-blocker eye drops may be contraindicated in this group)
- Multiple sclerosis (optic neuritis)

8) Medication history

Drug allergies can never be missed. You may also want to consider asking about their use of:
- Aspirin
- Warfarin (antiplatelet / anticoagulants can be contraindicated in some ocular surgeries)
- Ophthalmic medications / eye drops
- Hormone replacement therapy (increased risk of thromboembolic events including ocular and migraines)

9) Family history

Be sure to ask about certain conditions or attributes which can run in families:
- Squints
- Glasses
- Glaucoma
- Childhood cataracts
- Ocular tumours
- Retinal detachment
- Macular degeneration

10) Social history

- **Occupation**: *'Are you currently working? What do you do for work? What exactly does that involve? Have you had any difficulty performing at work because of the symptoms that you are experiencing?'*

- Ophthalmological disease may also have some implications on whether they will be able to continue to work in their current role (e.g. pilots, heavy machine operators).
- **Driving**: *'Did you drive yourself here today?'* If not, *'Do you usually drive?'*
  - Visual acuity must be at least 6/12 in both eyes in order to drive. Corrective glasses may be worn to meet this standard. Grade 2 drivers must meet a higher grade of visual acuity.
  - People are able to drive with cataracts as long as they meet the minimum requirement for visual acuity.
  - Patients with visual field defects such as bilateral glaucoma, bilateral retinopathy, bilateral retinitis pigmentosa, hemianopias or quadrantanopia may still be able to drive but they must notify the DVLA.
  - Those with diplopia must not drive and must notify the DVLA.
  - Those with night blindness must not drive and must notify the DVLA.
- **Smoking**: pertinent as a risk factor for thyroid eye disease and Leber's optic neuropathy.
- **Alcohol consumption**: heavy alcohol consumption has not been shown to be associated with any ocular conditions; however, your patient's alcohol intake may impact on their ability to cope with changes in vision or care for conditions requiring regular eye drops.
- **Recreational drug use**: IV drug use is a high risk of bacterial endocarditis and this can be picked up in an eye examination.
- **Social support**: who will care for them if they require eye surgery?
- **For more information about how to assess substance use, refer to *Chapter 7*: Psychiatry.**

11) Closing the consultation

Always use your basic communication skills according to the Calgary–Cambridge model. Remember to ***summarize*** and be sure to ***screen*** in order to ensure that the patient has had the opportunity to express anything else they feel is relevant.

Always close by ***thanking*** the patient and informing them of the next step in their ***plan of care***.

Summary of key points (GET YOUR MARKS):

Establish rapport (clear introduction of who you are, what your role is and why you are there).

History of presenting complaint: key symptoms to screen for – loss of vision, red or irritated eyes, floaters or flashing lights, diplopia, pain.

Systems review: rule out differentials – headaches, vertigo, focal neurological deficits (limb weakness or altered sensation), palpitations, nausea, joint pains or swelling, difficulty swallowing, back pain.

ICE.

Past medical history: previous cardiovascular disease, diabetes, hypertension, renal disease, thyroid disease, autoimmune disease.

Medication history: current medication, allergies, OTC medications and supplements.

Family history: first-degree relative with squints, refractive error, glaucoma, ocular tumours, retinal detachment, macular degeneration or childhood cataracts.

Social history: disease impact on occupation and ADLs. History of smoking, alcohol intake, recreational drug use and ability to drive.

Closing the consultation: let the Calgary–Cambridge Model be your guide. Remember your key skills of summarizing and screening. Always leave the patient with a plan of care even if it is that you need to speak with your colleagues. Thank the patient.

10.2 Information giving and shared decision making

The following section is a quick overview of what you might tell the patient during an information giving or shared decision making station. Use this section as a guide to what information might be relevant for the patient. Be sure to always assess the patient's starting point. Drawings and the use of models are very helpful for patients and also usually count for one or more marks. If you don't have anything to draw, writing long words for patients can also be helpful.

Review *Chapter 5* to get the most OSCE points possible.

10.2.1 Cataracts

What is it? The eye is very complex and contains many components. One of its components is the lens, which can become cloudy leading to cataracts. Cataracts usually occur in older people, developing gradually. Unfortunately cataracts are a major cause of blindness worldwide due to a lack of access to the surgery required for treatment.

Who gets it? Cataracts mainly affect us as we get older, with 1 in 3 of those over 65 years being afflicted. It is usual for both eyes to have this cloudiness but one eye can be more affected than the other. Indeed, many patients with early cataract will be unaware due to no significant effect on their vision. Both men and women are equally likely to get them but diabetics are at a greater risk. Other more uncommon causes are congenital cataracts (present at birth) and those related to trauma and damage to the eye.

Treatment: surgery as a day operation is the best way to manage cataracts. This is when a small cut is made in the corner of your eye using a microscope. Your eye will be numbed so as to avoid any significant discomfort. The cloudy lens is removed and a new plastic lens inserted. Usually no stitches are necessary but you may need to wear a pad over the eye for a short period. There are different plastic lenses available now, with some negating the need for the spectacles you may have used before the operation. There is a small risk of bleeding and infection in the eye after surgery but these risks are minimal.

10.2.2 Glaucoma

What is it? Glaucoma is a condition which can affect vision through damage to a special nerve at the back of the eye called the optic nerve. The damage is caused by increases in pressure within your eye also known as intraocular pressure (IOP). There are different types of glaucoma but the most common is known as chronic open-angle glaucoma. If left untreated it can result in significant damage to the optic nerve and even complete vision loss. Therapy offered aims to reduce this pressure and therefore prevent this damage from occurring. However, 1 in 5 people have normal pressures in the eye but still have evidence of optic nerve damage. This is known as normal pressure glaucoma.

In the early stages there are often no symptoms. However, with increasing damage to the optic nerve, patients may realize that they are increasingly bumping into objects. This is because the outer or peripheral vision is first affected and can give you "tunnel vision".

Who gets it? It is uncommon for people under the age of 35 to have glaucoma. It becomes increasingly common with age, with 1 in 10 of those over 75 having the condition. You're also more likely to get the condition if you are diabetic, short-sighted or have a family history of glaucoma.

Treatment: unfortunately any visual loss that is already manifested cannot be restored with treatment. The aim of therapy is to lower the pressure in your eye and to prevent and slow down any further damage. The first-line treatment is often eye drops. Your eye doctor or ophthalmologist will decide which eye drop(s) are most suited to you. If drops are ineffective then your doctor may try using laser therapy or refer you for surgery.

10.3 Practice scenarios

1. A 74-year-old patient has made an appointment at her GP surgery to discuss something her optometrist told her. You are the FY2 on duty in the practice that afternoon and see Mrs Eleanor Nutt. Her high street optometrist has informed her that she may have cataracts and she is now concerned that she will go blind. Your job is to explain what the condition means and reassure the patient about her visual prognosis.

2. You are the junior doctor working in the ambulatory care clinic near the acute medical unit. Mr Shahid Afridi is a 54-year-old gentleman who has been brought in by his anxious wife. She has a referral letter from their GP which states that the patient may have some peripheral visual field loss. His wife is worried that he has the same condition as his mother because he's constantly knocking into furniture like she did. Mr. Afridi appears completely unconcerned and does not want any further investigation. Explain to the patient the significance of what may be going on and what further tests are needed.

3. Mr Terence Jones is a 69-year-old with bilateral cataracts which have severely reduced his visual acuity. He has had three recent admissions with mechanical falls that have been put down to poor coordination. Even though his cataracts have been diagnosed for many years, he has previously refused any intervention for them. You are now seeing him in A&E for another fall which has caused him extensive soft tissue injuries. You decide to take it upon yourself to inform him of the benefits of cataract surgery and how it may impact his life.

4. You have been asked by your GP partner to see 48-year-old Mr Anant Sharma because the practice pharmacist has noted he has not been collecting his repeat glaucoma medication prescription. He reveals to you that he is not using his drops because of a rash on his face which only appears a few days after instilling the drops. You are immediately concerned that he may be having a reaction to the preservative and discuss several alternative options with him.

11

Cardiovascular medicine

RACHEL WAMBOLDT

Cardiovascular Medicine: Keys to Success

Patients with cardiovascular disease are likely to present with one or a combination of the following six symptoms:
1. Chest pain
2. Palpitations
3. Shortness of breath
4. Syncope or blackouts
5. Peripheral oedema
6. Intermittent claudication (signs and symptoms of peripheral arterial disease)

Any patient presenting with a cardiovascular complaint should be asked about all six of these symptoms. Be sure to take a thorough history (and get your OSCE marks). This chapter will illustrate how to elicit these complaints from the patient and explore them in more detail.

Red flags in cardiovascular medicine:
- Acute crushing chest pain radiating to the neck, jaw, back or arm
- Sudden 'tearing' pain radiating into the back
- Palpitations with syncope or pre-syncope
- Chest pain or dyspnoea associated with palpitations and new onset rapid heart palpitations

11.1 **Information gathering**

Complaints related to the cardiovascular system can present as an acute event or as the chronic development of symptoms. A thorough history is necessary in order to determine how the symptoms have progressed and to ascertain what risk factors the patient may have for cardiovascular disease.

1) Introduce yourself and your role on the healthcare team

2) Ensure consent and confidentiality

3) Confirm the patient's name and DOB; ask about occupation

It is sometimes helpful to ask the patient about their occupation early in the consultation. Asking about what the patient does for work along with a follow-up question such as *'What does that involve?'* or *'Do you enjoy your job?'* can establish rapport early and may provide some context later in the consultation when you are asking about limitations.

4) History of presenting complaint
'What has brought you into the clinic / office / A&E today?'

> **Allow for the Golden Minute:** If a patient presents with one or more of the key symptoms in their Golden Minute (chest pain, palpitations, shortness of breath, syncope, oedema or peripheral arterial complaints), each must be explored in further detail. Establish when they started having the symptoms, the frequency, duration, progression, severity, relieving and exacerbating factors. See below under the appropriate section for example questions.

If one or more of the six core symptoms are not mentioned in the Golden Minute, you must specifically ask about them, as the patient might not have associated the symptom with the reason that they have presented.

11.1.1 Chest pain

> **Key Knowledge: Differential diagnosis for chest pain**
>
> **Cardiac:** angina pectoralis, MI, pericarditis, myocarditis
>
> **Respiratory:** pulmonary embolism, pneumonia, pulmonary hypertension
>
> **Musculoskeletal pain**
>
> **Anxiety**
>
> **GI:** oesophageal pain, peptic ulcer pain, biliary colic

SOCRATES is a commonly used method of assessing pain of any type.

The questions do not have to be asked in the exact order and most times the patient will give you the answer to more than one question at a time. If at the end you have asked a question from each section, you can be fairly confident that you have taken a thorough pain history.

Site: *'Can you show me exactly where you felt the pain?'*

Pain typically associated with angina generally presents centrally (retrosternal) and is band-like across the chest. It may also present in the back, neck, jaw, arm or between the shoulder blades.

It is also helpful to look at the patient's non-verbal cues. The closed squeezing fist in the centre of the chest is more descriptive of cardiac pain, whereas pain that can be covered with one or two fingers is more likely to be musculoskeletal or pleuritic.

'Does that pain get worse when you press on it or take a big breath in?'

Onset: *'When did you first start to feel the pain?'*
'What were you doing when the pain came on?'
'How quickly did the pain come on (sudden or gradually)?'
'When did the pain stop?'

It is important in a cardiovascular history to assess the onset of the complaint and whether its severity has fluctuated with time. What the patient was doing at the time that the pain started is important, as exercise, cold weather and big meals can trigger angina. If the pain is coming on at rest, we become more concerned that this might be unstable angina.

Character: *'Can you describe to me what the pain feels like?'*

Pain associated with a myocardial infarction (MI) is usually described as 'heaviness', 'pressure' or 'tightness'. Pericardial pain is usually described as 'sharp' or 'stabbing'. Pain associated with aortic dissections is described as a severe 'tearing' or 'stabbing'.

If given enough time to think, most patients will be able to describe their pain. Too commonly, healthcare professionals rush this question. For many individuals, they may have never thought about how to describe pain. If the patient is really having difficulty, you could consider saying:

'It would be really helpful for me if I knew exactly how your pain might have felt. Would you say it was a tight pain, a heaviness/pressure or more like a stabbing/sharp type of pain?'

- It can sometimes be helpful to mimic the pain that you are describing using your hands, so that the patient has a better understanding of what you mean. In some cases, if the patient is unable to describe the character of the pain, they may make these signs themselves.
  - ○ Clenched fist to the chest: indicates a squeezing or tight sensation (Levine's sign)
  - ○ Both hands flat on the chest: indicates a heaviness
  - ○ A stabbing motion to the chest: indicates a sharp or stabbing pain
- A tight or heavy sensation is more typical of the pain associated with ischaemia.
- You can quantify a heaviness or pressure by asking, *'Did it feel like a 5lb or 10lb weight sitting on your chest?'*

Radiation: *'Did the pain stay in that one spot or did you find that it spread to another part of your body?'* The pain associated with an MI radiates up to the neck, jaw, back, one or both arms.

Associated features:
- *'Sometimes when people have chest pain, they may also experience trouble breathing, dizziness, nausea or vomiting. Did you experience any of these?'*
- *'Were you ever aware of your heartbeat or did you feel that your heart was racing?'*
- *'Have you experienced any recent weight gain or swelling in your ankles?'*

Time course:
- *'Have you noticed any pattern to the pain?'*
- *'How long does it usually last?'*
- *'Is the pain becoming more frequent?'*

Exacerbating/relieving factors: ask about triggers. Exercise, emotion, big meals, smoking and cold/windy weather can be associated with angina. Pericardial pain can be brought on by inspiration or certain positions (leaning forward). Ask about relieving factors such as rest or nitrates.
- *'What types of activities bring on the chest pain?' 'Does the chest pain come on at rest?'*
- *'Does the intensity of the pain change when you lie flat? What about when you sit forward?'*
- *'Does the pain change when you take a big breath in or cough?'*
- *'What do you do when you get the chest pain?'*
- *'Does the pain get better when you stop what you are doing and have a rest?'*
- *'How many times a week do you use your nitrate for chest pain?' 'Does it help?'*

Severity: *'On scale of 1 to 10 how bad is the pain? If 10 is the worst pain possible, how would you rate your pain?'*

Pain is subjective and as such, having the patient rate how their pain feels to them is extremely useful to monitor their response to treatment. Patients have different pain thresholds and therefore you should never assume that because somebody is laughing or talking on their phone, they are not in pain. The pain scale rating is the patient's own interpretation of what they are feeling.

11.1.2 **Palpitations**

Palpitations are the conscious awareness of one's own heartbeat. They can be benign (such as an extra beat or related to anxiety) or due to an abnormal rhythm. The goal of the history is to differentiate between the two.

Palpitations usually come on suddenly and can last for a variable amount of time. They may resolve spontaneously or the patient may have to perform a vagal manoeuvre to get them to stop. Explore this with the patient as they may not recognize that they are doing it (e.g. *'I can usually get them to stop when I bend my knees and hold my breath'*).

In order to assess palpitations, consider using the acronym PALPS which stands for **P**resentation, **A**ctivity, **L**ength, **P**recipitating and relieving factors and **S**ymptoms.

> **OSCE TIP**: One of the easiest ways to assess a patient's complaint of palpitations is to have them tap out the rhythm on your desk.

Presentation:
- *'When did you first notice that you were having palpitations?'*
- *'How often do you feel your palpitations? Have you noticed a particular pattern of when they come on?'*
- *'Do you find that you are getting these palpitations more often now?'*

Activity:
- *'So that I can have a better understanding of what you might be feeling, can you describe to me what they feel like?'* (Give the patient time to think about their answer. They may need prompting with words such as skipping, fluttering, missed beats or thumping.)
- *'Are they fast or slow? Are they regular or irregular?'*
- *'Have you ever taken your pulse when you have felt these palpitations? Do you remember how fast it was?'*

Length (timing): *'How long do they last for? Do they start or stop gradually or abruptly?'*

Precipitating and relieving factors: explore precipitating factors such as caffeine, alcohol or smoking.
- *'What are you doing when they come on?'*
- *'Do you find your palpitations are worse after you have had alcohol, caffeine or a cigarette?'*
- *'When you get these palpitations, is there anything that you can do to get them to stop?'*

Symptoms: if associated with pre-syncope or syncope, the patient needs to be assessed urgently.
- *'Do you get any other symptoms or abnormal feelings when your palpitations come on?'*
- *'Have you ever passed out or lost consciousness when you have had your palpitations? Do you ever feel light-headed?'*

11.1.3 **Shortness of breath**

Shortness of breath (SOB) is a very common complaint in patients with acute and chronic heart disease and can be exacerbated by chest pain or palpitations. It usually comes on initially with exercise but as the cardiovascular disease worsens, it can come on at rest, especially when lying flat.

Orthopnoea is SOB that increases when the patient lies flat due to the increased venous return to the right side of the heart leading to an accumulation of fluid in the alveoli of the lungs.

Paroxysmal nocturnal dyspnoea (PND) is SOB that wakes the patient up from sleep. It usually comes on 2–3 hours after the patient falls asleep and can be associated with coughing or wheezing. Like orthopnoea, it is associated with an increased venous return to the right side of the heart.

Shortness of breath is best assessed by considering the impact of the symptom on the patient's ADLs. Severe SOB can be associated with extreme fatigue which may limit their ability to complete daily tasks.

- *'How long have you been short of breath? Have you been short of breath in the past? What do you think was the cause of your shortness of breath?'*
- *'Did your shortness of breath come on gradually or all of a sudden?'*
- *'Do you ever wake up from sleep short of breath?'* (paroxysmal nocturnal dyspnoea)
- *'What types of activities cause you to feel short of breath? Does your shortness of breath restrict your daily activities?'*
- *'Do you get short of breath when walking on a flat surface or uphill? Can you keep up with people your own age?'*
- *'How many stairs can you climb before stopping for a breath?'*
- *'Do you get short of breath when lying flat? How many pillows do you sleep on at night?'*
- *'Do you ever get chest pain when you are short of breath?'*
- *'What relieves your shortness of breath?'*

11.1.4 Syncope and blackouts

A thorough history of syncope and blackouts is needed to determine if this symptom is cardiovascular or neurological in origin (see *Table 11.1*). Explore the symptom in more detail in order to differentiate between vertigo (inner ear problem), light-headedness and syncope. Syncope and light-headedness are more often associated with cardiovascular disease and can be divided into obstructive heart disease, arrhythmias, postural hypotension and neurocardiogenic syncope.

Patients may describe vertigo as the room spinning around them. Light-headedness may be associated with autonomic features such as nausea, sweating, breathlessness or chest pain. They may have to sit down in order for the symptoms to stop. Syncope is associated with complete loss of consciousness.

Assess a patient with a complaint of syncope with the **4 Ps** (**P**recipitating factors, **P**rodrome, **P**henomenon and **P**ost-syncope). In OSCE situations and in real life, it can be helpful to get the patient or their escort to walk you through the events that took place before, during and after the syncopal episode. A good collateral history can be very helpful.

Precipitating factors
- *'What were you doing before you had the faint?'*
- *'How had you been feeling earlier in the day?'*
- *'How was the temperature in the building/outside?'*
- *'Were you sitting or standing before the faint?'*
- *'Have you ever had something similar happen in the past?'* (explore previous episodes with the patient)
  - *'How often do you experience blackouts or faints?'*
  - *'Do you always lose consciousness?'*
  - *'Have you noticed any trigger to your blackouts?'* Give the patient a couple of common examples such as fear, smells, sights (like blood), lack of sleep, changing position, alcohol, exercise, not eating, etc.
- *'How are these blackouts affecting your daily activities? Are there any activities that you have stopped doing in fear that you will have one of these spells?'*

Table 11.1 Types of syncope and some possible causes

Type	Causes
Orthostatic	Prolonged sitting / standing
Neurally mediated	Warm / crowded area, pain, emotional distress, fear Certain activities (coughing, laughing, urination / defecation)
Cardiac	Head movement, tight collars, shaving During or after exertion
Medications	Anti-arrhythmics, antihypertensives, macrolides, anti-emetics, antipsychotics and tricyclic antidepressants. *This should be explored in the medication history.*

Prodrome (see Table 11.2)

- *'Can you describe to me how you were feeling just before you fainted?'*
- Allow the patient time to explore this and then ask specifically: *'Leading up to the faint, did you feel light-headed, have blurred vision, nausea, dizziness, sweating, chest pain or an abnormal sensation in the chest?'*
- *'Did anything happen before the faint that startled you, such as a loud noise?'*

Table 11.2 Types of syncope and their prodromal symptoms

Type	Prodromal symptoms
Orthostatic	Light-headedness, dizziness, blurred vision, vertigo
Neurally mediated	Nausea, diaphoretic, abdominal pain, focal neurologic deficit, auras (seizures)
Cardiac	Chest pain, SOB, dyspnoea, fluttering or palpitations

Phenomenon (see Table 11.3)

- *'Did you lose consciousness? Were you sitting, standing or changing positions when this happened?'*
- *'Did anyone tell you that they think you had a seizure?'*
- *'Did you wet yourself or bite your tongue?'*
- *'How long were you told that you were unconscious?'*

Table 11.3 Types of syncope and their phenomena

Type	Phenomenon
Orthostatic	Sudden change in posture, prolonged standing or sitting
Cardiac	Supine

Post–syncope (see Table 11.4)

- *'Where were you when you regained consciousness?'*
- *'How did you feel? Were you nauseous, confused, incontinent of urine or had you bitten your tongue?'*

Table 11.4 Post-syncope features

Type	Features
Neurally mediated	Nausea, vomiting, fatigue, focal neurological deficit, amnesia, incontinence, tongue biting
Cardiac	Immediate and complete recovery, chest pain, SOB and pallor

11.1.5 Oedema

There are many causes of peripheral oedema and therefore an accurate systems review will be important in order to eliminate other causes. Oedema of cardiac origin is usually dependent, meaning that it is associated with gravity. Patients who spend a lot of time on their feet will notice the fluid settling in their ankles and lower limbs; alternatively, those who are bed-bound will have fluid settling around the sacrum. The most common cardiac causes of peripheral oedema are heart failure and medications such as calcium channel blockers. It is usually painless.

- *'Have you noticed any swelling in your ankles? Do you ever have trouble putting on your shoes because your ankles are too swollen? Do they ever go back to a normal size?'*
- *'When did you first notice the swelling?'*
- *'What time of day does the swelling tend to be the worst? Do both of your legs swell equally?'*
- *'When you get your swelling do you ever feel short of breath as well?'*
- *'Do you ever sit with your legs up when you are in a chair? Does this help with the swelling?'*

11.1.6 Intermittent claudication

> **OSCE TIP**: Ask male patients if they have had any difficulty achieving or maintaining an erection. This will show your examiner that you are practising holistic medicine, which is crucial to having a patient-centred approach.
>
> This is something that patients are often too embarrassed to bring up themselves. It can be a sign of small and large vessel disease.

This is important to ask about in order to find out if the patient is suffering from peripheral arterial disease. Patients with lower leg arterial disease will often complain about pain when walking or pain that wakes them up. Use **SOCRATES** to establish the characteristics of the pain. Ask specifically:

- *'How far are you able to walk before you start to get the pain? Do you have to stop and rest? How long does it take for the pain to improve?'*
- *'Does the pain wake you up? How do you relieve the pain?'* Dangling the feet over the edge of the bed for relief is characteristic of arterial disease.
- *'Do your legs or feet change colour during these painful episodes? Is there a change in the sensation of your feet (e.g. numbness, tingling or burning)? Are they cold to touch?'*
- *'Have you noticed any hair loss from your legs? Do you have any sores that won't heal?'*
- *'This is a very personal question but is something that we ask all men in your situation: do you have any difficulty achieving or maintaining an erection?'*

After taking a thorough history of the presenting complaint, it is a good idea to summarize everything you have discussed up to that point. This shows the patient that you are listening and have understood what they have told you, allows you to clarify information that might not be clear and in an OSCE gets you that valuable summarizing mark. It also helps you gather your thoughts before proceeding to the second part of the consultation.

5) ICE

A patient presenting with symptoms of cardiovascular disease may be extremely frightened. Some conditions such as MIs and arrhythmias may leave patients with a sense of impending doom. Eliciting the patient's ICE and addressing them accordingly, offers the patient an opportunity to express these fears and allows the healthcare provider the opportunity to offer empathy and reassurance. Knowing their ICE also makes it easier in the long run to meet their needs.

- *'Do you have any idea about what might be causing your pain / shortness of breath / palpitations / leg pain?'*
- *'I know this all might be a little overwhelming, but is there anything specifically that you are concerned about?'*
- *'I have a few more questions to ask you but do you have any questions that I might be able to answer now before we continue? Is there anything specific that you are expecting from us today?'*

6) Systems review

A systems review should be conducted on every patient in order to establish a differential diagnosis. If the patient answers positively to questioning in a certain system, you should complete a full enquiry into the state of that system in order to remove it as a differential. Please refer to *Chapter 6* for more details.

General: *'Recently have you experienced any fever, chills or weight change? Have you felt more tired than usual?'* (anaemia can cause palpitations and heart murmurs due to a hyperdynamic state)

Neuro: *'Have you had any recent dizziness, headaches or change in vision? Have you experienced any numbness or tingling in your arms, legs, fingers or toes?'*

ENT: *'Any ear pain or tinnitus? Have you had any recent change in your hearing?'* (tinnitus can be a sign of carotid artery stenosis or aneurysm)
'Do you suffer from nosebleeds?' (important if the person is being anticoagulated)
'Do you have any problems with your teeth or gums? Have you had any recent dental surgery?' (important in patients with prosthetic heart valves, a history of endocarditis, abnormal valve function and congenital heart disease as they are at high risk for endocarditis).

Resp: *'Have you ever had problems with your breathing? Have you experienced wheezing, coughing up blood or chest pain that increases when you take a big breath in? Do you currently have a cough?'* (if yes to any of these, need to complete full respiratory history as chest pain / SOB may be related to a chest infection or pulmonary embolism)

Vascular: *'Do you have any veins that stick out or cause you any problems?'*

GI: *'Have you had any problems with your stomach recently such as pain, nausea, vomiting or constipation?'* (electrolyte disturbances can lead to rhythm abnormalities)
'Have you ever had trouble with stomach ulcers or reflux?' (differential to cardiac chest pain)
'Do you ever suffer from pain in your stomach after a meal?' (abdominal angina related to insufficiency in the mesenteric vessels can cause pain minutes after starting a meal which subsides over a few hours; can progress to ischaemic bowel)

GU: *'Have you noticed any changes in the number of times that you go to the bathroom in a day? Do you wake up during the night to use the bathroom? How often?'*
'Do you have any difficulty passing urine? Any pain or blood?'
'Do you have any difficulty achieving or maintaining an erection?'

MSK: *'Have you had any recent muscle cramps, weakness or stiffness?'* (important if the person is taking a statin) *'Any joint pain or swelling?'* (autoimmune disease)

Skin: *'Do you have dry or itchy skin? Have you noticed any new skin rashes, bumps or sores? Have you noticed any hair loss?'* Hyperthyroidism can increase the patient's heart rate, blood pressure and increases the risk of AF. Hypothyroidism can cause a lowered blood pressure and heart rate, which is usually not noticed by the patient, but can also increase the cholesterol levels in the blood, causing an increased risk of coronary artery disease.

7) Past medical history

When acquiring a past medical history from a patient with a cardiac complaint you assess the patient's general health and establish if they have any risk factors for cardiovascular disease.

Start by asking a couple of general questions.
- *'Is there anything that you see your doctor for regularly?'*
- *'Have you ever had to stay in hospital because of illness? Have you ever had surgery?'*

After asking for a general history of previous medical conditions, ask specifically about:

Previous cardiovascular disease
- DM
- Hypertension → Vascular disease – risk for myocardial infarctions, strokes and peripheral vascular disease
- Renal disease
- Hyperthyroidism (arrhythmias)
- Autoimmune or connective tissue disease (linked with pericarditis)
- Chronic respiratory conditions (risk for cor pulmonale)
- Childhood illness such as rheumatic fever.

8) Medication history

A good medication history can help to identify if there is any history of cardiovascular disease not picked up in the past medical history, whether the patient is on any medications that might exacerbate symptoms or any drugs that may cause mimics of cardiovascular disease (e.g. NSAIDs causing gastritis that may mimic an MI).

Be sure to ask about allergies, OTC medication and herbal remedies / vitamins / supplements.

Refer to *Chapter 21* on taking a drug history.

9) Family history

A family history of cardiovascular disease, especially in a first-degree relative (father, mother, siblings) under the age of 55, including unexplained deaths, is a risk factor for cardiac disease in the patient.

A family history of stroke, high cholesterol (familial hypercholesterolaemia), diabetes, hypertension or thrombosis (inherited thrombophilia disorders such as factor V Leiden) are also important risk factors for cardiovascular disease.
- *'Has anyone in your immediate family (mother, father, brother, sister) had a heart attack or any other heart problems? How old were they?'*
- *'Have you had anyone in your family die unexpectedly under the age of 55?'*
- *'Has anyone in your family suffered from a stroke?'*
- *'Has anyone in your family had trouble with blood clots, diabetes, high cholesterol or high blood pressure?'*

10) Social history
- **Occupation**: *'Are you currently working? What do you do for work? What exactly does that involve? Have you had any difficulty performing at work because of the symptoms that you are experiencing?'*

- Cardiovascular disease may also have some implications on whether they will be able to continue to work in their current role (e.g. pilots).
- **Effect on ADLs**: *'Are there any activities that you used to enjoy doing but are now unable to do because of your symptoms? Do your symptoms prevent you from doing everyday tasks such as cleaning the house or shopping?'*
  - The best way to provide patient-centred care is to ask specifically about how the symptoms are affecting their daily lives. This is more appropriate in patients with chronic symptoms or disease.
- **Smoking**: crucial in a cardiovascular history as it is the most preventable risk factor.
  - *'When did you start smoking?'*
  - *'Do you smoke cigarettes or a pipe?'*
  - *'How many cigarettes / pipes do you smoke per day?'*
  - *'Have you ever tried to give up smoking? What methods did you use?'*
  - For non-smokers ask about smoking in the household currently and in the past.
- **Alcohol**: *'Do you drink alcohol? In the last week, how much alcohol have you had to drink? If you think about the last three months, is this a typical amount for you? What type of alcohol do you drink?'*
  - Heavy alcohol consumption can increase the risk of arrhythmias and heavy drinkers can get dilated cardiomyopathy. If the patient is close to or over the maximum recommended intake of alcohol (14 units for both men and women), complete a CAGE score (see *Chapter 7*).
- **Recreational drug use**: IV drug use is a high risk of bacterial endocarditis and stimulant drugs such as cocaine and methamphetamines can cause arrhythmias, Prinzmetal angina, and MIs.
- **Caffeine**: *'In an average day, how many cups of coffee, tea, energy drink or cola do you drink?'* (relevant for a history of heart palpitations).
- **For more information about how to assess substance use, see *Chapter 7*.**
- **Dietary history**: for more information about how to take a dietary history see *Chapter 14*.
- **Exercise history** (see below).

Mnemonic for exercise history: think WORK IT

Week: in the last seven days, how many times did you engage in moderate physical activity for at least 10 minutes without stopping?

Ordinary activity: what type of activity do you ordinarily like to do? Moderate physical activity can be brisk walking, light jogging, gardening, housework, dancing, etc.

Routine: on the days that you do moderate exercise, how long do you do it for?

Keeping trends: when you think about the last three months, has your amount of exercise in the last week been more than normal, less than normal or about the same?

Intent: do you wish you could exercise more?

True motivation: what are the reasons you might want to become more physically active? What things are getting in the way? Refer to *Chapter 7* for motivational interviewing skills.

---

11) Closing the consultation

Always use your basic communication skills according to the Calgary–Cambridge Model. Remember to ***summarize*** and be sure to ***screen*** in order to ensure that the patient has had the opportunity to express anything else they feel is relevant.

Always close by ***thanking*** the patient and informing them of the next step in their ***plan of care***.

- *'Thank you so much for all of the information that you have given me. I am now going to quickly speak with my colleagues and then I will be back to discuss the plan with you.'*
- *'Thank you for all that information. The next step is to do a few blood tests and an ECG so that we can come up with a plan. Do you have any questions?'*

> **Summary of key points (GET YOUR MARKS):**
>
> Establish rapport (clear introduction of who you are, what your role is and why you are there).
>
> History of presenting complaint: key symptoms to screen for – chest pain, SOB, palpitations, syncope, peripheral oedema and symptoms of peripheral arterial disease (pain in legs, loss of hair, cold extremities, etc.).
>
> Systems review: rule out differentials. Main symptoms to ask about include SOB, cough/wheeze, fever, change in weight, skin changes (pallor, cyanosis, loss of hair, dryness), muscle pain, abdominal pain after eating and erectile dysfunction.
>
> ICE.
>
> Past medical history: previous cardiovascular disease, diabetes, hypertension, renal disease, thyroid disease, autoimmune disease, chronic respiratory disease, childhood illnesses.
>
> Medication history: current medication, allergies, OTC medications and supplements.
>
> Family history: first-degree relative with cardiovascular disease or unexpected deaths under 55. Included in family history is hypercholesterolaemia, diabetes, stroke, hypertension or thrombosis.
>
> Social history: disease impact on occupation and ADLs. History of smoking, alcohol intake, recreational drug use and caffeine. Dietary and exercise history if time permits.
>
> Closing the consultation: let the Calgary–Cambridge Model be your guide. Remember your key skills such as summarizing and screening. Always leave the patient with a plan of care even if it is that you need to speak with your colleagues. Thank the patient.

11.2 Information giving and shared decision making

The following section is a quick overview of what you might tell the patient during an information giving or shared decision making station. Use this section as a guide to what information might be relevant for the patient. Be sure to always assess the patient's starting point. Drawings and the use of models are very helpful for patients and often count for one or more marks. If you don't have anything to draw, writing long words for patients can also be helpful.

Review *Chapter 5* to get the most OSCE points possible.

11.2.1 Angina/myocardial infarction (heart attack)

What is it? (Drawing the heart and the coronary arteries or using a model can aid patient understanding.) Your heart is a muscle. Like any muscle in your body, it requires oxygen in order to work effectively. Oxygen is delivered to all of the surfaces of the heart by three major arteries (highways). These are called the coronary arteries. Over time fat and cholesterol can build up inside the walls of these arteries, forming a plaque. This narrows the artery reducing the blood flow (traffic) to certain areas of the heart. This causes the painful squeezing sensation felt as 'angina'.

If one of these plaques breaks open it causes a blood clot (massive pile-up car accident) which blocks the blood flow (traffic) from reaching the muscle beyond that point. This is called a heart attack but you might hear the doctors refer to it as a myocardial infarction or an MI. The muscle slowly starts to die due to a lack of oxygen. The longer the artery remains blocked, the more damage occurs. This causes permanent damage to the heart muscle. If the patient has had a heart attack it might be helpful to explain whether they have had a STEMI (full blockage) or NSTEMI (partial blockage).

Heart attacks feel different to everyone. They can come on suddenly and intensely or build up slowly. The typical symptoms include an uncomfortable squeezing, pressure or fullness in the chest, pain in the arms, back, neck or jaw, shortness of breath, sweating, nausea and dizziness.

Who gets it? Around 146 000 people in the UK have a heart attack each year. The risk increases with age (especially after 50) and it is three times more common in men. After menopause, the risk in women becomes equal to that of men. It has also been shown that people from Asian origins are at a higher risk of developing cardiovascular disease.

There are some risk factors for heart attacks that you can't change such as your age and your family history but there are many things that you can modify to reduce your risk. This includes stopping smoking, managing blood pressure, losing weight, reducing cholesterol levels, eating a healthy diet and controlling blood sugars if you are diabetic. (Risk factors should have been assessed prior to starting information giving. Discuss the patient's risk factors.)

11.2.2 Atrial fibrillation

What is it? (Draw the heart as four chambers.) Your heart is made up of four chambers; two on the top and two on the bottom. The top two chambers (atria) move the blood into the bottom two chambers (ventricles). The bottom chambers then move the blood to either the lungs to get oxygen (right side) or to the entire body (left side).

Normally one signal arises from the top right chamber (atrium). This signal tells the two atria to contract together to push the blood into the ventricles. In atrial fibrillation (AF) random electrical activity arises from the left atrium and disrupts the normal signals. This causes the atrium to quiver rather than giving one big effective contraction (show the difference by squeezing and quivering your hand).

You can live with atrial fibrillation but over time if the atria are not contracting effectively your heart becomes tired and you may develop heart failure. The major and worst risk of atrial fibrillation is stroke. Strokes happen because the blood remains stagnant in the quivering atria rather than being pushed along. The blood starts to stick together, forming clots that can break off and travel to your brain.

Not everyone can tell that they are in atrial fibrillation but some of the symptoms include a rapid and irregular heartbeat, palpitations, shortness of breath, sweating, fatigue and blackouts.

Who gets it? Atrial fibrillation is common and the risk increases with age. About 1 in 200 people have atrial fibrillation at the age of 50–60 and 1 in 10 over the age of 80. There are many causes of atrial fibrillation and in 10% of patients we are unable to identify a cause. Some of the causes include high blood pressure, problems with the valves of the heart and previous heart attacks. Atrial fibrillation can also be triggered by infections (like pneumonia), overactive thyroid gland or drinking too much alcohol or caffeine.

11.2.3 Peripheral arterial disease

What is it? Peripheral arterial disease is a disease of the blood vessels outside the heart and the brain. Your arteries are a network of blood vessels which deliver the blood that is pumped from your heart to all of your organs and tissues. The major cause of vessel disease is atherosclerosis which is the build-up of fat and cholesterol in the walls of the arteries. These build-ups are called plaques. Plaques narrow the blood vessel and block the normal flow of blood beyond that point. Think of it like scale that builds up in water pipes.

These plaques can occur in the blood vessels that supply your kidneys, intestines, arms, legs and feet. If left untreated, peripheral artery disease can cut off the oxygen supply to these areas, causing tissue death and gangrene which can ultimately require an amputation of the limb. People who have peripheral arterial disease are also more likely to have blood vessel disease in their heart and brain, putting them at a higher risk of heart attacks and stroke.

In the early stages, the main symptom is pain in one or both legs when you walk. This usually goes away when the activity stops. This is called intermittent claudication. In the later stages, you may notice cold feet, poor hair growth below your knee or ulcers that have difficulty healing. You can also sometimes get pain at rest and pain that wakes you up from sleep, which improves when you dangle your legs over the side of the bed. If this happens in the kidneys, it can cause high blood pressure and eventually reduced kidney function or failure.

Who gets it? Peripheral arterial disease increases with age. In the UK 1 in 5 men and 1 in 8 women have PAD in their legs. There are some risk factors that you cannot change such as age, being male or your family history but there are many risk factors that you can change and that we can reduce with medication. These include smoking, lack of physical activity, being overweight, unhealthy diets, excess alcohol, high blood pressure, high cholesterol and diabetes.

Treatment: lifestyle changes, risk factor modification (aspirin, statins, blood pressure medication) and surgery.
- Angioplasty – inserting a tiny balloon in the artery which is blown up in the narrowed area in order to widen the artery and allow blood flow.
- Bypass surgery – diverts the blood around the blockage by connecting a graft above and below the narrowed section.
- Amputation – used as a last resort when the above methods are not suitable.

11.3 Practice scenarios

1. You have been asked to speak to Robert McCaffery, a 56-year old-gentleman who has recently been admitted to hospital after an MI. He is being discharged today. The consultant has asked you to speak to him about his discharge plan. He would like to know about lifestyle changes he can make to minimize the chances of a future heart attack. He has been referred to cardiac rehab.

2. Fiona Spear has recently been admitted to hospital due to a fluttering sensation in her chest. She is 60 years old and recent attempts at cardioversion were not successful. The consultant has informed her that she has a condition called atrial fibrillation. She has been started on atenolol for rate control and will be starting on warfarin. You have been asked to explain to her why she needs to take these medications.

3. Rajender Kumar is a 72-year-old man. He has recently suffered from calf cramping bilaterally which was waking him during the night, and pain with walking. He thought it was just a case of 'restless legs' but the doctor has told him that it is a problem with the blood vessels in the legs. You have been asked to speak to Mr Kumar about his diagnosis of peripheral arterial disease and discuss the medications that he has been started on:
   A. Simvastatin 40 mg orally at bedtime
   B. Aspirin 75 mg orally daily

4. The GP has asked you to speak with Poppy Markings. Poppy is a 52-year-old woman who has recently been getting chest pain when she is working in her garden. The pain goes away when she rests. She does not feel short of breath with this pain and it does not radiate. After having an ECG and blood work done by the GP she was informed that she has

angina. She would like to know more about this condition and how to use the GTN spray that she has been prescribed.

5. Peter Cooke has come to his GP follow-up appointment after having suffered from an MI 6 weeks ago. He says that he has been free from chest pain since discharge and is slowly getting back to his regular lifestyle. His blood work shows the following:

- Total cholesterol   ↑ 6.8 (normal <5 mmol/L)
- HDL cholesterol   ↓ 0.6 (normal >1 mmol/L)
- LDL cholesterol   ↑ 3.2 (normal <3 mmol/L)
- Fasting triglycerides   ↑ 3.4 (normal <2 mmol/L)

Peter declined a statin therapy initially. He is now reconsidering his decision and has come to you for more information. Please explain the blood work to Peter and the risks and benefits of being on this type of treatment.

6. After a failed cardioversion for AF, the cardiology team has decided to manage Tiang Wu medically. She is 72 years old. The doctor has prescribed bisoprolol for rate control and plans on anticoagulating her with either warfarin or a new oral anticoagulant (rivaroxaban, apixaban or dabigatran). She has asked you to explain atrial fibrillation to Mrs Wu and then come to a shared decision on what anticoagulant to use. Mrs Wu wonders if there was something that she could have done to prevent it.

12

Respiratory medicine

RACHEL WAMBOLDT

12.1 Information gathering

When a patient presents with a concern related to the respiratory system, they may be too unwell or short of breath to give an accurate history. In these cases, medical management of their symptoms with airway security, oxygen administration and medication is the priority

(ABC approach). Once stabilized, a detailed history can be obtained to determine the cause of their acute event. Patients may also present with chronic respiratory illness. With these patients, a chronological history of their disease may be helpful in determining any recent changes in their status. In some cases, a collateral history of events may be required.

1) Introduce yourself and your role on the healthcare team

2) Ensure consent and confidentiality

3) Confirm the patient's name and DOB

4) History of presenting complaint

It is uncommon for a patient with respiratory illness to present with only one clinical symptom. Each of the following key respiratory symptoms need to be explored with any patient with a potential respiratory problem.

1. Dyspnoea
2. Cough
3. Chest pain
4. Wheeze
5. Sputum production
6. Haemoptysis

> **Allow for the Golden Minute:** establish when they started having the symptoms, the frequency, duration, severity, relieving and exacerbating factors. These factors are important to elicit, as respiratory symptoms can be manifestations of dysfunction in nearly any system of the body.
> - Cardiac – MI, heart failure, arrhythmia
> - Metabolic – diabetic ketoacidosis, drug overdose, sepsis
> - Vascular – pulmonary embolism
> - Endocrine – thyrotoxicosis
> - Psychogenic – anxiety or panic attack
> - Renal failure
> - Anaphylaxis

> **Key Knowledge: Medical Research Council Dyspnoea Scale**
> 1. Not troubled by breathlessness except with strenuous exercise.
> 2. Short of breath when hurrying or walking up a hill.
> 3. Walks slower than people of the same age on the level, or stops for breath while walking at own pace.
> 4. Stops for breath after about 100 m or after a few minutes on level ground.
> 5. Too breathless to leave the house or breathless when dressing or undressing.

12.1.1 Dyspnoea

Have the patient describe their history of dyspnoea in chronological order, collecting information about its onset, duration, severity and precipitating factors.

- *'When did the shortness of breath start? How quickly did it come on? What were you doing at the time?'*
- *'Did anything bring on your shortness of breath?'*
- *'How long did your shortness of breath last? While you were short of breath did you have to stop your regular activities?'* (severity) *'Did you do anything to help get your breath back?'*

- *'How often does your breathlessness come on? Do you get more short of breath when you are at work? Does the shortness of breath continue when you are not working, for example when you are on holiday or at the weekend?'*
  - Establish an occupational cause of lung disease.
  - Intermittent breathlessness may be due to an arrhythmia or psychogenic cause.
- *'Have you ever had difficulty with shortness of breath in the past?'* A previous history of shortness of breath can help establish a differential diagnosis. Conditions that have frequent exacerbations such as asthma or COPD may have been diagnosed.
- *'Do you feel short of breath when you are resting or only when you exert yourself? How far can you walk before you need to take a break?'*
- *'How many pillows do you sleep on at night?'* (orthopnoea) *'Do you become short of breath when you lie flat? Do you ever wake up in the night with a severe attack of shortness of breath and coughing?'* (paroxysmal nocturnal dyspnoea)
  - Need to rule out cardiac causes of shortness of breath such as heart failure. Pulmonary oedema is more common at night while the patient is lying flat and there is increased venous return.
- *'Does anything make your breathlessness better? Does anything make your breathlessness worse?'*
  - If the patient has relief with inhalers or nebulizers, consider reversible airway disease such as asthma.
  - Shortness of breath associated with dust, pollen, pets or exercise is likely asthma or atopy.

Differential diagnosis for acute shortness of breath: asthma attack, anaphylaxis, inhaled foreign body, pulmonary embolism, pneumothorax, pulmonary oedema, pneumonia or trauma.

12.1.2 Cough

Determine the onset of the cough in relation to other presenting symptoms. Because a cough is most commonly associated with upper respiratory tract infections, careful questioning about a history of coryzal illness and sore throat is helpful. The duration of the cough is important. A duration of less than 3 weeks is most commonly associated with an upper respiratory tract infection. Sudden onset of cough could be related to the inhalation of a foreign body. Coughs can also be manifestations of other conditions such as allergies, heart disease, medication use and gastric reflux.

- *'Is your cough wet or dry? What are you coughing up?'*
- *'Can you describe your cough for me?'*
  - A cough that is tickly is often due to irritation of the laryngeal mucosa by either infective pathogens or due to gastro-oesophageal reflux. Determine if there is a history of heartburn.
  - A chesty cough is usually productive and associated with increased phlegm or mucus.
- *'Is your cough worse at a certain time of day?'*
  - Night-time and early morning coughing can be associated with asthma, COPD or heart failure.
- *'Is there anything you have tried that makes your cough better? Does anything make your cough worse?'*
  - Patients with asthma may notice their cough is worse when they are angry, during exercise or at work. They will also report improvement with the use of salbutamol.
  - If the cough is associated with drinking fluids, there may be a neuromuscular problem.

12.1.3 Chest pain

Site: *'Where exactly are you having the pain?'*

Chest pain associated with inflammation of the parietal pleura of the upper six ribs can be localized by the patient. Irritation of the parietal pleura of the lower six ribs will be referred to the upper abdomen. Parietal pleura located near the central diaphragm is supplied by the phrenic nerve and therefore will be referred to the upper abdomen. Chest wall pain can be localized to the site of intercostal muscle injury or trauma.

Onset: *'When did the pain start? What were you doing when the pain came on? How quickly did the pain come on (suddenly, slowly)?'*

Character: *'Can you please describe the pain for me?'*
Pleuritic chest pain is sharp and stabbing in nature. Aching chest pain can be associated with pneumonia or heavy coughing.

Radiation: *'Does the pain travel anywhere else?'*
Pleuritic chest pain is non-radiating. If the patient is having radiation, especially to the neck and left arm, consider cardiac causes.

Associated features: ask about SOB and other respiratory symptoms, palpitations, syncope, peripheral oedema, nausea, vomiting and sweating. Have they had any recent calf pain or swelling?

Time course: *'Does the pain come and go or is it constant?'*
Develop a timeline for the chest pain. *'Has it been getting worse over time?'*

Exacerbating: *'Does anything make the pain worse?'*
Deep breathing / coughing can exacerbate pleuritic chest pain.

Severity: *'On a scale of 1 to 10 how bad is the pain?'*

Differential diagnosis (pleuritic chest pain): pneumothorax, pneumonia, pleurisy, pulmonary embolism, musculoskeletal chest pain. Be sure to rule out cardiac causes of chest pain – MI, pericarditis or aortic dissection. Oesophageal rupture can also cause chest pain and SOB.

12.1.4 Wheeze

Patients have difficulty with the concept of wheeze and will often refer to any noisy breathing as a 'wheeze'. Ask the patient directly *'Do you have a wheeze?'* but be sure to encourage the patient to describe exactly what they mean. If they present with an acute attack, this can be confirmed through auscultation of the patient's chest but it is a bit more tricky retrospectively.

Ask the patient if the sound happens when they breathe in or out, as this can help to distinguish between a true wheeze and stridor.
- *'When do you get your wheeze? Do you experience more wheezing at a certain time of day or night? How long does it last? How often do you have a wheeze? What makes it better or worse?'*
  - A wheeze that occurs in the night or first thing in the morning is suggestive of reactive airway disease such as asthma or COPD.
- *'What side do you get the wheeze? Does it get worse if you lie on your left or right side?'*
  - If the patient is complaining of a unilateral wheeze, it could be indicative of a large airway obstruction such as lung cancer or a foreign body.
- *'Is there anything that sets off your wheeze (e.g. pet dander, cold, perfumes)?'*

12.1.5 Sputum production

Any sputum production is abnormal. Patients don't often want to raise this on their own so it is important to ask about it.

- *'How long have you been coughing up mucus? Do you cough up mucus every day? How many days a week are you affected by excess sputum/mucus?'*
  - Coughing up sputum daily is a sign of a chronic lung disease. The Medical Research Council defines COPD as a productive cough occurring for more than three months per year, for two successive years. Alternatively, daily sputum production can be caused by bronchiectasis.
- *'How much sputum do you cough up each day?'* Get the patient to quantify it in measures such as a teaspoon or egg cup full.
  - Higher volumes of sputum are in favour of bronchiectasis.
- *'What does the sputum look like?'* Ask about colour, consistency and taste.
  - Clear sputum commonly occurs with chronic bronchitis and COPD. It indicates no active infection.
  - Purulent sputum indicates the presence of inflammatory cells.
  - Yellow sputum occurs in acute lower respiratory tract infections (live neutrophils) or asthma (live eosinophils).
  - Green sputum occurs in chronic chest infections (dead neutrophils). Common in COPD and bronchiectasis.
  - Brown/green sputum can be seen in *Pseudomonas aeruginosa* infections and is the result of pigments called pyocyanins.
  - Rusty sputum is seen in early streptococcal pneumonia infections.
  - Pink, frothy sputum is common in pulmonary oedema or heart failure.

12.1.6 Haemoptysis

Coughing up blood is considered lung cancer until proven otherwise. Start by distinguishing true haemoptysis from gastrointestinal causes or other sites (e.g. blood in the mouth without coughing could be from the oral or nasal cavity).
- *'How much blood are you coughing up?'* (streaks of blood versus small/large blood clots)
- *'How long have you been coughing up blood? How often is there blood in your sputum?'*
  - First-time episodes of large haemoptysis could suggest thromboembolism or infarction.
  - If the haemoptysis is daily, it is suggestive of lung cancer, tuberculosis or a lung abscess.

Differential diagnosis: lung cancer, infection (bronchiectasis, tuberculosis, infective bronchitis, pneumonia, lung abscess), pulmonary infarction, AV malformation, vasculitis, inhaled foreign body, iatrogenic (biopsies), heart failure, mitral stenosis, blood dyscrasias.

5) Systems review

A systems review should be conducted on every patient. As mentioned above, respiratory symptoms are a common manifestation of systemic illness. Likewise, some causes of respiratory diseases can have manifestations in other systems (e.g. cystic fibrosis, collagen vascular disorders).

Ask specifically about general symptoms of weight loss, anorexia, fevers, night sweats and fatigue as these might suggest tuberculosis or lung cancer. Establish daytime sleepiness or a history of snoring to determine if the patient may have obstructive sleep apnoea.

6) ICE

Establish the patient's thoughts and ideas about their symptoms. Patients with recent onset of SOB, haemoptysis, etc. may be concerned that they have lung cancer. Knowing the patient's concerns and expectations allows you to address these with reassurance and the proper investigations. Enquire about how the symptoms are affecting the patient's life, hobbies and jobs.

7) Past medical history

Ask specifically about:

- Allergies
- Asthma / atopy or COPD
- Pneumonia
- Tuberculosis
- Cardiac disease: MIs, heart failure
- Blood clot: pulmonary embolism or deep vein thrombosis
- Cancer: risk of secondary metastases and increased risk of venous thromboembolism
- Childhood illness: whooping cough or measles (as this may be a cause of bronchiectasis).

Establish whether the patient has ever been hospitalized for their respiratory disease. To establish asthma severity, ask about ITU admissions and whether they have ever been intubated. Ask if they have ever had any investigations into the cause of their presenting complaint (e.g. lung function tests, CT scans, bronchoscopy).

8) Medication history

Over 600 medications are known to potentially cause respiratory side-effects. Patients that are most at risk for the development of drug-induced lung disease include those receiving chemotherapy, those with inflammatory diseases (e.g. rheumatoid arthritis, ulcerative colitis) and those taking multiple toxic agents. The most commonly used drugs that can induce lung toxicity are methotrexate, amiodarone, NSAIDs, nitrofurantoin and ACE inhibitors.

- **Cough**: ACE inhibitors
- **Bronchospasm**: aspirin, beta-blockers, contrast media, nitrofurantoin, penicillamine, sulphonamides
- **Pulmonary fibrosis**: amiodarone, azathioprine, bleomycin, etanercept, GOLD, infliximab, methotrexate, nitrofurantoin, rituximab, sulfasalazine
- **Pulmonary oedema**: aspirin, contrast media, cyclophosphamide, methotrexate, sulphonamides, salbutamol, terbutaline
- **Pulmonary embolism**: oral contraceptive pill.

Ask about allergies and intolerances. Is the patient on long-term home oxygen therapy?

9) Family history

Many respiratory conditions have a genetic component. Ask about a family history of atopy (asthma, eczema, hay fever), lung cancer, COPD at a young age ($\alpha 1$ antitrypsin deficiency) and cystic fibrosis. If the patient is presenting with an acute illness, establish if anyone else in the household has been sick with an infective illness (cold/flu symptoms, pneumonia or tuberculosis).

10) Social history

- **Occupation**: *'What do you do for work?'* Ask about limitations and symptoms at work.
  - *'What other jobs have you had in your lifetime?'*
  - *'Have you ever been exposed to asbestos?'* (think plumbers, construction workers)
  - Miners are at risk for pneumoconiosis
  - Ask farmers if they have contact with poultry or other birds (allergic extrinsic alveolitis)
- **Smoking**: risk factor for COPD and lung cancer.
  - *'When did you start smoking?'*
  - *'Do you smoke cigarettes or a pipe?'*
  - *'How many cigarettes / pipes do you smoke per day?'* If they smoke cigars, do they inhale?
  - *'Have you ever tried to give up smoking?'* *'What methods did you use?'*
  - For non-smokers ask about smoking in the household currently and in the past.

- **Alcohol**: *'Do you drink alcohol? What types of alcohol do you drink? How many days a week do you drink alcohol? How much alcohol would you consume on an average day?'* If there is any concern, use the CAGE score to see if they may be dependent.
- **Recreational drug use**: inhaled drugs can increase the risk of lung cancer and COPD.
- **Exercise level**: *'Do you exercise?'* If so, how much and what type of exercise. Good for establishing a baseline.
- **Pets**: *'Do you own any pets? Do you own any birds?'* Always ask about birds separately as people don't often consider them to be pets. Bird owners are at risk of allergic extrinsic alveolitis. Pets can also be an exacerbating factor in atopic asthma.
- **Living situation**: *'Do you live in a house or a bungalow? Can you manage the stairs in your house? Does anyone help you with your activities of daily living?'*
- **Travel history**: *'Any recent long-haul flights?'* (consider pulmonary embolism). Hotel air conditioners could cause legionnaires' disease. Did they visit a country with a high prevalence of tuberculosis?

11) Closing the consultation

Always use your basic communication skills according to the Calgary–Cambridge Model. Remember to **summarize**. After collecting all of the relevant data, be sure to **screen** in order to ensure that the patient has had the opportunity to express anything else they feel is relevant.

Always close by thanking the patient and informing them of the next step in their plan of care.

> **Summary of key points (GET YOUR MARKS):**
>
> Establish rapport (clear introduction of who you are, what your role is and why you are there).
>
> History of presenting complaint: key symptoms to screen for – SOB, cough, haemoptysis, sputum production, wheeze and chest pain.
>
> Systems review: rule out differentials by asking about red flags including weight loss, fatigue, haemoptysis, night sweats and fever.
>
> ICE.
>
> Past medical history: ask about asthma, COPD, infections, previous blood clots, cancer or childhood illnesses.
>
> Medication history: current medications (including inhalers), allergies, OTC medications and supplements. Consider if any of their medications are causing their symptoms.
>
> Family history: first-degree relatives with asthma, atopy, lung cancer or cystic fibrosis.
>
> Social history: disease impact on ADLs and occupation. Establish a history of asbestos exposure, occupational hazards, smoking or exposure to second-hand smoke, recreational drug use, pets/birds, exercise tolerance, infectious contacts and travel history.
>
> Closing the consultation: use the Calgary–Cambridge Model throughout. Summarize and screen as you go. Develop a plan of care with the patient as your partner in the shared decision making process. Thank the patient.

12.2 Information giving and shared decision making

This section is a quick overview of what you might tell a patient during an information gathering or shared decision making station. Use this only as a guide. The most important message is that any explanation that you give a patient should be clear and free from medical jargon. Always use the Calgary–Cambridge Model to get your OSCE points. The main principles that should be applied include assessing the patient's starting point, 'chunking and checking', summarizing and signposting. Make use of paper in the station to help illustrate the information to the patient or to spell out difficult important words.

Review *Chapter 5* to get the most OSCE points possible.

12.2.1 Asthma

What is it and who gets it? Asthma is a disease affecting the small airways (bronchioles) of the lungs. It usually develops in childhood but it can develop at any point in a person's life. Approximately 1 in 10 children and 1 in 20 adults have the disease. An asthma attack can be triggered by many different things but it most commonly occurs when the person is exposed to an allergen, infections, cigarette smoke, exercise or stress. When an asthma attack occurs it is because of a process we call inflammation. The small airways react to a trigger by becoming constricted or narrowed (draw a picture of a normal bronchiole / alveoli versus an inflamed bronchiole). This is because the muscles that surround the airways are irritated so they squeeze the airways closed. The inflammation also leads to the production of mucus which can further restrict the amount of air that can pass to the alveoli, which is the area of the lung that helps to move the oxygen to our body.

When your asthma is active you might feel short of breath, feel a tightness in your chest and/ or hear wheezing which happens because the airway is narrow.

Treatment: there are many ways that we can prevent and treat asthma. By far the most important thing you can do to prevent your asthma from flaring up is to avoid any triggers you might have. Your doctor may prescribe you one or more inhalers to help with your symptoms.

The most common inhaler prescribed is a blue one called Ventolin. We call this type of inhaler 'the reliever'. You only need to take this inhaler when you feel breathless or experience wheezing. We encourage you to use a spacer when you need to use your Ventolin as this will optimize the amount of medicine that you will receive. I will show you how to do that shortly.

The second inhaler that you might be prescribed is a brown one. This is an inhaler that we like to call 'the preventer'. We prescribe this inhaler to prevent you from having an attack as it contains a steroid. You will need to take this inhaler once or twice daily, even if you are not having any symptoms. As with 'the reliever', we encourage the use of a spacer. Be sure to rinse your mouth out after using this inhaler, as the steroid can cause thrush. Most patients will use it in the morning and at night before brushing their teeth.

You may need more treatments if your asthma remains uncontrolled but your doctor will discuss these with you. Signs that your asthma needs better treatment include: breathlessness or wheeze at night, needing to use your reliever more often or if your peak flow readings are lower.

12.2.2 Chronic obstructive pulmonary disease (COPD)

What is it? COPD is a chronic disease of the airways which is an umbrella term used when someone has bronchitis and/or emphysema. Bronchitis involves inflammation of the larger airways of the lung called the bronchi and emphysema is a disease of the small airways and air sacs (alveoli). This leads to reduced air flow through the lungs and affects how well oxygen can move across the lung into the blood to supply the rest of the body.

People generally start by having a cough which is usually productive for phlegm. You may have heard of this being called a 'smoker's cough'. Eventually people become short of breath, at first when they are exerting themselves, for example walking upstairs, but eventually this can occur with only minor activity. Chest infections also occur more often when you have COPD. If this happens you may notice that you become more wheezy or that you are coughing up more phlegm.

Who gets it? COPD is a very widespread disease which commonly occurs in people over the age of 40, becoming more prevalent the older people get. Smoking is the cause of the vast majority of cases but it can occasionally be caused by second-hand smoking, air pollution, poor work conditions and sometimes due to a rare genetic condition.

Treatment: the damage to the airways is permanent and fixed, therefore treatment options to help open up the airways are limited. The most important way to prevent the progression of COPD is to stop smoking. It is never too late to quit. If you would like advice about how to quit, we can arrange for you to come back to discuss it further.

- Short-acting bronchodilator inhalers are often prescribed to open up the airways (dilate them). Examples include salbutamol / terbutaline (beta agonists) and ipratropium (antimuscarinic).
- Long-acting bronchodilator inhalers work by opening up airways for up to 12 hours. Examples include formoterol / salmeterol (beta agonists), tiotropium (antimuscarinic).
- Steroid inhalers are used when someone has regular flares or exacerbations of their asthma. They can sometimes be combined with long-acting beta agonists in a single inhaler. Examples include beclometasone, budesonide, fluticasone and mometasone.
- Mucolytic agents such as carbocysteine help to reduce the thickness of your phlegm, making it easier to cough up and making it harder for germs to infect the mucosa.
- We also recommend that you get your pneumococcus jab and your yearly flu vaccination, try to exercise regularly and lose weight (if appropriate) which can help relieve some of your breathlessness.
- Your doctor will need to review your COPD yearly but do call your doctor if you have any increase in your symptoms.

12.2.3 Respiratory treatments

Using your inhaler (metered dose inhaler – MDI)

- Inhalers are used to treat asthma and COPD because they help to deliver the medication directly to the lung where it is needed to help you breathe. They also have few side-effects because not much of the drug gets absorbed into the rest of your body.
- Many people use their inhaler incorrectly. This means that they do not get the entire dose of their medication which can lead to flare-ups in their condition.
- You will work with your doctor or nurse practitioner to develop a written action plan in the event that your asthma flares up, in order to help you take control of your condition rather than letting your condition control you.
- To get the most out of your MDI, you should use a spacer.
- Start by shaking your MDI. This ensures that the medicine and the propellant (the ingredient that turns the medicine into an aerosol) mix.
- If using your spacer, insert the 'puffer' into the opposite end of the mouthpiece. Press the button on the inhaler and then breathe normally for up to 5 breaths. The canister helps to collect the medicine so that you don't have to breathe it in all at once.
- If you do not have a spacer with you, you will need to time your breath with the delivery of the medicine. Breathe in and then all the way out. When ready, take a slow but deep breath in and press the button on your 'puffer' with the mouthpiece in your mouth and your lips closed around it. You should then hold your breath for up to 10 seconds and then exhale.
- If multiple sprays of your puffer are needed, allow 30 seconds between each puff. This allows enough time for the propellant and the medicine to mix together.
- If you are using your steroid inhaler, be sure to rinse out your mouth afterwards to avoid thrush.

Peak flow monitoring and asthma action plans

- Peak flow meters are used to monitor how well the lungs are functioning. *Establish if the patient has been prescribed their peak flow meter for investigating whether they have asthma or to monitor the status of their asthma.*
- **Investigation purposes**: in order to determine if you have asthma we will be having you complete a peak flow reading twice a day for the next 2–4 weeks. This will give us important information to help us determine if asthma has been the reason why you have been experiencing your symptoms.
  - Twice a day you will need to complete a reading. In order to complete a reading, you will need to blow three times into your peak flow meter and then record the highest reading on your peak flow chart.
  - You should be standing when you take your readings. Start by exhaling normally. Then take a big breath in and blow into your peak flow meter as hard and fast as you can. Your breath should take about 1 second.
  - Make sure that you keep your posture upright and that you close your lips (not your teeth) fully around the mouthpiece to ensure a good seal.
  - 'Here, let me show you how it is done and then we will let you have a try.'
  - After you have completed your 2–4 weeks of readings, we will review these. We then may prescribe you an inhaler to use and have you complete readings for an additional two weeks, just to verify the diagnosis and make sure that the treatment works for you.
- **Monitoring your asthma**: using your peak flow meter and asthma action plan can help you take control of your asthma and its symptoms. When you are well we will calculate your personal best peak flow. This is important because it will be used in your action plan to help treat your asthma symptoms if they occur.
  - Your asthma action plan is made up of a traffic light system. Research has shown that people who use their asthma action plans are four times less likely to visit the hospital because of their asthma symptoms.
  - The green part of your action plan is when you are well or have mild symptoms. Twice a day you will need to take your preventer inhaler. This will reduce the amount of asthma symptoms you have.
  - If you develop a wheeze, experience chest tightness or find it hard to breathe, you should complete three peak flow readings. Using your highest reading, plug it in to your action plan to find instructions as to what you should do. This may involve taking your reliever, increasing the amount of preventer you are using, visiting your GP or attending A&E.
  - If you have severe asthma, long-term daily monitoring of your peak flow readings can help you to detect early changes in your disease status.
  - Every year your GP or nurse practitioner will update your action plan and alter it to fit your needs. This may involve increasing, decreasing or keeping your medication regimen the same.
  - Keep a copy of your plan with you at all times in the form of a copy or as a picture on your phone. It is also helpful for close family and friends to have a copy of your form in case of an emergency.
  - Make sure that you bring your action plan with you when you attend your GP appointments so that adjustments can be made if necessary.

12.3 Practice scenarios

1. Mashrur Obama is a 65-year-old man who has been recently diagnosed with COPD. He has been started on salbutamol (PRN) and beclometasone inhalers (BD). He has never used an inhaler before. Teach Mashrur about COPD and how to use his inhalers at home.

2. Jessica Anderson, 22 years of age, has been suffering from night-time coughing and early morning shortness of breath. The GP is concerned that Jessica may have asthma and has asked you to talk to Jessica about performing two weeks of peak flow measures. Talk to Jessica about asthma and how the serial peak flow measures will help to determine if she has the condition.

3. Jane Ball is a single mother. She has recently found out that her only son Curtis (age 6 months) has cystic fibrosis. Jane is not in contact with the father. She has come to you to discuss the diagnosis and specifically how Curtis' breathing will be affected. She would like to know how the team will manage his respiratory symptoms.

4. Vanda Kwiatkowski is a 26-year-old lady who is two weeks postpartum. She presented to the hospital after a sudden onset of shortness of breath and right-sided chest pain. A pulmonary embolism was confirmed on CT scan. The consultant has asked you to speak to Vanda about her diagnosis and how it will be managed.

5. Bob Thomas is a 56-year-old man. His wife has presented with him as she is worried that he has been stopping breathing during his sleep. He is obese and smokes. Upon questioning, he admits that he takes a nap on his lunch break because he is tired. His wife also says that Bob naps after supper. The GP is considering sleep apnoea. Discuss how this will be investigated and what treatment options are available for him.

6. Janet Baldwin is a 54-year-old woman who has recently been diagnosed with COPD. She has been a smoker for over 34 years and wants to finally quit. Discuss the options available for her and establish a plan of care.

7. Bridget Russell is a 30-year-old woman who is being discharged after a life-threatening asthma attack which resulted in 4 days intubated on ITU. She was transferred to your unit 3 days ago and has been stable since. This is her second time being admitted to ITU due to her asthma exacerbations and she often attends A&E for nebulizer treatments. Discuss her current inhaler regimen with her and the importance of compliance. Try to come up with a shared plan of care.

13

Ear, nose and throat

RUPERT SMITH

Ear, Nose and Throat: Keys to Success

The nature of ear, nose and throat (ENT) as a specialty means that patients can present with a vast array of symptoms. Although this may seem daunting at first, once broken down into the constituent sub-specialties of otology, rhinology and head and neck, remembering what information you need to draw from the patient is relatively straightforward:

- Ears: hearing loss, otalgia, otorrhoea, tinnitus, vertigo
- Nose: congestion, rhinorrhoea, epistaxis, olfactory changes
- Throat: pain, dysphagia, odynophagia
- Larynx: hoarseness, vocal changes, noisy breathing, difficulty breathing
- Trachea: noisy breathing, difficulty breathing
- Neck: lymphadenopathy, new lumps and bumps, pain, swelling
- Face: facial pain, pressure, swelling, numbness.

Red flags in ENT:

Acute onset of hearing loss or unilateral hearing loss should raise suspicion of more sinister pathology including malignancy (e.g. acoustic schwannoma), abnormalities of cranial nerves in addition to hearing loss (also raises possibility of malignancy or other central nervous system (CNS) pathology), stridor or other sign of respiratory distress, drooling, muffled voice (often described as "hot potato"), visible bulge in the pharynx.

Red flags for head and neck malignancy:

- **Symptoms suggesting a localized malignancy**: anorexia and weight loss, dysphonia, dysphagia, odynophagia, dyspnoea, persistent hoarseness, otalgia, cough.
- **Symptoms suggesting a haematological malignancy**: fatigue, night sweats, fever, weight loss, bruising/bleeding, recurrent infections, bone pain, pruritis, lymphadenopathy at other site (leg groin).

13.1 Information gathering

The opening of the consultation is the same regardless of whether the patient is presenting with an ear, nose or throat problem, so be sure to open with the following three key points:

1) Introduce yourself and your role on the healthcare team

2) Ensure consent and confidentiality

3) Confirm the patient's name and DOB

It is sometimes helpful to ask the patient about their occupation early in the consultation. Asking about what the patient does for work along with a follow-up question such as *'What does that involve?'* or *'Do you enjoy your job?'* can establish rapport early and may provide some context later in the consultation when you are asking about limitations.

> **Allow for the Golden Minute:** always allow the patient to talk uninterrupted for the first minute of the consultation. Not only will this give you a solid starting point on which to base your consultation, but it will also give you time to think about the questions you will need to ask, based on what you have heard.

> **Key Knowledge**
> **Five causes of sensorineural hearing loss:**
> - Congenital causes (e.g. Usher's syndrome)
> - Fetal/childhood infection – rubella, cytomegalovirus, meningitis
> - Presbyacusis (age-related hearing loss)
> - Ménière's disease
> - Drugs – aminoglycoside antibiotics, chemotherapy agents, loop diuretics
>
> **Five causes of conductive hearing loss:**
> - Ear wax impaction
> - Otitis media with effusion
> - Perforated tympanic membrane
> - Malformation of external ear
> - Otosclerosis

13.1.1 The ear

4) History of presenting complaint
'What has brought you into the clinic/office/A&E today?'

There are five cardinal signs which must always be asked about when a patient presents with an ear complaint. Just think HOOT V (*five*): Hearing loss, Otalgia (ear pain), Otorrhoea (ear discharge), Tinnitus and Vertigo.

Hearing loss

Although many of the causes of hearing loss will be readily apparent on examination of the patient, a good history is important in order to identify causes which will not be detectable on examination.

Questions to ask:
- *'Have you noticed your hearing has decreased in one or both ears? Has anyone ever told you that they thought your hearing was getting worse?'*
- *'When did you first notice a decrease in your hearing?'*
- *'Did the decrease in hearing come on suddenly or has it been gradual?'*
- *'Have there been any recent events which you feel may have affected your hearing such as significant noise exposure, head injury or starting a new drug?'*

> **OSCE TIP:** The ear
> - Remember that you are dealing with a patient who may be very hard of hearing. If the patient is struggling to hear you – don't be afraid to raise your voice.
> - A request commonly made by OSCE examiners is to name five causes each of sensorineural and conductive hearing loss – make sure you have five of each ready to go if asked.

Otalgia

As with any other type of pain, use the SOCRATES mnemonic to ensure you cover all the important elements of pain.

Don't forget that pain in the ear does not always originate from the ear. Common origins of referred ear pain include the cervical spine, temporomandibular joint, teeth and the throat.

Otorrhoea

The discharging ear can be embarrassing for patients and should be approached sensitively. A thorough history of otorrhoea should always be taken (see *Table 13.1*) and should include the following key questions:
- *'How long have you been having discharge from your ear?'*
- *'What does the fluid coming from your ear look like? What colour is it? Is it thick/watery/bloody?'*
- *'Has anything been placed into the ear, for example a cotton bud?'*

Table 13.1 Types of ear discharge and their diagnosis

Type of discharge	Possible diagnoses
Purulent	Often infectious in origin – acute otitis media, recurrent episodes suggestive of chronic suppurative otitis media
Blood-stained	Trauma to tympanic membrane (often from cotton buds), chronic infection (bleeding from granulation tissue)
Clear, watery	May be suggestive of CSF leak, especially in cases where there is a previous history of trauma
Clear, mucoid	Chronic tympanic perforation, discharge through grommet
Foul-smelling	Raises suspicion of cholesteatoma or malignancy

Tinnitus

Tinnitus can be described as either subjective (most common) or objective.

A thorough history of tinnitus can be elicited from the patient through a similar approach to the SOCRATES method used in pain:

Site: *'Do you hear the noise in one ear or both?'* – unilateral tinnitus can be caused by earwax impaction and otitis media/externa.

Onset: *'When did you first start experiencing the noise in your ear/s? Was it a gradual or sudden onset?'* – noise exposure and head trauma can result in the sudden onset of tinnitus.

Character: *'How would you describe the noise? Is it high- or low-pitched? Does it sound like a pulsing or a heartbeat?'* – a low-pitched rumbling is suggestive of Ménière's disease, whereas a high-pitched pattern suggests sensorineural hearing loss. A pulsing thumping noise in time with the pulse is likely the result of a vascular abnormality.

Pattern: *'Is the noise always present or does it come and go?'* – continuous tinnitus often accompanies hearing loss, whereas episodic tinnitus should raise suspicion of Ménière's disease.

Exacerbating / alleviating factors: *'Is there anything you do which seems to make the noise better or worse? Does lying down seem to have any effect?'* – Eustachian tube dysfunction causing or contributing to tinnitus is sometimes relieved on lying down with the head in a different position.

Associated symptoms: *'Have you had any other symptoms with the tinnitus?'* – patients do not always recognize the links between symptoms and may not deem them significant enough to mention; therefore, whilst it is good to begin with an open question about other symptoms, you should also specifically ask about any associated vertigo, aural fullness and hearing loss.

Quality of life: *'How does the tinnitus affect you in your day-to-day life?'* – different patients can have very different experiences of tinnitus. For some, tinnitus can be incredibly debilitating while others consider it a minor annoyance they are willing to put up with. The impact on the patient is essential to understand as this will guide the management.

Vertigo

Vertigo is defined as an illusion of movement of the person's surroundings. Vertigo is always the result of a defect in the vestibular system.

Patients sometimes use different terminology when describing symptoms. A precise history is important in distinguishing true vertigo from dizziness or light-headedness which may have their origin in different systems (for example, cardiac abnormalities are a common cause of dizziness). You should try to avoid asking leading questions and allow the patient to describe the sensation using their own words. You can ask further questions to clarify meaning where you are uncertain.

Description: *'How would you describe the sensation you are experiencing?'* – always start with an open question. Patients will commonly use terms such as dizzy, or light-headed. Getting further detail by asking *'Does the world seem to spin during the episodes?'* should allow you to distinguish between dizziness and light-headedness, which are likely to be of non-ENT origin, and true vertigo.

Duration: *'How long does each episode last?'* – the duration of each episode of vertigo is one of the key questions to ask in order to come to a correct underlying cause (see *Table 13.2*).

Table 13.2 Duration of vertigo episode and likely cause

Duration	Cause
Seconds	Benign positional paroxysmal vertigo (BPPV)
Hours	Ménière's disease
Days	Labyrinthitis
Long-term (slowly progressing)	Possible malignancy (e.g. acoustic neuroma)

Alleviating/exacerbating factors: *'Does anything seem to make the sensation better or worse?'* – improvement on lying down with the head in a different position is suggestive of BPPV.

13.1.2 The nose

Nasal obstruction

Nasal obstruction is increased resistance to airflow through the nose and can be a result of structural deformity (such as deviated nasal septum) or vasoactive conditions (such as allergic rhinitis). Patients may describe obstruction as not being able to breathe through the nose. It is important to determine if the obstruction is unilateral or bilateral, and continuous or intermittent.

You should make sure you ask the following questions: *'Have you noticed if the obstruction is on one side or both? Does the obstruction seem to come and go or is it permanent? Does anything seem to make it better or worse?'*

Nasal discharge

Nasal discharge can occur anteriorly or posteriorly (post-nasal). The usual questions about frequency, severity and duration should be asked in the history. One specific question to ask the patient is what the discharge looks like (see *Table 13.3*). This can be particularly helpful in determining the cause.

Table 13.3 Appearance of nasal discharge and likely causes

Appearance	Causes
Watery	Allergic rhinitis
Serous	CSF leak
Mucusy, purulent	Inflammatory conditions such as chronic rhinosinusitis
Blood-stained	Post-epistaxis, tumour, foreign body, illicit drug use

If the discharge is recurrent you should also seek to clarify any relation to where the patient is when the discharge occurs, the season, or exposure to potential allergens (see past medical history section).

Epistaxis

The severity of nosebleeds can range from minor nuisance to severe, potentially life-threatening bleeding. The emphasis in an acute situation is to stem the bleeding, but you should remember to ask about the severity, frequency and duration.

Severity: *'Could you roughly guess how much blood you have lost from your nose since the bleeding started?'* – rather than using measurements you could ask the patient to estimate based on common household items. For example, *'Was it enough to fill an egg cup? Enough to fill a standard mug?'*, etc.

Frequency: *'How often do you get nosebleeds? Does anything seem to bring on your nosebleeds?'* – most nosebleeds are reported as spontaneous events but it is important to determine any history of facial trauma.

Duration: *'How long in minutes do your nosebleeds usually last? How do you usually try to stop the bleeding? Have you ever been to hospital because your nose wouldn't stop bleeding?'* – longer episodes of bleeding may increase the risk of significant blood loss which can be life-threatening.

History of bleeding disorders and use of anticoagulant medications is important to determine (see past medical history).

13.1.3 Throat, head and neck

Throat symptoms

Sore throat and tonsillitis are among the most common conditions of the mouth seen in ENT. You should ask about the course and duration of the symptoms and make sure you take a good general medical history (systemic conditions such as HIV infection and anaemia have oral manifestations):

- *'How long have you had a sore throat? Are you having difficulty swallowing?'* – sore throat of long duration with difficulty swallowing can result in the patient becoming dehydrated.
- *'Have you experienced any neck pain or stiffness?'* – indicative of more serious conditions such as epiglottitis and retropharyngeal abscess.
- *'Have you tried any self-care at home?'* – patients may have tried OTC medication and other measures at home; if not you can advise them appropriately (e.g. increasing fluid intake, paracetamol, ibuprofen, lozenges).

Patients presenting with hoarseness of the voice should be asked the following specific questions:
- Onset: *'Did the hoarseness come on suddenly or gradually over a longer period?'* – acute onset may be suggestive of viral or bacterial laryngitis, whereas a more chronic presentation may be a result of smoke exposure, malignancy or reflux.
- Exposure: smoking status, alcohol use (both increase risk of laryngeal cancer), previous head and neck surgery.
- Timing: *'Does the hoarseness seem to come on/is it worse at a particular time of day?'* Evening onset may be of neuromuscular origin (e.g myasthenia gravis); morning onset may be a result of reflux; constant hoarseness is more likely to be a result of a structural change in the larynx such as a tumour.

Lumps and bumps in the neck

Although your examination will give you a good idea of what the lump is like, you should always take a history from the patient rather than jumping straight into an examination. The ultimate aim of questioning is to distinguish possible malignancy from other causes of lumps in the neck. In order to do this, make sure you cover the following elements in your history:

Site: *'Where is the lump? Is it one lump or are there several?'* – you should ask the patient to show you where the lump is and if there is more than one.

Size: *'How big would you say the lump is?'* – sometimes patients struggle to objectively estimate size in centimetres. It can be useful to ask the patient to compare the size of the lump to common fruits such as a grape.

Shape: *'How would you describe the shape of the lump?'*

Consistency: *'Does the lump feel hard/soft? Does it feel like there may be fluid inside?'* – hard lumps are generally more likely to be of more sinister origin.

Pain/tenderness: *'Does the lump cause you any pain? Does it hurt when you touch it or perhaps when you shave?'* – painless lumps should raise suspicion of malignant disease. Don't forget to use SOCRATES if the patient says they are experiencing pain.

Onset: *'When did you first notice the lump? Did it come up quickly? Did anything seem to come on with the lump? Had you been ill at all around the time you first noticed the lump?'* – a rapid onset painful swelling suggests an inflammatory cause. A slow onset hard non-tender lump is more suggestive of malignancy.

Change over time: *'Does the lump seem to have changed at all since you first noticed it?'* – change may be in size, shape or consistency.

Symptoms suggesting a lump of infectious or inflammatory origin: recent history of illness (infection of the ear, nose, throat, scalp or dental infection), fever and rigors, sore throat, cough, earache, toothache, rash.

5) Systems review

- General: *'Recently have you experienced any fever, chills or weight change? Have you felt more tired than usual?'* (always ask about red flag symptoms which may point to malignant disease – particularly important in those presenting with neck lumps).
- Neuro: *'Have you had any recent dizziness, headaches or change in vision? Have you experienced any numbness or tingling in your arms, legs, fingers or toes?'* (central neurological problems may have an impact on hearing or balance).
- Respiratory / cardiovascular:
  - *'Have you had any chest pain or shortness of breath recently?'* (ENT conditions may require surgical intervention, therefore it is important to have an idea if the patient is likely to be fit for a general anaesthetic).
  - *'Have you ever had problems with your breathing?'* (there is a significant interaction between the upper and lower respiratory tracts; you should take a thorough history if the patient describes any previous or current breathing difficulties).
- GI:
  - *'Have you experienced any chest pain or reflux?'* (reflux is thought to have a role in the development of rhinosinusitis and also can be a cause of hoarseness).
  - *'Have you experienced any notable weight loss / gain?'* (may suggest altered thyroid function).
- MSK: *'Have you had any recent muscle cramps, weakness or stiffness? Any joint pain or swelling?'* (autoimmune disease).
- Skin: *'Do you have dry or itchy skin? Have you noticed any new skin rashes, bumps or sores? Have you noticed any hair loss?'* (also suggestive of autoimmune disease and altered thyroid function – relevant in patient presenting with neck lump).

13.1.4 General ENT history taking

6) Past medical history

The patient's past medical history can provide important clues to the underlying cause of ENT symptoms. Patients often unintentionally or deliberately omit information from the history, therefore it is important to lead the patient through the history with specific questions in order to avoid missing relevant and important points.

- Medical history: begin by asking the patient about their general health – *'Do you have any other medical conditions? Are you seeing a doctor regularly?'* You should enquire specifically about the following areas that are particularly relevant to ENT:
  - Neurology (symptoms of cranial nerve palsy, sensorineural causes of hearing loss).
  - Respiratory disease (asthma linked with chronic rhinosinusitis – Samter's Triad – see drug history).
  - Rheumatological / autoimmune conditions (may increase chance of thyroid pathology in central neck lump).
  - Haematological disease (particularly relevant in epistaxis).
- Surgical history: begin by focusing on the specific area where the patient is experiencing symptoms and then work out more broadly to other areas. This approach ensures that the most important information is elicited first and prevents you from getting bogged down in the details of irrelevant procedures. For example:
  - *'Have you had any previous surgery on your ... (insert relevant anatomy e.g. ear)?'*
  - *'Have you had any other procedures anywhere on your head or neck?' 'Have you had any other surgical procedures?'*
- Environmental allergies: at this point you may wish to ask about environmental allergies (some decide to ask about environmental allergies with drug allergies in the medication history). It is particularly important to ask about environmental allergies in patients presenting with sino-nasal symptoms. You should ask:

- o *'Do you have any confirmed allergies? If so, to what? How was this diagnosed?'*
- o *'Do you think there is anything you may be allergic to but have not had it confirmed?'*
- o *'Do you have any pets at home?'*
- o *'Do your symptoms seem to be any worse at any particular time of year?'*
- o *'Do you have or have you ever had eczema or asthma?'*

7) Medication history

Taking a good drug history is as important in ENT as any other specialty. A thorough history is particularly important in patients presenting with hearing loss as there are some commonly prescribed medications which are known to be ototoxic.

Not only is it important to know what medications patients are taking, but also why. If you are uncertain why a patient is taking a particular medication, always clarify with them before continuing.

Always remember to ask about allergies to medications. This is particularly pertinent in patients with sino-nasal symptoms, as sensitivity to aspirin is associated with chronic rhinosinusitis with nasal polyposis and asthma (known as Samter's Triad).

> **Key knowledge: Medications known to be ototoxic**
>
> **Aminoglycoside antibiotics** (particularly gentamycin)
>
> **Loop diuretics** (furosemide)
>
> **Chemotherapy agents** (cisplatin)
>
> **Aspirin** (at high doses – often reversible on discontinuation)

8) Family history

Asking the patient if anyone in the family has ever had a similar problem to what they are experiencing is a quick and easy way to identify any potential hereditary ENT issue. For example, family history of endocrine tumour in a patient with a neck lump raises the possibility of multiple endocrine neoplasia syndrome (MEN). In any patient where you suspect a malignancy you should ask about relatives who may have had a diagnosis of cancer, as a positive family history raises the risk in many cases.

9) Social history

Many ENT conditions can be very disabling for patients. Making an assessment of function by asking the patient what impact symptoms have on their function and quality of life is important for guiding management. For example, hearing loss can have a profound effect on patients' everyday lives. Make sure to ask how the patient is coping with day-to-day tasks. Have they found themselves at risk because of their hearing loss? (for example, difficulty in hearing traffic when crossing the road).

You should also remember to ask some specific questions about the patient's social history:

- Alcohol use: *'Do you drink alcohol? How much do you drink?'* – as when taking any history, you should make sure you have a reasonably accurate idea of how much alcohol the patient drinks.
- Smoking status: *'Do you smoke? How many cigarettes/pipes do you smoke a day?'* – this generic question should be asked of all patients. However, it is particularly important to ask in ENT as smoking can exacerbate many conditions of the upper respiratory tract and increases the risk of all types of malignancy.
- Occupation: *'Are you currently in work? What is it you do for work? Does your work mean you are exposed to noise? Does your work mean you are exposed to any chemicals or*

substances?' – occupational exposure to noise may be a cause of hearing loss. Exposure to chemical fumes or smoke may result in or exacerbate upper respiratory tract symptoms. Throat symptoms in a professional voice user (such as a professional singer) may be of particular concern.

- Personal / dental hygiene:
- *'Have you had a check-up with a dentist recently?'* – a particularly relevant question in patients complaining of facial or ear pain.
- *'Do you use cotton buds in your ears?'* – use of cotton buds can cause perforation of the tympanic membrane and impaction of wax.
- Recent air travel / diving: *'Have you been away on a plane or been diving recently?'* – ear symptoms such as 'popping' and a sensation of pressure in the ear may be a result of altered external pressure on the ear.

10) Closing the consultation

Remember to utilize your four key principles of summarizing, screening, discussing the plan of care and thanking the patient.

Summary of key points (GET YOUR MARKS):

Establish rapport (clear introduction of who you are, what your role is and why you are there).

History of presenting complaint: key symptoms to screen for – ears (hearing loss, otalgia, otorrhoea, tinnitus and vertigo), nose (epistaxis, rhinorrhoea), throat (difficulty swallowing, lumps / bumps, noisy breathing).

Systems review: rule out differentials.

ICE.

Past medical history: previous neurological conditions, respiratory conditions, environmental allergens, autoimmune conditions and previous surgeries on the head and neck.

Medication history: current medication, allergies, OTC medications and supplements. Consider ototoxic drugs.

Family history: first-degree relative with hearing loss and malignancies.

Social history: disease impact on occupation and ADLs. History of smoking, alcohol intake, recreational drug use and caffeine. Include questions about dental hygiene and recent travel / diving.

Closing the consultation: let the Calgary–Cambridge Model be your guide. Remember your key skills of summarizing and screening. Always leave the patient with a plan of care, even if it is that you need to speak with your colleagues. Thank the patient.

OSCE TIP: The order in which you tackle each of the parts of the history from the HPC through to the social history should be relatively fixed. However, asking questions particularly relevant to the presentation earlier in the consultation demonstrates that you know what is important to ask in that particular condition and are able to appropriately tailor your consultation.

For example, you may choose to ask about the possibility of occupational noise exposure earlier before getting to the social history, in a patient presenting with hearing loss.

13.2 Information giving and shared decision making

The following section is a quick overview of what you might tell the patient during an information giving or shared decision making station. Use this section as a guide to what information might be relevant for the patient. Be sure to always assess the patient's starting point. Drawings and the use of models are very helpful for patients and often count for one or more marks. If you don't have anything to draw, writing long words for patients can also be helpful.

Review *Chapter 5* to get the most OSCE points possible.

13.2.1 The ear – otitis media

What is it? (Draw a horizontal tube and divide it up into three sections; in the middle box draw a representation of the tympanic membrane ossicles – don't worry if it doesn't look realistic). The ear is divided up into three main sections, the outer, middle and inner ear. The middle ear is the section where the ear drum and small bones which allow you to hear sit. For a variety of reasons the eardrum can become red and swollen, which is what we call inflammation. The swelling and irritation of the eardrum mean that its ability to pass sound on through the ear is reduced; this explains why you may be experiencing a reduction in your hearing on that side. The middle ear also becomes very sensitive as a result of the inflammation and that results in ear pain. Most commonly this inflammation is due to a bacterial or viral infection.

How is it treated? The majority of cases of otitis media resolve on their own and don't require treatment beyond giving you medication such as paracetamol and/or ibuprofen to help control the pain. If your symptoms don't seem to be getting better after 3 or 4 days you may be given a short course of antibiotics to help resolve the infection faster.

13.2.2 The nose – chronic rhinosinusitis (CRS)

What is it? (Draw a basic representation of the nose and maxillary sinuses). The sinuses are small air-filled spaces within the cheekbones and forehead. The purpose of our sinuses is to provide acoustics for our voice. Basically they help determine how your voice sounds. For a variety of reasons the lining of these sinuses and the lining of the nose can become inflamed. This inflammation causes the three main symptoms of CRS, which are a runny nose (which can also drip down the back of the throat), facial pain, and reduced sense of smell. Some patients also develop nasal polyps, folds of the normal lining in the nose, which can also cause congestion in the nose.

How is it treated? CRS is initially treated with medications but surgery is considered for patients who see little improvement in symptoms. The following are often used in combination to manage symptoms:
- Lifestyle interventions – stopping smoking, practising good dental hygiene (dental infection is associated with CRS).
- Nasal douching – washing out the nose with a douche can help to reduce congestion in the nose.
- Warm face packs – to provide relief for facial pain.
- Steroid nasal sprays – help to reduce inflammation of the lining of the nose and sinuses (you should make sure the patient is aware of the side-effects of steroids).
- Simple analgesics – paracetamol and ibuprofen can be used to manage pain.
- Oral steroids – courses of oral steroids can be used.
- Functional endoscopic sinus surgery – aims to clear the sinuses and improve sinus drainage (you should inform the patient of the general risks of surgery, e.g. infection, bleeding, anaesthetic risk).

13.2.3 **Throat, head and neck – tonsillitis**

What is it? (You may wish to draw a basic picture of the throat; a circle with a midline uvula and a representation of the tonsils on either side will suffice). The tonsils are lumps of soft tissue which sit on either side at the back of your mouth. They play a role in fighting infection but they aren't essential and can be removed if necessary. Tonsillitis occurs when the tonsils themselves become infected. When this occurs the tonsils can become enlarged and sore which makes swallowing painful. Tonsillitis can also make you feel generally unwell; you may notice that you get a temperature, headache, and feel more tired than usual. You may also develop some lumps in the neck.

How is it treated? Tonsillitis is caused by either a bacterial or viral infection, which are treated in different ways. Both are managed with pain relief (such as paracetamol and ibuprofen) but antibiotics will only be given in particular circumstances where it is likely that you have a bacterial rather than viral infection. If you experience repeated episodes of tonsillitis, surgery can be performed to remove the tonsils and prevent further infections.

> **OSCE TIP**: Be sure to check the specific guidelines for when to refer for tonsillectomy – this could come up in an OSCE station.

13.3 **Practice scenarios**

1. Mitchell James is a 22-year-old man who has had several episodes of a sore throat over the past 12 months. Mitchell has seen his GP several times and has been prescribed penicillin V twice previously, but on this occasion the GP suspects a viral illness rather than bacterial tonsillitis. Mitchell is unhappy that he has not been offered antibiotics as he says this helped his sore throat before. You are asked to explain to Mitchell why he has not been prescribed an antibiotic today.

2. Marion Ellis is a 45-year-old lady who attends ENT clinic for treatment of her benign paroxysmal positional vertigo (BPPV). The GP has previously explained that the treatment for this particular type of dizziness is for a specialist to move Marion's head in a particular way while she is lying down. Marion doesn't understand how this could help and asks for more information. You are to explain to the patient the cause of BPPV.

3. A 30-year-old man is concerned about a small lump in his neck which he noticed while shaving. The GP has taken a history and found the patient had a common cold a week earlier. The GP is unconcerned and believes this to be a swollen lymph node from the viral illness which will resolve on its own. The patient is still concerned that he may have cancer. You have been asked to talk to the patient to explain why the lump is unlikely to be of malignant origin.

4. Samia is a 16-year-old girl who has had recurrent episodes of tonsillitis. Her parents have brought her to see the GP as they have become concerned at the amount of time off school Samia is having to take with a sore throat. The GP has asked you to discuss with Samia and her parents the option of tonsillectomy versus ongoing medical management of recurrent sore throat.

5. You have been asked to speak to Duncan, a 27-year-old rugby player, who suffered a broken nose in a match four weeks ago. Although the bridge of his nose is in alignment, it is clear on examination that he has a deviated nasal septum which is causing a degree of obstruction in his right nostril. You are asked to discuss with him the option of surgery to correct the deviation (septoplasty). This should include a discussion of the general risks of surgery.

6. Douglas is a 50-year-old man who attends the GP surgery complaining of hearing loss in his right ear. Examination reveals a build-up of wax which is fully occluding the ear canal and is responsible for the hearing loss. You are to discuss with Douglas the options for removal of the wax. This includes the use of ear drops, self-irrigation and syringing. You should also advise Douglas on how to avoid build-up of wax in the future (with particular reference to cotton bud use).

14

Gastroenterology and hepatology

SRIKIRTI KODALI AND OSCAR SWIFT

> **Gastroenterology and Hepatology: Keys to Success**
>
> The gastrointestinal (GI) and hepatology history is best approached systematically. When a patient presents with a symptom that may be related to this system, it is important to screen for other symptoms that may be occurring. The main symptoms that you should always screen for in every GI complaint include:
>
> - Abdominal pain
> - Nausea or vomiting
> - Change in bowel movements
> - Blood in emesis or stool
> - Weight loss
> - Jaundice.

> **Red flags in gastroenterology and hepatology:**
>
> - Weight loss
> - Haematemesis
> - Melaena
> - Fever
> - Severe abdominal pain
> - Signs of shock
> - Change in bowel habits
> - Dark urine
> - Pale stools
> - Diffuse itching
> - Jaundice

14.1 Information gathering

As with all areas of medicine, a thorough history is vital in order to ensure a valid differential diagnosis is obtained.

1) Introduce yourself and your role on the healthcare team

2) Ensure consent and confidentiality

3) Confirm the patient's name and DOB

It is sometimes helpful to ask the patient about their occupation early in the consultation. Asking about what the patient does for a living along with a follow-up question such as *'What does that involve?'* or *'Do you enjoy your job?'* can establish rapport early and may provide some context later in the consultation when you are asking about limitations.

4) History of presenting complaint

'What has brought you into the clinic/A&E today?'

Following this open question, allow for the Golden Minute and give the patient time to tell their story to you about what happened.

14.1.1 Abdominal pain

Pain in the abdomen is a very common presenting complaint that affects all ages either on its own or in association with other symptoms.

The characteristics of pain can be described systematically using the mnemonic **SOCRATES**. This is a good general rule for exploring pain as a symptom. Here, a gastrointestinal theme has been applied.

- **Site**: The abdomen is anatomically divided into nine areas (see *Fig. 14.1*). This narrows down differentials and the pathology and usually coincides with visceral anatomy in that area, unless of course the pain is referred or radiating.

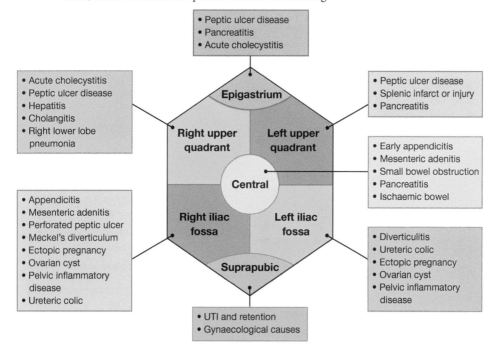

Figure 14.1 *The nine anatomical areas of the abdomen.*

- **Onset**: *'Did the pain come on suddenly? How long have you had it? What were you doing at that time? Is this new or have you had this before?'*
- **Character**: sharp, dull, colicky, deep or superficial. *'How would you describe the pain?'*
  - Colicky pain is characteristically described as pain that 'comes and goes'. The character of the pain is spasmodic or often described as 'coming in waves'. Luminal obstruction causes spasm of the smooth muscle in the wall of the structure, usually proximal to the obstruction.
- **Radiation**: *'Does the pain travel anywhere else? Where did the pain start? Has it moved?'*
  - Visceral afferent nerves project onto the same spinal intermediary neuron as somatic afferents. The area to which pain radiates can thus help identify its origin. For example, acute pancreatitis can present with pain radiating from the back to the epigastrium, renal colic presents with loin to groin pain and gall bladder pain is referred to the right shoulder.
- **Associated features**: ask about any constipation / diarrhoea, nausea / vomiting, lumps in their abdomen.
- **Timing**: subacute, chronic, cyclical. *'How long has this been going on for? Did it come on suddenly? Does it come and go?'*
- **Exacerbating factors or relieving factors**:

- ○ Positional component – *'Is there any position that makes the pain better/worse?'*
- ○ Analgesia – ask in detail what medication they have been using and in what dose and frequency. *'What seems to help?'*
- ○ Does ingestion/defecation/micturition have any effect on the pain?
- **Severity:**
  - ○ **Subjective**
    - – Pain has an emotional element to it. The patient might have their own comparative way of expressing it. It is important to allow them to do this, especially when establishing the doctor–patient relationship. *'How would you describe the pain? What would you compare the pain to?'*
    - – Some might say the pain of renal colic is *'like the pain of childbirth.'*
  - ○ **Objective**
    - – *'On a scale of 1–10, with 10 being the worst pain you have ever experienced, how would you rate your current pain?'*

Obstruction can be classified into luminal, mural (within the wall) or extramural causes (see *Table 14.1*).

Table 14.1 Locations of abdominal obstruction

	Luminal	**Mural**	**Extramural**
Small bowel	Twisting of the bowel on itself (volvulus)	Strictures	Organomegaly, pancreatic or ovarian cancer
Large bowel	Twisting of the bowel on itself	Carcinoma	Organomegaly, pancreatic or ovarian cancer
Biliary tree	Stone	Carcinoma, parasites (schistosomiasis)	Gall bladder, head of the pancreas
Ureter	Stone	Carcinoma	Complication from surgery

Abdominal pain overlaps with a number of other systems outside the gastrointestinal tract. It is important to also consider gynaecological and urological pathologies.

Pearls of Wisdom

- In a young female with acute/subacute abdominal pain: always rule out pregnancy by taking a menstrual history and ordering a urinary beta-hCG test. The intention is to rule out an ectopic pregnancy. Beta-hCG urine testing is routine in A&E now.
- Ask about menstrual pains.
- **Urological differentials**: pain radiating from the loin to groin is suggestive of urinary colic. Spasms of colicky pain due to obstruction of urinary tract are commonly due to renal stones. The pain is usually 10/10 with the patient often unable to stay still. Also consider urinary retention or urinary tract infection in patients with lower abdominal pain.

14.1.2 Haematemesis

Haematemesis is a medical emergency with significant mortality. It may be necessary to pursue an ABCDE approach in order to ensure haemodynamic stability prior to obtaining a history from the patient. Once the patient is stable haemodynamically the following should be established:

Tip: If it is possible to directly witness the haematemesis this can provide valuable information to help you when taking a history.

Amount of bleeding

'How much blood did you bring up? How many times have you vomited up blood?'

Often patients will find it difficult to quantify the amount of bleeding and so it can be helpful to give them a framework to help with this:

'Did you bring up a teaspoonful/egg cupful/small glassful or pint glassful of blood?'

Nature of haematemesis

'What colour was the blood that you brought up? Was it fresh red blood like when you cut your finger? Were there any clots in it? Did it look like "coffee grounds"?'

Haematemesis with fresh blood and clots is likely to reflect active bleeding in the proximal upper gastrointestinal tract. For haematemesis to occur, the bleeding source must be proximal or at the level of the duodenum (ligament of Treitz).

> **Key knowledge: Differential diagnosis for haematemesis**
> - Peptic ulcer disease (gastric ulcer/duodenal ulcer)
> - Oesophagitis/gastritis
> - Variceal haemorrhage
> - Mallory–Weiss tear
> - Oesophageal or gastric malignancy
> - Dieulafoy lesion (ectatic submucosal artery)
> - Vascular abnormalities (angiodysplasia, arteriovenous/vascular malformations, gastric antral vascular ectasia)
> - Aortoenteric fistula
> - Bleeding diasthesis
> - Alternative source of bleeding: epistaxis/haemoptysis

Associated PR bleeding

'Have you passed any blood or dark, smelly stool from the back passage?'

Passage of digested blood, in the form of black, tarry, sweet-smelling stool called melaena, suggests an upper gastrointestinal bleed. Haematochezia, the passage of fresh blood per rectum in the absence of a lower gastrointestinal bleeding source reflects brisk, significant upper gastrointestinal bleeding.

Abdominal symptoms

'Have you had any abdominal pain? How long have you had the pain for? Is the pain affected by you eating? Are you ever affected by bloating, indigestion or heartburn?'

Peptic ulcer disease as well as gastritis and oesophagitis are common causes of upper gastrointestinal bleeding. Haematemesis can occur when the peptic ulcer erodes into a blood vessel in the wall of the stomach or duodenum. Patients will often describe a history of abdominal pain associated with bloating, belching, indigestion and heartburn. Pain associated with a gastric ulcer is classically associated with eating, while pain associated with a duodenal ulcer classically occurs a few hours after eating, when the stomach has emptied its contents.

Recurrent episodes of severe vomiting

'Have you been vomiting a lot recently? Was this associated with anything? Have you had a stomach bug or drunk alcohol recently?'

A Mallory–Weiss tear, if large, can present with haematemesis. Mallory–Weiss tears often occur following previous episodes of recurrent, prolonged vomiting, most commonly in the context of recent alcohol intoxication or gastroenteritis.

Swallowing and associated problems

'Have you had any difficulties or pain with swallowing? Is it worse trying to swallow solids or liquids? Has this got worse at all? Has the amount of food you are able to eat changed? Have you noticed any weight loss recently? How much weight do you think you have lost?'

Oesophagitis is associated with odynophagia. Severe oesophagitis can lead to upper gastrointestinal bleeding. A less common but well recognized and very important cause of upper gastrointestinal bleeding is oesophagogastric malignancy. Often patients will report progressive dysphagia, initially worse with solids before progressing onto liquids. Early satiety is a common symptom in gastric malignancies. Quantification of weight loss should be performed when considering oesophagogastric malignancy as a potential diagnosis.

Episodes of epistaxis or haemoptysis

'Have you had a recent nose bleed? Did you cough rather than vomit blood?'

Epistaxis and haemoptysis can be confused with haematemesis and if there is doubt then you should check with the patient about the nature of the blood source.

When taking a history from a patient who has haematemesis, it is important to think about the underlying pathophysiology and have a differential diagnosis in mind to guide what questions you ask.

14.1.3 Jaundice

Onset of jaundice

'How long have you been yellow / jaundiced? Do you feel that you are getting more yellow? Have you ever been jaundiced in the past? If so, what were the circumstances surrounding that episode of jaundice?'

Information about the progression of jaundice and whether there have been any other causes of jaundice may be very helpful in elucidating the cause of the current presentation.

Associated abdominal pain

'Do you have any abdominal pain? Can you tell me about the nature of the pain? Does a particular position have any effect on the pain? Have you had any nausea or vomiting?'
Remember **SOCRATES**.

Abdominal pain may point towards gallstones, hepatitis or pancreatitis as the likely underlying aetiology. Pancreatic pain is often epigastric and radiates through to the back, improves on leaning forward and is worse on lying flat. Pain due to the gall bladder is often in the right upper quadrant and radiates around to the right side of the back or right shoulder tip. Nausea and vomiting often occur in conjunction with abdominal pain.

Fever

'Have you felt hot or had any shaking or shivering episodes? Is there any pattern to the shaking or shivering episodes that you experience? Have you taken your temperature before you came to hospital? What was the recording?'

A history of fevers, sweats or rigors in conjunction with jaundice is suggestive of biliary or hepatic infection. If the patient describes prodromal symptoms then this may be suggestive of viral hepatitis.

Weight loss

'Have you had any weight loss recently?' If the patient isn't sure then ask the following: *'Have you noticed that your clothes have become looser recently? Has anyone commented on your change in weight?'*

Jaundice and weight loss that is usually painless are associated classically with head of pancreas adenocarcinoma. Patients can also develop weight loss in the context of jaundice if they have hepatic malignancy (either primary (hepatocellular carcinoma) or secondary metastases). Hepatic malignancy can present with pain caused by stretching of the liver capsule.

Abdominal swelling

'Has your abdomen become more swollen? Does it feel tense or tight? Have you noticed any swelling in your legs?'

Abdominal swelling in a jaundiced patient commonly reflects the presence of ascites. This occurs in the context of decompensated liver disease. Ascites and jaundice (along with coagulopathy and encephalopathy) are markers of decompensation and are poor prognostic signs in patients with chronic liver disease. Patients may also have generalized oedema (and hence leg swelling) as a result of fluid overload and hypoalbuminaemia. Patients with fever and abdominal swelling should be investigated for spontaneous bacterial peritonitis.

Change in character of stools / urine

'Have your stools or urine changed colour in any way? Have your stools got lighter in colour or has your urine got darker at all? Have you noticed difficulty flushing your stools when they are in the toilet?'

Failure to excrete bile into the duodenum (in the setting of obstructive jaundice) leads to increased conjugated bilirubin in the blood and reduced levels in the gut. As conjugated bilirubin is water soluble it can be excreted into the urine, thus making the urine a darker colour. Reduced levels of bile in the gut lead to a decreased production of stercobilinogen, which when oxidized to stercobilin gives faeces its brown colour. As a result the stool is a paler, whiter colour in obstructive jaundice.

Itch

'Is your skin itchy?'

Itch in a jaundiced patient suggests that there is obstruction to biliary flow.

If you have in mind the information in *Tables 14.2* and *14.3* when you take your history, this will help to guide your history taking.

Table 14.2 Classification of jaundice

Prehepatic	Hepatic	Posthepatic
Haemolysis / large haematomas (increased bilirubin load)	Hepatitis (due to alcohol, viruses, medications or autoimmune pathology)	Common bile duct stones
Congenital or acquired defects in conjugation of bilirubin	Cirrhosis	Carcinoma (head of pancreas, cholangiocarcinoma)
	Intrahepatic cholestasis (due to medications, viruses or autoimmune pathology)	Benign biliary stricture
	Hepatic malignancy (either primary or secondary)	Pancreatitis

Table 14.3 Causes of chronic liver disease

Drugs and toxins	Alcohol (most common cause of chronic liver disease in the Western world)
	Methotrexate
	Amiodarone
Infection	Hepatitis B (most common cause of chronic liver disease worldwide)
	Hepatitis C
Metabolic	Non-alcoholic fatty liver disease
	Haemochromatosis
	Wilson's disease
	Alpha-1 antitrypsin deficiency
Autoimmune	Autoimmune hepatitis
	Primary biliary cirrhosis
Vascular	Budd–Chiari syndrome
	Cardiac failure
Biliary disease	Primary biliary cirrhosis
	Biliary obstruction
Miscellaneous	Ischaemic
	Malnutrition
	Sarcoidosis
	Amyloidosis

14.1.4 Weight loss

Many of the specific presentations described in this book will have weight loss as a presenting symptom. This section outlines how to approach a patient with malnutrition or a patient who is at risk of malnutrition.

Malnutrition is a common problem and affects over 3 million people in the UK. Between 25 and 34% of patients admitted to hospital are at risk of malnutrition. The following groups are at greatest risk:

- Patients over the age of 65, especially if they are a care or nursing home resident or an inpatient.
- Patients with chronic disease including diabetes, chronic lung disease and kidney disease.
- Patients with chronic progressive conditions including dementia and cancer.
- Patients who abuse alcohol or recreational drugs.

Patients with malnutrition are at increased risk of hospital admissions, have longer stays in hospital with more complications and are more likely to require support and care at discharge. Spending time with patients exploring if they have had any change in their weight or appetite and finding out what they eat may be helpful; however, the Malnutrition Universal Screening Tool ("MUST") is the best way to recognize malnutrition. It is a validated, five-step screening tool to identify adults who are malnourished or at risk of malnutrition. It can also be used to assess obese patients.

The 5 "MUST" steps are described as follows:

Step 1: Measure height and weight in order to calculate BMI (BMI = weight (kg)/height (m)^2)
BMI >20 = 0 points
BMI 18.5–20 = 1 point
BMI <18.5 = 2 points

Step 2: Calculate percentage of unplanned weight loss over the past 3–6 months
<5% = 0 points
5–10% = 1 point
>10% = 2 points

Step 3: Establish and score acute disease effect
If the patient has been acutely unwell and there has been or is likely to be no nutritional intake for more than 5 days = 2 points

Step 4: Add scores from steps 1, 2 and 3 together to obtain overall risk of malnutrition
Score = 0 (low risk)
Score = 1 (medium risk)
Score = 2 or more (high risk)

Step 5: Use management guideline and/or local policy to develop care plan.

For all risk categories
- Treat underlying condition and provide help and advice on food choices and eating and drinking, when necessary.
- Record malnutrition risk category.
- Record need for special diets and follow local policy.

Low risk
Routine clinical care and screening:
- Weekly if in hospital
- Monthly if in care home
- Annually if in community (only for special groups e.g. >75-year-olds)

Medium risk
Observe:
- Document dietary intake for 3 days
- If intake adequate and there is little concern:
  ○ Repeat screening weekly if in hospital
  ○ At least monthly if in care home
  ○ At least every 2–3 months in community
- If inadequate:
  ○ Follow local policy
  ○ Set goals
  ○ Improve and increase overall nutritional intake
  ○ Monitor and review care plan regularly

High risk
Treat (unless detrimental or no benefit is expected, e.g. imminent death)
- Refer to dietician, nutritional support team or implement local policy
- Set goals, improve and increase overall nutritional intake
- Monitor and review care plan:
  ○ Weekly if in hospital
  ○ Monthly if in care home or community

14.1.5 Blood in stool (see Fig. 14.2)

Blood in stool can be confusing sometimes as it appears in many shades depending on the oxidation of haem. This indicates the transit time along the gut. Darker stool (melaena) suggests bleeding from the proximal tract, whereas fresh bleeding suggests bleeding closer to the anus.

It is important to explore the colour of the stool in detail as the patient might not perceive this as blood.
- *'What is the colour of the stool?'*
- *'Is the blood mixed with the stool or separate?'*

- *'Is it fresh blood? Do you see it on the toilet paper?'*
- *'Is it associated with mucus?'*

Timing:
- *'How long have you noticed this for?'*
- *'What is your normal bowel habit – how often and what colour?'*

Associated symptoms:
- *'Pain – abdominal or anal? Does the pain come on after eating?'*
- *'Have you experienced any heartburn or reflux?'*
- *'Have you suffered from loose bowel movements or diarrhoea?'*
- *'Has your diet changed recently?'*

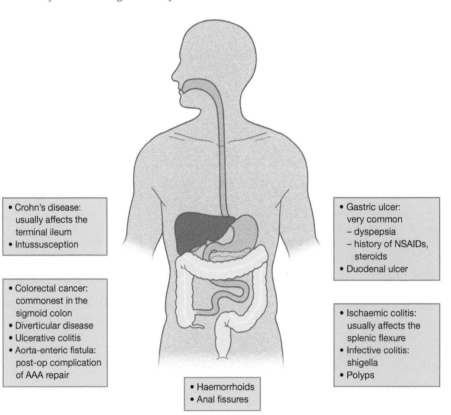

Figure 14.2 *Possible causes of blood in stool.*

14.1.6 Diarrhoea and vomiting

Loss of fluid and electrolytes are common complications of diarrhoea and vomiting. In an acute setting, immediate resuscitation and replacement of electrolytes is important to prevent dehydration and electrolyte imbalances.

The history and examination should be focused on two themes:
- How severe is the fluid and electrolyte imbalance?
- What is the underlying cause?

Diarrhoea

The World Health Organization defines diarrhoea as three or more episodes of loose/watery stools a day (or an increased frequency to the usual bowel habit).

Nature of the diarrhoea

'How often are you opening your bowels? What is your normal frequency?'
'What is the consistency of the motion? Is it soft, watery, porridge-like, difficult to flush?'

Timing: acute or chronic
'When did the problem start?'
'Is the frequency increasing or decreasing?'
'Is there any change in the consistency of the stool with time?'

Triggers:
'What seems to trigger it?'
'Does eating affect it? If so, are there particular foods that don't agree with you?'
'Have you been travelling recently?'
'What medications are you on and have they been changed recently?'
'Do you use laxatives?'
'Have you been incontinent of faeces at all?'

Associated symptoms:
- Vomiting / nausea
- Mucus or blood in stool
- Weight loss, nutritional assessment in the form of 'diet in a day'
- Systemic signs of sepsis, diabetes

The Bristol Stool Chart is widely used in clinical practice as a standardized assessment of the quality of stool.

Key Knowledge: Differential diagnosis

Infective:
- Gastroenteritis is commonly seen in children, caused by rotavirus
- Food poisoning – salmonella, campylobacter
- Travellers' diarrhoea – *E. coli*

Malabsorption:
- Lactose intolerance, reduced absorption
- Coeliac disease

Colitis:
- IBD
- *Clostridium difficile* infection

Tumour (usually watery stool):
- Carcinoid, VIPoma
- Zollinger–Ellison
- Villous adenoma

Pancreato-biliary:
- Chronic pancreatitis – steatorrhoea
- Bile acid malabsorption

Iatrogenic:
- Laxatives, antibiotics

Functional:
- Irritable bowel syndrome (IBS)

Vomiting

Vomiting is an expulsion of gastric contents secondary to contraction of abdominal muscles and the diaphragm. It involves both gastrointestinal and central neurological mechanisms.

Equally, functional / psychogenic and iatrogenic causes are also important to consider during history taking. Losing fluids and electrolytes as a consequence of vomiting will affect the fluid and electrolyte balance in the body.

Nature of the vomit:
'What is the colour and the content of the vomit? Is it bile / remains of the last meal / watery?'
'Did you notice any blood / mucus in the vomit?'
'How much did you bring up? Is it a cupful, a bowl- or a jugful?'

Timing:
'When did it start?'
'How many episodes have you had in the last 24 hours? Is the frequency increasing or getting better?'

Triggers:
'What seems to trigger it?'
'Is it associated with eating? If so, are there particular foods that aggravate it?'

Relieving factors:
'What seems to settle it?'
'Have you tried anything to control it?'

Associated symptoms:
Sepsis: fever, dizziness
Dehydration: *'How much urine have you passed in the last 24 hours and what colour is it? Do you feel thirsty? Do you feel light-headed when you stand up?'*
Abdominal pain, constipation, abdominal distension

Note: Vomiting can be an allergic reaction to certain food. If this is suspected, take an allergy history and encourage the patient to maintain a food diary.

5) Systems review

Review of systems is a screening questionnaire that serves many purposes. It helps you pick up on extra-gastrointestinal involvement of the primary disease, complications of disease and at times highlights relevant information or a separate concern that needs addressing. In this chapter the relevant general themes of questioning for each gastrointestinal presenting complaint have been addressed to help cultivate a habit of focused history taking.

Anaemia is a complication of blood loss. Iron deficiency anaemia is particularly common in lower GI bleeds and is one of the red flags for potential malignancy. Management for anaemia depends on its severity and complications. Common symptoms of anaemia include fatigue, malaise, SOB. *'Do you feel more tired than usual? Are you experiencing any shortness of breath?'*

Differential diagnosis
Gastrointestinal:
- Mechanical / obstructive: pyloric or small bowel volvulus, small / large bowel obstruction.
- Luminal: infection, oesophageal stricture, Mallory–Weiss tear, peptic ulcer disease, oesophageal cancer.
- Hepato-pancreato-biliary: acute pancreatitis, biliary tree obstruction.
- Neurological: the vomiting centre (chemoreceptor trigger zone) resides in the area postrema which is on the floor of the fourth ventricle. Some anti-emetics (e.g. ondansetron, prochlorperazine) act by antagonizing receptors in this area. Vomiting can be an associated symptom of the following pathologies:

- ○ Raised intracranial pressure
- ○ Vestibular pathologies
- ○ Migraine

Functional:
- IBS

Psychogenic:
- Bulimia
- Psychogenic vomiting

Iatrogenic:
Nausea and vomiting are common side-effects of many commonly used drugs. The timing and association of symptoms to a change in prescription is important to ascertain.

Commonly used drugs associated with nausea and vomiting: NSAIDs, opiates, chemotherapy agents, antidepressants.

Malignancy
'Have you lost any weight recently? If so, how much over how long? Was it intentional? Has your appetite changed recently?'

Weight is proportional to the total calorie intake or calorie spent with exertion. Any disproportional weight loss due to other metabolically active processes is a red flag symptom and requires urgent investigation to rule out malignancy.

6) Past medical history
For a patient with haematemesis it is important to establish the absence or presence of, and ask specifically about:
- Previous peptic ulcer disease
- *H. pylori* status and if they have previously received eradication therapy
- Chronic liver disease (CLD; see *Table 14.4*)
- Previous endoscopies
- Previous procedures, e.g. transjugular intrahepatic portosystemic (TIPS) shunting for portal hypertension
- Oesophagogastric malignancy.

For a patient with jaundice it is important to establish the absence or presence of, and ask specifically about:
- Chronic liver disease
- History of diabetes, hypercholesterolaemia (non-alcoholic fatty liver disease)
- History of autoimmune disease (autoimmune hepatitis, primary biliary cirrhosis)
- History of IBD (autoimmune hepatitis, primary sclerosing cholangitis)
- Gallstones
- Underlying malignancy, time of diagnosis, staging and previous treatments
- Previous surgery: hepatic damage can be caused by anaesthesia (halothane), hypoxic damage as a result of perioperative hypotension or damage to the bile duct during abdominal surgery
- Previous procedures: endoscopic retrograde cholangiopancreatography (ERCP), biliary stenting, percutaneous transhepatic cholangiography
- Haematological problems.

For a patient with abdominal pain it is important to establish the absence or presence of, and ask specifically about:
- *'Do you have any medical conditions that you have seen a doctor for in the past? Have you had any surgical procedures done in the past?'*

- It is important to get a medical and a surgical history particularly in ascertaining whether this is an exacerbation of an underlying problem or a potential complication of a procedure in the past. There are some GI-related important positives or negatives to ask the patient specifically about.
  - **Medical**: IBD, IBS, coeliac disease, recurrent urinary tract infections (UTIs)
  - **Surgical**: previous abdominal or gynaecological surgery, gallstones or renal stones
  - **Gynaecological**: history of endometriosis or ectopic pregnancy.
- If they do admit to a condition that you think is relevant to the history, exploring the most recent encounter with a specialist or a doctor will help establish their baseline severity.
  - *'When did you last see Dr Thorpe in clinic and how did that go? Have you had any recent investigations? (What were the results of those?) Have there been any recent changes to your medication? What led to that and has there been any improvement since?'*

For a patient with bloody stools, it is important to establish the absence or presence of, and ask specifically about:
- Previously diagnosed bowel pathology:
  - *'Have you ever been diagnosed with ulcers in the stomach? Do you have a background of IBD?'*
- Any history of haemorrhoids or fissures
- Haematological problems: any inherent tendency to bleed.

For a patient with diarrhoea and vomiting, it is important to establish the absence or presence of, and ask specifically about:
- **Diarrhoea**: IBD, coeliac disease, lactose intolerance, history of colorectal surgery or thyroid disease
- **Vomiting**: *H. pylori* treatment in the past, gastritis, previous upper GI endoscopy or oesophagogastroduodenoscopy, Mallory–Weiss tears or abdominal surgery.

7) ICE

It is important to address these. Often patients may open up regarding what is worrying them following open questioning. If they do not, the following questions are useful to gauge patients' thoughts and opinions:

'What do you think is happening at the moment?' 'What is worrying you the most at this point in time?' 'Is there anything that I have missed that you think is important and would like to tell me?'

8) Medication history

For a patient with haematemesis ask specifically about:
- Medications that can increase bleeding risk (aspirin, clopidogrel, warfarin, novel oral anticoagulant drugs)
- Medications that can cause gastritis / oesophagitis (aspirin, NSAIDs, bisphosphonates, steroids)
- Medications to treat peptic ulcer disease / oesophagitis / gastritis (proton pump inhibitors, H_2 histamine receptor antagonists)
- Drugs to lower portal venous pressure (non-selective beta adrenoreceptor antagonists)

For a patient with jaundice ask specifically about:
- Paracetamol overdose
- Recent history of medications that can cause obstructive / cholestatic or hepatocellular pattern of liver injury (see *Table 14.4*)
- Any non-prescription / OTC medications – these are a frequent cause of jaundice and must be specifically asked about.

Table 14.4 Medications that can cause chronic liver disease

Obstructive/cholestatic	Hepatocellular
Co-amoxiclav	Paracetamol
Oestrogens	Valproate
Chlorpromazine	Ethanol
Phenytoin	Isoniazid
	Carbamazepine
	Methyldopa

For a patient with abdominal pain ask specifically about:
- Opiates (constipation), laxatives, prokinetics, steroids and antibiotics. It is important to consider the presenting complaint as a side-effect of a drug.

For a patient with bloody stools ask specifically about:
- Anticoagulants: warfarin, aspirin
- Recent change in prescription and potential for interaction with existing medication; for example, drugs that affect the metabolism of anticoagulants (e.g. clarithromycin)

For a patient with nausea and vomiting ask specifically about:
- Commonly used drugs associated with nausea and vomiting (NSAIDs, opiates, chemotherapy, antidepressants)

9) Family history
- A family history of upper gastrointestinal bleeding may raise the possibility of hereditary haemorrhagic telangiectasia, an autosomal dominant condition associated with vascular malformations that can occur, and bleed, predominantly in the upper gastrointestinal tract.
- A family history of jaundice may raise the possibility of either a defect in erythrocytes (in the erythrocyte membrane, enzymes, or haemoglobin structure) or an underlying metabolic disorder causing chronic liver disease (haemochromatosis, alpha-1-antitrypsin deficiency, Wilson's disease).
- Specifically ask about family history of venesection, arthritis, diabetes and heart disease for haemochromatosis. A hepatitis B positive relative raises the possibility of either chronic hepatitis B infection (via vertical transmission) or acute hepatitis B infection (via horizontal transmission).
- For patients with abdominal pain, ask about any family history of IBD and cancer (colorectal, gynaecological).
- For patients with blood in stool ask about family history of previously diagnosed gastrointestinal pathology (for example peptic ulcers, IBD) and haematological problems.
- For patients with diarrhoea and vomiting ask if they have been exposed to close contacts with similar symptoms. Screening for a family history of IBD.

If there is an inheritance pattern of a condition/s relevant to the presenting complaint, representing this in a family tree will be easier to interpret.

10) Social history
Social history is crucial in patients with gastrointestinal or liver disease. Smoking, alcohol and drug use are often heavily implicated in the underlying disease process.
- **Smoking**: *'When did you start smoking? Do you smoke cigarettes or a pipe? How many cigarettes/pipes do you smoke per day? Have you ever tried to give up smoking? What methods did you use?'* For non-smokers ask about smoking in the household currently and in the past.

- **Alcohol**: *'Do you drink alcohol? In the last week, how much alcohol have you had to drink? If you think about the last three months, is this a typical amount for you? What type of alcohol do you drink? Do you know the percentage of the alcohol you drink?'*

***CAGE questionnaire (see* Chapter 7)**
- **Recreational drug use**: *'Have you ever used recreational drugs in the past?' 'Have you ever injected drugs in the past?'*
- **Sexual history**: it is important that this subject is broached sensitively and should often be left until towards the end of the history when you have built a rapport with your patient. *'Are you sexually active? Do you have a regular partner? Have you ever had sex with a casual partner? Do you use condoms? Have you ever been tested for sexually transmitted diseases?'*
- **Foreign travel**: a travel history is useful in patients who present with diarrhoea and vomiting. This will give you an idea of the causative pathogen that might be endemic to the area of travel. *'Where did you go on holiday? Did you receive any vaccines? Did you stay in a rural or urban area? Did you swim in any fresh water? Did you drink any unbottled water or use ice cubes in your drinks? Where did you eat? Did you use any precautions (insect repellant, mosquito nets)?'*

11) Closing the consultation

Always use your basic communication skills according to the Calgary–Cambridge Model. Remember to **summarize** and be sure to **screen** in order to ensure that the patient has had the opportunity to express anything else they feel is relevant.

Always close by thanking the patient and informing them of the next step in their plan of care.

'Thank you so much for all of the information that you have given me. The plan for your treatment will be... Do you have any questions or anything you would like to ask me?'

Summary of key points (GET YOUR MARKS):

Establish rapport (clear introduction of who you are, what your role is and why you are there).

History of presenting complaint: key symptoms to screen for – abdominal pain, weight loss, upper or lower gastrointestinal bleeding, jaundice, abdominal bloating, diarrhoea, nausea and vomiting.

Systems review: approaching the systems review by theme will help you determine the severity of the current illness and the likely underlying diagnosis.

ICE.

Past medical history: previous gastrointestinal disease, liver disease, diabetes, autoimmune disease, malignancy or haematological disease.

Medication history: current medication, allergies, OTC medications and supplements.

Family history: relatives with gastrointestinal or liver disease. Ask also about family history of gastrointestinal bleeding, jaundice or IBD.

Social history: disease impact on occupation and ADLs. History of smoking, alcohol intake, recreational drug use, sexual history and travel history. Utilize CAGE questionnaire as appropriate for those at high risk of alcohol misuse.

Closing the consultation: let the Calgary–Cambridge Model be your guide. Remember your key skills of summarizing and screening. Always leave the patient with a plan of care, even if it is that you need to speak with your colleagues. Thank the patient.

14.2 **Information giving and shared decision making**

The following section is an overview of what you might tell the patient during an information giving or shared decision making station. Use this section as a guide to what information might be relevant for the patient. Be sure to always assess the patient's starting point. Drawings and the use of models are very helpful for patients and often count for one or more marks. If you don't have anything to draw, writing long words for patients can also be helpful.

Review *Chapter 5* to get the most OSCE points possible.

14.2.1 **Cirrhosis**

What is it? Cirrhosis is scarring of liver caused by continuous, progressive damage to the liver over a period of time. The scar tissue replaces healthy liver tissue permanently and prevents the liver from working properly. Cirrhosis can be so extensive that it causes the liver to stop working completely. This is called liver failure.

The liver performs many important functions including:
- Fighting infection
- Removing poisons from the blood
- Helping the blood to form clots when you injure yourself
- Releasing bile, a liquid that breaks down fat and helps digestion.

Consequently, patients with liver problems are more likely to:
- Get infections
- Be at risk of toxins building up in their blood and making them unwell or drowsy
- Bleed or bruise easily
- Lose weight and become malnourished.

Who gets it? Every year in the UK around 4000 people die from cirrhosis and 700 people need a liver transplant to survive. The most common causes of cirrhosis in the UK are alcohol misuse, long-term infection with either hepatitis B or C virus, or a condition associated with fat build-up in the liver called non-alcoholic steatohepatitis. There are a number of other conditions that can lead to cirrhosis, including autoimmune conditions, where your immune system attacks your liver, rare genetic conditions, and conditions that cause the bile ducts to become blocked.

Treatment: the main aim of treatment is to manage symptoms and stop the disease getting worse. Treatment will take place at a hospital with a specialist hepatology (liver) unit. The treatment of cirrhosis depends on the cause; for example, antiviral medications for viral hepatitis or steroids and other medications that suppress the immune system for autoimmune hepatitis.

You can also change a number of things in your lifestyle to reduce your chances of developing further problems if you have cirrhosis, including:
- Completely avoiding alcohol
- Losing weight if you are overweight or obese
- Regular exercise to prevent muscle wasting
- Good hygiene to reduce your chances of developing an infection
- Going to your GP and getting travel vaccinations or the annual flu vaccine
- Eating a balanced, high protein, low salt diet
- Checking with your doctor or pharmacist about your medications.

You may also be prescribed tablets that reduce high blood pressure in the main vein that takes blood from the gut to the liver and prevent or treat infections. You may also be given medications to reduce itch.

There are certain treatments available that may be performed to manage complications of liver disease. These include:
- Endoscopy for swollen veins in the gullet, called varices
- Diuretics or abdominal drain insertion for fluid in the tummy, called ascites
- Laxatives for problems with brain function, called hepatic encephalopathy
- Liver transplantation.

14.2.2 Inflammatory bowel disease (IBD)

What is it? The term inflammatory bowel disease is used to describe two conditions – Crohn's disease and ulcerative colitis, both of which cause chronic inflammation of the wall of the bowel. These conditions can be distinguished from each other by histology (what they look like under a microscope), the pattern of disease, the areas affected, risk factors for the diseases and their associated complications. For example, ulcerative colitis tends to affect only the large bowel (draw the digestive tract, mouth to anus to illustrate this) whilst Crohn's disease can affect anywhere along the digestive tract and cause symptoms outside the tract.

Who gets IBD? IBD is thought to affect about 1 in every 250 people in the UK. Symptoms often begin in your late teens and early 20s but can occur at any age. The cause of IBD is currently unknown but it is thought to be caused by a combination of genetics (therefore you are more likely to develop the disease if you have a first-degree relative affected), the environment (exposure to different viruses and pathogens) and a dysfunction in your immune system (leading your immune system to attack your digestive system).

How do I know that I have IBD? The most common symptoms of IBD are abdominal pain and cramping, bloating, bloody diarrhoea, weight loss and fatigue. Your doctor will likely complete some blood work and test your stool to see if they can identify an alternative cause. To diagnose IBD and distinguish between the two types, a biopsy of the intestinal tract needs to be done. In order to get an appropriate biopsy, an endoscopy will have to be completed.

How is IBD treated? Management can be conservative, medical or surgical. Lifestyle modification is an important part of conservative management. This includes stopping smoking. Medication may be given with moderate disease in order to control the activity of your immune system. It may be given locally in the form of a suppository, or may be taken as a tablet to help control disease affecting other areas of your bowel. Surgery may be required if your disease cannot be controlled with medications. Always tell your doctor that you have IBD before starting any new medication (especially those that cause constipation or prevent diarrhoea).

14.2.3 Endoscopy (gastroscopy and colonoscopy)

What is it? These procedures allow direct visualization of the lining of gullet, stomach and bowel. Gastroscopy is the examination of the gullet, stomach and first part of the small bowel. Colonoscopy is the examination of the large bowel and the very end of the small bowel. Both procedures involve passing a small flexible tube either through the mouth (in the case of gastroscopy) or through the anus (in the case of colonoscopy).

This allows the person performing the procedure to see if there are any problems such as inflammation, ulcers or polyps. Sometimes samples of the lining are taken. These are called biopsies. Most people find this painless. Gastroscopy takes between 5 and 15 minutes and colonoscopy approximately 20 minutes.

Getting ready for the procedures: if you are taking blood thinners such as clopidogrel, warfarin or other anticoagulation medications it is important to let your medical team know prior to the day of your procedure, so that they can safely plan your procedure.

Prior to colonoscopy you will be required to take strong laxatives and adhere to a special diet called a low residue diet. This is called bowel preparation. You will be given specific information about this. You should expect frequent bowel movements that start within three hours of the first dose of bowel preparation. It is advisable to stay at home and near a toilet the day you start the bowel preparation. Drink as much clear fluid as possible. Do not eat or drink anything for four hours prior to gastroscopy.

Before these procedures you will be given a sedative and pain relief by injection into a vein. This will make you feel relaxed and drowsy but it will not put you to sleep in the same way a general anaesthetic does. You must ensure that someone is able to take you home after the procedure otherwise it will have to be cancelled.

What happens during the procedures?
Gastroscopy: to keep your mouth open so that you do not bite the endoscope a mouth guard will be placed between your teeth to stop you biting it. You may gag slightly as the endoscope is passed down into the gullet; this is normal. During the procedure some air will be put into your stomach to improve the view for the endoscopist; this may cause some burping.

Colonoscopy: after the colonoscope is passed through the anus into the bowel some air will be put into the bowel, which may cause a wind-like pain. This should not last for too long. You may also experience periods of discomfort and feel as if you need to go to the toilet. This is normal and there is no need to worry.

Potential risks
- Bleeding (0.1%)
- Tearing of the lining of the stomach or bowel (0.1%)
- Aspiration pneumonia
- Reaction to analgesia / sedative

After the procedure: you will go into the recovery area and be monitored until the sedation wears off. When you are more awake you can be taken home. You are advised not to drive, operate machinery, sign legally binding documents or go back to work until 24 hours after the procedure. Someone should stay with you until 12 hours after the procedure. You can eat and drink normally. If you have severe pain, bleeding or black tarry stools, you should seek urgent medical advice.

14.3 Practice scenarios

1. Steven Jones is a 49-year-old male admitted with jaundice and ascites. Ultrasound scan of the abdomen with Doppler identifies a small, irregular liver with increased echogenicity and an enlarged portal vein with hepatofugal blood flow. He drinks 90 units of alcohol per week. A liver screen that has been performed to examine for an underlying viral, autoimmune or metabolic cause for his chronic liver disease is negative. Your task is to explain the underlying diagnosis to Mr Jones and explain the proposed treatment plan for his condition.

2. Ahmed Khan is a 67-year-old male who has been found to have an iron deficiency anaemia. Your task is to inform Mr Khan of the diagnosis and explain upper gastrointestinal endoscopy and colonoscopy to him.

3. Natalia Stevens is a 21-year-old female who presents to A&E with diarrhoea, abdominal pain and fever; this is the second time in the last couple of years with these complaints,

except they are more severe this time. You are the FY1 and have been asked to take a history and perform a relevant examination. You will have to present this to the medical registrar on call, for a senior review.

4. Malcolm Morris is a 75-year-old man who had an urgent colonoscopy for recent weight loss and change in bowel habit. You have his histology results which confirm an adenocarcinoma. You have been asked to explain the results to him and the need for a CT scan to stage the disease. Explore his ideas, expectations and concerns around this issue. Explain to him briefly about the management options for colorectal cancers, introducing the idea of the multidisciplinary team approach.

5. Meera Patel is a 52-year-old lady with primary biliary cirrhosis. She has recently been admitted following a haematemesis and endoscopy has identified the presence of oesophageal varices. She was treated endoscopically with band ligation and pharmacologically with terlipressin. The bleeding has been controlled and she is now fit for discharge. She has been reading her discharge paperwork and identifies that she has been started on a new medication, propranolol, and that she is due for a further gastroscopy in 2 weeks. Your task is to speak to Mrs Patel and explain the rationale behind starting propranolol and repeat gastroscopy.

6. Juan Gonzalez is a 67-year-old male who has been admitted with jaundice and ascites. He is found to drink 110 units of alcohol per week. Your task is explore Mr Gonzalez's drinking habits and assess his risk of alcohol misuse.

7. Roy Mitchell is a 28-year-old male who has been diagnosed with Crohn's disease and is currently waiting to be seen in the gastroenterology outpatient clinic to talk about possible medical management options. He had recently been an inpatient with a flare of Crohn's and is a candidate for medical disease-modifying therapy. Briefly discuss the medication prednisolone which he will be started on. Explore any concerns that Mr Mitchell might have with regard to this. He mentions to you that he smokes 5 cigarettes a day. Please highlight the importance of smoking as a serious risk factor in Crohn's and explore his ideas on seeking help to quit.

8. Vinitha Khan is a 26-year-old student studying law at the local university. She has been doing a part-time job while trying to keep up with all of her assignments and exams. She is experiencing bloating and abdominal cramping as well as an increased number of soft bowel motions per day. After an appropriate work-up the doctor believes that she has IBS. Give information to Miss Khan about her diagnosis and explore options for management.

15

Nephrology and urology

BEN WARNER AND ALINA GOMEZ

Nephrology and Urology: Keys to Success

Nephrology cases are rarely used for OSCE communication skills stations; however, acute kidney injuries are very common in practice and a good working knowledge is important for working out a differential diagnosis. Urology is very closely related to nephrology and the histories should always be taken together. Be sure to always ask about:

- Haematuria
- Dysuria, urinary frequency, urgency and incomplete voiding
- Incontinence
- Flank or abdominal pain.

Red flags in nephrology:

- Weight loss
- Haematuria (malignancy)
- Urinary retention or difficulty urinating (cauda equina, acute retention – benign prostatic hyperplasia (BPH))
- Severe scrotal pain

15.1 Information gathering in nephrology

Before beginning any form of consultation it is important to cover the following points:

1) Introduce yourself and your role on the healthcare team

2) Ensure consent and confidentiality

3) Confirm the patient's name and DOB; ask about occupation

4a) History of presenting complaint (nephrology)

'What has brought you into the clinic/office/A&E today?

Allow for the Golden Minute. Nephrology (renal medicine) is a highly specialized field and is not a topic that easily lends itself to communication skills stations in an OSCE, i.e. many qualified doctors are not sufficiently informed to give pre-dialysis counselling. In this section we will discuss acute kidney injury (AKI), the main nephrology presentation you will meet in your working lives and the key communication scenario which presents in your OSCE examinations.

The key to effective history taking is having a clear understanding of the true purpose of your questioning. In real life, and in the OSCE, the purpose of your history taking is to answer one question *"Do I understand why this patient has an acute kidney injury?"* Depending upon the answer to this question, you will correct causative factors (e.g. give fluids or catheterize) and will then wait 48 hours, to see an improvement in the renal function, before launching into expensive, invasive and other necessary investigations.

15.1.1 Acute kidney injury (AKI)

AKI in adults is defined as:
1. A rise in the serum Cr ≥26 µmol/L in 48 hours **OR**
2. A rise in serum Cr ≥50% from baseline (proven to have or thought to have) occurred in the last 7 days, i.e. in a young fit person an increase from Cr = 50 to Cr = 85 (although still in the "normal range") constitutes an AKI; many junior doctors miss this, now you won't! **OR**
3. Oliguria (urine output <0.5 ml/kg/hr) for >6 consecutive hours.

Causes of AKI

AKI is divided into **pre-renal, post-renal and intra-renal causes of kidney injury.**

By far the most common, and accounting for >75% of cases, are the pre-renal causes. They are all based on the underlying mechanism of hypoperfusion of the kidney leading to kidney damage. The commonest cause of hypoperfusion is reduced blood pressure; this can be caused by dehydration, acute blood loss, third spacing of intravascular fluid, reduced cardiac output, or reduced peripheral arterial resistance e.g. vasodilatation in systemic inflammatory response syndrome (SIRS) seen in severe infection. The other, rare, causes of kidney hypoperfusion to consider are renal artery stenosis, renal vein thrombosis and fibromuscular dysplasia. Thus history taking should cover the following:

Information gathering for pre-renal causes of AKI

> **Key knowledge:** Concealed haemorrhage is unlikely in this setting, but if the patient is in shock consider retroperitoneal bleed, aortic dissection and abdominal aortic aneurysm.

Search for causes of dehydration:
- *'Are you eating and drinking normally?'*
- *'Are you suffering from any vomiting or diarrhoea?'*
- *'Are you peeing more than usual?'* (polyuric)
- *'Have you had a fever or any hot and cold sweats lately?'*

Search for acute blood loss:
- *'Have you had any rectal bleeding? Any black stools?'* (melaena)
- *'Have you been coughing or vomiting up blood?'*
- *'Have you noticed any blood in your urine?'*
- *'Do you suffer from nosebleeds?'*
- *'Do you bruise easily or have you developed any strange rashes?'*
- *'Have you noticed any unusually heavy, inappropriately timed or post-menopausal vaginal blood loss?'*

Search for third spacing:
- *'Have you noticed any unusual abdominal swelling?'* (looking for ascites)
- *'Have you ever suffered from pancreatitis / have you ever been diagnosed with cancer?'*
- *'Do you suffer from shortness of breath? Especially when lying flat?'*

Search for reduced cardiac output:
- *'Have you been experiencing any palpitations recently?'*

- *'Do you suffer from an irregular heartbeat?'*
- *'Do you have any history of heart disease?'*

Search for reduced vascular resistance:

- *'Are you currently taking any medication for your blood pressure or any nitrates?'*
- Ask about sources of infection that could be causing SIRS.

Renal artery stenosis (RAS), fibromuscular dysplasia and **renal vein thrombosis** are often asymptomatic. Ask about hypertension as this is seen in both fibromuscular dysplasia and RAS, where it is caused by increased renin release from the kidney in an effort to increase kidney perfusion. Ask about other arteriovascular disease i.e. ischaemic heart disease (IHD), peripheral arterial disease, stroke and transient ischaemic attack (TIA). Ask about personal and family history of RAS and renal vein thrombosis, and smoking and alcohol history. There is genetic predisposition to fibromuscular dysplasia but there is not a simple inheritance pattern and family history is very often unyielding.

So good, you've covered the vast majority of the workload and you've probably established by now that your patient has a bug causing vomiting and diarrhoea and is a bit dehydrated or has a SIRS and has a touch of left ventricular hypertrophy (LVH) which are together causing renal hypoperfusion. You're going to get her a side-room, rehydrate her, await stool cultures and optimize her cardiac function.

But what if you haven't found a pre-renal cause for the AKI?

Information gathering for post–renal causes of AKI

Next we need to discuss the post-renal causes of AKI, which account for around 15% of cases. Basically, this occurs when the kidney is not able to drain the urine it is producing. There are three levels at which this can go wrong:

- Bladder outflow level (most common)
- Vesiculo-ureteric junction (VUJ; entrance of the ureters to the bladder)
- Renal pelvis and the ureters themselves

The most common cause of bladder outflow obstruction in men is a benign or malignant enlarged prostate and, in women, its cause is most commonly by vaginal prolapse; usually a cystocoele. The other important causes are:

- Constipation
- Severe sepsis (interferes with autonomic control of the bladder).
- De-innervation of the bladder e.g. cauda equina, multiple sclerosis and diabetic autonomic neuropathy.
- Obstruction at the level of the VUJ is usually a bladder tumour (benign or malignant), renal calculi, transitional cell carcinoma (TCC) of ureters and occasionally bladder calculi.
- At the level of the renal pelvis and ureters, obstruction usually occurs from renal calculi, TCC of ureters, pelvic tumour invasion and occasionally retroperitoneal fibrosis.

Search for bladder outflow obstruction:

- *'Have you had any problems with passing urine lately? Have you been passing good volumes of urine?'*
- Ask men lower urinary tract symptoms (LUTS) questions and past and present history of BPH and prostate cancer – see *Section 15.2.*
- Ask women about past and present vaginal prolapse and atrophic vaginitis.
  - *'Have you felt any pressure or bulging coming from the vagina? Do you experience dryness in the vagina? Does it hurt when you have intercourse?'*

Search for obstruction from bladder masses:

- *'Have you noticed any blood in your urine? Have you had any recent UTIs? Have you noticed any lumps on your abdomen? Have you suffered from any unintentional weight loss? Have you noticed any gritty residue in your urine? Do you have any history of bladder cancer?'*

Search for renal calculi:
- *'Have you had any pain around your flanks? Have you ever had renal stones, or has anyone in your family ever had renal stones?'*
- Ask about personal and family history of hyperparathyroidism and Crohn's disease – these are the conditions you will see in your practice that predispose to stone formation.

Search for retroperitoneal fibrosis:
- *'Have you had any back pain recently? Have you noticed any unusual leg swelling? Have you recently had a blood clot in your leg (DVT)?'*
- *'Have you had any exposure to asbestos? Have you ever had to have radiotherapy on your abdomen? Are you currently taking any beta-blockers, methyldopa or hydralazine?'*

Information gathering for intra-renal causes of AKI

By this point you have covered >90% of the causes of AKI but you still have not identified the cause in your patient. You are now into the territory of intra-renal causes of AKI where the nephrologists get very excited. This is also the point in your enquiry that you need to start arranging the following expensive specialist tests:
- **Urine dipstick and MSU** – identifies presence or absence of proteinuria and screens for infection.
- **Protein:creatinine ratio** – a urine test which gives an indication of protein loss from the kidney.
- **An urgent ultrasound scan of kidney, ureters and bladder (USS KUB)** – in the request ask to:
  - Rule out hydronephrosis
  - Comment on kidney size
  - Measure cortical and medullary thickness
  - Measure Doppler flow of the renal arteries and veins.
- **An acute renal screen** – this typically includes blood tests for:
  - **Antinuclear antibody (ANA)** – most commonly associated with systemic lupus erythematosus (SLE) but also Sjögren's syndrome, scleroderma, polymyositis and dermatomyositis, all of which can cause a glomerulonephritis.
  - **Anti-neutrophil cytoplasmic antibody (ANCA)** – associated with small vessel vasculitis such as Wegener's granulomatosis, Churg–Strauss syndrome and microscopic polyangiitis, all of which can cause a glomerulonephritis.
  - **Anti-glomerular basement membrane antibody (anti-GBM)** – associated with Goodpasture syndrome.
  - **Complement levels** – complicated association with several autoimmune diseases and requires specialist nephrologist interpretation, e.g. high C3 levels correlate with up-regulation of the membrane-attack complex and a worse prognosis in lupus glomerulonephritis.
  - **Myeloma screen** – include serum immunoglobulins and serum electrophoresis.
  - **Hepatitis screen** – only if high clinical suspicion.

It is worth noting that urine microscopy for cell casts and 24 hour urinary protein collection were once widely requested tests but are now rarely used. Kidney biopsies are a specialist test with a significant risk of post-biopsy haemorrhage and should only be requested by specialist teams.

Information gathering for intra-renal causes of AKI

Your history taking thus far, for pre- and post-renal causes of AKI, has already achieved most of the workload. Your history taking for intra-renal causes should be focused on symptoms of auto-immune diseases, myeloma and a careful drug history. Thus your history-taking should cover the following:

Search for autoimmune disease:
- *'Have you had any unusual rashes lately? Do you notice that you bruise/bleed easily? Have you noticed any blood in your urine? Have you coughed up any blood? Have you noticed any pain in your eyes or visual disturbance (uveitis)?'*
- *'Have you lost any weight recently? If so, was this intentional? Do you suffer from night sweats? Have you had any unusual pain in your joints or muscles recently? Do you suffer from mouth/anal ulceration? Have you noticed any unusual pain or tingling in your limbs?'*

Search for myeloma:
- *'Have you had any bone pain recently?'* Ask about weight loss, night sweats, fatigue and breathlessness (anaemia). *'Are you having any recurring infections?'*
- Ask about symptoms of hypercalcaemia: poor appetite, nausea, constipation, thirst, confusion, depression and renal colic.

Search for nephrotoxic drugs:
- Ask about regular medications, OTC medications, herbal remedies, performance-enhancing drugs (muscle-building drinks/additives and anabolic steroids) and illicit drug use.
- Key nephrotoxins to elicit are NSAIDs, ACE inhibitors, furosemide, thiazide diuretics, penicillins, aminoglycosides (e.g. gentamicin), phenytoin, rifampicin, amphotericin, cocaine and ecstasy.

Hopefully you now feel forearmed and ready to face your communication skills station and, more importantly, are able to assess and start initial management of such patients in the real world setting. We now hand over to the surgeons for a discussion of the main communication skills scenarios in Urology.

15.2 Information gathering in urology

The most common symptoms to have in mind associated with different urological problems are:
- Lower urinary tract symptoms (LUTS)
- Dysuria
- Loin (flank) pain
- Haematuria
- Urinary incontinence

A thorough history needs to be taken pointing to different urological conditions, the details of which will be explained in this chapter.

> **Red flags in urology:**
> - Sudden onset of severe pain in the hemi-scrotum, sometimes waking the patient up in the night, radiating to the groin/loin suggests testicular torsion and is an emergency.
> - Difficulty voiding and urinary retention in any female and young male associated with back pain, sensory changes and muscle weakness in the lower limbs and bowel dysfunction would suggest cauda equina.
> - For urological malignancy: painless macroscopic haematuria, persistent UTI, constitutional symptoms, age >50, deteriorating renal function, abdominal mass on examination.

4b) History of presenting complaint (urology)
A good opening question can be: *'What has brought you into the clinic/office/A&E today?'*

It offers the patient the opportunity to express in their own words what is really bothering them. It often gives the most important clues as to where the problem lies, so listening attentively and allowing for the Golden Minute is more often than not the key to success.

Depending on the patient's story, we are guided to ask more questions, as in the examples below, adding in questions for other systems reviews which may or may not be associated with the presenting complaint.

15.2.1 Lower urinary tract symptoms (LUTS)

This term is classically associated with prostatism, although it has been coined in this generic form in order to include other causes for bladder outflow obstruction besides BPH (benign prostatic hypertrophy).

Symptoms can be scored in terms of frequency over the past month in order to create an index of severity – The International Prostate Symptoms Score (IPPS).

Questions to be asked are:
Incomplete voiding – *'Do you have the sensation of not being able to empty your bladder completely after urinating? How often does this happen?'*
Frequency – *'Do you feel that you need to urinate more often than normal/in the past? How often do you need to urinate again less than 2 hours after finishing urinating?'*
Intermittency – *'Do you feel that you need to stop and restart several times when urinating?'*
Urgency – *'Do you often find yourself having to rush to the toilet? Do you find it difficult to postpone urination?'*
Weak stream – *'Do you have a weak urinary stream?'*
Dribbling – *'Do you experience any dribbling after voiding?'*
Straining – *'Do you have to push or strain to initiate urination?'*
Nocturia – *'How often do you have to get up at night to urinate?'*

It is important to remember that there are different causes leading to LUTS, as this will guide the history taker and give differentials. Although there may be some rare congenital causes, most causes are acquired and can be split into:
- Local genitourinary causes/bladder outflow obstruction:
  - Prostatism, i.e. BPH or prostate cancer
  - Urethral stricture caused by infection or trauma
  - Bladder stones, bladder cancer
  - Constipation
  - Bowel malignancy
- Neurological causes:
  - Spinal cord or cauda equina compression. Symptoms will be associated with back pain, sciatica and loss of sensation in lower limbs and perineum.

15.2.2 Dysuria
- *'Any stinging or burning when you pass urine?'*

The classic symptom of a urinary tract infection (UTI); although the patient can often have a urinary tract infection without dysuria. Other associated symptoms may be:
- *'Any temperature or feeling hot and cold?'*
- *'Any nausea/vomiting?'*
- *'Have you noticed your urine being cloudier or foul smelling?'*
- *'Have you noticed any blood in your urine?'* (haematuria can have many causes – see below, but can also be associated with a UTI)
- *'Any abdominal pain? Any lower back pain?'*

LUTS symptoms may also be associated with a UTI; please see above for the relevant questions. A urinary tract infection can in itself cause obstruction and LUTS through urethral inflammation and pain, but it can also be the consequence of bladder outflow obstruction causing urinary retention, increasing the likelihood of an infection developing.

15.2.3 Loin (flank) pain

This is typically the pain of upper tract urinary stones. It is due to the obstruction and local distension of the urinary tract by the stone. The pain severity, location and radiation will vary with the patient and the location of the stone. The pain location may also change if the stone moves down the urinary tract. As with any kind of pain, **SOCRATES** is useful in history taking.

Site:
- *'Can you point to where the pain is?'*
- Typically patients will complain of severe flank pain for a ureteric stone, but a large stone in the renal pelvis obstructing the ureteropelvic junction may cause pain in the costovertebral angle just below the 12th rib. A stone in the intramural ureter will give suprapubic pain.

Onset:
- *'Did the pain come on suddenly or gradually over a period of time?'*
- The pain of urinary stones comes on abruptly and can wake the patient from sleep. A more chronic or gradual onset suggests disease within the kidney or renal pelvis.

Character:
- *'How would you characterize your pain? Would you say it is a sharp pain or more of a dull ache? Is it constant or does it come and go?'*
- The pain may vary from dull to unbearably sharp acute pain. The pain is constant and severe as long as the obstruction remains but could come in waves if the obstruction is intermittent.

Radiation:
- *'Does your pain spread or radiate anywhere?'*
- Stones of the renal pelvis will give pain radiation to the flank and also to the ipsilateral upper abdominal quadrant, and it is possible to confuse this with biliary colic when affecting the right side. Upper ureteral stone pain radiates to the flank and lumbar region and mid-ureteric stone pain can radiate to the iliac fossae, potentially being confused with appendicitis or diverticulitis, depending on which side is affected. When a ureteric stone has reached the distal ureter, the pain radiates to the groin and testicle in males and labia majora in females.

Associated symptoms:
- Are there any other symptoms associated with the pain?
  - *'Have you noticed any change in colour of your urine?'*
  - *'Any nausea or vomiting?'*
  - *'Have you been shivering/felt hot and cold?'*
  - *'Do you have to urinate more often than normal or do you feel that you have to rush to the bathroom? Any stinging or burning when passing urine?'*
- Urinary stones are usually associated with haematuria, at the least microhaematuria seen on a urine dipstick. Often there would be intermittent frank haematuria or dark urine due to old blood.
- Patients can frequently get nausea and vomiting with the pain, especially with stones obstructing the upper urinary tract.
- Infections can also develop secondary to the obstruction and patients may then develop pyrexia. If the stone approaches the bladder, LUTS and dysuria are associated symptoms as well.

Time:
- *'How long did the pain last for?'*
- How long the pain lasted, together with type of onset will suggest whether it is an obstruction and when and if the obstruction is relieved. Pain due to obstruction usually peaks within minutes to hours.

Exacerbating and relieving factors:
- *'What makes the pain better or worse?'*
- Patients with renal colic will be in agony and will try to move into different positions in an attempt to relieve the pain. In comparison, patients with peritonism will be very still. Drinking large amounts of fluid may set off the pain.

Scale:
- *'On a scale of 1 to 10 where 1 is very mild pain and 10 is the worst pain you could imagine, how would you grade your pain?'*
- The pain of renal colic is usually intense but not related to the size of the stones. Ureteric stones usually cause the most severe pain.

15.2.4 Haematuria

Haematuria can have different causes which need to be kept in mind when asking questions:
- Associated with loin (flank) pain / renal colic → urinary tract stones
- With suprapubic pain → bladder stones, cystitis (infective, drug-induced, radiation, autoimmune)
- Associated with LUTS → UTI or prostatism
- Painless → bladder malignancy, glomerulonephritis, coagulation disorders, BPH, vascular malformations
- At the end of micturition → bleeding from the prostate or bladder base
- Throughout micturition → bleeding from the bladder or above
- At the start of micturition with clear urine after → urethral lesion
- From ruptured cyst in polycystic kidney disease

'How long have you been noticing blood in your urine?'
'Does it happen every time you pass urine, just once or intermittently?'
'Do you have any abdominal or flank pain? Any pain when passing urine?'
'How much blood would you say that you have seen in your urine – small / large amounts, any clots?'
'Does it look like fresh or old blood?'
'Have you noticed the blood in your urine at the beginning, throughout or at the end of micturition?'
'Any symptoms of hesitancy, poor flow, dribbling, urgency?'
'Are you taking any medication to thin your blood?'

Note: A thorough past medical and drug history is vital. Also ask about any trauma. Any recent catheterization? Previous occupation and smoking are important in the context of risk for bladder cancer.

15.2.5 Urinary incontinence

Urinary incontinence may be:
- Stress:
  - *'Do you find yourself leaking urine if coughing, laughing, sneezing or exercising?'*
  - For women: *'Have you had any children? Were they born by vaginal delivery? Did you experience any tearing during the delivery? Were forceps used?'*
- Urgency:
  - *'Do you find that you can't make it in time to the toilet to pass urine?'*

- *'Do you ever have the urge when you are in a certain situation, e.g. when walking in the front door?'*
- *'How often do you have to pass urine during the day? Do you get up at night to pass urine?'*
- Mixed stress and incontinence
- Overflow
- Nocturnal enuresis
  - *'Do you get up at night to pass urine? How many times?'*

5) Systems review

Systemic features are important to ask for in order to establish differential diagnoses.

General: *'Recently, have you experienced any temperatures? Feeling hot and cold? Shivering? Any night sweats? Have you noticed any weight loss? Any lack of appetite?'*
- Rigors are a feature of pyelonephritis.
- Unintentional weight loss raises the suspicion of malignancy.

Neurological: *'Have you noticed any altered sensation in your lower limbs? Any symptoms of sciatica? Pain in your back/lower limbs? Loss of bowel control?'*
- Loss of sensation and pain in the lower limbs together with impaired bowel control point to a spinal or brain lesion.
- *'Have you had headaches, vomited, felt drowsy or had any fits?'* (this would suggest uraemia)

GI: *'When did you open your bowels last? Was this a normal motion?' 'How often do you normally open your bowels?'*
- Constipation can lead to urinary retention. Diverticulitis can lead to colovesical fistulas and the pain of diverticulitis can sometimes mimic ureteric stones.

MSK: *'Does your pain get worse with certain movements?'* (back pain differential)

Skin: *'Has your skin felt itchy?'* (symptoms of uraemia)

6) ICE

It is important to find out what the patient's main concerns are, which are not always what the doctor asking the questions may think. By checking that we have asked about ICE, we place the patient at the centre of our consultation, recognizing their needs empathetically and preventing any miscommunication.
- *'What are your thoughts on this pain/blood in the urine/problems urinating?'*
- *'Is there anything in particular that you are concerned about?'*
- *'Are there any questions which I have missed?'*
- *'What are your expectations from today's consultation?'*

7) Past medical history

Full past medical history can give clues towards possible predisposing factors, as well as patients' general physical condition and ability to cope with more medical problems. Let the patient tell you themself about previous conditions but make sure you ask about:
- Known BPH
- Previous UTIs – could point to congenital abnormalities
- Previous abdominal surgeries – can lead to adhesions and hernias
- Cardiovascular disease – think RAS leading to renal impairment
- Renal disease
- Diabetes – predisposing to renal disease and more likely to acquire infections
- Gout – uric acid crystals causing gout can also deposit to form renal stones
- IBD – more likely to develop urinary stones
- Previous stroke – can affect bladder function.

8) Medication history

- Certain medications can lead to urinary tract symptoms: drugs such as rifampicin can give a red-coloured urine; anticoagulants may cause haematuria and cyclophosphamide can give drug-induced cystitis.
- Acquire an up-to-date list of the patient's medications including the doses, frequency, route and reason for the medication.
- Ask about all OTC medications and vitamins / supplements.
- Ask about allergies.

9) Family history

Ask about family history of diabetes, hypertension, cardiovascular disease, malignancies, autoimmune disease, polycystic kidney disease and renal stones.

10) Social history

This is an important section, not to be forgotten.
- *'Do you have anybody with you at home? Who do you live with? Do you normally manage independently?'*
- *'Do you smoke? Have you ever smoked?' 'How much coffee / tea do you normally drink per day?' 'How much alcohol would you say that you consume per week?'*
- *'What is your occupation? Have you had any other jobs in the past?'*
- Smoking, as well as exposure to dyes, aromatic amines, paints, plastics and rubber manufacturing, increases the risk for bladder cancer.
- Coffee, tea, alcohol and smoking negatively affect incontinence issues.

11) Closing the consultation

Make sure you **summarize** and ask the patient if they think that there is anything you have missed **(screen)**. Always discuss the diagnosis and the **plan of care.** Close by **thanking** the patient.

> **Summary of key points (GET YOUR MARKS):**
>
> Establish rapport (clear introduction of who you are, what your role is and why you are there).
>
> History of presenting complaint: key symptoms to screen for – haematuria, dysuria, urinary frequency, urgency and incomplete voiding, incontinence, flank or abdominal pain.
>
> Systems review: rule out differentials. Main symptoms to ask about include fever, night sweats, weight loss, rigors, neurological symptoms, constipation, etc.
>
> ICE.
>
> Past medical history: diabetes, cardiovascular disease or a history of stroke, renal disease, gout, IBD, autoimmune disease, previous UTIs and abdominal surgeries.
>
> Medication history: current medication, allergies, OTC medications and supplements.
>
> Family history: first-degree relative with diabetes, hypertension, cardiovascular disease, malignancies, autoimmune disease, polycystic kidney disease and renal stones.
>
> Social history: disease impact on occupation and ADLs. History of smoking, alcohol intake, recreational drug use and caffeine. Occupation is important to assess for risk factors for bladder cancer.
>
> Closing the consultation: let the Calgary–Cambridge Model be your guide. Remember your key skills of summarizing and screening. Always leave the patient with a plan of care, even if it is that you need to speak with your colleagues. Thank the patient.

15.3 Information giving and shared decision making

15.3.1 Kidney failure and dialysis

What do the kidneys do? Our kidneys are responsible for filtering the blood in our body, removing excess water and waste products from it. This extra fluid and waste is then moved to the bladder and we excrete it as urine. When the kidneys aren't working properly, these waste products can build up in the blood and damage the body.

What is dialysis? If you have been told you have established kidney failure, there are some treatments which are able to take over the work of your kidneys and make you feel better. Kidney dialysis is one of these treatments. It works by carrying out some of the work of the kidneys by removing the extra fluid and waste products from your blood. Dialysis does about 10% of the work of normal healthy kidneys. This percentage ensures that enough toxins and fluids are removed from the body to keep it working. Dialysis doesn't cure chronic kidney disease and your failing kidneys will unfortunately keep getting worse.

Once you start dialysis, you will be on it for the rest of your life, or until you have a successful kidney transplant.

What types of dialysis are there? There are two main types of dialysis:

Haemodialysis: this is where a machine takes blood out of your body, usually through a vein in your arm or leg, filters out the waste products in it and puts the 'clean' blood back into your body.

Peritoneal dialysis: this is where you add and then remove a liquid from your abdomen. This liquid naturally draws out the waste from your blood using the natural lining in your abdomen (the peritoneum – hence the name peritoneal dialysis).

These types of dialysis can be carried out in different ways:

Looking at haemodialysis first, this can be carried out in your own home or in a hospital/ clinic environment:

- In both scenarios you will have to be attached to the machine for about 4 hours, 3 or 4 times a week.
- If you decide to have it in the hospital you will need to make time for appointments at least three times a week. If you are working, your employer is required by law to make reasonable adjustments to allow you to attend.
- Haemodialysis side-effects: tiredness and weakness, itchy skin, muscle cramps and restless legs. One thing which can happen during haemodialysis is a sudden drop in your blood pressure which can make you feel dizzy. You may get infections and blood clots where the machine needs to gain access to your venous system.
- You may need to restrict the amount of salt, potassium and phosphate in your diet. A specialist called a dietician can help you with this. You will also need to restrict the amount of fluid you drink.

Looking at peritoneal dialysis:

- **Automated peritoneal dialysis (APD)**: this involves having a machine at home which automatically takes the liquid with the waste products out of your abdomen every night while you sleep.
- As you will be having dialysis at night while you're sleeping you won't need to schedule your work and other activities around your treatment. It may be difficult to go on longer trips or travel far as you need to be attached to your dialysis machine at night.
- **Continuous ambulatory peritoneal dialysis (CAPD)**: this is where you get rid of the liquid from your abdomen and add more in its place for about 30 minutes, up to four times every day. This can be done at home or wherever suits you best.

- You will need to fit your daily activities around your dialysis. If you're working you can seek advice on how to do dialysis exchanges in your workplace.

For both APD and CAPD:
- You will need to spend one or two days in hospital having an operation to put in a catheter. You will need to have blood tests throughout the course of your treatment to check it is working well. Your treatment will be every day but you can move around and do other things while it's happening.
- You won't have to restrict the amount of fluid you drink as much as if you were having haemodialysis.
- Side-effects from peritoneal dialysis include fatigue, shortness of breath and restless legs. You may put on some weight. An important side-effect to be aware of is an infection of the peritoneum (the lining in your abdomen) called peritonitis which is more common in people having peritoneal dialysis.

With CAPD and APD, not everyone can stay on these treatments long term and some people will need to change treatments. It's common for people to live for many years on dialysis. The type of dialysis you choose has not been found to make much difference to how long you live.

15.3.2 Benign prostatic hyperplasia

What is it? Benign prostatic hyperplasia means an enlarged prostate gland. The prostate is a gland found in men just below the bladder, that usually enlarges with age. Its function is to produce fluid which is added to the sperm. Urine from the bladder flows through a tube called the urethra which passes through the prostate gland. When the prostate enlarges, it may press on the urethral tube, causing symptoms such as poor urinary flow, hesitancy, the feeling of incomplete voiding and increased frequency of urination, symptoms of urgency and dribbling after urination. These are called lower urinary tract symptoms.

Who gets it? Men after the age of 50. By the age of 90, 9 out of 10 men have an enlarged prostate.

Treatment:
- Lifestyle changes include avoiding coffee / tea and evening fluids, watchful waiting (surveillance), medical (α-blockers (e.g. tamsulosin), 5α-reductase inhibitors (e.g. finasteride) or phosphodiesterase type 5 inhibitor (tadalafil)) and surgical management:
  - Transurethral resection of the prostate (TURP) – a cystoscope (narrow tube) is inserted through the urethra to the bladder. Instruments can be passed via this tube and small pieces are cut off the prostate in order to reduce its size and pressure on the urethra. Between 80 and 90% get retrograde ejaculation. More rare complications are impotence and incontinence.
  - Laser prostatectomy.

15.3.3 Management of prostate cancer
- **Localized** (confined to the prostate)
  - Active surveillance – monitor PSA (prostate-specific antigen) blood test. PSA levels increase with the size of the prostate and the activity of the cancer. May repeat the biopsy.
  - Radiotherapy – external (high energy beams are directed towards the cancerous tissue) or internal (brachytherapy, where radioactive seeds are placed into or next to the tumour).
  - Surgery – prostatectomy (complete removal of the prostate gland); can be done as open surgery or laparoscopic.

- **Advanced**
  - ○ Hormonal – prostate cancer cells need the hormone testosterone to grow. Testosterone is made in the testis and its production is controlled by other hormones made by the pituitary gland. Medication targets either the production of testosterone by stopping the pituitary stimulating hormones (goserelin – implant under the skin; leuprorelin, triptorelin – injections), or by stopping the action of testosterone (flutamide, bicalutamide – tablets). Side-effects: impotence, hot flushes, sweating
  - ○ Surgery – castration
  - ○ Radiotherapy – for painful bone metastases.

15.3.4 Renal stones

What are they? Kidney stones can form in the kidney, in the ureter (tube from kidney to the bladder) or in the bladder. Ninety percent of them are calcium based. They can be different shapes and sizes, ranging from very small ones which can pass with the flow of urine (<6 mm), to larger, obstructing ones causing symptoms.

Who gets it? More common in males (3:1), 20–50 years old. Risk factors are: infection, obstruction, prolonged immobilization, low fluid intake, high animal protein intake, oral calcium supplements, hyperparathyroidism, diuretics, IBD, hot climate, congenital abnormalities, family history, previous renal stones (50% recurrence).

Treatment:
- Medical – analgesia and tablets (tamsulosin) which help to pass the stone.
- Ureteric stent – a tube is placed inside the ureter in order to relieve the obstruction and make it easier to pass the stone.
- Percutaneous nephrostomy – a tube is placed into the kidney through the skin in order to relieve an acute outflow obstruction which may otherwise damage the kidney.
- Lithotripsy – high energy shock waves are directed towards the stone to break it into smaller fragments which can be passed with the urine.

15.3.5 Urinary incontinence

What is it? Involuntary leakage of urine, which can be of different types:
- *Stress incontinence* – the muscles helping to keep the bladder outlet closed, i.e. the pelvic floor muscles, are too weak to withstand the extra pressure inside the abdomen caused by sneezing, coughing, laughing, jumping or running.
- *Urge incontinence* – different aetiologies:
  - ○ The bladder muscle (detrusor muscle) is overactive and contracts too early; the cause can be neurological (fault with the nerve system) or unknown – 'idiopathic urge incontinence'.
  - ○ The detrusor muscle is not elastic enough or has a change in its tone, so that it cannot distend well when filling with urine, increasing the pressure in the bladder – can be due to a neurological condition such as spinal cord injury or because of previous surgery (radical hysterectomy) or having had radiation therapy affecting the bladder.
- *Mixed* – as the name suggests, both stress and urge incontinence elements combined.
- *Overflow incontinence* – a bladder outflow obstruction, such as a large prostate, causes impaired voiding leading to a certain amount of urine being retained. This builds up with time and causes increased pressure behind the obstruction, with leakage of urine as a consequence. The increased pressure may also backtrack and lead to swelling and injury to the kidneys.

Who gets it?
- *Stress incontinence* → women over 40, in particular women who have had several childbirths – ask about vaginal deliveries and any associated complications. Obesity is

another risk factor; also men who have had prostatectomy or radiotherapy for prostate cancer. One in 5 women have some degree of stress incontinence.

- *Urge incontinence* – mostly in neurological disorders, such as PD, multiple sclerosis, spinal cord injury, post-stroke but can also be seen with constipation and uterine prolapse.
- *Overflow incontinence* – BPH, chronic constipation.

Treatment:
- Conservative: avoid caffeinated drinks and alcohol, avoid drinking liquids before going to bed, pelvic floor exercises, bladder retraining, weight loss, avoid constipation.
- Pharmacological:
  - **Urge / detrusor instability** – anti-muscarinic drugs (e.g. oxybutynin, solifenacin) or selective beta-3 agonist (mirabegron).
  - **Overflow** – BPH (see above); constipation treated with laxatives.
- Surgical/procedural:
  - **Stress:**
    - Tape procedures – a plastic tape is inserted via an incision in the vagina and threaded around the urethra, to hold it in the right position and give support. The side-effects include mild incontinence, increased urinary frequency and a feeling of incomplete voiding or the tape moves out of place / wears out.
    - Colposuspension – an incision is made in the abdomen. The bladder neck is lifted and stitched into a new position. The risks include incomplete voiding, recurrent UTIs and discomfort during sex.
    - Sling procedures – an incision is made in the abdomen. A sling is placed around neck of bladder to give extra support and create an artificial urinary sphincter. The risks include incomplete voiding and urge incontinence.
  - **Urge:** Botulinum toxin A (Botox), sacral nerve stimulation, posterior tibial nerve stimulation, augmentation cystoplasty, urinary diversion.
  - **Overflow:** clean intermittent catheterization, indwelling catheter, BPH surgery.

15.3.6 Haematuria and bladder cancer

Who gets it:
- 2nd most common urological malignancy and accounts for 3% of all cancer mortality.
- Male:female – 2.5:1
- Increased age
- Smoking
- Exposure to aromatic hydrocarbons (latent period 25–45 years) – ask about jobs in rubber manufacture, exposure to paints and dyes, gas and tar, diesel, hairdressers, leather workers, plumbers.
- Chronic bladder inflammation – bladder stones, long-term catheters.

How does it present?
- Microscopic haematuria → 5–10% urological cancers
- Macroscopic haematuria → 20–25% urological cancers

Investigations for haematuria: urine culture, urine cytology, renal ultrasound, intravenous urography (IVU), cystoscopy (flexible for diagnostic purposes and rigid if known malignancy and biopsy needed), CT, MRI.
- *Cystoscopy:* local anaesthetic gel is applied so you would not feel any pain and then a cystoscope (thin tube with a camera and light at the end) is passed through your urethra and into your bladder.
- *TURBT (transurethral resection of bladder tumour):* This is done under general or spinal anaesthetic. A thin telescope (cystoscope) is passed through the urethra and into the bladder and instruments are passed via this tube. This enables the surgeons to cut off

the tumour or part of the tumour from the bladder wall so that it can be sent for analysis in the lab. To prevent or stop any bleeding, a mild electric current is applied to the site (cauterization). The operation takes between 15 minutes and 1 hour. A urinary catheter is normally placed after the operation to help with the passage of urine during the next 24 hours. Risks include bleeding, burning sensation when passing urine for a few days, infection and perforation of the bladder (rare). The laboratory result (histopathology) will determine whether the tumour is benign or malignant and if malignant, the staging of the cancer.

Management of bladder cancer: TURBT, intravesical chemotherapy / BCG (bacille Calmette–Guérin), systemic chemotherapy, radiotherapy or cystectomy.

15.4 **Practice scenarios**

1. Mrs Deborah Wayne, a 60-year-old woman with painless haematuria, has just had intravenous urography and is awaiting cystoscopy +/- diagnostic biopsy. Mrs Wayne is a bit anxious and would like to know more about the procedure, what it involves and possible outcomes.

2. Mr Peter Sayer, a 77-year-old man with LUTS and BPH, comes to the outpatient clinic. Please take a history with regard to how severe his symptoms are and what treatment options are available.

3. William Stevenson, a 72-year-old man, had a high PSA after testing by the GP and has subsequently had a prostate biopsy which was positive for moderately differentiated prostate cancer. His CT scan showed only locally advanced disease. He is still not aware of the final diagnosis. Please explain to Mr Stevenson the results of his investigations and talk him through his treatment options, including both medical and surgical management.

4. Mrs Jane Silver, a 55-year-old woman, has been suffering for some time with stress incontinence which she finds very distressing. Please take a short history and talk her through medical and surgical management.

5. Alina Ibanescu is 30 years old and 12 weeks pregnant. She has been suffering for some time with intermittent severe left flank pain when urinating. She has had an ultrasound of the urinary tract showing a 6 mm stone in her left ureter, causing mild hydronephrosis. She is worried and frustrated. A doctor has told her that she might need a ureteric stent but she doesn't know what this means and she is worried about her pregnancy. She would like someone to explain her scan and why she has a stone, the treatment suggested and the risks she would run if she chose to have the treatment or not.

16

Obstetrics and gynaecology

GEMMA WILLIAMS AND RACHEL WAMBOLDT

Obstetrics and Gynaecology: Keys to Success

Obstetric and gynaecology consultations are complex so it helps to be systematic. Patients are often anxious when seeing a healthcare professional and this is particularly true when it comes to obstetrical and gynaecological concerns. Every consultation should be conducted in a professional manner so that patients are able to discuss their concerns free of judgment. Your history taking should be relaxed and in a private setting. It is preferable to speak to the woman alone unless they are a child, adolescent or have a mental impairment.

Red flags in obstetrics:
- Shortness of breath with chest pain
- Leg swelling with pain
- Rash with fever
- Headache with epigastric pain, vomiting or visual disturbances
- Abdominal pain with vaginal bleeding
- Rupture of membranes without labour within 24 hours
- Meconium-stained liquor
- Fever or mood changes in the first weeks following delivery

Red flags in gynaecology:
- Post-menopausal bleeding
- Pelvic pain +/- fever
- Unprotected sex in the last 5 days
- Inter-menstrual bleeding
- Breast lump

16.1 Information gathering in obstetrics and gynaecology

1) Introduce yourself and your role on the healthcare team

2) Ensure consent and confidentiality

3) Confirm the patient's name and DOB; ask about occupation

It is sometimes helpful to ask the patient about their occupation early in the consultation. Many pregnant patients may be a full-time parent already. Asking about what the patient does for work along with a follow-up question such as *'What does that involve?'* or *'How old are your other children?'* can establish rapport early and may provide some context later in the consultation when you are asking about limitations. Have something to say in case the patient is unemployed, e.g. *'You'll soon have your work cut out though.'*

4a) History of presenting complaint – obstetrics

16.1.1 Obstetrical history

Pregnant patients often present with several symptoms that may appear trivial, or that may be part of the natural physiological process of pregnancy. Each of these symptoms should be explored with an open question, and eventually with focused questions to rule out important differential diagnoses. If the patient is in pain, it may be appropriate to manage this prior to taking the history. If the patient has their partner or a family member present, ask them their name too and involve them in the consultation when appropriate.

Acknowledge that the patient is pregnant and ask about current gestation.
'What has brought you into the clinic / office / A&E today?'

> **Allow for the Golden Minute:** let the patient describe their symptoms, and ask open questions to prompt them, for example: *'Can you tell me more about that?'* After the first minute clarify features with more specific closed questions to characterize each symptom in turn. Firstly find out if the patient still has the symptom now. Then, establish when they started having the symptoms, the frequency, duration, progression, severity, relieving and exacerbating factors. Summarize what the patient has told you before moving on to another section of the history.

Explore each symptom in more detail. In this section we will cover the most common presenting complaints in pregnancy. See the *'Systems review'* for details of questions for some common obstetric differentials. For multiple symptoms, find out how they relate to one another in terms of onset, time, exacerbating factors and severity.

Key symptoms to ask about in a pregnant patient: nausea / vomiting, abdominal pain, vaginal bleeding, dysuria / urinary frequency, headache / visual changes / swelling.

Be sure to signpost the change in direction of the consultation before starting with the obstetric history.

History of the current pregnancy:
- *'Is this your first pregnancy?' 'How did you discover you're pregnant?'* (home test/US)
- *'How did you conceive?'* – naturally or assisted
- *'What was the date of the first day of your last menstrual period? How long is your typical cycle?'*
  - If the patient has had no period after stopping contraception, ask when they stopped contraception and what they were using for contraception.
- *'Are your periods usually regular?'*
- *'How many days are in your menstrual cycle?'*
- *'What is your estimated date of delivery?'*
- *'Have you been taking any vitamins before / during your pregnancy, particularly folic acid?'*
- *'Are you up to date with your scans?'* (dating scan, anomaly scan)
- *'Have you ever been pregnant before? What were the outcomes?'* It is helpful to start with the first pregnancy and work your way forward in time. For each pregnancy, enquire about the following:
  - Maternal age
  - Was this pregnancy with the current partner?
  - Ask about whether this was a multiple pregnancy or not

- ○ Miscarriages / stillbirths / terminations – ask about these in a sensitive manner
- ○ Gestation at birth or time of pregnancy loss
- ○ Complications (antenatal, during labour and postnatal)
- ○ Congenital malformations or concerns on prenatal screening
- ○ Mode of delivery and need for assistive devices such as forceps or vacuum
- ○ Current health of children
- Ask if they have any medical illnesses and if so, what medications they are taking.
- **Include a full gynaecological, contraceptive and sexual history.**

Vaginal bleeding in pregnancy

Vaginal bleeding in pregnancy can be alarming but does not always signify pathology. To determine the cause and severity, it is important to quantify the bleeding and ask about associated symptoms. See *Section 16.1.2* for more examples of questions relating to vaginal bleeding.

Rule out: miscarriage (1st or 2nd trimester), labour (bloody show, 3rd trimester), molar pregnancy, ectopic, placental abruption, placenta praevia and vasa praevia before considering other causes.

Time course:
- *'Have you noticed any pattern to the bleeding?'*
- *'When did the bleeding start?'*
- *'Is the bleeding intermittent or constant?'*
- *'Does the bleeding happen after sex?'*
- *'How many times a day are you bleeding?'*
- *'How long does each episode last?'*
- *'Is the bleeding getting heavier or more frequent over time?'*
- *'What day of your period would you compare it to?'*

Severity:
- *'Is the bleeding heavy or light?'*
  - ○ Patients may find it difficult to quantify bleeding. Asking how often they change sanitary towels is a good way to quantify this. Remember, visual blood loss may be disproportionate to actual blood loss if the bleeding is trapped within the abdominal cavity.
- *'Do you feel dizzy or faint?'*
  - ○ If patients feel light-headed it is likely that there is a high volume of blood loss.

Associations:
- *'Are you experiencing any other symptoms?'* – in particular, abdominal pain and dizziness.

Abdominal pain in pregnancy

SOCRATES is a commonly used method of assessing pain of any type. See *Chapter 14* and *Section 16.1.2* for details of questions relating to abdominal pain.

Rule out: Placenta abruption, miscarriage (2nd trimester), labour (3rd trimester), pre-eclampsia (after 20 weeks) and uterine rupture (3rd trimester) before considering other causes.

Remember to include:
- *'Have you had any recent trauma to your abdomen?'*
- *'Have you travelled abroad recently?'* (foreign travel may make infection or dehydration, i.e. renal stones, more likely)
- *'Does it feel like period pain / labour pain?'*

- *'Has anyone else around you complained of abdominal pain?'*
- *'Have you experienced a change in bowel habit?'*
- *'Have you been vomiting?'* (if so, find out the relation to meals)

Severity: record current analgesia and take this into account by asking for a rating for the pain now, and at its worst.

Associations: *'Are you experiencing any other symptoms?'* – in particular, vaginal bleeding and headache.

> **Key Knowledge: Non-obstetrical DDx for abdominal pain in pregnancy**
>
> **GI** – reflux*, constipation*, cholecystitis*, appendicitis, gastroenteritis, obstruction
>
> **Gynae** – uterine / ligament stretching, fibroid degeneration, ovarian torsion, ruptured ovarian cyst, pelvic inflammatory disease
>
> **Renal** – UTI*, pyelonephritis, renal colic
>
> **MSK** – muscle strain
>
> **Respiratory** – pneumonia
>
> **Cardiac** – inferior MI
>
> *most common

Vomiting in pregnancy

Vomiting in pregnancy is common, and benign morning sickness can occur in the 1st trimester. In history taking, emphasis must be put on determining whether the patient is becoming clinically dehydrated as a result of the vomiting. Asking about previous scans is important – if the patient has not been in touch with health services, this indicates that there may be a pathological cause for the vomiting.

Rule out: hydatidiform mole (2nd trimester), hyperemesis gravidarum, pre-eclampsia (after 20 weeks) and multiple gestation, before considering other causes.

Time course:
- *'Have you noticed a pattern to the vomiting?'*
- *'How often do you vomit?'*
- *'What time of day are you vomiting?'*
- *'How long does the vomiting last?'*
- *'Does the vomiting happen after meals?'*

Severity:
- *'Are you able to keep food and drink down?'*
- *'Have you lost any weight?'*

Associations: *'Are you experiencing any other symptoms?'* – in particular, headache, epigastric pain, diarrhoea (gastroenteritis), symptoms of hyperthyroidism (hydatidiform mole) and ear pain or tinnitus (vestibular neuritis).

Headache in pregnancy

When investigating headache in pregnancy, first find out whether the patient is prone to headaches – there may be a personal history of migraines. If so, ask whether this feels the same or different. If the headache presents with vomiting, this may be a sign of dehydration. Dehydration is common due to water retention as oedema and in amniotic fluid. Symptoms of headache and vomiting, however, also feature in pre-eclampsia.

Work through **SOCRATES** to sufficiently gather information about the pain. See *Chapter 8* for examples of questions related to headache. Determine if there are any triggers, any focal neurological deficits and consider medication use and medication overuse.

Rule out: pre-eclampsia (after 20 weeks), brain haemorrhage and meningitis before considering other causes.

Severity:
- *'Is the headache having an adverse impact on your daily life?'*
- *'Does the headache wake you up at night?'*

Associations:
- *'Are you experiencing any other symptoms?'* – in particular epigastric pain, visual changes, sudden leg swelling; rule out other neurological differentials by asking about photophobia, neck stiffness and rash.

Pre-eclampsia
- Know this condition inside out.
- It is common and can present with many different symptoms: vomiting, headache, sudden leg or hand swelling, shortness of breath, visual changes and epigastric pain.
- Ask about gestation and if it is the first pregnancy or multiple gestation.
- Note age and weight.
- Ask about hypertension, kidney disease and diabetes.

If the main symptom is bleeding:
- **Placental abruption**: pelvic pain and bleeding. Risk factors – previous abruption, trauma, smoking and hypertension.
- **Placenta praevia**: painless vaginal bleeding. Ask about scans, smoking, multiparity, advanced maternal age, previous placenta praevia and Caesarean deliveries.
- **Cervical or endometrial cancer**: intermenstrual, post-coital, post-menopausal bleeding. For cervical cancer, ask about number of sexual partners, human papillomavirus (HPV), smoking, COCP. For endometrial cancer, ask about whether they have ever been pregnant / had a baby, late menopause, tamoxifen treatment.
- **Fibroids and polyps**: painful periods, bloating / swelling, dyspareunia.

If the main symptom is vomiting:
- **Hydatidiform mole**: vomiting, vaginal bleeding and features of hyperthyroidism such as palpitations, diaphoresis, tremor, anxiety, diarrhoea, thirst and heat intolerance. Ask about scans, the patient's age and about family history.
- **Hyperemesis gravidarum**: quantify vomiting and weight loss, ask about hyper-salivation and symptoms of dehydration – headache, thirst, constipation and dizziness. Risk factors: first pregnancy, multiple pregnancy and family history.

If the main symptom is skin related:
- **Acute fatty liver of pregnancy**: jaundice with epigastric pain, nausea and vomiting in the 3rd trimester. If confirmed, the fetus is delivered to reduce the risk of severe complications to mother and fetus.
- **Intrahepatic cholestasis of pregnancy**: severe intractable pruritus after the 2nd trimester, similar symptoms in previous pregnancies. Jaundice is not always present and there is no rash, only excoriations. This condition carries high risk to the fetus.
- **Pemphigoid gestationis**: plaques around the umbilicus preceded by itch. Immune response can cause placental insufficiency.
- **Polymorphic eruption of pregnancy**: erythematous itchy papules that begin within striae, in late 3rd trimester.

If the main symptom is pain:

- **Ectopic pregnancy**: vaginal bleeding, bowel symptoms, shoulder-tip pain. If the Fallopian tube has ruptured the patient may present in shock. Ask about previous ectopic, PID, previous sterilization operation, abdominal surgery, endometriosis.
- **PID**: abnormal vaginal bleeding, dyspareunia, abnormal vaginal discharge, fever, back pain. Ask about sexual history, previous PID or STI, recent abortion, recent pelvic operation, recently inserted intrauterine device (IUD).
- **Ovarian cyst**: dyspareunia, irregular periods, sudden severe pain if cyst bursts, abdominal swelling.

If the main symptom is fever:

- **Retained products of conception**: ask about abdominal pain, fever, mode of delivery, how the placenta was passed, vaginal bleeding that is getting heavier or prolonged over 3 weeks, unusual colour, quantity or smell of vaginal discharge.
- **TORCH infections (toxoplasmosis, other (syphilis, varicella-zoster, Zika, parvovirus B19), rubella, cytomegalovirus, herpes)**: fever, fatigue, swollen lymph glands, muscle or joint aches. Ask about exposure to others who are unwell, exposure to cat litter (reservoir for toxoplasmosis), sexual activity and foreign travel.

Shortness of breath in pregnancy

Shortness of breath may be a normal physiological feature of pregnancy, which is attributed to increased abdominal pressure preventing diaphragm contraction, plasma volume expansion causing a relative anaemia, and progesterone-induced hyperventilation. Physiological dyspnoea of pregnancy is of gradual onset and there is a lack of red flag symptoms. If the onset is acute with inability to complete sentences, consider emergency diagnoses such as anaphylaxis or MI. An anaphylaxis-type presentation during pregnancy or in the puerperium may be due to amniotic fluid embolism, where fetal cells enter the maternal circulation. Also consider pulmonary embolism, which is more likely during pregnancy due to high oestrogen levels causing a hypercoagulable state, so ask about foreign travel and long-haul flights. See *Chapter 12* for more details of questions.

Rule out: pulmonary embolism and pre-eclampsia (after 20 weeks), before considering other causes.

Time course:

- *'Have you noticed a pattern to the shortness of breath?'*
- *'When did the shortness of breath start?'*
- *'Did it come on suddenly or gradually?'*
- *'Is there something that triggers the shortness of breath?'*
- *'Does it come on after exercise?'*
- *'Is the shortness of breath getting worse?'*

Severity: Assess during the history by seeing whether the patient is able to complete full sentences when at rest. How did they arrive at the department? Were they ambulatory or did they require assistance?

Associations:

- *'Are you experiencing any other symptoms?'* – in particular, headache, chest pain and palpitations.

Leg swelling in pregnancy

Mild oedema is a normal feature of pregnancy, due to large increases in circulating plasma volume accompanied by fluid retention. Normal physiological oedema is of gradual onset and there is a lack of red flag symptoms. If the onset is acute, consider diagnoses such as deep vein thrombosis (DVT) if unilateral or pre-eclampsia if bilateral. DVT is more likely during pregnancy due to high oestrogen levels causing a hypercoagulable state, so ask about foreign travel and long-haul flights.

Rule out: deep vein thrombosis and pre-eclampsia (after 20 weeks), before considering other causes.

Time course:
- *'Have you noticed a pattern to the swelling?'*
- *'When did the swelling start?'*
- *'Did it come on suddenly or gradually?'*
- *'Is it worse in the morning or at night?'*

Severity: if the swelling is unilateral, measure leg circumferences.

Associations: *'Are you experiencing any other symptoms?'* – in particular, leg pain, warmth and redness, and headache.

Skin changes in pregnancy

There are several normal physiological skin changes that occur during pregnancy. These include darkening of the linea alba to become the linea nigra, striae gravidarum (stretch marks), nipple areola hyperpigmentation and extension. Other less common but normal features are melasma, telangiectasia, palmar erythema, varicosities and hyperhidrosis. In history taking, you need to determine whether skin symptoms are physiological or pathological, having severe consequences for the fetus and/or mother. See *Chapter 17* for more guidance on taking a dermatological history.

TORCH is an acronym that stands for **T**oxoplasmosis, **O**ther (syphilis, varicella-zoster, Zika, parvovirus B19), **R**ubella, **C**ytomegalovirus and **H**erpes. When these infections are contracted during pregnancy there can be catastrophic congenital malformations in the fetus. Ask whether anyone in the family has been unwell – if so, the cause of a rash may be infective.

Rule out: pemphigoid gestationis, intrahepatic cholestasis of pregnancy (mostly 3rd trimester), acute fatty liver of pregnancy (3rd trimester), hepatitis and TORCH infections, before considering other causes.

Description: ask about site, colour, size and whether the lesions are raised.

Time course: ask about onset and whether the skin change has spread over time.

Associations:
- *'Are you experiencing any other symptoms?'* – in particular, fever, itch and pain
- *'Have you noticed that your skin or your eyes have become yellow?'*

Severity of itch or pain: *'Do these symptoms wake you up at night?'*

Mood changes during and after pregnancy

Low mood, or post-partum blues, is relatively common after delivery and may be a result of hormonal changes. This usually resolves within two weeks following delivery. It can be difficult to determine whether symptoms are due to depression or part of the normal adjustment of having a new baby. Ask about personal history and family history of depression and psychosis. A collateral history may be important in this instance. For further information on taking a psychiatric history, consult *Chapter 7*. It is good practice to consider other differentials causing anxiety, such as hyperthyroidism or phaeochromocytoma, and low mood, such as SLE and Cushing's disease.

Rule out: postnatal depression and postnatal psychosis, before considering other causes.

Time course:
- *'When did the low mood start in relation to your pregnancy and delivery?'*
- *'How long has it been going on for?'*

Symptoms of depression: ask specifically about low mood, anxiety, poor concentration, irritability and insomnia within six weeks of delivery.

Symptoms of psychosis: is the patient within the first two weeks after delivery?
- *'Do you hear, see or smell things that other people do not seem to?'*
- *'Do you have any particular beliefs about the world?'*
- *'Have you ever thought about taking your own life?'*
- *'Do you ever have any thoughts about harming your baby?'*

Remember, depression and psychosis can happen at any time, but are classified as postnatal when within the time scales above.

Ask about support: social issues predispose patients to depression.

Ask about the baby, its health and behaviour: the risk of depression is increased when the baby has congenital abnormalities.

Fever during and after pregnancy

Pregnant patients may develop fever in response to any usual infective differentials such as influenza, appendicitis, etc. Important obstetric differentials to rule out are TORCH infections that may invoke lasting damage to the fetus, and retained products of conception if the fever occurs with pelvic pain after delivery, miscarriage or termination. In sepsis, initiate the Sepsis Six as soon as possible (high flow oxygen, blood culture, broad-spectrum antibiotics, lactate and full blood count, intravenous fluids, measure urine output).

Rule out: TORCH infections and retained products of conception (after delivery), before considering other causes.
- *'How have you measured your temperature?'*
- *'Do you get sweaty or do you get shaking episodes?'*
- *'Have you travelled abroad recently?'* – consider endemic areas of Zika virus.

Ask about time course: *'When did the fever start?'*

Ask about the mode of delivery, if appropriate:
- Caesarean sections: *'Was the Caesarean section planned or did it have to be done as an emergency? Why did you require a Caesarean section?'*
- Vaginal delivery: *'Did the doctor or midwife have to use forceps or the vacuum to assist with the delivery? How quickly was the placenta delivered?'*
- Miscarriage or termination: *'How was your miscarriage managed?' 'How was the pregnancy terminated?'*

Ask about associated symptoms:
- *'Are you experiencing any other symptoms?'* – in particular, rash, pelvic pain and vaginal discharge. This is also a good time to take a thorough systems review.
- *'Do you have any breast pain, redness or swelling?'* – consider mastitis.

Sexual history: in practice, if a partner is present you could ask them to leave for a couple of minutes or for the examination, and ask these questions at this point. Ensure the patient that you do not mean to be intrusive, and questions are voluntary, but the answers may be key to reaching a diagnosis. See *Section16.1.2* for how to take a sexual history.

Infertility

Infertility can be very stressful for the couple involved. The period in which the couple has been trying to conceive can vary significantly. Those concerned about their fertility should be informed that 80% of couples in the general population will conceive within a year if they do not use contraception and have intercourse regularly (every 2–3 days). Infertility can be an issue with either partner, therefore both should be assessed.

Both partners
- *'How long have you been having unprotected intercourse?'*
- *'How long have you actively been trying to conceive?'*
- *'How many times per week do you have intercourse?'*
- *'Do either of you have children from another partner?'*

Females
- Start by enquiring about her general health. Ask about past medical history, medication history, family history of infertility and lifestyle (smoking, alcohol, recreational drug use, exercise, diet).
- Take a complete obstetrical, gynaecological and sexual history, including the contraception methods that they have used in the past.

Males
- Start by enquiring about his general health. Ask about past medical history, medication history, family history of infertility and lifestyle (smoking, alcohol, recreational drug use, exercise, diet).
- Complete a sexual history.
  - *'Have you ever been seen by a urologist?'*
  - *'As a child, did you have undescended testes, mumps, chemotherapy, bladder, penile or hernia surgery?'*
  - *'Do you have difficulty achieving or maintaining an erection?'*
  - *'Do you ejaculate semen every time you have intercourse or masturbate?'*
  - *'Have you ever conceived with another woman?'*
  - *'Have you ever had a semen analysis?'*

4b) History of presenting complaint – gynaecology

16.1.2 Gynaecological history
- **Cervical cytology**: cervical smears are a form of primary prevention aimed at preventing cervical cancer. In the UK, women are invited for cervical screening at the age of 25– 49 (every 3 years), 50–64 (every 5 years) and over 65 if they have not been screened since the age of 50 or have recently had an abnormal test.
  - *'When was your last cervical smear?'*
  - *'Have you ever had an abnormal smear result?'* If so, *'How was it treated?'*
- **Breast cancer screening**: a mammogram is offered to women between the ages of 50 and 70 in the UK and earlier if there is a family history.
  - In women over the age of 50, *'Have you been invited to the breast screening programme for a mammogram?'* If so, *'What were the results?'*

Menstrual history
Start by signposting to the patient that you would like to ask them a few specific questions about their menses. *'At this time, I would like to ask you a few specific questions about your menstrual cycle.'*

- **Age of menarche**: women typically begin their periods around 12–13 years of age (range is 8–16). It is initially anovulatory in nature, therefore the menses may be heavy and irregular.
  - ○ *'How old were you when you started having periods?'*
- **Last menstrual period**
  - ○ *'What date did you start your last period?'*
  - ○ *'How many days did it last?'*
- **Typical menstrual pattern**
  - ○ Cycle length: ovulatory cycle length varies between 23 and 40 days, with the median cycle length around 28 days. A recent change in cycle length can indicate a problem.
    - – *'How many days do you go between periods?'*
    - – *'Is your cycle regular? For example, can you anticipate what day you will start your period?'*
  - ○ **Duration of flow**: the length of menstrual bleeding varies from 1–7 days. Women who are taking oral contraceptive pills typically experience shorter withdrawal bleeds than a natural menstrual period.
    - – *'How many days do you typically bleed?'*
  - ○ **Amount of flow**: the amount of menstrual bleeding is difficult to quantify. The average amount of blood loss is approximately 30 ml but can vary between 10 and 80 ml. Clinically, the actual amount of menstrual bleeding is not relevant. It is more important to establish if there are any recent changes in the amount of blood and whether the patient finds the amount of bleeding tolerable.
    - – *'Have you noticed any recent changes in the amount of menstrual bleeding that you experience?'*
    - – To establish whether they suffer from troublesome, heavy periods, ask: *'Do you have to use double protection, i.e. tampons and pads? How many packets would you get through in a typical cycle? Do you suffer from flooding?'*
  - ○ **Physical and emotional symptoms**: most women experience physical and/or emotional symptoms in the premenstrual period but they usually resolve at the end of menstruation. Physical symptoms include abdominal pain, breast tenderness, weight gain and abdominal distension. Emotional disturbances include mood instability and irritability.
    - – *'Do you find your premenstrual symptoms particularly disturbing?'*
    - – *'Do you ever have to miss school or work because of your premenstrual symptoms?'*
    - – *'Are your periods painful? Does this pain affect your day-to-day activities?'*
  - ○ **Intermenstrual / post-coital bleeding**: a small amount of spotting mid-cycle can occur in some women; however, if bleeding occurs at any other time of the cycle (with the exception of menstruation) or after intercourse, this is abnormal.
    - – *'Do you ever experience bleeding when your period is not due / between your periods?'*
    - – *'Do you ever experience bleeding after sexual intercourse?'*

Menorrhagia

Menorrhagia is defined as heavy bleeding during menstruation that interferes with daily life.

Rule out: pregnancy-related (miscarriage), endometrial polyps / fibroids, anovulatory cycles (polycystic ovarian syndrome – PCOS), hypo- or hyperthyroidism, Cushing's disease.
- Establish whether the blood loss is causing them to feel symptomatic. *'Have you experienced an increase in shortness of breath, fatigue, decreased exercise tolerance, palpitations or dizziness? Has anyone commented that you look paler than normal?'*
- *'Have you experienced any abdominal pain?'*
- Complete a thorough obstetrical, gynaecological, menstrual and sexual history.
- *'When was your last cervical smear?'*
- *'Have you experienced any bleeding in between your periods or during / after intercourse?'*

Impact on everyday life
- *'How does your vaginal bleeding interfere with your everyday life?'*
- *'Do you ever suffer from flooding?'*
- *'Is there anything that you aren't able to do when you are experiencing your bleeding?'*
- *'Do you use pads or tampons? How many packets do you get through per cycle?'*

Oligo- / amenorrhoea

Amenorrhoea is the absence of menstruation. Primary amenorrhoea occurs when a girl has never had menarche (her first period). It should be investigated at age 16 or, if there has been a failure of breast development, at age 14. Secondary amenorrhoea is the cessation of menses for greater than 6 months once they have already started (with the exception of pregnancy). Oligomenorrhoea is defined as infrequent menses. It is quite common at the extremes of the reproductive age. The most common cause of oligomenorrhoea during the reproductive years is PCOS.

The first step in the assessment of oligo- or amenorrhoea is to determine if the patient is pregnant.
- Complete an obstetrical, gynaecological and sexual history.
  - *'Have you ever had a period? When was your last period?'*
  - *'When did you first develop breasts? When did you first develop pubic hair?'*
  - *'Are you currently using contraception? What forms of contraception have you used in the past?'*
- Complete a past medical history, medication history, family history and social history.
  - *'Were you born with any medical conditions?'* – establish whether there are any congenital conditions and abnormalities
  - *'Did anyone else in your family start their periods late?'* – assessing for a constitutional delay in puberty
  - *'Do you have any facial hair? Have you had any trouble with acne?'* – these can be signs of PCOS.
  - Determine exercise habits and dietary pattern. Determine if there are any causes of stress. These can cause hypothalamic amenorrhoea.
- Determine if they are experiencing any neurological symptoms (headache, vision changes) or galactorrhoea (prolactinoma).

Pelvic pain and dysmenorrhoea

Dysmenorrhoea is defined as painful periods. Primary dysmenorrhoea is not associated with organ pathology and is usually present from menarche, whilst secondary dysmenorrhoea is associated with pathology.

Rule out: ectopic pregnancy, endometriosis, ovarian cysts, pelvic inflammatory disease (PID) and non-gynaecological causes (e.g. appendicitis, renal colic, UTI, IBD)
- Ask about **SOCRATES**.
- *'When was your last period? Are you currently sexually active? Are you currently using contraception?'* – establish the risk for ectopic pregnancy.
- *'Have you had any bleeding in between periods, or after sexual intercourse?'*
- Enquire into urinary and bowel symptoms.
- Complete a thorough obstetrical, gynaecological and sexual history.

Menopause

Menopause is defined as the absence of menses for 1 year. The cessation of menses can occur between the ages of 40 and 59 with a mean age of 51 years.

Rule out: pregnancy, hyper- or hyperthyroidism, medication side-effect.

- Bleeding: as women go through the perimenopausal period their menstrual bleeding patterns can become irregular and can change in the frequency and amount of bleeding.
  - *'When was your last menstrual bleed?'*
- Symptoms: approximately 70% of women are affected by menopausal symptoms. Women experience a variety of symptoms due to changes in their hormones, particularly oestrogen.
  - *'Have you been experiencing any disturbing symptoms?'*
  - Physical symptoms: hot flushes, night sweats, palpitations, difficulty sleeping, joint aches and headaches.
  - Emotional symptoms: mood swings, irritability, anxiety, difficulty concentrating and memory disturbances.
  - Sexual symptoms: vaginal dryness / itching / discomfort and low libido.
  - Urinary symptoms: increase in urine infections, incontinence and urinary frequency.
  - Hormone replacement regimen (if applicable).
  - *'Have you ever taken hormone replacement therapy? Have you ever been given medication to help with your menopausal symptoms?'*
  - *'Have you had any changes in your weight, palpitations or night sweats?'*

Post-menopausal or intermenstrual bleeding

It is important to address post-menopausal and intermenstrual bleeding as they can be a sign of cancer or infection.

Rule out: pregnancy (miscarriage), endometrial or cervical cancer, cervicitis (STI)
- Complete a thorough obstetrical, gynaecological, menstrual and sexual history.
- Acquire a past medical history as PCOS, obesity, diabetes, hypertension and breast cancer (tamoxifen use) are all risk factors for endometrial cancer.
- Consider family history as hereditary non-polyposis colorectal carcinoma is a risk factor for endometrial cancer.
- *'When did you first notice the bleeding? Have you had more than one episode of bleeding?'*
- *'How long did the bleeding last?'*
- *'What day of your period does the amount remind you of?'*
- *'Is there any associated pain or discomfort?'*
- *'Do you experience any pain when you are having intercourse?'*
- *'When was your last cervical smear? What were the results? Have you ever had a positive result?'*

4c) History of presenting complaint – sexual health, contraception and the breast

16.1.3 Sexual health and contraception history

Sexual health history

Completing a sexual history can often be as difficult for the interviewer as the interviewee. Each sexual history needs to be approached in a sensitive manner. After establishing the reason for the consultation, the doctor should explain the need to ask questions that may seem a bit personal (signposting). You should always start with questions that are non-threatening in nature (e.g. contraception and menstrual history) before moving on to more sensitive questions (e.g. same-sex relations and injection drug abuse).
- **Menstrual history**: menstrual information should be gathered to identify the risk of pregnancy, the need for emergency contraception or a pregnancy test to avoid prescribing drugs that are contraindicated in pregnancy. It is also a trigger for providing contraceptive advice.

- **Obstetrical history**: determine the number of pregnancies, the outcomes and any pregnancy-related complications.
- **Cervical cytology results**
- **Contraception (for both men and women)**: important for providing the opportunity for health promotion and information giving.
  - *'Are you currently using any form of contraception?'*
  - *'Do you use condoms? Do you ever have sex without using a condom?'*
  - *'Are you currently taking birth control? What type? Do you have any concerns with your current contraception method? Is there anything you wish could be better about it?'*
  - If applicable, *'On average, how many pills per month do you take late or miss? Do you know what to do if you are late taking a pill or if you miss a pill?'*
- **STIs**
  - *'Have you ever been diagnosed with a sexually transmitted infection?'* If so, when, what type, how was it managed and were there any complications?
  - *'Have you ever had a blood test for HIV?'*
- **Last sexual contact**: *'I would now like to ask you a couple of questions about your last sexual contact.'*
  - *'Was your last sexual contact male or female?'*
  - *'What type of sex did you have?'* (oral, vaginal, anal) – used to identify what sites need to be sampled.
  - *'Did you use a condom or barrier device?'*
  - *'What was your relationship with this person?'* (casual, regular, dating, married) *'How long did you have relations with this person?'*
  - *'How long has it been since your last sexual contact?'*
  - *'Did this partner have any symptoms or risk factors for sexually transmitted infections or HIV?'* – see high risk behaviours below.
- **Previous sexual partners (in the last three months)**
  - Gender of partner(s)
  - Type of sex (oral, vaginal, anal)
  - Use of barrier methods
  - Relationship to partner and whether they are high risk
- **High risk behaviours**:
  - *'Have you ever injected drugs? Do you share needles or drug preparation equipment?'*
  - *'Have you ever had a sexual relationship with someone who injects drugs?'*
  - *'Have you ever paid or been paid for sexual intercourse?'*
  - *'Have you ever had sex with someone who comes from somewhere with a high prevalence for HIV, like Africa?'*
  - *'Have you ever had sex with someone who is HIV positive?'*
  - *'Have you been vaccinated for hepatitis B? When?'*
  - *'Have you ever received medical treatment or a tattoo in a place where sterility should be questioned?'*
- **Safety**
  - If underage, you need to assess for **Gillick competence** and for sexual safety. Enquire specifically about:
    - The age of their sexual contacts and how they know them.
    - Is there an age gap? An inappropriate age gap would be greater than 5 years in an adolescent or if one of the partners is under 16 years old.
    - Is this person in a position of power or trust?
    - Where are they engaging in sexual activity?
    - Have they ever been forced to engage in sexual activities by force or threats of violence (both physical and psychological)?
    - Have they ever received gifts, money, drugs or alcohol for sexual favours?

- Have they ever been involved with the police or child protection agencies?
- It is also important to do a complete HEADSSS assessment. See *Chapter 20.*
  ○ Screen for **domestic abuse** by asking the following SAFE questions:
    - **Stress / safety**
    - *'What stresses do you experience in your relationship?'*
    - *'Do you feel safe in your relationship?'*
    - **Afraid / abused**
    - *'People in relationships sometimes fight. What happens when you and your partner disagree?'*
    - *'Have you ever been in a situation with your partner where you have felt afraid?'*
    - *'Have you ever been threatened or physically hurt by your partner?'*
    - *'Has your partner ever forced you to do sexual activities that you didn't want to do?'*
    - **Friends / family**
    - *'Are your friends and family aware of what is going on?'*
    - **Emergency**
    - *'Do you have a safe place to go in case of an emergency?'*

When closing a sexual history, it is important to thank the patient for their honesty, acknowledge the difficulty of answering such questions and reinforce why it was so important to ask those questions.

Vaginal discharge

The role of the history and examination when a patient presents with vaginal discharge is to distinguish between physiological and pathological discharge. Signs of abnormal discharge include an increase in the amount, foul smell, accompanying itching or soreness, burning on urination and grey or yellow / green discharge.

- *'When did you first notice a change in your discharge?'*
- *'What has been bothering you the most about the discharge?'*
- *'What does it look like? Does it smell?'*
- *'Have you experienced any itchiness or irritation down below? Have you had any pain during intercourse? Do you have any pain when you urinate?'*
- *'Have you had any bleeding after sex or in between your periods?'*
- *'Have you ever been tested or treated for an STI in the past?'*
- Take a full sexual history and consider obstetrical, gynaecological and menstrual histories as appropriate.

Dyspareunia

Dyspareunia is defined as pain that occurs in the vagina, labia or clitoris during or after sexual intercourse. It is most commonly experienced in women who are sexually inexperienced or in women who are peri- or post-menopausal. Vaginismus is the painful tightening of vaginal muscles that makes penetration impossible.

- *'How long have you had this discomfort? When do you feel the pain (before, during or after sex)? How long does this pain last?'*
- *'Is the pain you are having on the outside, deep inside or both?'*
- *'Do you ever experience pain when you are not having intercourse, for example during your periods or during bowel movements?'*
- *'Are you able to have intercourse?'*
- *'Do you ever have sex when you don't want to? Are you ever forced to have sex?'*
- *'Do you and your partner use foreplay or lubricant?'*
- Take a complete sexual, obstetrical (including a history of episiotomy and traumatic childbirth), gynaecological and menstrual history.

Differential diagnosis includes STI (PID, vaginitis, cervicitis), UTI, menopause (atrophic vaginitis), endometriosis / adenomyosis, sexual assault, breast-feeding, genital prolapse, post-operative hysterectomy, skin conditions (lichen planus, lichen sclerosis), Sjögren's syndrome, diabetes, chronic constipation.

Contraceptive advice

Women vary vastly in their knowledge of the various forms of contraception. As the physician, your job is to explore their medical history, lifestyles and goals to see what forms of contraception will work best to meet their needs. When performing your consultation, you should always consider the *UK Medical Eligibility Criteria for Contraceptive Use* (UKMEC), which is a clinical guideline for contraceptive prescribing. Its contents will be summarized in *Section 3*.

If a girl is under the age of 16, you need to ensure that she meets the Fraser Guidelines to be considered Gillick competent and able to consent to her own medical treatment without parental consent. According to the House of Lords (1985), a doctor can give advice and treatment if the girl meets the following criteria:

1. "The girl (although under the age of 16 years of age) will understand his advice;
2. That he cannot persuade her to inform her parents or to allow him to inform the parents that she is seeking contraception advice;
3. That she is very likely to continue having sexual intercourse with or without contraceptive treatment;
4. That unless she receives contraceptive advice or treatment her physical or mental health or both are likely to suffer;
5. That her best interests require him to give her contraceptive advice, treatment or both without parental consent."

Rule out: contraindications to the UKMEC system.

- Start by obtaining a complete medical history including obstetrical, gynaecological, sexual and menstrual history.
- Ask specifically about a past medical history of migraines with aura, blood clots and breast / cervical cancer as these are all contraindications to the combined oral contraceptive pill.
- Family history – ask about family history of breast cancer, thrombophilia, venous thromboembolism (VTE).
- Medication history – some drugs can interact with the combined oral contraceptive pill (COCP), e.g. anti-epileptic drugs.
- Smoking history – smoking can increase their risk of a blot clot.
- Family planning should be addressed. If she is considering conceiving within the next two years, a short-term method is preferred. The depot injection should also be avoided as it can sometimes take up to 18 months for normal fertility to resume.
- Ask about previous contraception use. What worked and didn't work for her? Does she have any current preferences?
- Discuss whether she is confident that she could remember to take a daily tablet or whether she could tolerate injections.
- It is also important to reinforce the use of condoms to protect against STIs.

16.1.4 Breast history

Breast lump

When a woman discovers a breast lump, she automatically associates it with breast cancer. This fear is also related to an increase in societal awareness of the disease and the promotion of screening and education programmes. Patients will undoubtedly be anxious.

Rule out: breast cancer
- *'When did you first notice the lump? How has it changed since that time?'*
- *'Are you currently or have you recently been breast-feeding?'*
- *'Have you had a fever?'*
- *'Is the lump causing you any pain or discomfort?'* If so, this needs to be addressed with **SOCRATES** questioning.
- *'Have you ever noticed any other lumps?'*
- *'Have you noticed any change in the skin of your breast?'*
- *'Have you noticed a change in your nipple? Have you experienced any discharge from your nipple?'*
- *'Do you notice that lump change during the course of each month?'*
- *'Is there a family history of breast or any other type of cancer?'*
- *'Have you had any bone pain, numbness or tingling, change in your vision or headaches? Have you noticed any recent change in your weight?'* – assess for possible symptoms of metastases.
- Complete an obstetrical, gynaecological and menstrual history to look for risk factors: first child after the age of 30, not having breast-fed, early menarche or late menopause, use of hormone replacement therapy.

5) Systems review
Think about what you have to exclude and ask questions relevant to risk factors and symptoms of obstetric and non-obstetric disorders that may be causing the presentation.

If you have time, finish off by running through each body system. If the patient answers positively to questioning in a certain system, you should complete a full enquiry into the state of that system in order to remove it as a differential. Refer to *Chapter 6* for more details.

6) ICE
Pregnant patients, especially primigravidae, may be extremely worried and generally unsure about what is normal. Patients have often already conducted an internet search, and the more severe diagnoses for their presentation would have stuck in their minds. They will look to doctors to reassure or confirm. Often concerns cannot be alleviated at the history stage, but you can acknowledge them and explain that further tests are necessary.

7) Past medical history
- *'Is there anything that you see your doctor for regularly?'*
- *'Have you ever had to stay in hospital because of illness?'*
- *'Have you ever had surgery?'*

Ask specifically about common conditions which may account for or lead up to their particular presentation.
- **Hypertension** – risk factor for pre-eclampsia.
- **DM** – risk factor for pre-eclampsia and may correlate with PCOS. Diabetes can also lead to vaginal dryness, urinary symptoms, dyspareunia and an increased risk of candida and other vaginal infections.
- **Thrombophilia** – makes VTE more likely, or if the patient needs anticoagulation this makes bleeding more likely.
- **Migraine** – may be a contraindication for certain types of contraception.
- **Hiatus hernia** and/or **reflux** – increased abdominal pressure may be exacerbating this and cause vomiting.
- Known **malignancy** – unusual, but some patients may defer cancer treatment until completion of a pregnancy. This could result in vaginal bleeding.
- **Asthma** or **COPD** – can account for increased SOB in pregnancy.

- **Eczema** – this may get worse during pregnancy, and may explain an itchy rash.
- **IBD** or **IBS** – can lead to dyspareunia.
- **Depression** – may predispose patients to increased mood instability.

8) Medication history

Take a thorough drug history, including when each medication was started and ones that have been stopped in the past. Include allergies, OTC medication and herbal remedies. Give advice on supplementation (folic acid is important pre-conception and during the first 12 weeks). Ensure the patient is not taking any medication contraindicated in pregnancy, such as high dose vitamin A (cod liver oil), warfarin, NSAIDs, methotrexate, retinoids, ACE inhibitors and thiazide diuretics. Refer to *Chapter 21* for more information.

9) Family history

- *'Is there any family history of trouble getting pregnant?'*
- *'Is there any family history of babies born with congenital problems?'*
- *'Is there any family history of breast or ovarian cancer? Has anyone in your family had genetic testing for the BRCA1/BRCA2 gene for breast cancer?'*
- *'Is there anything else that runs in your family?'* – in particular, DM and genetic disorders such as cystic fibrosis, sickle cell disease and hereditary thrombophilias.

Ask about family history in both the patient's family and the partner's family. If there is strong family history of a disorder, draw a family tree to determine genetic inheritance. Familial conditions include hyperemesis gravidarum, hydatidiform moles and pre-eclampsia.

10) Social history

Signpost the change in consultation topic, and reassure the patient that we ask everyone these questions. Talking about lifestyle can be intrusive so let the patient know that these are optional, and that knowing some answers may help you to offer support where it is needed.

- Details of **partner**: male or female? Are they happy about the pregnancy? What does the partner do for a living? It may sometimes be appropriate to ask about consanguinity.
- Details of **support**: emotional, financial and practical.
- Ask about **living arrangements** – where does the patient live and who do they live with?
- Ask about **occupation** –is she self-employed? Are there any occupational hazards?
- What is their **diet** like? Are they vegetarian?
- Ask for **weight** and height, then calculate BMI – obesity is a risk factor for miscarriage, pre-eclampsia, thromboembolism.
- Ask about **smoking** and quantify. In non-smokers ask about past smoking and about second-hand smoke exposure.
- Does the patient drink **alcohol**? If so, quantify by glasses / bottles, and calculate units later.
- Does the patient use **recreational drugs**? If so, ask which ones, and quantify use.
- Ask about **foreign travel and activity**, both of which can affect the likelihood of a clot.

11) Closing the consultation

Always use your basic communication skills according to the Calgary–Cambridge Model. Remember to summarize and be sure to screen in order to ensure that the patient has had the opportunity to express anything else they feel is relevant. Always close by thanking the patient and informing them of the next step in their plan of care.

'Thank you so much for all of the information that you have given me. I am now going to quickly speak with my colleagues and then I will be back to discuss the plan with you. Do you have any questions?'

Summary of key points (GET YOUR MARKS):

Establish rapport: introduce yourself and explain why you are there.

History of presenting complaint: investigate each symptom in turn, thinking about differentials. Find out how each symptom relates to one another.

Systems review: exclude differentials, and run through each system if time permits.

ICE: acknowledge any concerns.

Obstetric history: include the details of current and past pregnancies.

Gynaecological and menstrual history: ask about cycle length, regularity, menorrhagia, any abnormal bleeding, cervical screening and breast screening.

Sexual history: ask about last sexual partner, previous sexual partners, any previous STIs, high risk behaviours, contraception.

Past medical history: used to establish whether there is a relation with the current presentation and helps to prepare for potential complications.

Medication history: ensure medications are safe in pregnancy.

Family history: establishes whether the presentation may be genetic.

Social history: including social support and lifestyle.

Closing the consultation: summarize and always leave the patient with a plan of care, even if it is that you need to speak with your colleagues. Thank the patient.

16.2 Information giving and shared decision making

16.2.1 Pre-eclampsia

What is it? This is a state that can lead to a dangerous condition called eclampsia that includes seizures. You may feel fine, but we can detect this state by measuring your blood pressure and testing your urine for protein. Your blood vessel lining becomes disrupted, allowing protein to leak into your urine, and fluid to leak into your tissues that can result in swelling in your hands and also into your liver, which can result in liver damage. Your blood vessels also tighten, which causes the high blood pressure.

Who gets it? The exact cause is not known, but pre-eclampsia is a sign that your body is not adapting to the pregnancy well. This happens in the second half of the pregnancy, and is more likely if it is your first pregnancy or if you are having twins. Other risk factors are high blood pressure, kidney disease and DM, as well as obesity and older age. Pre-eclampsia affects up to 8 in 100 pregnancies in the UK.

How do you treat it? To manage the condition we'll prescribe some antihypertensive medication to lower your blood pressure. The only "cure" is delivery of your baby, but this will only be recommended if the risks to you because of pre-eclampsia are greater than the risks of preterm delivery to your baby.

16.2.2 Placental abruption

What is it? This happens when the placenta comes away from the lining of your uterus. If the placenta is high, bleeding may not be apparent because the baby is preventing the blood from draining out. We can assess severity of the abruption by checking on your baby's heartbeat to see whether it is distressed.

Who gets it? Risk factors for abruption include previous abruption, trauma, smoking, high blood pressure, advanced age, low body mass index and having had more than one baby. Placental abruption affects up to 1 in 100 pregnancies in the UK.

How do you treat it? This depends on the volume of blood loss and whether your baby is distressed or not. You may just be monitored for a while, or you may need to have a transfusion and if it is safer for your baby, it may need to be delivered.

16.2.3 **Gestational diabetes**

What is it? This is when you develop diabetes during pregnancy. It is usually detected by blood tests, but you may get symptoms such as thirst and frequent urination. The hormones that play a role in pregnancy make developing diabetes more likely, and it usually resolves after delivery. Managing gestational diabetes is important because too much sugar in your blood can be passed on to your baby, making it grow too large and thus making delivery difficult. Also, the baby has a risk of a sudden drop in blood sugar after birth, as well as seizures.

Who gets it? Risk factors include previous gestational diabetes or pre-diabetes, older age, Afro-Caribbean ethnicity, PCOS, obesity and smoking. However, approximately half of women have no risk factors, which is why you are all screened for the condition. Gestational diabetes affects up to 18 in 100 pregnancies in the UK.

How do you treat it? It is safest to manage the condition by diet. We'll help you with knowing which foods are sensible. If the diabetes is severe we might recommend insulin injections.

16.2.4 **Chlamydia infection**

What is it? Chlamydia is a small bacteria that is usually transmitted through sexual contact with a person who is infected. Approximately 50% of men and 80% of women do not experience any symptoms and therefore it can spread to others without anyone knowing. If they do experience symptoms, women can have vaginal discharge, pain when they pee, pain in their lower abdomen, fevers, pain or bleeding during intercourse or bleeding in between periods. Men can have pain when they pee, discharge from their penis or testicular pain.

Who gets it? People are more likely to acquire the infection if they have multiple partners or do not use a condom when having sex. It is the most common STI in the UK.

Complications: although chlamydia can be treated with antibiotics, occasionally it can be associated with some serious complications. Women who have acquired chlamydia are at risk for severe infections of the womb (PID), ectopic pregnancies and infertility.

How do you treat it?
- The treatment involves either a single dose of azithromycin 1 g or a 7-day course of an antibiotic called doxycycline. We will also treat you for gonorrhoea with an injection of ceftriaxone into the muscle.
- You should refrain from having sexual intercourse for 1 week after taking the single dose treatment or after the entire 7-day course. You should not have sex with your partner until they too have completed treatment as there is a high risk of recurrence.
- We would recommend also having a blood test done for HIV and hepatitis B.
- Sexual partner tracing will need to be done so that they too can be tested and receive treatment. You can either inform them yourself or they can be informed by the health team.
- You should have a test for chlamydia every year and after a change in sexual partners. It can be done as a urine sample or as a vaginal swab in women.
- Discuss the importance of condom use and contraception in women.

16.2.5 **Contraceptive advice**

Contraception advice should begin with a thorough history to ascertain patient preference, lifestyle and any contraindications. The physician should consider the UKMEC when offering choices to the patient, as some options may be inappropriate or contraindicated. The major points to take away from the UKMEC (see *Table 16.1*) are as follows:

- In **post-partum** women, the combined hormonal contraceptive pill should be avoided in breast-feeding mothers <6 months post-partum and in non-breast-feeding mothers <6 weeks. The copper coil (IUD) and levonorgestrel-releasing intrauterine system (IUS) can be placed within 48 hours post-partum but placement should be avoided after this time until after 4 weeks.
- Insertion should be avoided whenever there is a risk of **infection** transmission.
- In women who **smoke,** the combined oral contraception (COC) is not the best choice. If they are over 35 years of age, COC should be avoided as the risk of complications is greater than the benefit. Consider all other forms of contraception.
- Avoid the COCP in women with a **BMI** >35. Caution in those with a BMI of 30–34.
- COCs should be avoided in patients with **IHD** or risk factors for cardiovascular disease (e.g. dyslipidaemia, hypertension, obesity, smoking, diabetes).
- If there is a previous medical history of VTE, COCs are contraindicated. If a relative has had a VTE <45 years of age, they should not be given.
- COC should not be given to women with **migraines with auras**.
- Some **anti-epileptics** interfere with the bioavailability of hormone contraceptives. Always check for interactions.
- If there is a risk for genital tract **malignancy** (e.g. abnormal smear results, undiagnosed vaginal bleeding), contraceptives should be avoided until it has been investigated.
- In patients with **breast cancer**, the copper coil is the only safe form of contraception, with the exception of barrier methods. COC should also be avoided in patients with a known gene mutation for breast cancer.

Table 16.1 Contraceptive choices, their pros and cons

	Description	Pros	Cons	Failure rate
Barrier methods – condoms (male/female)	Prevent sperm from entering the vagina. A male condom is placed on the penis and the female condom is inserted into the vagina.	They help prevent the transmission of STIs. Generally not associated with side-effects. Reliable method of contraception.	Some couples find them uncomfortable. Some people have allergies to latex, plastic or spermicide.	<2% if used correctly\n\n22% with actual use
Combined oral contraceptive pill (COCP)	A tablet that is taken daily, containing oestrogen and progesterone. Prevents ovulation, thickens mucus and thins the endometrium.	Periods are lighter and less painful. Alleviates acne, reduces the risk of ovarian, endometrial and colon cancer.	Can cause headaches, nausea, breast tenderness and mood swings. It can increase your blood pressure. Provides no protection against STIs.	<1% if used correctly\n\n8% with typical use
Progesterone-only pill (POP)	A tablet that contains progesterone that is taken at the same time every day. It thickens cervical mucus and can also stop ovulation.	It can be used in patients who are unable to take oestrogen. It can reduce the incidence of painful periods and occasionally stops periods altogether. It can be used in breast-feeding women.	Patients may not get regular periods and may have spotting. It does not protect against STIs.	<1% if used correctly\n\n13% with typical use

Depo-Provera	An injection containing progesterone that thickens the mucus in the cervix, thins the lining of the womb and may prevent ovulation. Given every 3 months.	Injections last for up to 12 weeks. It is a good option if patients are unable to take oestrogen-containing contraception. No daily pill. May reduce the heaviness of periods and premenstrual syndrome (PMS).	Periods may become irregular or cease. Side-effects include headaches, acne, breast tenderness and weight gain. Can cause osteoporosis.	<1%
Implanon	A small flexible tube containing progesterone that is inserted under the skin in the upper arm. Thickens cervical mucus and thins the endometrium.	Works for three years and is a good option if patient cannot take oestrogen. Fertility returns to normal once removed. Can reduce heavy periods.	Side-effects include headache, acne, nausea, breast tenderness and mood change. 20% of women have no bleeding and 50% have infrequent periods.	<1%
Sterilization	Performed in men or women under general or local anaesthetic. Disrupts the path of the egg or sperm to prevent fertilization.	Rarely has long-term effects on sexual health. The vasectomy is simpler and more reliable than female sterilization.	Does not protect against STIs. Very difficult to reverse. Small amount of surgical risks. Post-operative pain.	<1% (males) 5% (females)
Levonorgestrel-releasing IUS	A small T-shaped plastic device that is inserted in the neck of the uterus (cervix). It releases progesterone into the womb, thickening the mucus and thinning the lining. In some women, it may stop ovulation.	It is one of the most effective contraceptive devices. There is no need to worry about taking pills. It works for five years (Mirena) and when removed, fertility returns to normal. Periods may be shorter, lighter or stop. It is also good for patients who can't take oestrogen.	Some women can experience headaches, acne or breast tenderness. Irregular bleeding/spotting is common for 6 months. No protection against STIs.	<1%
Copper-bearing IUD	A small T-shaped device made of plastic and copper that is inserted into the neck of the womb (cervix). It works by causing a toxic environment for the sperm, preventing fertilization and implantation.	Contraception for up to 10 years without worrying about daily pills. Fertility returns to normal once it is removed.	Periods may be heavy, longer and more painful. No protection against STIs. Untreated STIs can lead to PID.	<1%

16.2.6 **Emergency contraception**

Emergency contraception (see *Table 16.2*) should be considered following sexual intercourse when contraception has failed, been used incorrectly or in cases of sexual assault. Before prescribing emergency contraception, the doctor should conduct a pre-counselling history which includes:

- The time elapsed since unprotected intercourse and the type of contraception that was used at the time.
- Discuss current contraception method. Education should be provided and long-term contraception should be prescribed if they are not using any.
- Menstrual history including:
  - ○ Date of last menstrual period
  - ○ Was the last period normal?
  - ○ Ask about cycle length to determine if ovulation is likely to have taken place and whether fertilization may have occurred.
- Has there been any other unprotected intercourse this cycle? This is a contraindication to giving emergency contraception.
- Have they previously used emergency contraception?
- Obstetrical, gynaecological and sexual history to determine if there is risk of PID, current vaginal discharge or history of ectopic disease. These are contraindications to the insertion of an IUD.
- Ask about previous medical conditions, looking for contraindications such as liver disease and porphyria.
- Enquire into medication history for enzyme-inducing agents (e.g. phenytoin and St. John's wort) as these may make the contraception ineffective.

Table 16.2 Emergency contraception

	Description	Timing	Side-effects	Failure rate
Levonorgestrel (progesterone-only)	If it is used in the early part of the cycle, it inhibits ovulation. It's unclear how it works later in the cycle.	Should be used within 72 hours of unprotected sex.	Nausea, vomiting, menstrual irregularity, dizziness, breast tenderness	Effective in 95% (first 24 hours), 85% (24–48 hours) and 58% (up to 72 hours)
Ulipristal acetate (selective progesterone receptor modulator)	Inhibits or delays ovulation. In the mid-follicular phase, suppresses the further development of follicles.	One tablet of ellaOne is licensed for up to 120 hours after unprotected sex.	Vomiting, nausea, dizziness, menstrual irregularities, abdominal pain, back pain, headache, mood disorders	Failure rate 0.9–1.8%
Copper IUD	Copper is toxic to both the ovum and sperm, inhibiting both fertilization and implantation. It also has an inflammatory effect on the endometrium.	Can be used for up to 120 hours following sexual intercourse.	Pain of insertion, heavy or painful menstrual period.	Failure rate <1%

16.3 **Practice scenarios**

1. Branka Marshall has presented for her first obstetrical appointment. This is her third pregnancy. Take a thorough obstetrical history.

2. Elizabeth McDonald is a 24-year-old medical student who has just returned from her medical elective in the USA. Whilst completing her elective she had three sexual contacts. Take a thorough sexual history.

3. Jennifer Chloe is a 20-year-old hockey player. She has come to the office as she has not had a menstrual period in over 8 months. Prior to this her menses were irregular. Take a menstrual history.

4. Alice Byron is a 30-year-old lady who is 30 weeks pregnant. She has been started on labetolol for pre-eclampsia. She is happy to take this if it is necessary for her baby, but she feels very well and is unsure exactly what the condition is. You have been asked to explain what pre-eclampsia is to her, and to explain why taking anti-hypertensives is important.

5. Chioma Uwak is a 22-year-old university student who has presented with vaginal discharge. She has had unprotected sex three times in the last 6 months. You suspect that she may have chlamydia and prescribe azithromycin and intramuscular (IM) ceftriaxone, both as a single dose. Explain the management plan, other investigations that might be needed and the importance of barrier use in the future.

6. Elspeth Frashton is a 40-year-old lady who is pregnant with her fourth child. Her last delivery was a Caesarean section due to placenta praevia. The placenta is high in this pregnancy. She has been advised that she may choose whether to have a vaginal delivery or opt for Caesarean section again. Please discuss risks to her and her baby, of vaginal birth after Caesarean versus risks of repeat Caesarean.

7. Georgia Haywood is a 19-year-old lady who is pregnant with her first child. A blood test has shown that her baby is high risk for Down syndrome. She has been offered amniocentesis. Please briefly explain what the test involves and any major complications. You have also been asked to explain what Down syndrome is, what may have caused it, and how it affects the baby.

8. Jessica Anderson has come to the office today to discuss various contraception options. *To mix up the scenarios, use the UKMEC Standards to determine the best form of contraception.*
   A. She is a 17-year-old with epilepsy and is currently taking phenytoin.
   B. She is a 36-year-old landscape gardener, who is a smoker and has completed her family.
   C. She delivered a healthy baby boy 7 weeks ago and is currently breast-feeding.
   D. She had unprotected sex 36 hours ago and would like emergency contraception.

17

Dermatology

SABRINA AHMED

Dermatology: Keys to Success

Dermatological conditions affect up to 30% of the population at any given time and can be a sensitive topic for many patients. The very physical nature of the disease can often have poor psychological impact on a patient, and hence a sensitive approach to the dermatological consultation is fundamental. Chronic skin disease can lead to physical and emotional scarring, and can result in social isolation or occupational struggles.

Remember the use of ICE here. Eliciting a patient's ideas, concerns and expectations can often provide more information than you can obtain from a generic history taking, and will demonstrate how skin disease impacts on a person's quality of life.

Many dermatological conditions are chronic conditions; however, a few can be life-threatening.

Look out for the red flag symptoms that appear in this chapter, and the skin conditions they may appear in. As skin disease appears as a more visual clinical presentation, good information gathering of the condition with a concise and detailed history taking will provide a helpful foundation to the clinical examination, in making a timely and accurate diagnosis.

Red flags in dermatology:
- Hives/respiratory compromise
- Pain
- Discharge
- Blistering
- Change in appearance of existing lesion
- Systemic symptoms

17.1 Information gathering

1) Introduce yourself and your role on the healthcare team

2) Ensure consent and confidentiality

3) Confirm the patient's name and DOB

4) History of presenting complaint

OSCE TIP: Occupation is a vital part of the dermatological history, as it can provide clues towards the diagnosis. Contact dermatitis often presents following use of chemicals or products at work.

'What has brought you in today?'

Start with an open question, giving your patient time to explain what is troubling them. Allow the patient to describe the nature of the problem, the onset of its presentation and the duration of time it has been occurring. They could be describing a lesion that has appeared, or a change in an existing lesion. They may describe any of the symptoms described in *Sections 17.1.1–17.1.5.*

17.1.1 Skin lesions / rash

Ask your patient how many lesions they've noticed, when they first came on and what they look like.

- What is the distribution of the lesions across the body?
- Are the flexor surfaces mainly affected (e.g. eczema) or extensor surfaces (e.g. psoriasis)?
- Is the rash confined to the trunk (e.g. pityriasis versicolor) or to the peripheries (e.g. lichen planus)?
- Take note if your patient mentions any of the following **ABCDE** features when describing their lesion:
  - **Asymmetrical** – *'What shape is the lesion?'*
  - **Border irregularities / Bleeding or itching lesion** – *'Would you describe it as a well-defined lesion? Have you noticed it bleeding or itching?'*
  - **Colour change / irregularity** – *'Has it changed colour recently? Does it seem to be more than one colour?'*
  - **Diameter >6 mm** – *'How large is the lesion?'*
  - **Evolution**, i.e. change in general appearance – *'Has there been any change in the appearance of the lesion?'*

> **Key Knowledge:**
> Pigmented lesions which have changed over time could be indicative of **malignant melanoma**.

17.1.2 Itching

For any lesions that may be present, ask if there is any associated itching. Some conditions are known to be itchy, whereas others don't present with this symptom.

- *'Are there any specific areas where it is itchy?'*
  - Contact dermatitis resulting from certain washing detergents or clothing may present with an itchy localized rash.
- *'Have you noticed any thickening of the skin over areas you have been itching?'*
  - Known as lichenification, this can occur with excessive excoriation of the skin.

17.1.3 Tenderness

- *'Is the area painful? At rest or only when it is touched?'*
- *'How bad is the pain?'*
  - Tenderness is a common presentation in many dermatological conditions; allow your patient to describe the nature of the pain in relation to the skin disease. If possible, ask them to rate the pain on a scale of 1–10.

17.1.4 Swelling

- *'Have you noticed any swelling of the skin?'*
  - Pain in association with swelling, erythema and warmth is a classic sign of cellulitis (infection of the deep subcutaneous layer of the skin) or erysipelas (infection of the superficial dermis layers).

- ○ Remember for inflammatory conditions: calor, dolor, rubor and tumor. Swelling in acute situations involving the superficial dermis (urticaria) and dermis, tongue or lips (angioedema) is an emergency, as it could result in anaphylaxis. Needless to say, in this instance you would have abandoned history taking and are hopefully commencing a management plan!

> **Key Knowledge:**
> Swollen itchy wheals and swelling of the tongue or face are indicators for allergic reactions and can result in anaphylactic shock; be sure to manage early.

17.1.5 Bleeding

Suspicious malignant lesions often spontaneously bleed and this is a red flag for possible melanoma.

- 'Have you noticed any spontaneous bleeding from the site?'
  - ○ Auspitz sign (see *Section 17.2.4*) is a classic sign of psoriasis.
- 'When you itch, does it bleed?'
  - ○ Purpuric lesions indicate bleeding into the skin or mucous membranes, such as in vasculitic disease. They can be pinpoint areas (petechiae) or larger bruise-like regions (ecchymoses).

17.1.6 Exacerbating / alleviating factors

- 'Does anything make the condition worse?'
  - ○ Patients may recognize certain factors as making their skin disease worse. These include alcohol, smoking or pet fur. Inflammatory conditions are commonly associated with these exacerbating factors.
- 'Have you noticed that it is worse at work than at home?'
  - ○ Occupational triggers such as dust or stress can sometimes exacerbate skin conditions (e.g. in eczema and psoriasis). Exposure to the sun may make some skin conditions worse or more prevalent (e.g. pityriasis versicolor).
- 'Does anything improve the skin condition?'
  - ○ Occasionally patients may report their skin condition improves after returning from a holiday in a warmer climate. Ultraviolet (UV) radiation has been known to improve the condition of psoriasis.

> **Key Knowledge:**
> Excessive UV exposure can lead to **basal cell carcinoma**, **squamous cell carcinoma** and **malignant melanoma**.

17.1.7 Skin type / tanning history

- 'When you go in the sun, how does your skin usually react? Do you burn easily? Do you tan easily?'
- 'How often do you use sunbeds?'
- 'How often do you apply sunscreen? What factor SPF do you use?' 'Do you use tanning oils?'
  - ○ Eliciting your patient's skin type and tanning history can give you important indicators to their risk of developing UV exposure-related skin cancers. The Fitzpatrick classification of skin types (see *Section 17.2.1*) categorizes skin types in relation to their reaction in the sun, and thus allows you to identify vulnerable patients.

17.1.8 Previous treatments and efficacy

- 'Have you tried any treatment for it? How has this worked for you?'

○ Some of your patients will not be presenting with a new onset condition, but due to management of their chronic condition, for which they may have already tried previously unsuccessful treatments.

○ Show empathy towards your patient if they feel disheartened by previously ineffective treatments. Now is a good time to ask about possible adverse side-effects to certain treatments that have been tried.

○ See *Section 17.2.5* for advice to give patients about topical steroid application and the 'fingertip unit'.

5) Systems review

Obtain as much information as you can gather from the above history taking. A nice way to wrap up the consultation is to explore other systems to learn about any symptoms that may have been missed previously. It is helpful to warn your patient that you are going to do this. *'Thank you for what you have told me so far. I am now going to run through some questions about your health in general.'*

Please refer to *Chapter 6* for more details.

General: *'How have you felt in yourself lately? Have you been fit and well? Any recent fever, chills or weight change?'* Systemic bacterial infections with malaise and pyrexia can result in exacerbations of dermatological conditions.

Common dermatological manifestations – mouth, nails, joints, scalp and hair: these areas are important to mention specifically to your patient as they are the common sites for spread of skin diseases. Lichen planus can cause white streaks in the mouth called Wickham's striae, and ulceration to the mouth and genitals arises in Behçet's syndrome. Psoriasis can cause arthritis and nail changes.

Neurological: *'Have you noticed any changes in your vision, migraines, weakness in your body? Have you had any difficulties with balance and coordination?'* Conditions such as neurofibromatosis can result in neurological signs with skin manifestations of benign growths over the body and café-au-lait spots.

Psychological: *'How have you been dealing with this recently?' 'Have you noticed any change in your mood?'* Dermatological disease can often impact patients psychologically and lead to anxiety and depression. Explore their quality of life and offer help in the form of support groups or counselling if required. Conditions can arise from a background of psychological illness, such as dermatitis artefacta, whereby lesions are self-inflicted.

6) ICE

Given the physically debilitating nature of dermatological disease, the psychological impact on a patient can be overwhelming. Explore their ideas, concerns and the expectations they have of what you can provide them or what they would like from the consultation.

- *'Do you have any ideas about what might be causing your skin to react in this way?'*
- *'Are there any specific concerns that I can address for you, or anything you are worried about?'*
- *'Is there anything in particular you were expecting from today's consultation that I can help you with?'*

7) Past medical history

Skin manifestation of other medical conditions is common, so obtaining a thorough past medical history can give you vital clues towards reaching a diagnosis. *'Do you suffer with hayfever or asthma?'* History of atopic disease increases the prevalence of conditions such as atopic eczema.

- *'Do you have any chronic condition of the joints?'*
  - Conditions such as psoriasis can be associated with polyarthritis.
- *'Have you had any previous skin cancers excised?'*
  - A history of skin cancer or suspicious-looking lesions is an obvious risk factor for further skin cancers.
- *'Any chronic lung or bowel conditions, or diabetes?'*
  - Conditions such as erythema nodosum have an association with sarcoidosis and IBD. Diabetes may point towards necrobiosis lipoidica or ulcerations.

8) Family history

- *'Does anyone in your family suffer with a similar sort of thing?'*
  - Obtaining a family history can help to identify genetic dermatological conditions such as neurofibromatosis, and conditions which carry a genetic component e.g. psoriasis.
- *'Does anyone in your household currently have the same symptoms?'*
  - This suggests a contagious or environmental aspect to the condition (e.g. scabies).

9) Medication history

- *'Are you taking any regular medications? Any over-the-counter medications? Are you on the oral contraceptive pill?'*
  - Certain medications can predispose to dermatological disease; for example, sulphonamides, sulphonylureas, penicillin, allopurinol, and captopril have all been known to cause erythroderma (an exfoliative dermatitis).
  - The oral contraceptive pill can cause erythema nodosum.
- *'Are you allergic to any medication? Any other allergies?'*
  - As previously mentioned, urticaria, angioedema and anaphylaxis can occur as a result of allergic reactions to certain medications (NSAIDs, antibiotics, morphine, etc.) and from food allergens such as nuts, shellfish and dairy products.
  - Certain washing products and nickel can cause contact dermatitis.

10) Social history

Exploring your patient's social history can detect contributory factors towards disease and also allow you to address management plans tailored to your patient's specific needs.

Occupation / hobbies: as previously mentioned, a patient's occupation can provide clues towards diagnosing a dermatological condition. Hobbies such as gardening can indicate contact dermatitis caused by nettles or poison ivy.

Recent travel: travel to a warmer climate can alleviate psoriasis, or alternatively can cause the skin to tan and make pityriasis versicolor / alba lesions appear more apparent. Travel to exotic locations may point you towards more tropical diseases.

Smoking and alcohol

Stress: stress has been known to exacerbate some skin conditions. Recent life events or stressful jobs may not be topics your patient thinks are relevant to their skin condition, so take the time to ask *'Have you been under any stress lately?'*

11) Closing the consultation

- Always use your basic communication skills according to the Calgary–Cambridge Model. Remember to summarize and be sure to screen in order to ensure that the patient has had the opportunity to express anything else they feel is relevant.
- What will follow on from the history taking is usually an examination of your patient, so now is a good time to do a brief run-through of what information has been gathered

and what the next steps are. Your brief summary should be no longer than a couple of sentences, and should only include relevant positive findings from the history taking.

- Don't forget to thank your patient!

> **Summary of key points (GET YOUR MARKS):**
>
> **Establish rapport** (clear introduction of who you are, what your role is and why you are there).
>
> **Presenting complaint:** establish the nature, onset and duration of the presenting symptom.
>
> **History of presenting complaint:** explore the nature of the problem – rash/lesion evolution, associated symptoms, alleviating and exacerbating factors, skin type and tanning history.
>
> **Systems review:** ask specifically about any mouth, nail, joint, scalp and hair involvement with their condition.
>
> **ICE:** explore your patient's ideas, concerns and expectations from the consultation.
>
> **Past medical history:** identify common conditions associated with dermatological disease, and history of skin malignancy.
>
> **Family history:** establish genetic predisposition to skin conditions in the family, and identify any family members currently exhibiting the same symptoms for contagious disease.
>
> **Medication history:** any regular medications, OTC preparations and oral contraceptive pills.
>
> **Social history:** identify stressors, smoking and alcohol history, as well as recent travel and hobbies.
>
> **Summarize and close the consultation:** let the Calgary–Cambridge Model be your guide. Remember your key skills of summarizing and screening. Always leave the patient with a plan of care, even if it is that you need to speak with your colleagues. Thank the patient.

17.2 Information giving and shared decision making

This section focuses on information giving on common dermatological presentations and health education, and allows for your patient to better understand their condition. By highlighting the nature, causes and management for common conditions your patients might present with, you can share this information in a clear and concise way. This results in a shared decision making process for patient management, and gives your patient an opportunity to ask questions. Using ICE (addressed earlier in your information gathering) will help you to pre-empt possible avenues your patient may want to explore for their management.

> **OSCE TIP:** Consider the use of models and diagrams to aid your information giving process. Remember to avoid medical jargon where possible.

17.2.1 Sun exposure

Giving advice on sun exposure is crucial! Prevention of excessive exposure to UV radiation is the leading way to reduce risk of skin cancer. Identify your patient's Fitzpatrick skin type by using *Fig. 17.1* and asking them to categorize themselves.

Type I	Type II	Type III	Type IV	Type V	Type VI
Light, pale white	White, fair	Medium white to olive	Olive to light brown	Brown to dark brown	Dark brown, black
Always burns, never tans	Usually burns, hardly tans	Mildly burns, slow tanning	Rarely burns, fast tanning	Very rarely burns, tans fast and easily	Never burns, easily tans to deep pigment

Figure 17.1 *The Fitzpatrick scale.*

Skin types that easily burn when exposed to the sun, such as types I and II, are at the highest risk of developing skin cancer. Once your patient's skin has been categorized into a Fitzpatrick type, you can give beneficial health promotion advice on how to keep safe in the sun. Use SOLAR to remember handy information to give to your patients.

> Mnemonic: **SOLAR**
> **S**tay in the shade from 11am to 3pm
> **O**utfit: protect yourself with sunglasses, a T-shirt and hat
> **L**ittle children have delicate skin; take extra precautions
> **A**void getting sunburn
> **R**emember to wear sunscreen, at least factor SPF30+, to protect against UVA/UVB

17.2.2 Atopic eczema

What is it? The most common type of eczema, it usually presents in infants (on the extensor surfaces; see *Fig. 17.2*) and can continue into later childhood and adulthood (on the flexor surfaces). It is characterized by inflamed, red, itchy patches, which can become weepy and blistered in a flare-up.

What causes it? A breakdown in the skin's protective barrier properties and a family history of allergic tendencies (atopy) with conditions such as eczema, asthma and allergic rhinitis (hayfever) is usually an indicator for eczema. Common culprits for exacerbations are pet fur, household dust, certain foods, heat and stressful situations.

How is it best managed? Prevention is better than cure – avoiding exacerbating factors will help to reduce acute flare-ups. Itching can lead to roughening of the skin, which can be managed with emollient creams and cream soap substitutes. Anti-allergy medication can provide relief from the itching, and in severe acute cases, a topical steroid cream may be indicated.

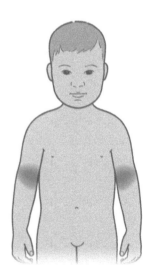

Figure 17.2 *Atopic eczema on extensor surfaces in infants.*

Don't forget to mention the fingertip unit (see Section 17.2.5) when showing your patients how to apply topical steroids!

17.2.3 **Psoriasis**

What is it? Psoriasis is an inflammatory condition of the skin, characterized by red scaly patches. There are many types of psoriasis, but the most common type is plaque psoriasis, commonly affecting the elbows, back of the forearms, scalp and behind the ears (see *Fig. 17.3*). The plaques are typically silver/pink in colour and present as dry patches. Scalp psoriasis can appear as severe dandruff, and disease can spread to affect the nails (50% of cases) and joints (in 5–10% of cases).

Remember your systemic review in patients with psoriasis to identify all affected areas.

What causes it? It is unclear what causes psoriasis, but genetics does play a part, as around 30% of those affected also have a close relative with psoriasis. Environmental triggers include trauma, stress, smoking and alcohol. Some patients often describe acute flare-ups following infection or with the use of certain medications, e.g. beta blockers, angiotensin-converting enzyme inhibitors and non-steroidal anti-inflammatory painkillers.

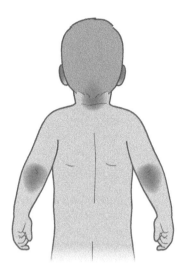

Figure 17.3 *Psoriasis on extensor aspects of the body.*

> **Key Knowledge:**
> Auspitz sign is when the removal of psoriatic plaques leads to pinpoint areas of bleeding.

How is it best managed? Many patients have noted an improvement in their psoriasis when exposed to the sun. Emollient creams reduce skin dryness and vitamin D-based creams (sometimes in combination with steroids) also have desirable benefits. Coal tar preparations have been used for some years; however, they can have an unpleasant smell and stain clothing and hence do not appeal to most patients. As always, prevention is best, so avoid triggers which may exacerbate your condition.

17.2.4 **Acne vulgaris**

What is it? An inflammatory condition of the hair follicles and glands which are found primarily in the face and torso. Inflammation can lead to solid raised lesions and/or pus-containing lesions.

What causes it? Typical onset for acne vulgaris is during puberty, when increased amounts of the sex hormone androgen promote the production of sebum which fills and blocks the pores. These plugged pores can be open (blackheads) or closed (whiteheads). In addition to the hormonal changes of puberty, other triggers include certain medications (e.g. corticosteroids, androgens), certain foods (e.g. carbohydrates and dairy products) and stress.

How is it best managed? The patients most often affected are teenagers, and it can be a psychologically sensitive topic, so approach with sympathy and reassurance. Topical creams with antibiotics (to reduce infected areas) and anti-inflammatory properties are effective. Treatments need to be persevered with for a minimum of 6 weeks to reach desired effect. More severe acne can be managed with oral medications (such as antibiotics and retinoids).

17.2.5 Topical steroids – 'the fingertip unit'

Why use topical steroids? Topical steroids are lotions, ointments or creams that are applied directly onto the skin and contain anti-inflammatory properties. They work by reducing inflammation in the skin and are used effectively in a variety of dermatological conditions. They come in different strengths, often defined as a percentage. As this is a specialist treatment, and not like a regular topical cream, the amount applied to the skin is important. The standard used is known as the fingertip unit (FTU; see *Fig. 17.4*).

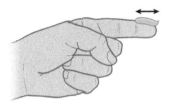

One FTU is the amount of cream squeezed out from the tube to cover an adult's fingertip (defined as the tip of the finger to the first crease). One FTU is enough product to treat an area of skin twice the size of an adult's flat hand surface; 1 g of topical steroid equates to approximately 2 FTUs.

This method can be used to prescribe an adequate amount of topical steroid to cover the targeted area, and can be used to give patients information on how much cream to apply.

Figure 17.4 *A fingertip unit.*

17.3 Practice scenarios

1. Eddo Mpofo is a 22-year-old male who has presented to your clinic today with itchy, erythematous rashes in the anterior surfaces of his forearms and the backs of his knees. He has recently noticed they have become worse since his roommate got a cat. Itching is causing excoriations on his skin and he has a history of asthma. Give Eddo information on his condition and arrange an appropriate management plan.

2. Sandra Quentin is a 45-year-old lady with a history of basal cell carcinoma. She has presented to your clinic today for a follow-up appointment and all looks well. She is planning a holiday to Greece in the summer and would like advice on how to prevent further UV damage to her skin. She is classified as Fitzpatrick skin type I. Summarize for her what this indicates and how best she can protect herself from excessive sun exposure.

3. Philippa Olsen is a 35-year-old female who has presented to your clinic with silvery-pink plaques covering her elbows and forearms. She complains of itching in her scalp and has pitting in her nails. Recently she has been experiencing pains in her knees. She is concerned she may have psoriasis. Explain this condition to her and possible therapies which would have benefit.

4. Mary Kite is a 52-year-old female who recently discovered a lesion on her face which appears to have grown in size and colour over the last few months. She has noticed the middle of the lesion darkening and occasionally it will bleed. It is not causing her any pain, but she is concerned as to what it might be. She has a history of sunbed use. Discuss with Mary her options for management of this condition, and some health promotion tactics to address this in the future.

5. Daniel Smith is an 18-year-old man who has presented to your clinic today having completed a two-week course of topical antibiotics and steroids as treatment for his acne vulgaris. His has noticed more pustules and papules appearing over the last week and doesn't think the previous ones have cleared up with the current therapy. He is concerned that the treatment is not working and would like to step up his regime to oral medications. He is finding it hard to concentrate in school. Speak to Daniel to address his concerns and arrange an appropriate management plan.

18

Endocrinology

RYAN LOVE AND TOM SYER

Endocrinology: Keys to Success

The endocrine system comprises many organs and physiological pathways. The key to truly understanding the endocrine system is the knowledge of other body systems and functions – endocrine pathologies manifest themselves in a variety of ways, often non-specific or vague.

The commonest presenting complaints with potential underlying endocrine causes are:

- Fatigue
- Palpitations
- Puberty issues
- Neck swelling
- Visual disturbance
- Weight changes
- Menstrual disturbance
- Libido and fertility issues
- Changing appearance
- Excessive thirst.

Red flags in endocrinology:

- Excessive, unexpected weight loss
- Syncope
- Confusion or delirium
- Steroid use
- Malignant hypertension
- Visual disturbance
- Decreased level of consciousness
- Sweet smelling breath

18.1 Information gathering

1) Introduce yourself and your role on the healthcare team

2) Ensure consent and confidentiality

3) Confirm the patient's name and DOB; ask about occupation

It is sometimes helpful to ask the patient about their occupation early in the consultation. Asking about what the patient does for work along with a follow-up question such as *'What does that involve?'* or *'Do you enjoy your job?'* can establish rapport early and may provide some context later in the consultation when you are asking about limitations.

4) History of presenting complaint

'What has brought you into the clinic / office / A&E today?'

Allow for the Golden Minute.

This section is presented according to the various axes and key hormones that comprise the endocrine system (a hormonal axis describes the interaction between endocrine glands, their hormones and the corresponding feedback mechanisms). Rather than an exhaustive run-through of the multitude of possible presenting complaints and their potential differential diagnoses, this section outlines key presenting complaints and provides possible questions you may wish to consider for further exploration. With any endocrine complaint, you must explore for possible symptoms in other glands, as many hormonal deficiencies are interlinked.

18.1.1 Pituitary gland

Problems affecting the pituitary gland may cause excessive or inadequate secretion of pituitary hormones, disrupting the normal homeostatic cycles.

The pituitary gland is located beneath the optic chiasm and can be damaged by a mass (benign adenomas are most common) or space-occupying lesion (SOL) such as a craniopharyngioma. A pituitary mass may lead to the characteristic bitemporal hemianopia, whereas a SOL is more likely to cause III, IV or VI nerve palsy. These may be elicited on examination. Other symptoms that may lead you to suspect SOL may be **nausea and vomiting**, **morning headaches** or **diplopia**. These symptoms may be suggestive of **raised intracranial pressure**.

- *'Have you noticed any changes in your vision?'* – particularly diplopia which is caused by oculomotor nerve compression
- *'Have you experienced any headaches recently?'*

The pituitary gland may also be damaged by radiation, brain injury or haemorrhage (known as pituitary apoplexy). Sheehan syndrome describes ischaemia of the pituitary due to infarction post-partum and may present with subsequent failure to **lactate** or **menstruate**.

See *Chapter 8* for further information about taking a headache history.

18.1.2 Thyroid gland

Hypo- and hyperthyroidism have many opposing symptoms (see *Table 18.1*) and during a consultation you may only suspect one or the other, hence your questions may be more directed and specific to that particular diagnosis, compared to those outlined below.

Table 18.1 Symptoms of hypo- and hyperthyroidism

Hypothyroidism	Hyperthyroidism
Fatigue	Irritability
Weight gain	Weight loss
Anorexia	Increased appetite
Cold intolerance	Heat intolerance
Menorrhagia	Oligo-/amenorrhoea
Constipation	Diarrhoea
Dry skin	Tremor
Hoarseness	Palpitations
Dry thin skin/alopecia	Pruritis
Myalgia	Ophthalmopathy
Depression	Anxiety/psychosis

- *'Have you noticed any unintentional weight change?'*
- *'Have you had a change in your appetite?'*

Often a patient will experience weight gain with hypothyroidism and weight loss with hyperthyroidism; however, an increased appetite, common in hyperthyroidism, can also lead to weight gain.

- *'Have you been more uncomfortable or sensitive in hot or cold environments?'*
- *'Have you suffered from night sweats?'*
- *'How have your energy levels been recently?'*

Malaise can be a symptom of either thyroid level dysfunction but is more prominent with hypothyroidism. Hyperthyroidism, however, can also present with irritability and restlessness which could manifest as higher than normal energy levels.

- *'Have you noticed any change in your skin or hair?'*
- *'Has there been a change in how often or how heavy your periods are?'*

If a patient has a goitre it is important to take a history of iodine intake (ingestion of kelp or seaweed, iodinated salt and country of origin), medications, family history of thyroid disease (both benign and malignant) and a history of irradiation to the head and neck. It is important to ask about symptoms of obstruction including dyspnoea, cough or stridor.

18.1.3 Parathyroid gland

The main role of the parathyroid hormones is to control calcium metabolism, and problems manifest as either hypo- or hypercalcaemia. More often than not patients are asymptomatic and an abnormal calcium is noted on routine bloods; however, they can present with chronic symptoms.

Hypercalcaemia

An easy way to remember the symptoms of elevated calcium is *"renal **stones**, painful **bones**, abdominal **groans**, and psychiatric **moans**"*.

- *'How have your energy levels been recently?'*
- *'Have you needed to pass water/urinate more often? Have you noticed any blood in your urine? Have you had any abdominal pain?'*
  - Abdominal pain can be caused by constipation or renal stones.
- *'Have you felt particularly achy or sore? Have you felt weaker than normal?'*
  - Painful bones are the result of abnormal bone remodelling. Proximal muscle weakness is sometimes seen with high levels of calcium.
- *'Have you had any difficulty concentrating? How has your mood been lately?'*

Hypocalcaemia

Hypocalcaemia most commonly presents with neuromuscular instability which manifests clinically as peri-oral numbness, numbness of the hands and feel, muscle cramps and seizures. Patients may also present with symptoms that are less specific, including fatigue, irritability, anxiety and depression.

- *'Have you had any numbness or tingling in your hands or feet?'*
- *'Have you suffered from any muscle cramps or aches?'*
- *'Have you been feeling more tired recently?'*
- *'How has your mood been? Have you felt more irritable recently?'*

18.1.4 Adrenal gland

There are multiple hormones controlled via the adrenal gland: glucocorticoids, mineralocorticoids, androgens and catecholamines. Diseases affecting this axis can therefore present with symptoms of just one hormonal abnormality or a combination, so exploring each in the history can be helpful.

- *'Have you noticed any unintentional weight change?'*
- *'Have you felt more dizzy recently? Have you had any fainting episodes?'*
  - Syncope secondary to postural hypotension is a common feature of hypoadrenalism.
- *'Have you noticed any changes to your skin?'*
  - Hyperpigmentation of sun-exposed areas, palmar creases and scars are common signs of primary hypoadrenalism (see *Table 18.2*). In Cushing's, thin skin, bruising and purple or red striae on the abdomen are indicative features.
- *'Are you feeling more tired or weak compared to usual?'*
- *'Has there been a change in how often or how heavy your periods are?'*
- *'How has your mood been recently?'*
  - Abnormally high and low glucocorticoids frequently lower mood and cause depression, although more rarely anxiety or even psychosis can present in Cushing's syndrome. Intermittent anxiety and panic attacks are also a feature of phaeochromocytoma.

Table 18.2 Features of hypoadrenalism

Glucocorticoids	Mineralocorticoids	Adrenal androgens
Weight loss	Postural hypotension	Decreased body hair
Anorexia	*Hyponatraemia* – nausea, vomiting, headache, confusion, irritability, muscle weakness and seizures	Loss of libido
Fatigue and weakness	*Hyperkalaemia* – nausea, vomiting, fatigue, numbness/tingling, chest pain, palpitations	
Hyperpigmentation		
Vomiting		
Diarrhoea or constipation		

18.1.5 Growth hormone (GH)

> **OSCE TIP**: A history of increasing foot or ring size in an adult may be suggestive of acromegaly.
> Asking to see old photos of the patient for comparison may assist you.

Excess secretion of GH may cause acromegaly in adults or gigantism in children. Conversely, under-secretion may lead to short stature in children. Acromegaly generally has an insidious onset, developing over many years; therefore patients may not notice a change in their appearance.

- *'Have you or has anyone else noticed a change in your appearance? Have you noticed that your hats or gloves do not fit as well?'*
- *'Do you suffer from headaches? Have you had any double vision?'*
  - In patients with large tumours there may be compressive symptoms such as headaches and cranial nerve palsies.

Associated symptoms of lethargy, sweating, and mood changes may also narrow your index of suspicion. A thorough systems review is also necessary due to visceral enlargement. A higher associated risk of colon cancer with acromegaly should always prompt screening questions.

- *'Have you had any weight loss recently?'*
- *'Have you had any changes in your bowel movements?'*
- *'Have you noticed any blood in your stool?'*

18.1.6 Sex hormones – follicle-stimulating hormone (FSH) and luteinizing hormone (LH)

Symptoms related to the sex hormones may present in a multitude of ways, and at various ages. A patient presenting with amenorrhoea, loss of libido or pubertal delay may have a problem with their hypothalamic–gonadotropin-releasing hormone axis, which may be primary, secondary or tertiary in nature.

- 'Have you experienced any changes or irregularities with your menstrual cycle?'
- 'Have you ever had difficulty conceiving a baby?'

> Mnemonic: **in menopause, think DASH**
> **D**yspareunia
> **A**trophic vagina
> **S**leep disturbance
> **H**ot flushes

When consulting a patient about abnormal menstruation, ask them to outline their 'normal' cycle for comparison. For patients presenting with amenorrhoea, it is difficult to rule out the possibility of pregnancy by discussion alone; this may be a sensitive issue and enquiries should be phrased in a considerate fashion.

- 'Are your symptoms interfering with your normal sex life?'

In women, dyspareunia and heat intolerance may be indicative of the menopause, which may be distressing for the patient. Patients may describe symptoms consistent with vaginal atrophy, such as itch or dryness.

It is important to note that patients may use euphemisms to refer to symptoms they perceive to be embarrassing; they might refer to their "waterworks" or "down there". Whilst rapport can be developed by adopting the use of a patient's own terminology, you must remember to confirm exactly what they mean, because this may save further confusion or embarrassment.

- 'When you say you have pain "down there" does that you mean that you are experiencing pain during sex?'

For information on how to take a full obstetrical and gynaecological history, please see *Chapter 16*.

18.1.7 Anti-diuretic hormone (ADH)

An affirmative answer to the following questions may indicate polydipsia due to diabetes insipidus (DI). Polydipsia is also a common presenting symptom in undiagnosed Type 1 diabetes mellitus (DM).

- 'Have you found yourself to be excessively thirsty?' (polydipsia)
- 'Have you been urinating more frequently?' (polyuria)

Polyuria may be due to cystitis, DM or DI. To understand more about change in urinary frequency, ask the patient to define what is normal for them first.

18.1.8 Prolactin

Prolactin stimulates milk production as well as suppressing gonadotrophs, so common complaints are galactorrhoea which can be spontaneous or expressible by the patient. Men may have reduced libido, erectile dysfunction or gynaecomastia. Women often have irregular or absent periods as well as a reduced libido.

- 'Have you noticed any change in your periods? How many days do you bleed? How many days do you go between your periods? Has this changed from your previous periods?'

- *'Has your interest in sex changed recently?'*
- *'Have you had any trouble getting or maintaining an erection?'*
- *'Have you noticed your breasts change or produce any liquid?'*

18.1.9 Diabetes mellitus (DM)

Alongside asking about polydipsia and polyuria, the following questions may reveal a developing Type 1 DM.

- *'Have you recently unintentionally lost weight? How much have you lost in the last three months?'*
- *'Has anyone commented that your breath has a sweet smell?'*

The patient may also complain of itchy genitalia, which can occur as a result of candida infection (thrush) associated with glycosuria. Type 1 DM may also present with collapse, or coma.

Type 2 diabetes is often asymptomatic, but a patient may present with one of its associated complications, such as visual change due to retinopathy, oedema due to nephropathy, or ulcer due to neuropathy.

5) Systems review

A systems review should be conducted on every patient in order to establish a differential diagnosis. If the patient answers positively to questioning in a certain system, you should complete a full enquiry into the state of that system in order to remove it as a differential. The systems review in a patient with a possible endocrine complaint is very important to help expose the big picture because many issues affect multiple systems.

Please refer to *Chapter 6* for more details.

6) ICE

Attempting to elicit a history from a patient with a suspected endocrine pathology may be a confusing or difficult process for you both – the multi-system nature of endocrinology means that their symptoms may be vague, previously unnoticed, or assumed to be unimportant or unrelated. For example, in hyperthyroidism, a patient may be most concerned about issues affecting their skin or hair, but take no issue with sudden weight loss. Regularly assessing the patient's own ICE can be a useful tool to make sure you are practising in a holistic manner, with a patient-centred approach. Some key points for consideration are:

- Be alert to patient sensitivity over their appearance and changes in this.
- Symptoms or signs may be perceived as embarrassing (e.g. dyspareunia). Considerately phrasing questions can alleviate this situation, making the patient feel more comfortable. For example *'It is quite common for those with a diagnosis of diabetes to have some troubles with gaining or maintaining an erection – do you mind if I ask whether you have experienced any issues like this?'*

7) Past medical history

'Is there anything else that you regularly see the doctor for?'

Always explore previous or concurrent medical conditions and hospital stays. Patients may often forget seeing the doctor for hypertension or hyperlipidaemia.

Ask specifically about:

- Autoimmune conditions – thyroid and Addison's are associated with other autoimmune diseases.

- Previous surgery, especially in the neck / thyroid area (parathyroid glands commonly damaged).
- Exposure to chemotherapy and radiation.
- In women, ask about pregnancy – post-partum thyroiditis and gestational diabetes may be relevant. Also ask about any concerns about fertility.
- Recent illness, accidents or surgery – may precipitate an Addisonian crisis.
- Hypertension – if resistant to medication, may be a sign of hyperaldosteronism or phaeochromocytoma.
- Kidney stones – recurrent renal stones could indicate chronic hypercalcaemia.

8) Medication history

Some medications commonly have side-effects that may lead to endocrine problems. Exploring symptoms in relation to past medical history and treatments is particularly relevant for the following medications:

- Lithium – may lead to the development of hypothyroidism and goitre. Long-term use can cause hyperthyroidism.
- Anti-psychotics and dopamine antagonists – may increase risk of developing diabetes, or affect prolactin homeostasis.
- Amiodarone – can disrupt thyroid function.
- Corticosteroids – exogenous steroids are a common cause of Cushing's syndrome.

Also remember to ask about OTC medicines and remedies; in the menopause herbal remedies and dietary supplements are often used.

9) Family history

'Do you have any family history of diabetes, thyroid problems or cancer?'

- If uncertain over type, explore diabetes by asking how they managed it. Ask specifically about first-degree relatives – type 2 diabetes has a large genetic component in its aetiology.
- Multiple endocrine neoplasia (MEN) is a familial condition with an autosomal dominant inheritance pattern. Each sub-type leads to development of combinations of characteristic endocrine tumours – pituitary, pancreatic, parathyroid and phaeochromocytoma.

> Mnemonic: remember the characteristics of multiple endocrine neoplasia with the following phrase:
> "Dominant MEN are PPPPretty bad."
> MEN follows an autosomal dominant pattern and involves a combination of endocrine tumours – Pituitary, Pancreatic, Parathyroid and Phaeochromocytoma.

10) Social history

- Always explore presenting symptoms in relation to their impact on the patient's ADLs.
- **Driving**: *'Do you drive? Does your job involve driving?'*
    - For a diagnosis of diabetes that is treated by insulin, or tablets that may cause hypoglycaemia (e.g. sulphonylureas) the patient **MUST** inform the Driver and Vehicle Licensing Agency (DVLA). This may come as a surprise to patients, who may be very reliant on their ability to drive.
        - Patients also need to notify the DVLA if they have had two severe episodes of hypoglycaemia in the last 12 months where they have been completely dependent on another person for treatment.
        - OR if they develop impaired awareness of hypoglycaemia.
    - This is especially important for coach, bus, or heavy goods vehicle drivers because there are separate, stricter requirements for them. These drivers must also inform the DVLA if they have Addison's disease.

- **Diet**: *'How much coffee, tea, fizzy drinks or energy drinks do you drink on an average day?'*
  - Caffeine in excess amounts may lead to palpitations.
  - *'Would you describe your diet as balanced?'* – explore fruit, vegetables, etc. Iodine deficiency is a cause of thyroid disease.
- **Alcohol**: excess alcohol consumption can give a cushingoid appearance (pseudo-Cushing's syndrome).
- **Smoking**: is associated with Graves' disease, especially in more severe forms.

11) Closing the consultation

- *'Thank you for talking with me today. Before we finish, is there anything else you would like to talk about, or anything you think it is important I know?'*
- Remember to summarize; give the patient the opportunity to ask questions, and ensure they understand and agree with the proposed next steps.
- In endocrinology, this may include planning multiple visits (e.g. glucose tolerance testing) or future annual reviews.

Summary of key points (GET YOUR MARKS):

Establish rapport (clear introduction of who you are, what your role is and why you are there).

History of presenting complaint: tailor your questions depending on what hormonal axis or part of the endocrine system you think is affected. Ask questions specific to these disorders.

Systems review: endocrine symptoms are typically non-specific and involve multiple systems, so it is important to carry out a systems review to rule out any other potential causes.

ICE: symptoms experienced in endocrinology can be very sensitive and may be embarrassing for the patient. Pay close attention to their feelings and elicit what is affecting them the most.

Past medical history: enquire about other autoimmune conditions, previous surgery (especially neck) and exposure to chemotherapy and radiation. In women, ask about pregnancy including gestational diabetes, recent illness/accidents, hypertension, kidney stones.

Medication history: current medication (e.g. lithium, anti-psychotics, dopamine antagonists, amiodarone, corticosteroids), allergies, OTC medications and supplements.

Family history: especially diabetes, thyroid problems or cancer, MEN syndrome.

Social history: ask how their symptoms are affecting their ADLs and about driving, diet, alcohol, smoking.

Closing the consultation: let the Calgary–Cambridge Model be your guide. Remember your key skills of summarizing and screening. Always leave the patient with a plan of care, even if it is that you need to speak with your colleagues. Thank the patient.

18.2 Information giving and shared decision making

The following section is a quick overview of what you might tell the patient during an information giving or shared decision making station. Use this section as a guide to what information might be relevant for the patient. Be sure to always assess the patient's starting point. Drawings and the use of models are very helpful for patients and often count for one or more marks. If you don't have anything to draw, writing long words for patients can also be helpful.

Review *Chapter 5* to get the most OSCE points possible.

18.2.1 Diabetes mellitus

What is it? Diabetes is a common, long-term condition where glucose (sugar) cannot enter the cells (building blocks) of our body properly. Glucose is the fuel that almost every cell in our body needs to do its job. To enter the cell, glucose needs insulin. You can think of insulin like a key that is needed to unlock the cell to let the glucose in. Insulin is a hormone that is made in the pancreas in our body. Diabetes can develop when:

- **There is no insulin** – this is known as **type 1 diabetes**. This happens when the cells in the pancreas that make insulin get destroyed. Nobody knows for sure why this happens, but usually it is because the body has an abnormal reaction to the cells (autoimmune). This means that the body cannot make insulin any more, and the cells cannot be 'unlocked' to let glucose in.
- **There is not enough insulin**, or the insulin does not work properly – this is known as **type 2 diabetes**. This can happen for a number of reasons including being overweight, not eating a balanced diet, or having a close relative with the condition (genetics). In type 2 diabetes the cells are only partly 'unlocked' by insulin, so they cannot let all the glucose in.

There are other types of diabetes, but type 1 (~10%) and 2 (~90%) are the most common. If you have diabetes, glucose can build up in your blood and this can cause problems with many parts of your body, such as your eyes, blood vessels and kidneys (in a consultation, you will **be expected to relate pathology to presenting symptoms**).

Who gets it? Anybody can develop diabetes. Type 1 diabetes usually develops before the age of 40, especially in childhood. You are at a greater risk of developing type 2 diabetes as you get older (40+), if you have a family history of diabetes, are overweight, or of Asian, Chinese, African-Caribbean or black African origin.

How do you treat it? There are lots of ways to manage diabetes. These include lifestyle changes and medicines that lower the amount of glucose left in your blood. You can't change some of the reasons why you might have developed diabetes (age, ethnicity) but the following lifestyle changes are always recommended:

- Regular exercise, e.g. walking 20 minutes every day.
- Balanced diet, e.g. reducing how much food with lots of fat in you might eat.
- Losing weight, if overweight or obese.

There is no cure for type 1 diabetes, so we need to replace the insulin that your body cannot make any more. This is usually done by teaching you how to give yourself 2–4 small injections of insulin during the day. Unfortunately insulin cannot be made as a tablet because the normal acid in your stomach will break it down before it gets a chance to unlock cells to let glucose in.

In type 2 diabetes there are a number of different medicines that can help the cells in your body to let glucose in. Sometimes making lifestyle changes might help you to manage the amount of glucose in your blood, but usually over time people with type 2 diabetes will need these medicines, or insulin injections as well.

18.2.2 Thyroid disease

What is it? The thyroid gland is located at the front of the neck just below where the Adam's apple is in men. Normally it is not visible but in some conditions it can increase in size and appear as a lump or swelling at the front of the neck. The gland produces, stores and secretes thyroid hormone which helps regulate many processes in the human body. Its main role is controlling the body's metabolic rate, in other words how quickly your cells use up energy. In a healthy individual the amount of thyroid hormone released is controlled by the hypothalamus and pituitary gland in the brain.

For a variety of different reasons the body can produce too much or too little thyroid hormone (hyper- / hypothyroidism, respectively), and this usually means a problem with the thyroid gland itself or, much less commonly, the areas which control it, the pituitary or hypothalamus.

Hyperthyroidism

If there is too much thyroid hormone in the body it causes symptoms such as weight loss, intolerance to heat, increased appetite, tremor, irritability, irregular menstrual cycle, palpitations and needing to pass stools more often. The most common cause of hyperthyroidism is Graves' disease, which is an autoimmune condition where the body's own immune system attacks the thyroid in a way which forces it to release more thyroid hormone. It can also be caused by infections, tumours and various drugs.

Who gets it? Hyperthyroidism is common and affects 2–5% of all females at some point during their life, whereas men are five times less likely to suffer. Most cases occur between 20 and 40 years of age. Depending on the underlying cause there are other risk factors such as family history for Graves' disease or other autoimmune conditions, high iodine intake, smoking, trauma to the thyroid gland (e.g. surgery), childbirth.

How do you treat it? This will depend on the underlying cause but for Graves' disease there are three main methods of reducing the amount of thyroid hormone: anti-thyroid drugs (carbimazole, propylthiouracil), radioactive iodine or surgery. These all aim to reduce the function of the thyroid gland.

Hypothyroidism

On the flip side, if not enough thyroid hormone is being produced it can cause opposing symptoms: fatigue, weight gain, reduced appetite, cold intolerance, low mood, lower heart rate. The most common cause in the UK is again autoimmune but it can also occur due to iodine deficiency, infections, tumours or post-surgery / irradiation.

Who gets it? Hypothyroidism is one of the most common endocrine abnormalities with prevalence in the UK of 2% in women and 0.1% in men, but over a lifetime it is 9% and 1% in respective sexes. An average age of diagnosis is later than that for hyperthyroidism, at around 60 years.

How do you treat it? For hypothyroidism, replacement drug therapy is often started using levothyroxine, beginning with a low dose daily and adjusting every few weeks, until symptoms have settled.

18.3 Practice scenarios

1. You are requested to speak to Helena Youssef, a 65-year-old female, with a recent diagnosis of type 2 DM. She has come to see her GP because she does not understand why she has been prescribed a new medication; she has told the practice nurse that she wants to stop taking it. In the same appointment, she was told she has an HbA1c of 60 mmol/mol (her previous HbA1c was 64 mmol/mol). You are requested to discuss Helena's new diagnosis, her medication and her blood results with her.

2. Elisabeth Holmes is a 59-year-old female. She saw her GP because she felt tired and cold all the time. The GP arranged some blood tests which showed:

   TSH: $\uparrow$6.7   (normal 0.5–5.7 mIU/L)
   T_4: $\downarrow$35   (normal 70–140 nmol/L)

   Elisabeth wants to know what this means, and how she will be treated. Discuss her blood results with her, and explain how she will be managed.

3. Adeeb Singh is speaking to you from his hospital bed. After a long period of unexplained symptoms he collapsed at home and was brought to hospital. He was eventually told that he has Addison's disease and will need to take medicines for the rest of his life. Mr Singh has been prescribed hydrocortisone and fludrocortisone. He wants to know why he has to take these medicines.

4. Sandra Smith, a 60-year-old female, comes to see you in the endocrinology clinic at the local hospital. She is hot, flustered and fed up. Two years ago she was told she has Graves' disease and she took tablets for 18 months until it got better. She wants to know whether she can go back on these tablets, or if there are any other options for her. Discuss the options available to Sandra.

5. Andre Lukovnic is a 57-year-old male, and has type 2 diabetes. He currently takes 500 mg metformin BD. His last HbA1c was 71 mmol/mol. His GP has suggested he start another medication to lower his blood glucose. Andre is unsure about this and has asked to speak to someone to find out if there is anything else he can do as well. Please explain to Andre the options available to him and agree a treatment plan.

6. Tony Charles is a 53-year-old male who has type 1 DM. He has come to see the GP because his partner George got concerned when the chiropodist recently told Tony at his annual review that he was losing the sensation in his feet. Tony does not understand what this has to do with his diabetes. He and George are concerned and want to know what they can do about it. You are asked to explore how Tony's diabetes is currently managed and formulate a plan to ease their concerns.

19

Older people's medicine

JOSEPH BEECHAM AND HARRIET TUITLE-DALTON

Older People's Medicine: Keys to Success

- Geriatric presentations are multiple, therefore it's not always appropriate to focus on one organ system.
- Tailor your communication to your patient. OPM patients may have cognitive issues, sensory impairments or simply be forgetful.
- Clinical presentations in older people are atypical. Keep an open mind as to the cause of the patient's symptoms.
- Iatrogenic illness is incredibly common.
- Don't forget your Systems Review as this will pick up lots of symptoms which many patients dismiss simply as "just part of getting old".
- Functional enquiry is essential – can the patient perform their Activities of Daily Living (ADLs)?
- Does the patient require support, and if so, who provides it?
- Is there someone with Power of Attorney, is there an Advance Directive, and do they have a next of kin?

Red flags in older people's medicine:

- Recent weight loss
- Acute confusion
- Impaired memory or disorganized thinking
- Lack of personal hygiene and other signs of neglect
- Recurrent falls

19.1 Particular issues in communicating with older people

Older people's medicine (OPM) can present challenging scenarios in both clinical practice and in OSCE settings. It's important to remember that these patients often present with more than one complaint, which are often due to a multitude of causes, and which may be complicated by complex social factors, cognitive decline, polypharmacy, as well as the features of normal ageing.

19.1.1 How to assess capacity in the elderly

Elderly patients can be affected by a variety of conditions that can impair cognitive functions and thus affect their capacity, e.g. dementia, delirium, stroke and mental health issues. This kind of OSCE station is often used to assess students' awareness of the Mental Capacity Act.

Capacity is specific to the individual situation – the patient may have capacity to make a straightforward decision like having a wound dressing, but not for a complicated decision like whether to be started on warfarin for AF.

Some fundamental points from the Mental Capacity Act:
- A patient always has capacity until proven otherwise.
- You must do everything possible to support a patient to make a decision.
- If you decide a patient does lack capacity then you must act in their best interests.
- Any decision made on a patient's behalf must be least restrictive of their rights.
- A patient is allowed to make a strange or irrational decision.

When applying this to a station, you first of all need to establish:

Is there damage to their brain or disturbance to mental function? If so, does that mean this patient cannot make a decision at this particular time, regardless of this changing in the future?

If you determine YES to the first part you now need to perform a short test that has four parts:
- Does your patient understand the information relevant to the decision?
  - Break the information down to be as simple as possible.
  - Use terms that are familiar or even gestures or pictures, as visual information can especially help those with dementia.
- Is your patient able to retain the information you have given them relating to the decision?
  - It may be important to perform an Addenbrooke's Cognitive Examination or Abbreviated Mental Test Score (AMTS) at this point to assess memory.
- Is your patient able to weigh that information as part of the decision making process?
  - Do they understand what will happen if they have the treatment? Do they understand what will happen if they don't?
- Can your patient communicate their decision back to you?
  - Involve interpreters/relatives to maximize the patient's ability to communicate to you.

Remember to **CHECK** if any previous advanced directives had been put in place or if anyone has been appointed to make decisions, e.g. Lasting Power of Attorney or Independent Mental Capacity Advocate.

Useful phrases for these conversations:
- *'Do you know why we've asked you to come in today?'*
- *'What's your understanding of the problem?'*
- *'Can you remember what we were saying about the possible future risks of this condition?'*
- *'Can you summarize what we've spoken about today so I can check I've explained it properly?'*
- *'If I told you* [new piece of information], *would that help you make a decision?'*

Some important concepts to understand
- **Advance directive**: this is a legal document signed by the patient when they had capacity and is only used by those over 18. This document can outline what treatment the patient DOES NOT want in the future and not ones they do.
- **Lasting Power of Attorney (LPA)**: this is a trusted person appointed by the patient to make decisions for them when they cannot. Again, the LPA can only refuse treatments on behalf of patient but not choose them.
- **DNAR (Do not attempt resuscitation)**: this is a document signed by a doctor (ideally the most senior member of the team), which instructs the medical team not to attempt resuscitation on the patient.

- ○ If the patient has capacity, the risks and benefits of resuscitation should be discussed with the patient and a shared decision should be made; however, if the patient wants cardiopulmonary resuscitation (CPR) despite limited chance of success, the doctor is not obliged to agree.
  - ○ If the patient lacks capacity, the doctor should establish whether the patient has an LPA or an advance directive. The decision should always be made in the patient's best interest.
- **Independent Mental Capacity Advocate (IMCA)**: legally appointed individual who acts as a safeguard for the patient. They advocate for the patient and make difficult social and healthcare decisions when the patient is not capable.

19.1.2 How to communicate with the sensory impaired

A mild degree of sensory impairment of one or multiple types is extremely common in elderly patients. When approaching an OSCE station with a patient with sensory impairment, make sure you read the instructions carefully; this may reveal the patient's impairment and help you prepare. If you begin the consultation and the patient reveals a sensory impairment (such as wearing a hearing aid), make sure you acknowledge the impairment and offer to make reasonable adjustments to your consultation (such as speaking more slowly). There are likely to be marks for 'spotting' an impairment, so make sure you're explicit about noticing these.

- *'I notice you're wearing a hearing aid – is there anything I can do to make sure that you catch everything I say?'*
- *'I can see your white stick* [indicating visual impairment]; *is there anywhere you'd prefer me to sit so that you can hear better or see better?'*

There is no guarantee that the patient's impairment in an OSCE station is related to their presenting complaint. Elderly patients have a multiplicity of pathologies, and you may be asked to assess chest pain in a patient with unilateral hearing loss. This is not an unreasonable station to sit, especially as these presentations are common for F1s.

- *'I understand you've come in to talk about the tightness in your chest, but would you mind if I asked some general questions about your health, just to check I haven't missed anything?'*

Remember, sensory impairment is not an excuse for taking a poor history. It's important that you take a thorough history, even if it requires additional effort.

You may find a patient brings a friend, relative or carer with them to the consultation. They can be very helpful in rephrasing your questions in ways that the patient understands, and it's perfectly acceptable to use their help. However, you should always address the patient themself when gathering information, and make sure you acknowledge that they are the patient.

Hearing impairment

Many patients may be wearing a hearing aid. Ask if it's switched on, and if they need you to speak more loudly or slowly. You should try to ascertain if one ear is better than the other, and make sure that you are sitting closer to the better ear. Ensure that the patient can see you speak, as many patients with hearing impairment use lip-reading, even if they have some residual hearing function. If the patient has significant deafness, it may help to get closer to the patient, so that you don't have to raise your voice. In cases of total deafness, which are unlikely to come up in OSCE stations, write short sentences legibly (in capitals if necessary).

- *'Would you like me to speak louder or slower to help you understand everything I say?'*

> **Example:** Adjustments that can help sensory-impaired patients
> - Lighting: make sure the room is well lit.
> - Noise: suggest moving to a side room if in a noisy environment.
> - Breaks: communication in sensory impairment can be exhausting for patients; consider having a break in consultations.

Visual impairment

Elderly patients have a variety of visual pathologies, including cataracts, macular degeneration and glaucoma. These can partially or totally obscure vision, and different pathologies affect different parts of the visual field. Find out which eye, and where in the visual field the patient has most vision, and ensure you are sitting where they can see you. Some patients with residual vision will still be able to make out different shades of light and dark, or may be able to see outlines, so it may help to sit closer. When explaining concepts to the visually impaired, don't forget to describe verbally any results you may have been given.
- *'Where is the best place for me to sit so that you can see me?'*
- *'I've got an X-ray of your fracture here, would you like me to describe it to you?'*

19.1.3 How to take a collateral history and use alternative sources of information

Collateral history taking involves speaking to a patient's relative, carer or other person involved in their care about their medical history. This represents an important source of information when planning care, when patients are unable to communicate. The most common circumstances when this is encountered in OPM are confusion, dementia and loss of consciousness.

In an OSCE setting, you may encounter a station featuring a patient and their relative, and be asked to take a collateral history from the relative. Alternatively, the station may just feature the relative, and the patient may not be present. Nevertheless, some key principles apply to both types of station.

Depending on the mental state of the patient, it may be appropriate to gain consent and explain to the patient the need for collateral history taking. Explain this in sensitive terms, and allow the patient to contribute to the history; they may feel the need to interject.
- *'Mrs Richards, because you're having some trouble remembering what happened, would you mind if I chatted to your daughter for a few minutes, just to see if she can help? Please don't hesitate to interrupt if you feel we're going down the wrong path.'*

You should also be aware that sources of collateral histories may be inaccurate, misleading or may have hidden motives. Elderly patients may not share their medical history with relatives or may not be aware of it in the first place. You should also be aware that carers may gain from presenting a particular picture of patients, such as gaining power of attorney or moving patients out of the family home. If you have any concerns, you should document them, and consult your local Adult Safeguarding team.

Key tips to remember:
- When talking on the phone, ensure that you are both talking about the correct patient, that you are talking to the appropriate person about the patient, and that you have permission to talk about the patient.
- Always identify yourself and the purpose of the consultation.
  - *'Hello, my name is Joe Bloggs, I'm the F1 at the London Hospital. I'm calling to get some medical information about one of our patients who's had a fall. Could I check who I'm talking to?'*

- Document the conversation in the patient notes.

Important components of the collateral history
- Identify yourself, the source of the history, and their relationship to the patient.
- Standard components: presenting complaint, history of presenting complaint, past medical history, family history, drug history, social history, systems review.
- Risks:
  - to themselves (wandering, neglect, diet, home)
  - to others (violence, careless behaviour)
- Mood
- Onset, time course and progression of symptoms (especially important in confusion).

Alternative sources of information, together with their method of examination in an OSCE setting, are shown in *Table 19.1*.

Table 19.1 Alternative sources of patient information

Alternative source of information	In an exam the candidate will be:
GP	asked to phone a GP and take a focused collateral history
Relative/neighbour	asked to consult either with or without patient present
Patient's list of medications	asked to review medications, write up drugs in hospital drugs chart, and spot dangerous interactions
Hospital medical records	given time to review a patient's set of notes and then clerk a patient based on a consultation
Other organizations	asked to phone a care home and ask specific questions about presentation and pre-morbid state

19.2 **Information gathering**

1) Introduce yourself and your role on the healthcare team

2) Ensure consent and confidentiality

3) Confirm the patient's name and DOB; ask about occupation

4) History of presenting complaint

> **Key Knowledge: Causes of delirium**
> Remember – VINDICATE
> - Vascular – stroke, migraines, MI
> - Infection/inflammation – UTI, pneumonia, meningitis, encephalitis, malaria, sepsis
> - Neoplasm – primary, secondary or paraneoplastic
> - Degenerative – organ failures (heart, liver, renal), urinary retention, constipation
> - Iatrogenic – post-operative pain, sedatives, analgesia, opiates, anti-parkinsonism meds, anti-cholinergics, steroids, alcohol, benzodiazepine withdrawal
> - Congenital – epilepsy
> - Autoimmune – SLE
> - Trauma – haematoma
> - Endocrine/metabolic – dehydration, hyponatraemia, hypercalcaemia, thyroid dysfunction, hypoxaemia, thiamine deficiency

- Start with an open question – *'What has brought you here today?'*
  - This can be helpful as it allows you to determine whether the patient themself is worried about their symptoms or if a worried family member has made them come to see you.
- Ask about the onset of symptoms – this helps you separate dementia and delirium.
- If you suspect delirium try to gather more information on what the underlying cause may be.
- If you suspect dementia, what was the progression like? Slowly progressive (Alzheimer's) or step-like (vascular)?
- Do they have memory impairment? Alzheimer's disease (AD) causes defects in anterograde episodic memory e.g. the ability to remember an address after five minutes or longer, whereas delirious patients may be unable to retain any information for any length of time. Those with Lewy body dementia (LBD) may have fluctuating memory loss.
- Those with delirium have difficulty concentrating and therefore struggle with counting backwards from 20.
- Do they have any associated symptoms?
  - Parkinsonian features (such as bradykinesia, tremor, rigidity) suggesting LBD
  - Mood changes which may indicate depression
  - Psychotic symptoms, e.g. hallucinations in LBD or delusions in AD
  - Behavioural changes, e.g. agitation, disinhibition or aggression which may indicate fronto-temporal dementia (FTD)
  - Cognitive disturbances:
    - Aphasia – language production and comprehension difficulties
    - Apraxia – difficulty performing tasks when asked
    - Agnosia – difficulty interpreting sensory information such as faces, smells and sounds
    - Difficulty planning and organizing
- How is the patient's sleeping pattern? Do they wake at night (AD), have early morning waking (depression) or fluctuating consciousness (delirium)?
- Have they had previous episodes like this? What was their cognitive functioning level before this incident?

19.2.1 Screening for cognitive impairment

Being asked to assess confusion and cognitive impairment is a common OSCE station. You may be asked simply to perform a screening test, which is likely to be the Abbreviated Mental Test Score (AMTS), or you may be asked to perform a full assessment of a presentation of confusion. This may require history taking, screening tests, physical examination and review of investigations and medication. It's important to explain sensitively why you're doing the test, as some patients will not understand its purpose and may become offended.

'Hello Mrs Richards, my name is Dr Bloggs and I understand that you've had a fall. Your neighbour was a bit worried that you couldn't remember everything. Would you mind if I ask you a few questions? These are just to see that you haven't got any problems remembering things. Some of the questions are a bit silly, but we have to ask them to be thorough. Would that be OK?'

The AMTS involves 10 questions, and each question scores 1 for a correct answer and 0 for an incorrect answer. A score of <6 is considered significant for cognitive impairment.

1. **Age:** *'Would you mind telling me how old you are?'*
2. **Time:** *'Do you know what the time is?'*

3. **Address for recall** (no points at this stage; see Question 11): *'I'd like you to remember this address – 42 West Street – can you repeat that? I'll be asking you to remember this in a couple of minutes.'*
4. **Year**: *'Do you know what year it is?'*
5. **Name of the place**: *'Do you know where we are at the moment?'*
6. **Identification of two people**: *'Do you know who I am? Do you know who that man in the uniform is?'*
7. **DOB**: *'Do you know your date of birth?'*
8. **Dates of the First World War**: *'Do you know the dates of the First World War?'*
9. **Present monarch**: *'Do you know who's on the throne at the moment?'*
10. **Count backwards from 20 to 1**: *'Could you count backwards from 20 to 1 for me?'*
11. **Address recall**: *'Can you tell me the address that I told you earlier?'*

> **Key Knowledge: Other cognitive screening tests to be aware of**
>
> **MMSE**: no longer widely used due to copyright issues
>
> **GPCOG**: widely used in primary care
>
> **6CIT**: used in primary care but complicated scoring
>
> **ACE III**: more in-depth test used in secondary care

Assessing dementia / delirium / other causes

Both in OSCEs and in real life, you will be presented with patients who are confused or have memory deficits. It is important for you to be able to take a history from them and work out what is going wrong, e.g. whether they are depressed, delirious or suffering from dementia (see *Table 19.2*). This requires you to glean as much information as possible from them and also from any carers or family. This can be a delicate matter so needs to be approached with care.

Table 19.2 The different features of delirium, dementia and depression

Features	Delirium	Dementia	Depression
Onset	Acute, e.g within hours	Insidious; months–years	Varying from weeks to months
Course	Fluctuates even throughout the day	Progressive	Varies
Conscious level	Decreased	Fine	Fine
Attention	Impaired	Normal unless severe	Decreased – difficulty concentrating
Mood	Fluctuating	Can have depressed mood	Lack of interest in activities, low self-esteem, suicidal ideation
Memory	Difficulty recalling recent events	Difficulty recognizing people and places in more severe	Difficulty remembering details
Sleep pattern	Disturbed	Normal	Insomnia – early morning wakening
Hallucinations	Yes, normally visual	Usually none unless LBD	Yes, in severe disease
Cure	Reversible if treat underlying cause	Irreversible	Reversible

Practical points to make the consultation easier: use a quiet, well-lit room with few distractions; speak slowly and clearly; use short, simple sentences but avoid patronizing them; show respect; if they don't understand a question first time try rephrasing it or asking it in sections; listen carefully and don't be afraid to ask them to repeat or clarify something.

19.2.2 Falls and 'funny turn' history

A history of falls is easier if you approach it chronologically. Ask the patient what happened before, during (this may need a witness account) and after the fall/funny turn.

Before the fall
- 'What were you doing leading up to the fall?'
- 'Were you sitting or standing?'
- 'Had you eaten/drunk anything?'
- 'Did you have any warning you were going to fall/pass out?'
- 'Did you feel light-headed?'
- 'Did the room spin? How did it spin?'
- 'Did you have a fast heart rate or chest pain?'
- 'Did you notice any vision changes?'

During the fall
- 'Did you pass out and if so, for how long?'
- 'Did anyone witness the fall?'
- 'Did you put your hands out to stop yourself?'
- 'Did you hit your head?'
- 'Did anything cause you to trip?'
- 'Did you bite your tongue?'
- 'Did you experience any shaking/seizing?'

After the fall
- 'Could you get straight up after the fall?'
- 'Were you in pain after the fall? Did you have any headaches?'
- 'Did you suffer any incontinence, either faecal or urinary?'
- 'Did you have any muscle aches?'
- 'Did you have any memory loss? Did you remember the event?'
- 'Did you feel sleepy afterwards?'

Additional questions
Past falls history – 'Have you had any episodes like this before?'
Mobilization – 'What is your mobility usually like? Do you use a stick/frame?'
Past medical history – 'Do you suffer from diabetes/heart problems/neurological problems?' 'Have you been feeling unwell recently?'
Family history – 'Is there any family history of heart disease/seizures?'
Social history – 'Do you have pets and are they trip hazards? What kind of house do you live in? Are there stairs? Is your house particularly cluttered?'
Drug history – 'What medication are you on? Have you had any recent changes?'

5) Systems review

6) ICE

7) Past medical history
Ask about any history of Parkinson's, risk factors for stroke (diabetes, high cholesterol, AF, smoking, sedentary lifestyle, etc.), head injury, and recent infections as these may

indicate aetiology. Do not forget to ask about psychiatric history and a history of depression, including any suicide attempts.

8) Drug history

A detailed drug history can be helpful for determining if they have vascular risk factors, if they are on any drugs that can cause confusion or any previous medication for dementia. Remember to check if any medication has changed recently. Some examples of drugs to look out for/ask about:

- Antihypertensives
- Diabetic medication
- Sedatives
- Opiates
- Parkinson's drugs
- Alzheimer's drugs

Do not forget the normal drug questions: Any over-the-counter medication? Any herbal / alternative medicines? Do they have any drug allergies?

9) Family history

There may be a genetic association in early onset AD. Also ask about a family history of cardiovascular and cerebrovascular disease, Parkinson's disease and psychiatric disorders.

10) Social history

- Assess baseline functional ability. Can the patient:
  ○ Bathe and dress by themself and use the toilet?
  ○ Cook meals?
  ○ Manage money?
  ○ Complete daily household tasks?
  ○ Take medicines on schedule?
  ○ Drive safely and get around in usually familiar areas?
- Who do they live with at home? What kind of house do they live in – are there stairs?
- Alcohol intake – this can be helpful for establishing whether delirium tremens may be a cause.
- Assess risks – these include driving, abuse and suicidal ideation.

19.2.3 Functional assessment of patients

In elderly patients, a functional assessment is an essential part of general history taking. Your intention here is to ascertain how a patient is managing at home, whether they require additional support and whether they are safe to return home after discharge. This requires an assessment of a patient's "Activities of Daily Living" (ADLs). When asking questions about patients' independence, be aware that elderly patients may be wary of your intentions, and believe that you may wish to change their housing situation. Patients wish to maintain their independence for as long as possible and this kind of history taking needs a sensitive, caring demeanour, as well as a good initial explanation.

'Hello Mrs Richards, my name is Dr Bloggs. I've got a few questions about how you're managing at home. I'm asking this because it's important to know whether you're OK to go home. This way if we find that you could use some extra help, we could put you in touch with services like Meals on Wheels or someone to come in and help. Would that be OK?'

There are formal ways to assess functional ability, such as the modified Barthel index, but many clinicians like to divide their questions into basic and advanced ADLs in clinical practice.

Basic ADLs can be remembered using the unfortunately named mnemonic **DEATTH** (we recommend you not say this out loud in front of your patient).

- **D**ressing – *'Are you able to get dressed in the morning without any help?'*
- **E**ating – *'Are you able to eat your meals?'*
- **A**mbulation – *'Are you able to walk around the house and pop out to the garden?'*
- **T**ransfers – *'Can you easily get in and out of chairs? Can you get in and out of bed?'*
- **T**oileting – *'Are you able to go to the toilet without any help?'*
- **H**ygiene – *'Are you able to have baths or showers, and keep yourself clean without any help?'*

Advanced ADLs can be remembered using the mnemonic **SHAFT-TT**:

- **S**hopping – *'Are you able to pop to the shops, and carry your shopping home with you?'*
- **H**ousekeeping – *'Are you able to look after the house, and do any vacuuming, dusting or cleaning?'*
- **A**ccounting – *'Are you able to look after your own money?'*
- **F**ood preparation – *'Are you able to prepare your own meals?'*
- **T**elephone – *'Are you able to use your home telephone or a mobile phone to call people?'*
- **T**ransportation – *'Are you able to drive, or to go on the bus or tram?'*
- **T**aking medications – *'Are you able to take your medications, and remember to take them?'*

There are a variety of causes for functional impairment, ranging from cognitive, medical and iatrogenic. The polymorbid nature of elderly patients mean that they often struggle with advanced ADLs. When faced with functional impairment, your aim is to maximize the patient's independence, in accordance with their wishes. In an OSCE setting, you may also be asked by the examiner to list some members of the multidisciplinary team who could assist with particular functional impairments.

> **Summary of key points (GET YOUR MARKS):**
>
> **Establish rapport:** clear introduction of who you are, what your role is and why you are there.
>
> **History of presenting complaint:** ask an open question initially. Ask about onset of symptoms, progression, memory impairment, associated symptoms, parkinsonian features, mood changes, hallucinations, behavioural changes, sleeping patterns and a history of previous episodes.
>
> **Systems review.**
>
> **ICE.**
>
> **Past medical history:** cardiovascular disease / diabetes, Parkinson's, head injuries, recent infections and psychiatric history.
>
> **Drug history:** ask about antihypertensives, diabetic medications, sedatives, opiates, drugs for Parkinson's, drugs for AD. Ask about OTC drugs and allergies.
>
> **Family history:** heart disease, psychiatric disease, memory disorders.
>
> **Social history:** ask about their living arrangements (do they live alone or with family? Do they have carers?). Try to gain an idea of how independent they are. Ask if they drive and about alcohol intake. Carry out a functional assessment to determine their ability to perform ADLs.
>
> **Closing the consultation:** Let the Calgary–Cambridge Model be your guide. Remember your key skills including summarizing and screening. Always leave the patient with a plan of care, even if it is that you need to speak with your colleagues. Thank the patient.

19.3 Information giving and shared decision making

The following section is a quick overview of what you might tell the patient during an information giving or shared decision making station. Use this section as a guide to what information might be relevant for the patient. Be sure to always assess the patient's starting point. Drawings and the use of models are very helpful for patients and often count for one or more marks. If you don't have anything to draw, writing long words for patients can also be helpful.

Review *Chapter 5* to get the most OSCE points possible.

19.3.1 Fractured hip

What is it? Your hip is a joint that connects your pelvis to the top of your thigh. It's a joint made up of a ball and a socket (consider drawing a diagram at this point), which allows the joint to move around. A fractured hip is when the joint becomes broken. The type of hip fracture depends on the bone affected. Intracapsular means that the bone inside the joint is broken and extracapsular means that the bone outside the joint is broken. You have the [describe type here] type of fracture. The reason it's important to know what kind of fracture you have, is because we have different treatments depending on the type.

Who gets it? Hip fractures tend to affect women more than men, and they tend to affect older people. It's really common in the over 80s, but some younger people can get it as well. It's one of the most common conditions seen by the bone specialists, so there's quite a lot of experience in treating these injuries. For most people, a hip fracture happens because of a mixture of problems. One problem is that bones can become thinner, more porous and more fragile with age, and this is called osteoporosis. Another reason is that you can become more likely to fall with age. This can be due to your blood pressure, fainting, tripping over things or problems with your balance.

What are the symptoms? Most people who get a hip fracture fall over and are unable to get up. It's often really painful around your groin and your thigh. If you are able to have your legs out in front of you, you might notice that the broken side is often a bit shorter than the other leg.

How do you treat it? Nearly all people with a broken hip need some sort of surgery by the bone specialists to fix it. Depending on the type of fracture you have, the surgeon can join the broken bones together using screws, nails, and plates. However, if there are quite a lot of bone fragments floating about, you might need a hip replacement, which is when the surgeon gives you a new metal hip joint.

Depending on how old you are, and how generally well you are, you might get a general anaesthetic, where you'll be put to sleep, or a local or spinal anaesthetic, which will numb the area. After the operation, you'll have to stay in hospital for a few days, and you'll meet the physiotherapists and occupational therapists who will help you get out and about and back to normal.

How do I stop this happening again? For some people at risk of falls, we can see if there's anything to reduce that risk, such as rearranging furniture in the house, or reviewing medication or treating any underlying conditions. Likewise, if you've got thin and fragile bones, your GP may consider giving you a bone scan, and possibly starting you on medication to strengthen your bones.

Will the operation fix everything? The operation will help the fracture, but it is possible that you experience some pain or find it difficult to walk as you previously did. This depends on a lot of things such as how serious the injury was, how much rehab you were able to do and how fit you were before the injury; but these are all things which can be helped.

Complications: as with all surgery, there are some complications. Infection and blood loss are possible but unusual. There's also a risk of a blood clot in your leg – which is known as a

DVT – and also getting an ulcer. These are caused by not being able to move around, which is why we like to start the rehab process quite quickly after the operation and start you on a medication to prevent clot formation.

19.3.2 Dementia

Background: dementia is a complex topic to explain to a patient but it is also common so you may well find yourself in this difficult situation. Life-changing diagnoses are best given with a senior colleague present and with additional written information to hand, so that the patient can come to terms with the diagnosis in their own time.

What is it? This is a disorder that affects a person's ability to remember, think and reason. It affects 1 in 100 people over 65. Unfortunately it can get worse over time but this can be very slowly over years. It is important to remember there is good support and care for those with early diagnosis so they can develop strategies of living and coping with their symptoms.

The most common dementia is Alzheimer's disease. Other less common types include: vascular, fronto-temporal and Lewy body. In your case we believe you have....

What are the causes? (In these situations it may be helpful to draw diagrams to try to help the patient visualize their condition.)

The different types of dementia have different causes:
- Alzheimer's – this is caused by the brain shrinking and nerve fibres reducing. Also a number of brain chemicals reduce; one you may hear mentioned is acetylcholine. Usually these chemicals and nerves carry messages around the brain and help with its different functions. In Alzheimer's the number of messages and functions are reduced, which is why memory and cognitive function are impaired.
- Vascular dementia – the result of multiple little strokes. When a stroke occurs parts of the brain are deprived of oxygen due to blockages, and die. This causes mental ability to gradually decline.
- Lewy body dementia – small deposits of protein develop all over the brain, though the cause of this is unknown.
- There are over 60 diseases which can cause dementia, but these tend to be rare.

What are the symptoms? You or your close family may notice changes in mood, behaviour and personality. It is important to be aware of these symptoms and any worsening or relief from them. Make a note of things that make them worse, such as time of day or unfamiliar places. Dementia forums and support groups are excellent resources for dealing with issues that may arise.

What happens next? Some people can go many years without needing any intervention in particular. Usually a referral to a specialist is needed to confirm diagnosis and find an underlying cause if there is one. It is important to start planning for the future early on in the disease progression as you may not be able to make the decisions as easily later on.

How do you treat it? Simplify daily routine – make sure you have a structure to the day including meals and activities. Discuss this at various intervals e.g. at breakfast talk about plans for the day, at dinner talk about what you did in the day. Write reminders for things to do and label what's in cupboards in your kitchen, etc. It's all about adaptation and not mourning the memory ability you used to have.
- Reality orientation – in the morning take the time to know what day, date, time, season it is and where you are.
- Cognitive stimulation – practise logic puzzles and quizzes.
- Sensory stimulation – involves using light, sounds and smells to stimulate brain and improve mood / agitation.

- Regular physical activity has been shown to help slow decline in mobility and elevate mood.

Can medications help? The difficult answer is there is no cure for dementia and there is no way to reverse the disease progress. The medication is aimed at helping to improve symptoms such as problems with thinking and mood. One type is called acetylcholinesterase inhibitors, e.g. donepezil, rivastigmine and galantamine. As mentioned earlier, Alzheimer's has been linked with low levels of acetylcholine. These drugs increase the level of this in the brain, which may help your thinking. It is important to say that these drugs only work in about half of patients.

Side-effects of these drugs include nausea, muscle cramps, tiredness, headache and diarrhoea. If the side-effects become too much for you to cope with you can come back and we can discuss other options.

Another medication option we can talk about is memantine. This medication works by reducing the amount of a brain chemical called glutamate, which may slow damage to brain cells in Alzheimer's. However, it only slows down the disease progression in some cases.

Antihypertensives / aspirin may be used in vascular dementia.

19.3.3 Explaining driving safety with an elderly patient

Background: GPs and medical professionals are commonly asked, either by the patient themselves or by a concerned relative about whether a patient can continue driving. You are expected to be aware of your professional obligations, as well as the ethical issues surrounding patients who may not be fit to drive. Older people are often extremely concerned about maintaining their independence, and all your decisions should try to maximize their wishes, whilst keeping them and the public safe. You should emphasize this throughout the consultation.

Can I still drive at my age? Legally, once you reach the age of 70, you have to tell the DVLA if you have a medical disability. You also need to get your licence renewed every 3 years, rather than every 10 years. Now that describes the legal bit. If you have any health problems that might interfere with your driving, and this includes eyesight problems, you may not be able to drive.

Are there any particular conditions that stop me from driving? Unfortunately, as we get older, there are a few conditions that can affect driving safely. Any kind of visual problem will need to be discussed with the DVLA, but cataracts, glaucoma and macular degeneration are common problems affecting driving. You should also get your eyes tested regularly, and you're entitled to a free eye test over the age of 60. Hearing is also important when driving, and while deafness isn't a total bar to driving, it can be improved by things like hearing aids. Some medical conditions are also quite dangerous to drive with; examples are dementia, diabetes, Parkinson's, stroke and fainting. There are lots of heart conditions that can also affect your ability to drive. If you have any concerns, it's really important that you contact your GP and the DVLA.

Doctor, I feel that I'm still safe to drive but it's not as easy as it used to be. There are alternative measures to consider before you have to stop driving completely. Some people find getting a smaller car with bigger windows and mirrors to be helpful. You can also adjust when and where you drive. You may feel more comfortable avoiding especially busy roads and poor weather conditions.

Doctor, what happens if you think I can't drive but I disagree? Whether you continue to drive or not is a decision for you. It's also your responsibility to tell the DVLA that you can't drive, not me. Having said that, if you continue to drive despite being unfit to, I will need to tell the DVLA myself. The reason for that is that I have a responsibility to protect others, as well as ensure that you are safe. However, I would always tell you what I'm going to do before I do it.

> **Key Knowledge: Conditions which must be reported to the DVLA (not exhaustive)**
> - Heart attack (stop driving for 6 weeks)
> - Fainting
> - Stroke (if still symptomatic 1 month after stroke)
> - Bilateral macular degeneration
> - Bilateral cataracts
> - Epilepsy, seizures, fits or blackouts

I really value my independence – what alternatives are there to driving? Walking and cycling are healthy ways to get around, and are important for maintaining your mobility as you age. If there is public transport available, there are often concessions for older people. In areas where public transport isn't often available, there may be 'community transport' options available, such as Dial-a-Ride and community buses. Don't forget that mobility scooters are also an option, as is car sharing.

19.4 Practice scenarios

1. A concerned daughter is worried that her father, Brian Potter (69 years old) is showing signs of dementia. She has noticed his memory has "not been as good as it used to" and he has completely forgotten to meet her for dinner on several occasions. She has also noted he seems slow to answer questions and has recently forgotten the name of his grandson. You note that his mood seems low and he doesn't seem interested in speaking in the consultation. On further questioning you elicit that his wife died 6 months ago. You suspect he is suffering from depression rather than dementia. Explain your diagnosis and treatment plan.

2. Greta Davies, 71, presents to A&E with severe abdominal pain and a fever. She complains that she is off her food. She is worried she has appendicitis. On examination she is tachycardic and has a temperature of 39°C. Tenderness is localized to her left lower quadrant. Blood results show a high white cell count and a CT scan helps you reach the diagnosis of diverticulitis. Explain your diagnosis and treatment plan.

3. Alexander Smith is a 68-year-old man who has just been diagnosed with prostate cancer after a TRUS biopsy and a staging CT. He has a low-grade cancer that is limited to the prostate and has not spread beyond the capsule. He has come to see you in primary care to discuss the options available to him, as he felt that his consultation in secondary care was not helpful. Explain the options available to him, which may include active surveillance, surgery and radiotherapy. Explain the risks and benefits of each and help him reach a decision.

4. Rose Welby is an 88-year-old woman and an inpatient in hospital after a broken hip. After several weeks of rehabilitation, she is still relatively immobile but medically fit for discharge. Physiotherapy and occupational therapy have written that it is not suitable for her to live independently due to her limited mobility and frailty. A placement has been found for her in a residential home; alternatively she may be able to return home and receive personal care several times a day. Explain these options to her and reach a shared decision on the next step.

5. Roger Marentette is a 92-year-old patient admitted with heart failure and an acute kidney injury. His daughter Violet has power of attorney and has requested to speak with a physician regarding his current state. The medical staff has already decided to initiate a DNAR order. Discuss the DNAR with the patient's daughter and options for palliative care.

20

Paediatrics

HELEN PORTE AND GEORGINA CLARK

The Paediatric Consultation: Keys to Success

Taking a paediatric history differs from the usual consultation as you need to use several sources to gain the full picture as the patient may not be able to communicate for themselves. You will generally have more than one person in the consulting room so your attention will be necessarily divided. **Each person will have their own ideas and agenda for the consultation, and your job will be to assess each of these in turn.**

Extra challenges arise as you must tailor your consultation to the age and development of the patient that comes through the door. The approach for a new baby with a tired first-time mum will be different to that required for a six foot truculent teenager – and therein lies the fun and challenge of paediatrics.

With this in mind, important skills to utilize during the paediatric consultation include:

- **Summarizing** – there is often a lot of information to be covered so a summary will help the interviewer gather their thoughts and may prompt the parent to provide further information.
- **Setting an agenda** – with several people in the room, it can be helpful to explicitly state a structure for the consultation from the outset.
- **Signposting** – again, with several people in the room, the structure and organization of the consultation can greatly facilitate its success.

The key to mastering a paediatric consultation is to be logical and organized throughout. Not only does this gain you marks, but it allows you to maintain control and gather relevant information in good time.

Red flags in paediatrics:

- Physical and mental signs of abuse or neglect
- Failure to achieve developmental milestones
- Regression
- Poor social behaviour (aggression, self-injurious behaviours)
- Poor weight gain or loss of weight
- Bruising
- Recurrent infections
- Worsening headaches

20.1 Information gathering

The presenting complaint in paediatrics can be anything – it may cover a wide range of topics and may be an acute or chronic problem. With this in mind, a full and comprehensive history from each informant, where possible, should allow you to ascertain the full picture and formulate your differential diagnoses.

Whilst taking the history, remember that much can be gained from observing the family as well. For example, does the toddling child make a beeline for the toybox and happily pull the contents out on to the floor? Or does the child sit quiet and subdued on mum's knee? A well child is usually a happy, active being who is pleasant to observe and interact with. An unwell child looks far less happy.

1) Introduce yourself and gain consent
- First impressions matter at this stage and a friendly, warm approach will establish rapport with the parents and child immediately.
- Don't forget to greet and introduce yourself to the child using an age-appropriate greeting. For younger children, using your first name may be less intimidating for them.

2) Consider your first impression
- Consider your body language and try to be open, relaxed and calm.
- Consider your seating arrangements and positioning – try to prevent barriers between you and the family, and consider how you appear from a small child's perspective.
- When practising, get a colleague to sit on the floor and another on a chair, side by side, then practise your introduction. Your colleague on the floor can feed back on how you appear from different positions – are you overly large and a little overwhelming from that angle?
- Try to balance looking professional to the parents with being welcoming to the child.

3) Confirm the patient's name and age
- Ask the child their name and age (*'How old are you now, Duncan?'*), if age appropriate, as this is a good way to break the ice. Try to establish who's who in the room by asking the child (if possible) *'and who have you brought with you today?'* This allows the child to communicate, whilst also allowing the older individuals an opportunity to introduce themselves.

4) History of presenting complaint
- Begin with an open-ended question, such as *'What has brought you to the clinic today?'* or *'How can I help you today?'* Think about phrases that work best for you.

> The Golden Minute is crucial in paediatrics. Parents will often be worried and want to get the problem off their chest. Try not to interrupt and listen carefully at this point – use body language, facial expressions and short phrases to facilitate active listening.
>
> During this time, try to pick out the key symptoms which will need to be explored in further detail as the consultation progresses. Following the Golden Minute, an initial summary will allow you time to gather your thoughts whilst also allowing the opportunity to signpost the consultation accordingly.

20.1.1 Differences in the history – adapting to age

When taking a paediatric history, different information must be gathered that would not necessarily feature in an adult history. In this section, we will consider each age group in turn.

Newborn

- With any newborn history, an accurate obstetrical history should be taken from the mother. For more information, see *Chapter 16*.
- *'How are you feeding baby?'* Try to establish if the baby is being breast- or bottle fed, or maybe a mixture of both, and ask about intake and frequency. Feeding can also be stressful for new mums so screen for any feeding difficulties with *'How are you finding feeding baby?'*
- *'How much is baby taking?'* If baby is breast-feeding, ask if they seem settled after feeds and sleep well, or if they sleep fitfully and seem hungry again. If baby is bottle-feeding, check the overall volume. For extra brownie points, a baby's intake should be 150 ml/kg/day, divided roughly into 8 feeds. This is beyond the knowledge expected of a finals student, but is practical, useful knowledge that will impress a paediatric examiner in a viva.
- To ensure adequate feeding and that the baby is gaining weight properly, ask *'How much did your baby weigh when he/she was born?'* Ensure a weight is taken at each visit and plot it on the growth curve.
  - Most babies lose weight after birth but 80% regain it by 2 weeks of age. When weight loss is greater than 10% or slow to recover, a clinical assessment is required.
- Adequacy of feeding can also be established by asking about the frequency of wet and soiled nappies. *'How many wet nappies does baby have each day? How many dirty nappies (stools) does the baby have each day?'*
- *'When did baby first open his/her bowels?'* A baby should have passed meconium within 24 hours. Any longer than this can signify a congenital issue or inadequate feeding.
- *'Did baby ever look yellow?'* Jaundice is common (60% of term babies) but if present, try to establish at what age this occurred. If this occurred within 24 hours of birth or persisted for more than 2 weeks, it needs further investigation.
- Observation of baby's activity levels during the consultation is also important – is baby very sleepy or irritable? If unusual, ask the parents if this is the baby's normal behaviour.
- Don't forget to ask mum *'How are you feeling?'* She will most likely be exhausted and will appreciate some acknowledgement of this. It is also useful as a screening question to check that she is coping adequately.

Infant

- Asking *'How are you feeding baby currently? What type of food does baby tend to eat?'* allows you to gain more information about weaning and which foods are now being eaten.
- Developmental milestones should be assessed and therefore you should have a good working knowledge of the major milestones at each age. Consider asking about whether they have achieved a milestone in each category – gross motor, fine motor, social and communication. For example, with a 6-month-old child:
  - *'Can your baby sit without any support?'*
  - *'Can your baby pass an object from one hand to another?'*
  - *'Does your baby smile at you?'*
  - *'Does your baby babble at you?'*
- Remember to ask about weight gain and growth – the red book will also be a handy source of information.
- Check that baby is up to date with all vaccinations.
- In an acutely unwell child, assess for dehydration by asking about oral intake as well as urine / bowel movements. Try asking *'How many wet nappies has baby had today?'*
- Take an obstetrical history and a history of the neonatal period.

Pre-school age (2–5 years)

- Try to establish the child's eating habits and diet – it should now be an adult-style diet. Ask *'What is their diet like currently? What foods do they like to eat?'*

- Developmental milestones – don't forget!
- Vaccinations – don't forget!
- Nursery / playgroup attendance – have they had any problems or concerns?
- Toileting – this is a common source of problems and family tension. Ask *'Do they have a toilet schedule?'* and try to establish whether the child is dry during the day and the night, whether they are still using nappies, and if their bowel habit is regular and consistent. 'Peas and carrots' diarrhoea is common in toddlers and is due to an immature gastrointestinal system, but it must be differentiated from other, more serious conditions. The key is to look for red flag symptoms such as blood in the stool, opening bowels regularly during the night, weight loss or failure to thrive.

Primary school age (5–12 years)

- Developmental milestones – don't forget!
- Vaccinations – don't forget!
- Using an open question such as *'Tell me about school'* allows you to gain a large amount of information quickly, whilst also building rapport. Some children may not be very expressive and therefore a closed question approach may be necessary. Try asking questions such as *'Do you like going to school? What's your favourite class? Who is your best friend?'*
- Remember to ask the parent about attendance and performance as well as social interactions at school.
- Asking *'What do you like to do when you are not at school?'* can ascertain any hobbies and can assess their social skills.
- Ask the parent about behaviour and if there are any significant differences between behaviour at home and at school.

Teenager

At this age, young people are establishing their independence, which may bring them into conflict with their parents as they test the boundaries and assert themselves in the world. A consultation may well consist of a grumpy parent and a grumpier teenager disagreeing with each other. The young person may have their own agenda and have issues that they are not willing to discuss with their parent – for example, drug or alcohol consumption and sexual activity. It can therefore be helpful to split the consultation into two sections; one with both parent and teenager present, and one with teenager alone, if appropriate for their age and the situation. However, this must be approached carefully – a parent may feel excluded and dislike the loss of control. A useful approach could be to state that as children make the transition to an adult, it can be useful to have part of the consultation with the child alone as preparation for adulthood. It may be helpful to signpost this at the beginning of the consultation so that it does not come as a surprise.

Adolescents may be reluctant to talk to doctors about their problems and conversely, doctors may find it difficult to talk to teenagers about personal problems. However, the psychosocial history in this age group is extremely important in highlighting risk factors and stressors which may be causing or impacting on a symptom or illness. In this case, a useful framework to use is the HEADSSS assessment. You should not think of these questions as a rigid structure to follow but more as prompts, beginning with less threatening questions (e.g. about home life or hobbies) to build rapport before moving on to more personal questions.

- Home – *'Who lives with you at home? Do you get on well with your family?'*
- Education and employment – *'How do you feel about school? How many days have you missed this term? Could you tell me about your friends from school? Do you have a job?'*
- Activities – *'What do you like to do in your spare time? Who do you like to spend your free time with?'*

- Drugs – you may choose to approach this topic by first asking about their friends or family. For example, *'Do any of your friends or family smoke? Drink alcohol? Use other drugs? Have you tried any of these things?'*
- Sexuality – *'Are you currently in a relationship? Are you sexually active? Are you using any contraception, for example a condom?'*
- Suicide / depression / self-harm – *'Do you feel sad or down frequently? Have you ever wanted to hurt yourself before? Do you know of anyone who has hurt themselves or tried to end their life?'* (this is a risk factor for suicide). *'Do you have anyone that you can talk to if you feel this way?'*
- Safety – *'Have you ever been bullied at school before? Have you ever felt threatened or unsafe because of someone? Have you ever got into a car with someone who has been drinking?'*

Consider the need to explore sensitive questions and tailor your consultation accordingly – for example, in a consultation for a twisted ankle while playing football it would not be appropriate to explore drugs and sexuality, but in a consultation for low mood and poor school performance, these factors could be crucial. If appropriate for the consultation, explore gynaecological issues in girls – pubertal development, onset of menses and any problems with irregularity. See *Chapter 16* for more information on how to take a menstrual and gynaecological history. Most importantly, try to be relaxed and not overly formal, but don't try too hard to "get down with the kids"; you'll risk looking like a fool!

20.1.2 The Fraser Guidelines

These cover the issue, also known as 'Gillick competency', where a child under the age of 16 seeks medical treatment – in this particular case, contraception. Lord Fraser stated, "Provided the patient, whether a boy or a girl, is capable of understanding what is proposed, and of expressing his or her own wishes, I see no good reason for holding that he or she lacks the capacity to express them validly and effectively and to authorise the medical man to make the examination or give the treatment which he advises." With regard to contraception, the guidelines are as follows:

"The doctor will, in my opinion, be justified in proceeding without the parents' consent or even knowledge, provided they are satisfied on the following matters:
- That the girl (although under 16 years of age) will understand their advice;
- That they cannot persuade her to inform her parents or to allow them to inform the parents that she is seeking contraceptive advice;
- That she is very likely to begin or to continue having sexual intercourse with or without contraceptive treatment;
- That unless she receives contraceptive advice or treatment her physical or mental health or both are likely to suffer;
- That her best interests require them to give the contraceptive advice, treatment or both without the parental consent."

In day-to-day life, it is best practice to gently encourage the young person to inform their parents themselves, while reassuring them (if they fulfil the above criteria) that they have a right to confidentiality. In an OSCE, it is important to elicit any worries that your patient might have about telling their parents – ICE is critical in this situation.

20.1.3 The fearful child

When children feel unwell, they regress in terms of their emotional maturity and find challenging situations more upsetting to deal with. You may be faced with a child who is crying, having a tantrum or alternatively sitting wide-eyed and mute. There are a range of tactics you can try to help.

- **Distraction**. In every paediatric consultation room, there should ideally be a range of toys for children of different ages to play with. During an OSCE situation, offering an age-appropriate toy to a child breaks the ice and helps settle the child down.
- **Investigation**. Allow a toddler or preschool child to touch or hold your (cleaned!) stethoscope while you take the history from the parents. They will be much more willing to let you touch them with it if they've had a chance to have a good look at it.
- **Demonstration**. If your young patient looks dubious at the idea of you examining them, let them watch you examine a parent or their teddy first. Once Mummy or teddy have gone through it unscathed, they'll be happier to let you do your assessment.
- **Turn it into a game**. For example, while examining the abdomen and listening for bowel sounds, get them to give you a wiggle while you 'guess' what they've had for breakfast. In the OSCE, don't forget you are dealing with children and you are allowed to have a little bit of fun with them – the examiner will appreciate a child that giggles their way through being examined.
- **Ask concrete questions to break the ice**. For example, ask how old they are and if they have any brothers and sisters.
- **Reward**. Finish a consultation on a good note. Offer younger children a sticker with lots of praise.

5) Systems review

Try to ascertain if any systems have been overlooked during your previous history taking and particularly focus on emotional and psychiatric symptoms here, as these are frequently overlooked.

6) ICE

Ideas, concerns and expectations feature heavily in the paediatric history and can make or break the consultation. Parents often have ideas as to what may be causing the problem in their child and it is important to elicit and acknowledge these. They may also have certain expectations as to the outcome of the consultation: for example, they would like their child to have some imaging. Establishing the parents' agenda can help to guide the consultation and will save crucial time during an OSCE station. It is also important, especially in older children and teenagers, to explore their ICE. Their agenda may be completely different from that of their parents; for example, they may be more concerned that they are not able to "go out with their friends". Try to incorporate both the child's and the parents' concerns.

- *'Have you had any thoughts about what could be causing these symptoms?'*
- *'Is there anything that is particularly worrying you currently?'*
- *'Do you have any specific questions that you wanted answered today? Or is there anything in particular you were expecting from me today?'*

What seems important to the patient may seem to be rather less important to you or the parents. Despite this, it is incredibly important to treat the patient's ideas with respect – if you seem dismissive of a young patient's ideas, you risk losing that ever-important rapport and engagement of the child with their treatment. Fitting in, socializing and participating in social activities are an important factor in a young person's quality of life, and so they may dislike interventions that mark them as being different.

7) Past medical history

Typically, this includes asking for the previous illness and operations of the child, but it is also important here to establish the state of the mother's health too. Start from the beginning:

- Ask about any antenatal problems or maternal health issues at conception – important things to screen for are abnormal scans or extra interventions, e.g. consultant-led care:

- ◦ *'Did you have any problems during your pregnancy?'*
- ◦ *'Were you referred to the hospital during your pregnancy?'*
- Ask about the birth history including the gestation and mode of delivery. Assess if there were any problems including need for resuscitation, an extended stay in hospital (e.g. in neonatal intensive care unit or special care baby unit) or any abnormalities found during the newborn baby check. It may also be helpful if you establish the baby's birth weight, either by asking or looking at the red book.
- Ask about developmental milestones – when assessing if toddlers have achieved their developmental milestones, it might be easier to watch them interact and play during the consultation. However, for newborns and infants, you will need to ask the parents about what they have observed.

8) Family history

'To your knowledge, do any diseases run in the family?' is a good opening question. If a child is acutely unwell, it is also helpful to ask *'Has anyone else in the family had similar symptoms recently?'* This may indicate an infectious cause. When taking a full history, it is good practice to sketch out a small family tree of the immediate family.

9) Drug history

This should be familiar from all other consultations. Establish if they are taking any prescribed medications, as well as OTC or herbal medicines. In teenagers, it is also important to ask about recreational drug use. Try using phrases such as:

- *'Do you currently take any medicines, prescribed or over the counter?'*
- *'Do you use any recreational drugs, including legal highs?'*

These issues can be tricky to explore. A discussion can be facilitated by explaining using a phrase such as, *'I'm just going to ask you some questions which we ask everyone.'* Always ask about allergies and establish the details of the reaction – it is not uncommon for minor reactions in childhood to be labelled as allergies.

10) Social history

This will vary depending on the age of the child – for older children, normal questions about smoking, alcohol and drug use as well as occupation may be relevant, but for younger children, the social history is attempting to understand the household that they currently live in. Try to establish who else lives there, including who has parental responsibility and if there are any siblings. Ask about the parents' occupation, if they own any pets or if smoking occurs in the house. If the child is older, enquiring about school performance, outside activities and their friendships may also be useful. Sensitively ask if there is any social service input.

11) Closing the consultation

Remember to use the Calgary–Cambridge Model and close the consultation with a summary. This allows you to gather and organize your thoughts, whilst also allowing you to screen for any further issues by asking *'Do you have any further questions or concerns for me?'* Make sure to thank both the patient and their parents, before explaining what your next actions will be. For example, *'Thank you for speaking to me today. I am going to discuss your history with the consultant and I shall be back shortly to explain the next steps.'*

Summary of key points (GET YOUR MARKS):

Establish rapport: tailor your introduction to the age of the child. For example, with younger children it may be less intimidating if you introduce yourself using your first name. Explain purpose of consultation, gain consent and ensure confidentiality.

History of presenting complaint: ask an open question and allow for the Golden Minute. During this time allow both the child and parent to speak.

Set an agenda: obtain the agendas of both parent and child and together with your own agenda, set out a plan for the consultation.

Adapt history to age:

- Newborn → enquire about feeding, when first opened bowels, bowel/bladder routine, baby's birth and current weight, screen for jaundice, baby's normal behaviour, mother's mood
- Infant → feeding, developmental milestones, nursery, toilet training
- Primary school age → developmental milestones, school life, social skills
- Teenagers → ascertain their agenda, employ the HEADSSS assessment.

Systems review including emotional and psychological wellbeing.

ICE for both the parent and the child.

Past medical history: if appropriate go right back to antenatal/birth history and include developmental milestones and vaccination history.

Family history: particularly congenital diseases.

Drug history: with teenagers, enquire about recreational drugs.

Social history: ask how things are at home and at school, hobbies, friends, etc. For teenagers use the mnemonic HEADSSS.

Closing the consultation: check you haven't missed anything, encourage them to ask questions if they have any. **Summarize and signpost** throughout. Thank the patient and their family.

20.2 Information giving and shared decision making

This section can be used as a guide to two important topics which are frequently encountered in paediatrics. Establishing the patient's or parents' ICE at the start of the consultation can help you tailor your information, but also make sure to assess the patient's starting point. If the child is old enough to be involved, try to use a level of language that they can understand and try to avoid any jargon. If appropriate, gain extra marks in OSCEs by drawing diagrams, writing a clear plan or offering leaflets.

Review *Chapter 5* to get the most OSCE points possible.

20.2.1 Immunization advice

However daunting the UK immunization schedule (see *Table 20.1*), it is important to get to grips with its basics, as parents naturally have numerous questions about vaccinations. These questions may range from the simple *'What are they and when do they have them?'* to the more complicated *'I'm not sure he/she should have them – what do you think I should do, Doctor?'* Again, try to be logical and organized when giving information. Try to clearly signpost sections, which you can pause between and use that time to chunk and check.

What are they and when do they need them? Vaccinations are injections which are given to people who are at risk of a particular disease. They work by prompting our bodies to produce antibodies, which would usually fight a disease, without us becoming infected. The aim is that you will then be protected from that disease for life.

What are the benefits? The aim of vaccinations is to force our bodies to mount an immune response to fight off infection, without actually infecting us with that disease. This produces antibodies which fight disease and stay in our body to protect us from that disease if we catch it in the future.

What are the risks? After a vaccination, the child may have some swelling at the injection site and may feel unwell and feverish for the first 24–48 hours following it. Sometimes, they may have mild symptoms of the disease they have been vaccinated against, but these will resolve on their own. Vaccinations do not "overload" a baby's immune system and even multiple vaccines only use a small percentage of a child's immune system.

What about the MMR vaccine? Dr Andrew Wakefield wrote a paper in which he claimed there was a link between the MMR vaccine and autism. However, since then, his work has been discredited and further studies have shown there is no proven link between the vaccine and autism.

What if they do not get vaccinated? Unfortunately, it means your child will not be protected from these diseases and may become infected in the future. This can cause long-term complications, which can be severe and sometimes life-threatening.

Table 20.1 UK immunization schedule

Age of immunization	Vaccine	How it is given
Two months old	Diphtheria, tetanus, pertussis, polio and haemophilus influenza type b (Hib)	One injection
	Pneumococcal conjugate	One injection
	Meningococcal group B (MenB)	One injection
	Rotavirus	Orally
Three months old	Diphtheria, tetanus, pertussis, polio and Hib	One injection
	Rotavirus	Orally
Four months old	Diphtheria, tetanus, pertussis, polio and Hib	One injection
	Pneumococcal conjugate	One injection
	MenB	One injection
Between 12 and 13 months old	Hib and Meningitis C	One injection
	Pneumococcal conjugate	One injection
	Measles, mumps and rubella (MMR)	One injection
	MenB	One injection
Two to eight years old	Influenza	Nasal spray – one spray into each nostril
Three years four months old	Diphtheria, tetanus, pertussis and polio	One injection
	Measles, mumps and rubella (MMR)	One injection
Girls aged 12–13 years	Human papillomavirus (HPV)	Course of two injections, 6–24 months apart
Around 14 years old	Tetanus, diphtheria and polio	One injection
	Meningococcal groups A, C, W and Y disease	One injection

20.2.2 Staying for further assessment

This can be a challenging scenario. An example situation may be that a child has been noted to have some bruises that are perhaps unusual in shape or location. This delicate situation may have been caused by an organic pathology, such as a clotting disorder, by non-accidental injury, or simply by accidents encountered by the child in the normal course of their life. Your job may be to explain to the parents that their child needs to stay on the ward for further investigation into the cause of the bruising.

Why does my child need to stay in hospital? Your child has some bruises which both you and we have noticed. We don't know what has caused them and there could be several reasons why they have occurred. While we try to sort through the reasons, we need to observe your child on the ward.

Why could my child have these bruises and why can't we have these investigations from home? There could be several different reasons for the bruising. Your child might have a problem with how their blood clots, or have problems with their skin, for example. They may have also hurt themselves in an accident. The other cause of bruising that we worry about is when another person hurts them and gives them bruises. We need to observe them on the ward to see how the bruises progress and see if they get any more of them.

What are you going to do while we are on the ward? We will need to do some tests on your child. These will include blood tests, X-rays and taking pictures of the bruises. We can also talk to you, your partner and your child to see if you have any problems that you would like help and support with.

What are the benefits of staying on the ward? While you are here, we can do all the tests more quickly and efficiently. We can also offer you any support you might need at home.

What if I want to take my child home? We would very much encourage you to stay with us while we try to find out why your child has these bruises. If you have any particular questions or worries about staying, please let me know and I can find a senior doctor to answer them for you if I can't.

20.3 **Practice scenarios**

1. You are in a GP surgery seeing 3-year-old Sophie Cook, who has come in with a 2-day history of a sore throat. She has been unwell for a few days and complains of a temperature (37.8°C), cough and runny nose. Her mum, Carol, has been giving her Calpol but is worried about her. On examination, she is apyrexial with a clear chest and normal ENT examination, except for a red throat. You have been asked to explain to the mother that this is likely a viral infection and explain further management.

2. You are in the diabetic clinic and have been asked to speak to 15-year-old Sam Foster. He was diagnosed with type 1 diabetes at the age of 7 and has had good glycaemic control since. However, in the past 6 months, his HbA1c has risen to 70 mmol/mol. You have been asked to speak to Sam about his diabetic control to try to establish why his control has worsened.

3. You are in A&E when a 2-year-old, Robert Brown, is admitted with a seizure. He is usually well, but for the past 3 days he has been unwell with a cold he picked up from nursery. All investigations are normal, but when you assess his observations chart, he is noted to have a temperature above 40°C on a number of readings. You have been asked to explain to his parents, Danny and Claire, about febrile seizures and what this means for the future.

4. You are in A&E and you see Daniel Kowalski, a 3-year-old boy who has tripped and bumped his head in the garden. He has been seen by a registrar, who arranged for him to have a short period of observation in A&E. At the end of this, he is alert and well. The registrar advises you that he is safe to go home and asks you to explain this to the parents.

5. You are the foundation doctor on the paediatric ward. Kelsey Black is a 14-year-old girl with cystic fibrosis who has been admitted with an exacerbation of her chest symptoms. You have clerked her in and relayed the information to your registrar, who tells you she will need to stay for at least a week of IV antibiotics. Your registrar asks you to explain this to Kelsey.

6. Ingrid Bauer is a 32-year-old woman who has attended for her 6-week check at the GP surgery. She is concerned about the child immunization programme and is worried about the effect it may have on her newborn daughter. Currently, she does not want her to be immunized. You are asked to speak to Ingrid regarding her concerns and come to a decision about her next steps.

7. Bethany White is a 15-year-old girl who has come to the GP surgery alone. She is asking for the contraceptive pill for the first time. You have been asked to answer her questions about the contraceptive pill and to decide if she is Fraser competent.

8. Jennifer Harris is a 29-year-old woman who has just delivered her first baby. You are the neonatal junior doctor and you attend to perform the 6-hour baby check on her baby on the post-natal ward. She asks you about feeding her baby and wants to discuss breast- and bottle-feeding.

21

Taking a drug history

JAMES PLATT AND JOE PANG

The Drug History: Keys to Success

When taking a drug history, consider the following factors for each prescribed medication:

- Medication ownership
- Duration of use
- Assessing compliance
- Indication for drug
- Prescribed dose and frequency
- Adverse effects.

Be sure to also enquire about known drug allergies, OTC medications and illicit substance use. During the OSCE this will often be assessed as a focused history taking station; however, it is important to take into account any further information from the patient's general history. This chapter will illustrate how to take a thorough drug history, and explore the factors listed above.

Red flag drugs:

- Anticoagulants (warfarin)
- Steroids
- Methotrexate
- Benzodiazepines
- Antibiotics (be aware of allergies)
- Diuretics
- Opiates
- Hypoglycaemics (insulin and sulphonylureas)

21.1 How to take a drug history

Medication histories are usually conducted when first clerking a newly admitted inpatient to the ward or completing a medication review as a GP. A medication review is done in order to know which medications are necessary to prescribe, and secondly to elicit whether the medications have contributed to their presenting state. It is also an opportunity to investigate compliance with medication and identify interactions.

1) Introduce yourself and your role on the healthcare team

2) Ensure consent and confidentiality

3) Confirm the patient's name and DOB; ask about occupation

It is sometimes helpful to ask the patient about their occupation early in the consultation. Asking the patient what they do for work along with a follow-up question such as *'What does that involve?'* or *'Do you enjoy your job?'* can establish rapport early and may provide some context later in the consultation when you are asking about limitations.

4) Medication history

> **OSCE TIP**: To prevent forgetting, always ask about allergies before exploring a patient's medical history.

21.1.1 Allergies

> **Key Knowledge:** Be aware of the difference between an allergy and a side-effect. For example, many people describe flushing when they take aspirin as an allergy but this is just a side-effect.

Often missed but crucially important. Medication allergies are frequently neglected in OSCE stations, as well as in everyday practice. It is also important to enquire about the nature of their reaction to any declared medication; patients often consider side-effects as an 'allergic' response.

'I am here to take a look at your medications, and see how you have been getting on with them.'

Patients will usually have their medications in a green pharmacy bag or in a dosette box. Patients sometimes bring a list of their medications with them to hospital. In any situation, always ask the patient if they have brought this bag with them.

21.1.2 Medication ownership

There are two main tasks that are required to complete this section.

Check the medication label

This is done to know what medication it is but also to confirm that it has been prescribed for the patient involved. It is not uncommon to sometimes find the medication of a spouse or relative mixed in with the patient's own bag of medications, hence it is vitally important to identify this at the start.

Confirm ownership with the patient

'I see that this drug has been prescribed to you, is this correct?'

Subsequently, check with the patient that the medication in question is indeed theirs. This acts as a failsafe to confirm ownership and also may give the patient the opportunity to express any issues or uncertainties.

21.1.3 Indication for drug

Patient's understanding

'What are you taking this medication for?'

Often, patients are prescribed medication without being fully aware of its purpose. A careful approach to this can expose areas where additional education is required. Furthermore, drugs prescribed a considerable time ago may remain amongst current medications as the patient may have forgotten to dispose of them. This can lead to unnecessary consumption and adverse effects.

Discussing these matters with a patient may also reveal other important elements, i.e. significant past medical history or co-morbidities.

21.1.4 **Duration of use**

Determine a timeline of use

'How long have you been taking this medication?'

It can be very helpful to get an idea of the exact periods in which this drug has been prescribed and consumed. If the medication is new to the patient, it may be that it has contributed in some way to the presenting complaint. On the flip side, you may be able to elicit drugs that have been consumed for much longer than required and are now not required.

21.1.5 **Prescribed dose and frequency**

Confirming suitability

'How much of it do you take, and how many times a day?'

Initially, ensure the prescribed dose and frequency is suitable for the patient's condition. Consequently, confirm the patient understands this, and has previously been taking that quantity. If not, this will provide a good opportunity to give information and educate the patient for future use.

21.1.6 **Assessing compliance**

Correct use

'Have you been taking this drug every day?' (frequency varies between drugs)

Medication compliance may affect a new patient in two ways. Firstly, the person may not be taking their medication correctly and consequently develops a problem. Alternatively, the patient may be taking the drug perfectly; however, it may have led to a medication-induced issue (i.e. toxicity or organ damage).

It is also important to screen for single instances where medication has not been taken correctly. This can be done by asking if there have ever been instances, intentional or otherwise, where the medication has not been taken.

'On average, how many days per week do you forget to take your medication?'

In addition to checking whether the patient is taking the medication as prescribed, the doctor should ascertain if the patient is also attending their follow-up appointments and undergoing appropriate drug monitoring (e.g. blood tests). This will require a working knowledge of the monitoring schedule for certain medications.

Exploring non-compliance

'On the occasions where you haven't taken your medication, what has been the reason for this?'

Discussing the reasons for non-compliance can shed light on a number of influencing factors. Determining what these are can assist in modifying the prescription or providing the necessary support to the patient. It is also possible to assess to what extent the patient is non-compliant.

> **Key Knowledge: Factors affecting compliance**
> - Indication of the drug not clear to patient.
> - Perceived risks and the patient's own concerns and expectations of the medication.
> - Perceived ineffectiveness of the medication.
> - Physical difficulties: e.g. swallowing difficulties, handling the medication.
> - Non-pleasant formulations: e.g. taste of medication.
> - Complicated regimens / instructions for regimen not explained clearly.
> - Prescription not collected or not dispensed.

21.1.7 Adverse effects

'How have you been getting along with the medication?'
'Have you noticed any problems or side-effects that you feel may relate to the drug?'

Understanding the nature of any adverse effect is an essential part of any drug history. It is important to consider the impact that these effects are having on the patient, and in addition what they could mean for the patient's overall health.

For some patients, a given side-effect may be totally manageable, with the benefit of the treatment far more vital in their eyes. In other cases, the same adverse outcome may be life-changing and have a considerable influence on the person's quality of life. Hence, it is important to understand the true meaning of these effects to each individual patient. Adverse effects may also come to light due to a problem with the patient's underlying health. Certain drugs are toxic to particular organs, and damage to these structures can occur in parallel to the beneficial effects of the drug. Therefore, it is important to pick up early on signs of damage.

In some instances, a patient may not recognize the relationship between a particular medication and an adverse effect they have been suffering with. A screening technique is to ask direct closed questions about significant or dangerous side-effects.

21.1.8 Over the counter purchases

'Have you purchased anything over the counter, which is not included in your prescription?'
'Do you take any medications you have purchased from elsewhere, for example vitamins or herbal remedies?'

It is not uncommon for patients to take medications, supplements or herbal remedies alongside their prescription. Whilst most of these are quite safe, it is important to be wary of interactions with prescribed drugs e.g. St John's wort in addition to SSRIs. Many patients will forget to mention these drugs when describing their medication, so it is vital that you ask specifically.

21.1.9 Illicit drugs

> **OSCE TIP**: When approaching the topic of recreational drug use, it is best to be forthright, direct and honest in your questioning.
> Not only will this allow for a more succinct history but it conveys objectiveness more efficiently. Apply this approach to smoking and alcohol as well.

'Do you take any recreational drugs?'
'Do you use any drugs that are not for medication purposes?'
'Do you take any prescription medications that have been prescribed to another person?'

Doctors and medical students often assume that patients do not use illicit substances, or neglect the importance of this information when taking a wider drug history. The reasons for asking this are twofold:

- First, this may have an influence on care and prescribing for this patient.
- Secondly, this information may help give an indication of a patient's general wellbeing.

This may be a very sensitive topic to some patients, therefore it is essential to approach this in a non-judgmental manner. A handy tip to maintain rapport is to guide the patient into this section of the history:

'This is a question we have to ask everyone...'

21.1.10 Oral contraceptive pill

'Are you taking any tablets for contraception/protection?'

Many women may not perceive the oral contraceptive pill to be a form of medication, and as a result, this can be missed. Take particular care to ask about oral contraceptives in women of childbearing age.

21.2 Encouraging compliance

Therapeutic compliance has been a major medical issue for some time, with non-compliance being very common. Many factors affect the rates of compliance, e.g. acute prescriptions tend to have better compliance than long-term therapies. There are various types of non-compliance:

- Receiving a prescription but not collecting the medication.
- Taking an incorrect dose.
- Taking medication at the wrong times.
- Increasing or decreasing the frequency of doses without medical advice.
- Stopping the treatment too soon.
- Failing to follow doctor's instructions.
- 'Drug holidays' – where a patient stops a therapy for a while before starting again.
- 'White-coat compliance' – where patients are only compliant around the time of seeing the doctor.

It is recommended that any non-compliant patient should be offered a constructive discussion which revolves around the following points:

- The purpose of their medication.
- Complications that can arise from not taking the medication as prescribed.
- Pharmacological and non-pharmacological alternatives.
- Reducing or stopping long-term medicines.
- Fitting medicines into their routine.
- Having a choice of medicines.

NICE recommends suggesting the following options for non-compliance, if suitable:

- Suggesting patients record their medicine-taking.
- Encouraging patients to monitor their condition (e.g. home blood pressure monitoring or daily weighing for patients with heart failure).
- Simplifying the dose regimen; for example, changing a regimen from twice per day to once per day.
- Using alternative packaging, for example switching to dosette boxes if the patient has difficulty opening the bottles or has difficulty remembering when to take their medications.

21.3 Special groups

It is important to understand how prescribing differs in these special patient groups. This will help you in assessing both a person's drug history and their prescriptions, writing up new regimens and making changes. You should always review the safety of prescribed medication in each of these groups.

21.3.1 Pregnancy

> **Key Knowledge: Drugs contraindicated in pregnancy**
> - ACE inhibitors
> - Various anti-epileptic drugs
> - Various antibiotics
> - Statins
> - Various herbal medications
> - Products containing vitamin A

Some drugs can be harmful to the embryo or fetus during pregnancy:
- **First trimester** (1–13 weeks): most of the organs are developing and being formed. Drugs can have teratogenic effects at this stage, manifesting in congenital malformations. The fetus is at highest risk between weeks 3 and 11.
- **Second and third trimesters** (14–27 and 28 weeks onwards, respectively): drugs may affect growth or function of the fetal tissues, causing stunted growth or toxic effects.

It is important to note that drugs prescribed during pregnancy are only considered if the benefits to the mother outweigh the risks to the fetus; for example, preventing withdrawal symptoms in opiate-dependent mothers with methadone prescriptions. Although there are many drugs that are safe during pregnancy, it is safer to avoid medications entirely, especially during the first trimester.

21.3.2 Breast–feeding

> **Key Knowledge: Drugs contraindicated in breast-feeding**
> Remember – BREAST
> Bromocriptine/benzodiazepines
> Radioactive isotopes/rizatriptan
> Ergometrine/ethosuximide
> Amiodarone/amphetamines/antimetabolites
> Stimulant laxatives/sex hormones
> Tetracycline/tretinoin

Breast-feeding is incredibly beneficial for infants, therefore mothers are usually encouraged to feed their babies until they are at least 6 months of age. Breast milk has higher nutritional value than formula feeds and contains antibodies, which provide passive immunity to children, thereby reducing the risk of infections and sudden infant death syndrome (SIDS).

Medications rarely interfere with the mother's ability to breast-feed; however, there are certain situations where breast-feeding is discouraged. The main concerns relate to the mixing of active drug metabolites with the mother's milk, leading to potential adverse effects on the infant.

21.3.3 Children

When completing a drug history in children, it is worth bearing in mind certain differences between them and adults.

Dosages vary greatly. Unlike most medications in adults, the dose is often based on weight, surface area or age ranges. Despite this, no dose for children should exceed the maximum adult dose, irrespective of the new calculated values. Extra care should be taken to avoid drug toxicity (especially in neonates); reduced drug clearance and differences in organ sensitivity can increase the risk of toxic effects.

There may be logistical influences on a child's prescription. Intramuscular (IM) injections may be avoided due to their painful nature, and regimens may be altered to fit with a child's routine. Parents are often the ones responsible for medication compliance in a child. Compliance issues should therefore be considered for both the parent and the child.

21.3.4 Elderly patients

With an ever-ageing population, elderly patients are becoming increasingly common, many of whom have co-morbidities that require long-term management. Potential dangers arise when multiple drugs are prescribed for one patient. Polypharmacy describes the concurrent use of multiple medications in one individual. Problems associated with polypharmacy may include:

- Drug interactions – potentially leading to adverse effects and fatal outcomes.
- Increasing 'pill burden' – may be unacceptable to the patient, leading to poor adherence.
- Additional medications being required – prescribed to counteract current medication side-effects, introducing further adverse effects of their own.

Furthermore, elderly patients are generally more sensitive to commonly used medications, due to altered pharmacokinetics. This leads to higher drug concentrations in tissues, in addition to the effects of ageing (e.g. postural hypotension). Care must be taken to identify and omit drugs that may be causing more harm than benefit. Common drugs to look out for in the elderly include:

- **Hypnotics**: drugs like benzodiazepines are commonly found on the prescriptions of the elderly; they can cause side-effects such as drowsiness, unsteady gait, and confusion, which all increase the risk of falls.
- **Diuretics**: often excessively prescribed in the elderly to treat simple gravitational oedema. They should be used with caution as they can lead to dehydration and confusion, thus increasing the likelihood of injury or fall.
- **NSAIDs**: bleeding associated with aspirin or other NSAID use is more commonly reported in the elderly. Unfortunately, the elderly are also at higher risk of more serious or even fatal outcomes from such events.
- **Antihypertensives**: may contribute to hypotension, increasing risks of falls and fractures.

21.3.5 Renal / hepatic impairment

Many drugs are metabolized by the kidneys and liver. Impairment of these organs can have a huge influence on a patient's prescription. Impairment can lead to reduced drug metabolism, and thus lead to toxic levels of the drug or reduced efficacy. For this reason, doses may need to be altered or avoided completely to accommodate and reduce risk to the patient. For example, hepatic impairment may lead to reduced clotting ability, which would increase sensitivity to any anticoagulants.

Certain drugs are also toxic to the organs themselves. These drugs may need to be avoided, or carefully monitored, to reduce or avoid any toxic consequences in those with pre-existing disease of the liver / kidneys.

Summary of key points (GET YOUR MARKS):

Establish rapport (clear introduction of who you are, what your role is and why you are there).

Confirm ownership of the medications with the patient and check the medication label if it is available to you.

Check the patient's understanding of why they are taking that medication.

Check how long they have been taking the medication and if they have been taking it appropriately, i.e. correct dose and frequency.

Assess the patient's compliance to the medications and if there is an issue with this, explore why, making sure to clarify any misconceptions.

- If appropriate you may need to encourage compliance (see *Section 21.2* on common ways to solve this).

Check if they are experiencing any adverse effects from their medication.

Check for any drug allergies and confirm the nature of the patient's reaction.

Enquire about OTC purchases and any illicit drug taking.

Always consider whether this patient falls into a 'special group' of patients, who have specific medication needs / contraindications.

Mnemonic for taking a drug history: OUT RACES

Ownership: Is it the patient's medication?

Understanding: Do they understand why they are taking it?

Timeline: When did they start the medication? How long should they be taking the medication?

Route, dosage and frequency in which they take their medications.

Adverse effects to their medications and allergies.

Concordance: Are they taking the medication as it is ordered? Do they attend scheduled appointments and follow-up investigations?

Extra medications and recreational drug use: Does the patient take any OTC medications, supplements or vitamins? Does the patient smoke cigarettes, drink alcohol or use recreational drugs?

Special groups: Does the patient have any medical issues that may interfere with the pharmacokinetics of the drug?

21.4 **Practice scenarios**

A drug history OSCE station will probably provide you with a clinical scenario. It will then usually ask you to complete a full drug history and make any changes to the prescription that you feel are necessary. The following scenarios are designed to help you practise making changes based on a clinical incident.

1. Marjorie Neal is a 74-year-old lady who has been admitted to the hospital following a fall at home. After you have taken a full history of the event, she reveals to you that she felt very dizzy upon standing from her chair. The next thing she knew, she was on the floor calling for help. This is the first time she has fallen. She has a past medical history of hypertension, IHD, OA of her left hip and asthma. Her blood pressure is 116/68 when supine and 94/52 when standing. Take a complete drug history and answer the questions that follow. *The following information is for the actor.*

   She takes the following medications:
   - Aspirin 75 mg PO OD
   - Simvastatin 40 mg PO ON

- Amlodipine 5 mg PO OD
- Ramipril 10 mg PO OD
- Paracetamol 1 g PO QDS
- Salbutamol INHALER PRN

There are no known drug allergies. There is no use of OTC drugs or illicit substances.

(a) Which of Marjorie's medications may have contributed to this state?

(b) How might you alter her prescription to prevent further events?

2. Teresa Novak, age 19, is admitted to the hospital with persistent vomiting. A pregnancy test is carried out, which comes back positive. The medical team estimate a gestation of approximately 10 weeks. She is started on cyclizine, which helps bring the sickness under control. The pregnancy has been otherwise uneventful. Whilst on the evening ward round, you have a look at Teresa's drug chart, and see the following prescribed medications:

- Cyclizine PO TDS
- Paracetamol 1 g PO QDS
- Ibuprofen 200 mg PO TDS
- Folic acid 400 mg PO OD
- Omeprazole 30 mg PO OD
- Isotretinoin PO OD

She has a past medical history of back pain, acne and gastric reflux.

She has no known drug allergies. There is no use of OTC drugs or illicit substances.

Review these medications and make any changes you feel may be necessary.

3. Kevin Morgan is a 74-year-old man who has been admitted to A&E for haematemesis earlier in the evening. His past medical history includes a heart attack one year ago and AF, for which he takes rate-control therapy. He also suffers from hypertension, and is taking medication for that. His current medications are as follows:

- Aspirin 75 mg PO OD
- Warfarin 5 mg PO OD
- Atorvastatin 80 mg PO ON
- Bisoprolol 10 mg PO OD
- Ramipril 2.5 mg PO OD
- Paracetamol 1 g PO QDS

Mr Morgan has no known drug allergies. There is no use of OTC drugs or illicit substances. He has since been investigated with an emergency endoscopy, which revealed a severe peptic ulcer.

Take a drug history and then answer the following questions. Consider his medications, listed above.

(a) What are some of the modifications you would make to Mr Morgan's medication list and why?

(b) What would you prescribe for Mr Morgan, given his history?

(c) What are some of the basic investigations you would perform immediately?

4. Lucy Parker is a 53-year-old lady seen in primary care for a sore throat and flu-like symptoms. She has been recently diagnosed with hyperthyroidism after a month-long history of weight loss despite ravenous appetite and intolerance to warm environments. She has started some medication for it, and has been tolerating it well, but recently has fallen a little ill as there seems to be a seasonal bug going around. Her medication history is as follows:

- Atorvastatin 40 mg PO ON
- Carbimazole 20 mg PO OD
- Adcal-D3 1 tab PO OD
- Alendronate 35 mg PO once weekly

Ms Parker has no known drug allergies and there is no use of OTC drugs or illicit substances. Take a drug history from the patient and answer the following questions.

(a) What are some of the medications you would like to review with Ms Parker?

(b) What would you do to manage this patient appropriately?

(c) What are some of the basic investigations you would perform immediately?

21.4.1 Answers to scenarios

1a) Amlodipine, ramipril.

1b) Consider altering antihypertensives e.g. removing ramipril to see if BP can be controlled with first-line therapy and lifestyle modifications. Also consider non-pharmacological approaches, e.g. modifications to household environment.

2. Ibuprofen – stop if not essential and patient can manage on paracetamol (risk vs. benefit situation)

Isotretinoin – STOP (this is teratogenic).

3a) Stop aspirin, warfarin and paracetamol (due to risk of gastric bleeding).

3b) Proton pump inhibitor (e.g. omeprazole) for at least 2 months, probably followed by a repeat prescription for peptic ulcer protection.

3c) Full blood count, urea and electrolytes, liver function tests, clotting screen, cross-match; followed by an urgent endoscopy.

4a) Given the onset of recent illness, you should always review all medications. However, given the scenario there should be a focus on carbimazole, due to risk of agranulocytosis.

4b) Stop the carbimazole immediately, carry out a full blood count and admit to hospital (treatment will then often involve granulocyte-CSF).

4c) Full blood count (with differential), blood film, exclude other causes and manage any sepsis.

22

The consultation through an interpreter

RHIANNA DAVIES

Consultation Through an Interpreter: Keys to Success

- Whenever possible, use an interpreter, not a relative or friend.
- Maintain your history taking structure throughout including signposting, summarizing and using both open and closed questioning.
- Don't forget to explore the patient's ICE. Recognize, acknowledge and validate any concerns that the patient may have.
- Address the patient NOT the interpreter.
- Avoid raising your voice or speaking unnaturally slowly.
- Allow the interpreter time to interpret your last sentence without interrupting.
- Close the consultation clearly and give the patient the opportunity to ask questions.

22.1 Language barriers in medicine

The most recent census from the Office of National Statistics suggests there are around 800 000 people living in Britain today with little or no English. The prevalence of non-English speakers is area-dependent but the percentage is higher in bigger centres such as London (see *Fig. 22.1*).

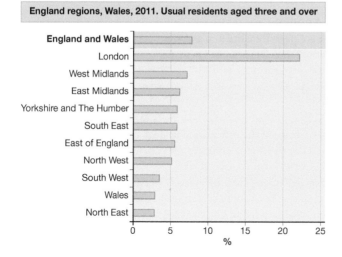

England regions, Wales, 2011. Usual residents aged three and over

Figure 22.1 Percentage of residents of England and Wales whose main language is not English, by region.

Doctors cannot be expected to speak multiple languages, but they should make the effort to ensure that they can communicate effectively with their patients. Patients who lack a proficiency in English (see *Fig. 22.2*) may have difficulty navigating the healthcare system. They may not engage with primary prevention strategies or delay seeking help for their ailments in an effort to avoid awkward encounters with healthcare professionals.

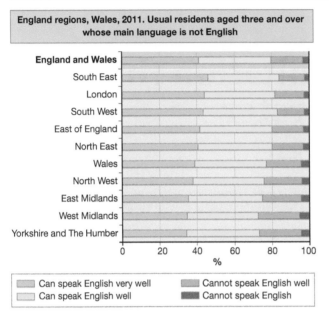

Figure 22.2 *Proficiency in English of residents of England and Wales, by region.*

22.2 **The consultation**

22.2.1 **Pre-consultation**

- Use a professional interpreter whenever possible. A relative or friend may not be able to interpret perfectly (due to insufficient knowledge of medicine or one of the two languages), may have their own agenda or may find it embarrassing to interpret for sensitive subjects.
- Where at all possible have an interpreter physically present in the room. If this is not possible, be aware of local or hospital interpretation services.

Briefing with the interpreter

- Ensure the interpreter is able to translate into and from the appropriate language.
- Discuss the type of consultation, whether bad news will be broken and whether there are to be any procedures or examinations.
- Discuss how the interpreter likes to interpret: taking turns to talk or longer chunks of speech.
- The interpreter will likely have a better understanding of the socio-cultural and religious aspects of the country of origin of the patient, so they may be able to brief you.
- Informing the interpreter of the demographics of the patient will help them to plan their use of language.
- Establish that the interpreter understands the necessity of confidentiality and impartiality.
- Ask how the interpreter likes the chairs to be arranged. It is generally felt that the 'triangle' seating arrangement must be avoided when sitting with a doctor, patient and interpreter. Having the three parties looking between each other breaks up the patient–doctor

dynamic. It is more appropriate to sit the interpreter slightly behind the patient so eye contact and rapport can be maintained between the doctor and the patient (see *Fig. 22.3*).

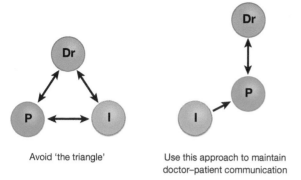

Avoid 'the triangle'   Use this approach to maintain doctor–patient communication

Figure 22.3 *Positioning of doctor, patient and interpreter.*

22.2.2 Initiating the consultation

- Introduce yourself to the patient as you would any patient, using appropriate name, handshake, etc.
- Explain the role of interpreter to the patient and assure confidentiality.

22.2.3 Throughout the consultation

- Maintain proper positioning, avoiding the 'triangle'.
- Address the patient not the interpreter. This allows you to take note of non-verbal cues and develop rapport.
- Maintain an open body position and eye contact with the patient.
- Pose questions to the patient not the interpreter – 'you' not 'she/he'.
- Maintain your normal structure of history taking throughout. Be sure to explore the patient's ICE as you would with any consultation.
- Speak in a normal tone and volume of voice.
- Be respectful towards the patient's lack of English.
- It is inadvisable to have a family member act as an interpreter, but if this is your only option be respectful of their efforts, regardless of ability.
- Break bad news in the same sensitive way you would to an English-speaking patient, including facial expressions and touch as appropriate. Your own non-verbal language will be even more important in these situations in order to comfort the patient.
- During the examination of the patient it is more appropriate for the interpreter to remain outside the curtain. If the interpreter is on the phone, use them to brief the patient as to what you will be doing throughout the examination before moving onto this stage of the consultation.

22.2.4 Ending the consultation

- Summarize the information in small chunks and check that you have not missed anything.
- Give the patient the opportunity to ask questions.

22.2.5 Debrief with the interpreter

- If it is a professional interpreter take the time to discuss what they feel you did well and what you could improve upon for future consultations via an interpreter.

> **Summary of key points (GET YOUR MARKS):**
> **Treat the consultation the same as any other:** maintain your normal history taking / information giving structure throughout.
> **Maintain proper positioning,** avoiding the 'triangle' arrangement.
> **Introduce yourself to the patient,** ask their name and DOB, obtain consent and ensure confidentiality.
> **Address the patient throughout,** not the interpreter.
> **Establish the patient's ICE.** There may be variations in cultural concerns and expectations for care.
> **Closing the consultation:** check the patient's understanding and your own. Give the patient the opportunity to ask questions. Thank the patient.

22.3 Practice scenarios

1. You are a doctor in a gynaecology outpatient department. Mrs Kosika is a 58-year-old Polish lady who speaks very little English. Having gone through the menopause several years ago she presents to you today having experienced several episodes of vaginal bleeding. She has brought her 15-year-old grandson with her who is fluent in both Polish and English. Take a history from the patient using a telephone interpreter service, after explaining why it is better not to have her grandson as the interpreter.

2. You are a doctor in a gastroenterology outpatient department. A 22-year-old Indian man presents with a history of change in bowel habit, weight loss and passing blood and mucus per rectum. An interpreter who speaks the appropriate language has been arranged. Please take a history using the interpreter provided.

23

Safeguarding vulnerable adults and children

ADAM WALTON

Safeguarding: Keys to Success

- Remember that there are many forms of abuse: physical (also known as non-accidental injury or NAI), emotional/psychological, sexual, financial, discriminatory and neglect.
- Remain non-judgmental in tone and avoid accusatory statements – this will only result in the suspected abusers becoming defensive and unwilling to cooperate.
- A clear diagnosis can be made through structured history taking, full examination and appropriate investigations. It is also helpful to gather information from collateral sources including witnesses, social services, other professionals, case notes, etc.
- The six principles of safeguarding are:
  1. Empowerment
  2. Protection
  3. Prevention
  4. Proportionality
  5. Partnership
  6. Accountability.

Red flags in safeguarding:
- Frequent attendances to A&E or the GP
- Delayed presentations
- Injuries that are inconsistent with the history
- Delayed developmental milestones
- Lack of concern from parent or guardian
- Poor attendance at school due to frequent illness
- Physical signs of injury or neglect

23.1 Safeguarding and abuse

It is the duty of all doctors to safeguard their patients from harm. The Department of Health defines safeguarding as "protecting children from maltreatment" and "protecting the rights of adults to live in safety, free from abuse and neglect". Safeguarding is a Care Quality Commission inspection criterion for all healthcare providers, from nursing homes to hospitals.

In England a total of 103 900 adult safeguarding referrals and 48 300 child protection plans were initiated in 2014. All patients should be safeguarded against the four categories of abuse (see *Table 23.1*). Financial abuse and discriminatory abuse have been recognized as two additional categories (see *Table 23.2*). Abuse can occur as isolated events or upon an institution-wide scale.

Table 23.1 The four categories of abuse

Category	Characteristics	Examples
Physical or non-accidental injury (NAI)	Infliction of pain and/or injury	Slapping, hitting, kicking, force-feeding, striking with objects, burning, female genital mutilation (FGM)
Emotional or psychological	Infliction of mental anguish or harm	Verbal aggression, malicious threats, deliberate withdrawal of love or attention, persistent degrading statements
Sexual	Coercion into sexual activities	Sexual assault, non-consensual exposure to explicit material, suggestive talk, sending pornographic images electronically ("sexting")
Neglect or acts of omission	Failure of carer(s) to meet needs required for patient's wellbeing; can be intentional or unintentional	Failure to provide adequate food, clothing and warmth, medical care, and attention/social interaction

Table 23.2 Additional categories of abuse

Category	Characteristics	Examples
Financial or material	Exploitation for financial purposes	Theft, fraud, demanding money, pressure in connection with wills, restricting access to personal finances
Discriminatory	Discrimination against protected characteristics (Equality Act 2010)	Racist abuse, sexism, abuse based on disability, abuse based on age, slurs and forms of harassment
Institutional or organizational	Acts of abuse within an institution or healthcare organization	The Mid Staffordshire Foundation Trust, Winterbourne View care home

23.2 Safeguarding children

> **OSCE TIP**: Safeguarding is often a sensitive and emotional subject. When dealing with suspected cases of abuse, it is important to remain non-judgmental in tone and to avoid accusatory statements. Developing a positive rapport with the patient and his/her carer(s) will be beneficial in future discussions.

A child is legally defined as anyone less than 18 years of age. In the UK one child in every 2000 suffers from significant physical abuse and up to 100 children are killed per year as a complication of maltreatment. Those who commit child abuse are more commonly young male adults of lower socioeconomic status. A history of substance misuse or criminal behaviour could also be present. When interacting with children, an abuse perpetrator may appear aggressive, hostile, or unemotional and lacking in concern.

Recognizing child maltreatment remains challenging. Abuse might be considered as part of a differential diagnosis, or suspected based on patient observation. Presentations suggestive of child abuse include:

- Delayed and/or unusual attendance patterns to medical services.
- A discrepant clinical picture (including fabricated and induced illnesses).
- Poor school attendances attributed to ill health.

A diagnosis of child abuse is possible through structured history taking, examination and appropriate investigations. All clinical findings need to be documented. Work-related stress, fear of parent / guardian complaints and worries surrounding personal safety might prevent clinicians from acting upon safeguarding concerns. Apprehension of wrongly implicating a parent / guardian who is innocent can also hinder discussion. It is vital, however, to overcome such barriers and for actions to be taken in the best interests of the patient. Staff members such as paediatric nurses can sit in during difficult consultations to provide support.

23.3 Information gathering

1) Introduce yourself and your role on the healthcare team

2) Ensure consent and confidentiality

3) Confirm the patient's name and DOB
Always remember to remain calm and introduce yourself fully to the patient and the accompanying adult(s). Gain consent to ask questions before proceeding. Start with an open question (for example *'What brought you into hospital today?'*) to identify the reason of admission.

4) History of presenting complaint

23.3.1 Physical abuse

Presentations of physical abuse include abrasions, bites, cuts, scalds and burns. Accidental bruising is uncommon in children who have yet to mobilize, i.e. those younger than six months. Detailed descriptions of the circumstances surrounding injury should be sought: *'Can you tell me exactly how this happened?'* If an incomplete explanation is provided then abuse is more likely. Asking the parent / guardian to repeat this explanation can check for any inconsistencies: *'Just to make sure I fully understand, can you confirm how X got these bruises?'* Remain calm and non-judgmental throughout this discussion. Witnesses should be identified and questioned if possible.

In addition to questioning adults, the patient should also be asked for their account of events. This should be away from any potential abuser(s) and in a non-threatening, calm environment. Abuse disclosure is a difficult process and sufficient time should be allocated for completion. Barriers to disclosure include a lack of patient understanding of what constitutes abuse, shame and self-blame, and being afraid of the consequences from speaking out. Abuse perpetrators might resort to emotional blackmail to prevent disclosure; for example, promising the victim that the abuse will not happen again or that it is a secret. It is important to reassure patients that they will not be in trouble should they disclose.

When communicating with the patient, open questions (for example *'Can you tell us what happened when you were hurt?'*) can often be a good starting point. Asking children *'Are you happy at home?'* may also help to initiate further discussion. Protection from further maltreatment is a crucial issue for many patients. Reassuring statements such as *'We will keep you safe'* and *'If someone is hurting you, then you don't have to see them again'* have been utilized during patient interviews to successfully promote disclosure.

23.3.2 **Emotional abuse**

Alerting features of emotional abuse include **child fearfulness, aggression, indiscriminate affection-seeking**, and **low self-esteem**. Children may display behaviours such as body rocking, self-harm, running away from home, and bedwetting. Such behaviours might be observed during the consultation. Initially ask the parent / guardian open questions.

- *'Does your child have any challenging behaviours?'*
- *'Has your child experienced any difficulties at school?'*
- *'Can you give me a specific example of what your child does to cause these difficulties?'* if any behavioural concerns are identified.

23.3.3 **Child sexual abuse**

Sexual abuse is difficult to detect in most cases. Enquiring about the possibility of child sexual abuse should be done with care and only after a rapport has been established with both patient and parent / guardian. Anogenital injuries are typically minor and produce minimal physical symptoms. Pain, pruritis, fever and discharge all suggest STI. If sexual abuse is suspected, ask the child closed questions to identify or exclude these features.

- *'Have you noticed any itchiness or pain in your private parts?'*
- Early pregnancy symptoms include nausea and/or vomiting, late period, fatigue, urinary frequency, mastalgia and food aversion.
- Vulval soreness is common amongst young girls and is a poor predictor of sexual abuse.

Raising the possibility of sexual abuse during the consultation might be appropriate if the suspected perpetrator is not present and there is sufficient clinical evidence to justify this. Although difficult, accompanying adults may also share this suspicion and could be willing to openly disclose their concerns. If the patient becomes upset during the consultation then the best course of action might be to consider admission to ensure their safety and continue the discussion at a later time. The presence of a senior and the relevant safeguarding lead should always be sought.

23.3.4 **Neglect**

Child neglect presentations can be insidious and healthcare professionals need to be persistent in order to recognize any alerting features. These include symptoms of undernutrition such as abdominal aches or pains, constipation, fatigue, muscle weakness and delayed growth. The patient can be asked closed questions to swiftly identify or exclude these symptoms.

- *'Does your tummy ever hurt or growl a lot?'*
- *'Do you often feel tired or have trouble staying awake during school?'*
- *'Can you tell me what food you like to eat?'* and *'How many times do you eat in a day?'* can also prove useful.
- *'Do you ever have to stay home on your own? Do you ever have to look after your younger brother or sister? Do you ever have to cook your own food?'*

Itching and rash can indicate infestations such as scabies. The circumstances surrounding accidental injuries can also expose the possibility of neglectful parenting; for example, a lack of adult supervision when performing dangerous activities.

- *'Who else was with you when you hurt yourself?'*

5) ICE

Always remember to give patients and their parents / guardians the opportunity to discuss their concerns and ask questions.

6) Past medical history

Previous hospitalizations and enquiring about **hereditary bleeding or bone disorders** is advisable. Patient medical conditions might be poorly managed due to an overall lack of parent / guardian concern. Seizures without fever or a past history of seizure disorder might raise the suspicion of head injury. The patient and their family could be known to the hospital child safeguarding team; if so, previous records might be of use. **Frequent attendances to the emergency department** can serve as a red flag for NAIs, whilst **delayed presentations** might indicate neglect.

Developmental history: developmental milestones may be delayed due to any ongoing abuse. A lack of concern on the part of the parent / guardian, or unwillingness to work with healthcare professionals to address any developmental delays, suggest neglect.

7) Family history

Shared health problems in the family such as tendency to bruise may suggest the presence of a hereditary medical condition. You should also screen for parental mental health problems and stress. Other siblings may be at risk of maltreatment and could have safeguarding records.

- *'Do any of your other children have any health problems?'*
- *'Are there any mental health problems in the family?'*

Reinforce that these are routine questions that everyone is asked. It is also useful to fall back on these screening questions in the event that you need to keep the child in hospital.

- *'I know you mentioned that there was no history of bleeding problems in your family but I think it's a good idea if we keep X in hospital and investigate this a bit further. This way we can be certain that this is not the cause of the bruises.'*

8) Social history

Important points to cover include any financial stressors, a history of family violence and/ or substance misuse as well as disciplinary practices. **Asking how the parent / guardian is coping at home** might provide useful information. Overcrowded and/or unhygienic living conditions can predispose children to infection and asthma. Smoking around children is a known health risk, although not legally considered to constitute abuse.

Educational history: children who are victims of abuse are more likely have poorer educational attainment when compared to their peers. Teachers might have also raised safeguarding concerns on previous occasions. Behavioural difficulties and bullying in school can both result from maltreatment. School absenteeism can indicate child neglect.

- *'How are things at school? Do you enjoy school? How often do you miss school?'*

9) Examination

Physical examination should identify NAIs and any alerting features of neglect. Inflicted injuries can occur on protected regions such as the neck, back, buttocks and thighs (see *Fig. 23.1*). Injuries at multiple sites and at different stages of healing also suggest maltreatment. The involvement of a medical photographer may be necessary. Suspect fracture sites include the sternum, scapulae, posteromedial ribs in infants, the digits, and vertebrae. Chest and abdominal examination may detect signs of internal injuries in extreme physical abuse cases. Intracranial injuries (including subdural haemorrhage) can present with impaired consciousness level and focal neurological signs. Fundoscopy should be performed if there is any suspicion of retinal haemorrhage.

Key Knowledge: In cases of suspected NAIs, detailed descriptions of circumstances surrounding the injury can be achieved through open questioning and the identification of witnesses who can provide a collateral history.

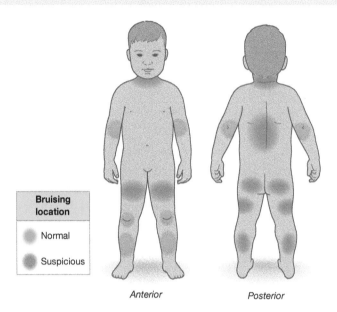

Figure 23.1 Normal and suspicious bruising patterns in children.

Key Knowledge: Confidentiality can be waived in safeguarding concerns involving children (those under 18) and adults who lack capacity. Disclosure without patient consent is also necessary when others are believed to be at risk of harm.

Height, weight and (in very young children) head circumference can be recorded and compared to previous measures. Failure to thrive might indicate underfeeding but can also result from malabsorption and food allergies, inborn errors of metabolism, and other medical conditions such as congenital heart disease. Dirty clothing and an unkempt appearance can indicate child neglect. **Unsuitable clothing** (e.g. lack of a warm coat during winter) can also be an alerting feature. Maltreatment should be considered in cases of **persistent or recurrent infestations**, e.g. scabies, pediculosis. Mouth examination can reveal tooth decay (considered as neglect when free NHS dental services are available).

Genital examination is required in cases of suspected sexual abuse. Always consider the need for a chaperone and/or sedation. Inappropriate or promiscuous behaviour can be observed amongst victims of child sexual abuse. If present, genital trauma can be mild and often difficult to detect. Urethral or vaginal discharge and genital skin changes (such as warts) indicate sexually transmitted diseases. Swabbing for forensic DNA evidence and infection diagnosis may be indicated. In girls the hymen can remain intact following vaginal intercourse, whilst perforation does not necessarily indicate sexual activity. Female genital mutilation (FGM) is a form of physical abuse and must be reported to the police.

10) Investigations and management
Keeping a child in for treatment and observation can produce hostility from abuse suspects. Explaining the reasoning behind a decision to admit will help to justify this decision, although if any of the accompanying adults are suspected perpetrators then it might be best

to withhold the details. *'Your son/daughter appears to have some worries, and we should investigate these further'* could be a good way to start. Barriers to effective communication include time constraints, the use of jargon, language difficulties and poor listening skills.

> **Key Knowledge:** An emergency protection order (EPO) permits the removal of a child to a place of safety by a Local Authority for up to 8 days (extendable to a maximum of 15 days). Any individual can apply for an EPO, should they believe a child is in imminent danger. Police protection orders serve as an alternative method of child protection, and last for a total of 72 hours.

Acknowledging patient and carer concerns (*'I can see that this is difficult for you'*) and informing the parent/guardian that you are **following procedure and acting in the best interests of their child** may help to ease the situation. **Establishing a rough time frame** for admission duration might also help. Avoid attributing blame and remain calm throughout the discussion. Letting the parent/guardian verbally express their anger and not interrupting during this process can be beneficial. The presence of a senior should also be sought.

The treatment and investigation of suspected child abuse is likely to include the following:
- Immediate medical or surgical treatment for any physical injuries.
- Full blood count and clotting studies to exclude bleeding disorders.
- Calcium, phosphate, albumin, alkaline phosphatase and parathyroid levels may identify malnutrition or bone mineralization disorders.
- Skeletal surveys are recommended in children under 2 years or those unable to report pain. Follow local guidelines to prevent unnecessary investigation and radiation exposure. Appendicular and axial films will be taken and the skeleton should be viewed in multiple planes.
- Referral to the designated child safeguarding lead, social services or local domestic abuse services, and your senior clinician.
- Emergency or police protection orders if the child is deemed to be at risk and his/her carers are unwilling to cooperate.

23.4 Safeguarding adults

There is a growing recognition of the need to safeguard adults against abuse. An adult at risk is defined as an individual with health and/or social care needs and who is unable to safeguard themself as a consequence. The term "vulnerable adult" is now used less frequently, and is sometimes regarded as stigmatizing and disempowering for patients. Adults at risk are likely to display a number of different characteristics:
- Physical impairment including frailty, chronic medical conditions such as cardiac failure, and loss of mobility.
- Sensory disability including visual impairment and hearing loss.
- Mental illnesses including depression and other mood disorders, schizophrenia, personality disorders and dementia.
- Homelessness.
- Living with someone who abuses recreational drugs and/or misuses alcohol.
- Learning disability or significant learning difficulties.
- Women left vulnerable due to isolating cultural factors.

Carers who commit acts of maltreatment are often unpaid, overburdened, under significant stress, and socially isolated. Abuse rarely manifests as a presenting complaint and is often discovered as an incidental finding. An adult at risk could be in receipt of home care or be a resident in an institution such as a nursing home. In such settings, a patient being unable to reach for a drink or failure to record fluid and food intake can both indicate neglect. An unkempt physical appearance, weight loss and poor skin care all suggest abuse. Additional red flags of maltreatment include unexplained injuries, behavioural changes such as emotional lability, recent anxiety or depression, and mentioning of a change in personal circumstances.

Red flags for abuse in adults:
- Unexplained injuries
- Changes in patient behaviour and low self-esteem
- Lack of mental capacity
- Neglect of appearance and hygiene
- Weight loss
- Mental illness
- Mention of a change in personal circumstances including financial difficulties

23.4.1 History

Key Knowledge: It is important to seek support from other healthcare professionals when addressing safeguarding concerns. Always inform your senior and the relevant safeguarding lead for assistance in cases of suspected abuse.

Victims will often be frightened to disclose abuse due to fears of care withdrawal or repercussions from the perpetrator. It is vital that patients are reassured that confidentiality will be respected and will only be broken if others are found to be at risk. Patients should be interviewed without the suspected abuser present, either alone or ideally with a trusted friend or relative who can provide emotional support. An interpreter of foreign languages or British Sign Language might be required in certain instances. Support from an IMCA may be necessary if the patient lacks capacity.

Acknowledging the impact that the abuse has had on the patient and providing an adequate consultation time will increase the likelihood of an abuse disclosure. Patients should be asked directly whether they have experienced abuse, with the clinician explaining why he or she is concerned. Permission may be sought to speak to others who can provide collateral information. Third party allegations of abuse may arise and will require an appropriate response. For instance, maltreatment in a nursing home could be witnessed by a visiting relative, necessitating further investigation.

23.4.2 Management

The management of proven or suspected abuse should be underpinned by the six principles of safeguarding outlined by the Department of Health (see *Table 23.3*). Striking a balance between the safeguarding principles of protection and proportionality can, however, prove challenging. For example, the exact severity or likelihood of maltreatment might be unclear, or a patient may be reluctant to enact changes to their personal circumstances despite ongoing safeguarding concerns. In such cases decisions should be discussed and shared on an MDT level, with no single clinician being burdened with sole responsibility (an example of partnership). Patient involvement and informed choice in this process adheres to the principle of empowerment. However, if there is any risk of serious harm or loss of life then immediate intervention is always required. Refuge is available if a patient cannot return to their home.

Table 23.3 The six principles of safeguarding (**Department of Health, 2011**).

1. Empowerment	Presumption of patient-led decisions and informed consent
2. Protection	Support and representation of those in greatest need
3. Prevention	It is better to take action before harm occurs
4. Proportionality	Proportionate and least intrusive response appropriate to the risk presented
5. Partnership	Local solutions through services working together with their communities, which have a part to play in preventing, detecting and reporting neglect and abuse
6. Accountability	Accountability and transparency in delivering safeguarding

As in cases of suspected abuse, any physical injuries or health concerns should be addressed. The appropriate investigation of symptoms such as weight loss may detect a medical cause and help rule out neglect. Referral to local safeguarding services and the implementation of a protection plan will likely be the next best step. Hospitals and many other institutions will have a designated adult safeguarding lead. Counselling may play a role in mitigating the psychological effects of abuse. If a criminal offence is likely to have been committed, then the police should also be informed. Most forces will employ officers specially trained for safeguarding, and who can decide whether an investigation is warranted. Monetary safeguards such as monitoring bank statements and withdrawing only small amounts of cash may be beneficial in cases of possible financial abuse.

> **Summary of key points (GET YOUR MARKS):**
>
> Initiating the consultation: introduce yourself, obtain patient's name and DOB, consent, confidentiality.
>
> Ask an open initial question.
>
> History of presenting complaint: obtain detailed descriptions of circumstances surrounding injury. Ask parent/guardian to repeat explanation to check for inconsistencies. Ask questions specific to the type of abuse you are suspecting.
>
> ICE: it is always important to elicit the patient's ICE and those of the parent/carer.
>
> Past medical history: previous injuries/hospitalizations, bleeding/bone disorders, developmental history.
>
> Family history: hereditary medical disorders, health of other siblings, parental mental health.
>
> Social history: enquire about how things are at home, e.g. ask about stress in the family at the minute, history of family violence, substance misuse. Ask how the parent/carer is coping. Enquire about living conditions e.g. how many people are living in the house? Is there enough room? Education and school life.
>
> Management: provide only minor details as to why the patient has to stay in for some observation. Acknowledge concerns of patient/carer. Explain you are following procedure and it is in the best interests of the patient. Give a rough time frame if you can.
>
> Closing the consultation: check you haven't missed anything, encourage them to ask questions if they have any. Summarize and signpost throughout. Thank the patient and their family.

23.5 **Practice scenarios**

1. Matthew Stoker is an 8-year-old boy admitted to A&E following injury to his right hand. X-ray reveals distal phalangeal fractures of the 3rd and 4th digits. Matthew is accompanied by his mother, who explains the injury was obtained by Matthew trapping his hand in the car door. On meeting Matthew, you notice he has poor eye contact and appears socially withdrawn. His clothing appears inappropriate for the cold weather outside and he has an

old bruise on his left cheek. Your consultant requests you take a full history from Matthew and his mother, and establish the likelihood of physical abuse.

- When examining Matthew what signs would be suggestive of maltreatment?
- Which further medical investigations might you wish to consider?
- What steps could be taken to protect Matthew if he was found to be at risk of serious harm?

2. Sophia Chalmers is a 13-year-old girl who presented to her GP requesting oral contraception. On further questioning, Sophia informs the doctor that she has started a sexual relationship with her boyfriend Steven, whom she met three months ago at the local cinema. Steven is 18 years old and works as an apprentice for a plumbing company. Sophia has informed her parents that she is dating Steven and they appear happy with this arrangement, although she has not disclosed that she is sexually active. Conduct the appropriate consultation with Sophia.

- Would you prescribe the oral contraceptive?
- What safeguarding and physical health concerns are raised by this case?
- Do the police need to be informed and would it be justifiable to break patient confidentiality? If so, how would you approach this conversation with Sophia?

3. Eleanor Burns is an 81-year-old lady who is a nursing home resident. She is admitted to hospital as an elective patient for right hemicolectomy of stage 2 colonic carcinoma. During her pre-operative assessment Eleanor confides that she is unhappy with her living arrangements and becomes tearful. She suffers from hip OA and cannot mobilize well without analgesics, which are often not administered by the nursing home staff. Sometimes she is left alone in her room unable to attend mealtimes or socialize with other residents. She is a widow and has no living relatives or friends remaining. On appearance Eleanor appears kempt with no obvious evidence of neglect. Discuss the above with Eleanor to establish risk of vulnerable adult abuse.

- What safeguarding concerns have been raised and how could these be best addressed?
- Who else should be informed of Eleanor's case?
- Are other nursing home residents also at risk?

24

Breaking bad news

RACHEL WAMBOLDT

Breaking Bad News: Keys to Success

- Gather information from the patient to determine their current knowledge about their condition as well as their readiness to hear the bad news.
- Provide clear information according to the patient's needs and desires.
- Support the patient through the use of skills that reduce the emotional impact of the news.
- Develop a plan of care with the involvement of the patient.

Breaking bad news is one of the most difficult aspects of a doctor's job; however, it is an essential skill that we will all have to do throughout our entire career. Bad news is defined as anything that will lead to changes in an individual's life, and even those who are the best at delivering bad news or have the most practice do not always get it right. Whether it is something that seems relatively minor, such as starting a new medication, or a major life-changing diagnosis, such as cancer, it is impossible to predict how a patient or their family is going to react.

Delivering bad news is as much dependent on verbal skills as non-verbal ones. It is crucial for the deliverer of the news to be aware of their own verbal and non-verbal cues as well as those of the patient. If the delivery of the bad news is done well, patients are able to continue with the consultation and maybe even help contribute to the decision making process. Breaking bad news can be complicated by the involvement of multiple family members. In some cases, a repeat appointment may be necessary to plan future care. Evidence has shown that the way in which a doctor or other healthcare provider delivers the bad news will inevitably influence the professional–patient relationship going forward. Good communication allows for adequate exploration of the patient's expectations of treatment and encourages their involvement in the development of the plan of care.

A successful breaking bad news consultation can be achieved using the six-step SPIKES protocol discussed in *Section 24.1.1*.

Mnemonic: SPIKES
Setting up the interview
Patient's perception
Invitation
Knowledge
Empathetic response to patient's emotions
Strategy and summary

24.1 **Six steps to breaking bad news**

24.1.1 **SPIKES protocol**

Step 1   Setting up the interview

Be prepared:
- Rehearsing the information that you would like to deliver to the patient will not only prepare you for its delivery but will help with managing your own stress and anxiety.
- Familiarize yourself with the patient's history, test results and management up to that point in time. In an OSCE situation, be familiar with the clinical vignette and do not enter the station until you feel confident with the information that has been provided.
- Reviewing the plan of care prepares you for answering any difficult questions or concerns that the patient may have.

Environment:
- Bad news should always be given in person, not over the phone, if possible.
- Ensure adequate privacy. Find a private room. If this is not possible, ensure that the curtains around the bed are closed.
- Make sure there are enough seats for everyone involved in the consultation. This will show that you are not in a rush and that everyone has a role in the consultation.
- Ensure that this time is protected, by turning off all bleeps and mobile phones for the duration of the consultation.

Patient comfort:
- To the best of your ability, ensure that the patient is as comfortable as possible. This includes adequate pain management and the presence of support networks such as family, significant others and key members of the interdisciplinary team.
- In an OSCE, this can be achieved by asking the patient if there is anyone else that they would like to be present during the consultation.
- It is strongly recommended that if possible the patient's named nurse or a nurse specialist accompanies you so that this individual can remain with the patient to offer continuing support after the completion of the consultation.

Build rapport early:
- Maintaining eye contact is important for building rapport and promoting trust.
- Start the consultation as you would any other:
  - Introduce yourself and your role. This may be obvious to the patient, but will be important if there are significant others present that you have not met.
  - Confirm the name and DOB of the patient, checking to see what they prefer to be called if you have not been their primary doctor.
  - Ensure confidentiality.

Step 2   Assessing the patient's perception

Check starting point:
- Start by asking patient about the events that have taken place up to this point. This helps to clear up any misconceptions the patient might have and helps to bring the family / significant others up to speed. This will also help to judge whether there is any degree of denial.
- Discuss their ICE. This will help to gauge how they might take the news.
- Questions you could consider asking include:
  - *'What do you understand about your condition?'*
  - *'Have you been worried about your illness or your symptoms? When you first started having your symptoms, what did you think it might be?'*

- ○ *'What is your understanding of the reasons why we did the MRI / blood test?'*
- ○ *'What are you expecting from today's appointment?'*
- Clarify any misinformation.

Step 3   Obtaining the patient's invitation

- Ideally, patients should be primed at the time the test is completed. This is done by simply asking the patient at that time about how much information they would like to receive about the test results.
- If this has not been done, you can ask the patient the following questions:
  - ○ *'Would you like to hear all the information about the test results or spend more time discussing the future plan of care?'*
  - ○ *'Would you like me to tell you the full details of your condition or would you prefer that I speak to someone else?'*

Step 4   Giving knowledge and information to the patient

Giving the bad news:

- Giving the patient a 'warning shot' can help to lessen the emotional impact and facilitate information processing. Examples include:
  - ○ *'I am afraid I have some bad news...'*
  - ○ *'The results have come back and unfortunately it is not as we hoped.'*

Try to avoid saying *'I'm sorry'* as it can be interpreted as physician responsibility or failure. You can, however, follow it up by saying, *'I'm sorry that I have to be the one to tell you this...'*

- Be sensitive but straightforward. Tell the patient the bad news and then stop.
- Patients will respond to the bad news in a variety of ways. It is very important to give the patient time to react, even if it makes you uncomfortable. Empathy can be shown by non-verbal actions such as moving your chair forward, providing comfort through appropriate touch or offering tissues.
- Silence is very powerful in these situations.
- The patient will be ready to continue with the consultation when they start to ask questions or with the use of non-verbal language, such as making eye contact.

Giving the information:

- Before proceeding with giving information, ask the patient if they have any immediate questions.
  - ○ *' I would like to give you some information about your condition and discuss the plan going forward. Before I do this, do you have any particular questions that you want answered?'*
- Establish a **shared agenda** with the patient to ensure that both of your goals for the consultation are being met.
- Use simple language so that it is easier for the patient to process. Avoid medical jargon and technical language such as "biopsy". Instead use words such as "tissue sample".
- The amount of honesty will depend on the patient. Avoid being blunt but being truthful and realistic is important.
- When the prognosis is poor, never say to a patient *'There is nothing we can do for you'*. Instead discuss other therapeutic options such as pain and symptom control. There is always something you can do.
- Don't forget your basic communication skills. **Chunk and check** and allow plenty of time for the patient to ask questions. Check that it is OK with the patient to continue with the next bit of information. Allow them lots of opportunities to ask questions.
- If the patient is clearly having difficulty keeping up with the information, it is OK to re-schedule another appointment for when the patient is ready to discuss the plan.

- Whenever possible, give verbal information in writing too. It is also important to ensure that the MDT (i.e. nursing staff) is aware of what the patient knows, so that they can provide the appropriate support.

Step 5   Addressing the patient's emotions with empathetic responses

- Patients can respond to bad news in a multitude of ways. Allow the patient to express their emotions so that you can provide the appropriate support and empathy.
- Giving an empathetic response to the patient consists of four steps:

1. **Identify the emotion** – anger, denial, sadness, shock, grief, acceptance, indifference or relief.

2. **Acknowledge the emotion** that the patient is experiencing. Use open questions to help the patient express and clarify their emotions. Allow time for silence and tears.
   - *'I see this news has come as a bit of a surprise, can you tell me how you are feeling?'*
   - *'I know you were hoping for a better result. How are you feeling?'*
   - *'Are you frightened by this news?'*
   - *'What worries you most about what I have just told you?'*

3. If you are uncertain of the reason for the emotion, **clarify with the patient.**
   - *'You said you were concerned for your children, can you tell me more about that?'*

4. Let the patient know that you have connected the emotion with the reason they have provided.
   - *'I know this isn't what you wanted to hear. I wish the news could have been better.'*

   Never say to a patient, *'I know how you feel'*, even if you have similar experience dealing with this situation. Remind the patient that their response is normal. Provide reassurance that they will be supported throughout the entire process.
   - *'I know this might seem very frightening but we will be with you every step of the way.'*
   - *'We will do everything in our power to make sure...'*
   - *'We will support you throughout this process and are always happy to address any questions or concerns you might have about your future care.'*

Step 6   Strategy and summary

- Having a clear plan for the future will help the patient manage their anxieties and uncertainty.
- Before continuing, be sure that the patient is ready to discuss the next step.
- Shared decision making will help the patient feel involved with their care. It is a legal requirement for patients to know all of their options going forward, but it also tells the patient that the medical team cares about their wishes.
- Explore the patient's knowledge, concerns and expectations about the disease. They may already be aware of the seriousness of the illness. Use this knowledge to facilitate the conversation.
- Address their concerns and expectations. Explore personal goals that they may have for treatment (e.g. pain or symptom control).
- Provide information about the medical plan of care and also support services available.
- Finish the consultation by summarizing the details that have been discussed. Reiterate the plan of care and let the patient know of support systems that are in place in case of need. Give them contact information to these lines of support.
- Screen for any more questions that the patient might have. Encourage them to write down questions at home and bring the list to their next appointment.
- Document the consultation in the patient's notes, being sure to use the specific words used to describe the disease and treatment.

24.2 Informing family of a patient's death

Breaking the news of a death to family members can at times be more challenging than breaking bad news to the patient themselves, especially if the death has been sudden. In practice, this conversation should be conducted by the senior doctor caring for the patient. The emotional response from family members can vary, depending on the circumstances surrounding the death as well as their cultural and social background. The team should be prepared to deal with any reaction that may occur.

This is a very important part of the doctor–patient relationship. Kindness shown by the healthcare team during their initial stages of grief can help influence the grieving process moving forward. Families often remember how the news was delivered and the way they were treated by hospital staff. Kindness can also help to reassure the family that the team gave their full efforts in the treatment of their loved one.

The six steps of the SPIKES protocol can be adapted and implemented in this situation.

Step 1 Setting up the interview

- Ideally the family member should be at the hospital when delivering the news. If the family is not present when the death occurs, a senior member of the team should call the family. Every effort should be made to have them come to the hospital before delivering the news.
- Inform the family that the patient has suddenly become very ill and has required life-sustaining treatment. Suggest that a member of the family comes to the hospital immediately.
- As above, the news needs to be delivered in a comfortable and private environment.
- If possible, deliver the news to as few people as possible. This will reduce the range of emotional reactions and allows more time for answering questions.
- If possible, have a nurse in attendance to provide continued support to the family, especially if the family is known to a particular member of staff.
- If this is not possible due to long distance, continue to follow the SPIKES protocol. Ensure that the person receiving the news has someone with them when receiving the news, so that they can be comforted at the end of the consultation.

Step 2 Assessing the family's perception

Ask the family to discuss their knowledge of the events leading up to this point. What do they know about the current situation? This gives the clinician a better idea of what kind of information needs to be communicated to the family.

Step 3 Obtaining the family's invitation

This may be implicated verbally by family members asking directly about the state of their loved one or by non-verbal cues of restlessness.

Step 4 Giving knowledge and information to the patient

Start by giving a "**warning shot**". Usually by this stage the family is aware of the news they are about to receive. Some may even start experiencing an overwhelming emotional reaction before they are told of their loved one's death. Use plain language. Tell the family that the patient has "died" or is "dead". Avoid using phrases such as "we lost him/her" as this can imply guilt.

- *'This is very difficult for me to tell you but unfortunately your father has died.'*
- *'I am saddened to tell you this but unfortunately your father has died.'*

Allow the relatives time to express their grief. Remain silent and provide non-verbal empathy using touch or facial expressions of sadness, if appropriate. Shape your reactions around the way the relatives are behaving. Encourage the relatives to express their feelings. Express to them that every effort was made by the healthcare team to conserve the patient's life. If appropriate, praise any effort on the part of the relatives for their care towards the patient while they were unwell.

Wait for the family to start asking questions. Answer any question that does not conflict with rules of confidentiality. Try to avoid medical jargon and ensure that the message that you have given them is clear. Remember your core communication skills of **chunking and checking**. **Recognize, acknowledge** and **validate** the family's emotions.

Step 5   Addressing the relatives' emotions with empathetic responses
Allow for the expression of emotion and encourage them to talk about the patient using the tools above. Respond to non-verbal communication and listen to the family's ICE.

Step 6   Strategy and summary
If the body is still in the department, ask the family whether they would like to view the deceased. Be sure that the patient has been prepared by the nursing staff before they are invited into the room. Make sure that there are enough chairs and that a member of staff is available for any needs or questions they may have.

If there are medico-legal implications to the case, inform the relatives about the possibility of an autopsy. Have a member of staff advise them on practical matters involved with the death (i.e. registering the death and the processing of the death certificate).

> **Summary of key points (GET YOUR MARKS):**
> Prepare yourself.
> Assess patient's starting point / what has been happening up until that point.
> Check how much they wish to know.
> Give a warning shot, e.g. *'Unfortunately things are more serious than we had hoped…'*
> Give information – using chunking and checking (do not overwhelm them with information).
> Check the patient's understanding of the information.
> Allow time for silence and shut-down.
> Identify the patient's main concerns and be sensitive to them, responding to any non-verbal cues.
> Elicit the patient's coping strategies, personal resources.
> Give realistic hope.
> Avoid false reassurances.
> Provide support by identifying a plan of care, emphasizing your partnership with the patient.

24.3 Practice scenarios

1. Mandy and Preston Kindling have come to your clinic for genetic testing. Mandy is a known carrier for the CFTR gene and Preston's cousin has cystic fibrosis. After genetic testing, it is revealed that Preston is also a carrier for the gene. They are planning on starting a family in the near future. Break the news to the family and discuss the future risk of acquiring the disease.

2. Kristen Samson is a 28-year-old woman who has been admitted to the obstetrical unit. She presented with vaginal bleeding and clots along with lower abdominal cramping. A urine hCG is negative and serum results indicated that the pregnancy has failed. An ultrasound has shown that there are retained products in the uterus. You are instructed to inform this patient of the failed pregnancy and the future plan of management.

3. Jimmy Gannon (56 years of age), was told two years ago that his small cell lung cancer was in remission after several courses of chemotherapy and radiotherapy. He presented to the clinic last week with increasing SOB. He underwent a CT scan of his thorax and a biopsy which has revealed that his lung cancer has returned and there has been invasion into the mediastinum and pericardium. He is a T4N2M1. He will now undergo palliative management. It is your job to break the bad news to the patient.

4. Amanda LaFromboise is a 38-year-old teacher. She is 13+1 weeks pregnant and has recently undergone her 12-week screening ultrasound and combined test. The results of the screening tests reveal that there is a 1 in 25 chance of Down syndrome. Disclose the news of the screening tests and discuss the future investigation and management options.

5. Josh Carson is a 25-year-old man who has recently returned from 6 months of travelling abroad. Whilst in Thailand, he had sexual intercourse with three men and did not use a condom. He has come to the genitourinary medicine (GUM) clinic and is awaiting the results of his blood test for HIV. His blood test has come back positive. Deliver the bad news and discuss the treatment options and implications for his future lifestyle.

6. Richard Park is a 24-year-old man who had a road traffic accident whilst riding his motorcycle home from his girlfriend's house. CPR was in progress when he arrived at the hospital. Despite 46 minutes of resuscitation efforts, the patient has been pronounced dead. His mother and brother are waiting in the private room. As the senior member of the team, you have been tasked with informing the family of Richard's death.

25

Communicating error and conflict resolution

MICHAEL PARKER

The Angry Patient: Keys to Success

There are three things one must always consider when dealing with an angry patient:
1. Background to the situation – what happened?
2. The emotional aspect of the situation – how does the patient feel?
3. The threat to identity – how has this situation made the patient feel about themself? (For example, they feel bad because they're not able to help their loved ones as much as they should.)

One must take a holistic, "helicopter" view of the situation and try to put all of the above into context whenever you communicate with an angry patient. Only by doing so could you turn a negative situation into a positive one.

25.1 Background

The French have a saying, *"tout comprendre, c'est tout pardonner"*. In English, this translates as "to understand all is to forgive all". This small piece of philosophy is the key to addressing an angry patient, relative or orthopaedic registrar! Communicating with angry patients, relatives and colleagues is one of the most difficult situations to find yourself in, be that in an OSCE setting or during life as a doctor. It is important, however, to fully reflect on why the person with whom you are communicating is angry. Think of anger in this context as a reaction to an environment the person has found themselves in. One of the most common triggers of anger is fear (remember the fight or flight response). If you can dissipate their fearfulness of a situation, their anger (more often than not) will subside with it. Without further ado, let's get to the matter in hand – how exactly we should approach angry patients – not only to ace an OSCE but to improve both our own satisfaction and that of those people we encounter on a professional level. This chapter will give you preparation for how to approach these situations, not just for OSCEs but for life on the wards and beyond!

As previously mentioned, anger is a secondary emotion. Anger is always a result of another more basic emotion (hunger, fear, tiredness, etc.) and subsequently it must be explored to be understood. It has been suggested that doctors dealing with angry patients often utilize four flawed techniques:
1. Disregarding the anger;
2. Attempts to placate the angry party;
3. Returning anger for anger;
4. Premature validation.

Ideally, this chapter will help you to avoid these mistakes that doctors commonly commit. Disregarding the anger will not allow you to find exactly its root cause, and subsequently you cannot address it sufficiently. Efforts to offer mere placation to the angered person will undoubtedly make you sound uninterested and could fan the flames of their anger even further! Responding angrily to the angry party will only result in both of you focusing on your strong emotions (and pride) and not allow for productive conversation. Finally, premature validation is a dangerous concept. We shall discuss in greater detail later on how important validation is; however, if we try to reduce anger before exploring it, we can inadvertently manipulate the patient to follow our own set of thoughts and beliefs, instead of letting them explore their emotions themselves.

Somebody directing anger towards you is a threatening situation. It is only natural to feel flustered when on the receiving end of strong emotion. During these episodes it is essential to keep calm, take a deep breath and think clearly. Try to remember that empathy is by far and away the best approach to reducing a person's anger. Don't just offer hollow platitudes, actually try your best to put yourself in that person's shoes and think exactly why they are so cross. Sometimes no matter what you do they won't calm down. In these situations, don't be afraid to directly ask them, *'What is it you are hoping to get out of talking to me?'* or *'What can I do to rectify this situation?'* Put the onus on them without being confrontational and allow them to either tell you directly what is causing them concern, or, failing that, give them an opportunity to reflect on how they're feeling.

How to avoid finding yourself in a sticky situation:
- Ensure you recognize strong emotions, such as anger, sadness and fear. Try to put yourself in the shoes of the person you're talking with. Sometimes people won't openly admit they're angry, sad, etc., and therefore you need to pick up on subtle hints (clenching fists, lack of eye contact, etc.).
- Do your best to explore a person's feelings and allow yourself to get involved in the quagmire of emotion. If you give people an opportunity to express themselves, it will be invaluable in helping them to feel better about the situation.
- Do not doubt your own empathetic abilities. Humans are social and empathetic animals. We all have it in us, so trust your gut.

Now we have done the basic background, it is time to look at a few more in-depth strategies in dealing with angry patients.

25.2 Communication skills

1) Introduce yourself and your role on the healthcare team

2) Ensure consent and confidentiality

3) Confirm the name of the person you are talking to and the patient they are concerned about

25.2.1 Why are they angry?

Start with an open question without any presumption. Usually the individual will approach you and ask if they can speak with you. An easy one is *'How may I be of service?'* or *'What can I help you with?'*

Allow for the Golden Minute: when dealing with an angry patient, the Golden Minute may feel like the golden hour! However, in this context it is absolutely vital to allow the patient to get everything they are dissatisfied with off their chest. Keep an ear out for any subtle hints they may drop. Later in the chapter we will discuss Maslow's Hierarchy of Need which will explain this better. Ensure you listen for words such as 'tired', 'hungry', 'pain' etc. These are all simple causes of anger which are all easily rectified if picked up on!

OSCE TIP: Body language
- If the patient is standing / stomping around, sit down and ask them politely to join you somewhere quiet or where you can sit down.
- Be wary of crossing your arms; this can often be interpreted as a defensive stance. Keep it open.
- Maintain eye contact.
- The use of non-verbal signs that you are listening is key.

Get them on your side! It is almost impossible to be angry with someone who is acting rationally, let alone if you are viewed as their advocate!

Once the Golden Minute has run its course, **apologize**! This isn't an admission of guilt, and even if you are in no way associated with the events which have caused the person with whom you are talking to become angry, an apology is always appreciated. An empty 'Sorry 'bout that' will win you no favours though. Make it pertinent to them. If they say they are cross they have been kept waiting, use that. Something as easy as 'I am sorry you have had to wait so long' can start to get the patient to acknowledge you're on their side and will make the rest of the consultation flow in a more positive way.

Many people struggle with certain empathetic concepts, and below are a few of the most common:
- What do you say and do after giving an empathetic response?
- What if I just cannot empathize with this person?
- I don't have time for this!
- Surely this isn't relevant for a doctor? This isn't my forte.

So how can we avoid the above? First of all, one of the most useful things to do after offering an empathetic response is to simply **do nothing**. You'll be in a highly emotive environment. Sitting quietly for a few seconds with the other person will allow both of you to take a chance to think about the situation you're in.

If you think you cannot empathize with someone, you are wrong. We all have the base ability to relate to those around us – it is an important survival mechanism. Many of us are fortunate enough to have never experienced the loss / illness of a loved one, but we have all been scared of something. Try to sit back and think of what you want to hear when you're scared, how somebody could help you. Use these overall concepts to offer support to your patients, and you will both benefit from it.

Obviously exploring strong emotion is a lengthy process, and in an OSCE or a busy ward you may feel like you do not have time to get involved in such situations. Realistically, however, it can make a consultation all the more efficient by addressing the elephant in the room at the onset of a conversation, to allow for a more open discussion later on.

Finally, anybody who thinks empathy is not for doctors is really rather wrong. We have a duty of care for our patients. This is not limited to abnormal physiology, but also to their mental and emotional health. If a person were to have a negative experience during their stay, they may avoid healthcare professionals in the future, which might subsequently have a long-term effect on their health. By allowing people to explore how they are feeling, you can make the world of healthcare more accessible to them in the future and optimize their health going forward.

25.2.2 If it looks inflamed – use ICE!

By now you should all be familiar with the concept of ICE (ideas, concerns and expectations). This is essential for the "angry patient" as the best way to get them on a happier agenda is to make them feel valued. After you've apologized for the trigger they have offered as to the cause of their anger, ICE them to cool them down further. Let's use an example of a man who is cross his wife has been in A&E with a sore throat for three hours and has not been seen by a doctor yet:

Ideas

- *'What is your understanding about why your wife hasn't been seen yet?'*
- *'Why do you think this has happened?'*
- *'What is your opinion on the way this has unfolded?'*

The above phrases can all prove to be quite useful. By looking at them closely, you can see that not only are they nice, open questions, but they are all entirely neutral. No blame is apportioned one way or the other by opening in this way, and in addition, it gives the patient further chance to express how they're feeling. It also allows for a portion of self-reflection on the part of the patient – is their wife not as sick as they initially thought? Are they cross because of something else and this is merely the chance they've taken to let it all out? More importantly, they should give you bits and bobs to take away for when you use recognizing, acknowledging and validating (RAV) a little while later in the consultation.

Concerns

- *'What, in particular, is concerning you the most?'*

The "in particular" is of utmost importance in aceing an OSCE. Usually there will be only one or two reasons a patient is angry in an OSCE setting. If you directly ask them, not only will you find out exactly what the root of their problems is, but it is also quite therapeutic for them to truly share what is really causing them grief. By this point in your consultation, you could already know why someone is cross and their reasons for feeling that way – and all you've done is ask them three simple questions!

Expectations

- *'How can I help fix this situation?'*
- *'Is there anything I can do to help?'*

Now it's time to seal the deal! By now they should have told you exactly what is bugging them and why they are so angry (annoyed about waiting times, angry as worried about the health of loved ones, etc.). Now here is their opportunity to let you know exactly how you can fix it. They may say something like *'Doc, I just want to know what's going on – I'm worried sick, I've not eaten all day and I'm absolutely exhausted'* – this seemingly simple question will allow you to fully take control of what has been an awful situation and make things right. Really try to pay attention to each bit of the explanation they offer and break it down into an action plan. If we were to use the above sentence as an example, we should be able to seal the deal on bringing the patient on our side:

- *'I just want to know what's going on.'*
- *'I'm worried sick.'*
- *'I've not eaten all day.'*
- *'I'm absolutely exhausted.'*

Before we address these issues, Maslow's Hierarchy of Need (see *Fig. 25.1*) is a really important concept to grasp. If you can get your head around it, it should make any consultation with an unhappy person much easier and more successful!

Figure 25.1 *Maslow's Hierarchy of Need.*

Maslow's Hierarchy of Need is a theory of what really motivates us, and is relevant in any consultation. To simplify it, Maslow stated that we all have base needs, and once we have fulfilled one we move onto the next level of higher needs. Putting this into context – often people who are hungry or thirsty are more concerned with resolving that than trying to get on top of the meaning of life.

If we relate this to our example consultation above, we can see a few things:

1. Physiological need – they are hungry and tired.

2. Safety needs – they are concerned about the impact on their health and wellbeing.

3. Emotional needs – they're worried about someone they care for.

4. No real self-esteem issues noted.

5. No existential troubles reported.

So we can see here that there are a few base needs we can address immediately. Although this is a hypothetical situation, in the OSCE (or real life!) offer them a seat and a cup of tea. Even if they decline they'll take note that you're addressing their base needs. Then you can come up with a plan to help them regarding their emotional concerns.

25.2.3 Summarize and signpost

By this point we should (hopefully) have found out what the salient points are that are causing this person's concerns. Your mind is probably going to be going a mile a minute, so take a deep breath and summarize. Useful phrases such as *'Just so I can ensure I haven't missed anything, I'd like to recap what you have mentioned so far'*, make you look both competent and empathetic. After this, ask the patient if there's anything else they'd like to discuss. This way you can come up with a nice succinct plan of how to go forward (and it makes you look super slick).

So we've summarized and we have a good idea of what the person you're talking to would like to discuss – ideally the OSCE actor would have told you if you'd missed anything after summarizing. Come up with three important points to discuss and then ask the patient if that's OK and if there's anything else they'd like to talk about. This is really important as the actors are trained to pick up on cues just as you are – if there's something they're supposed to talk about they'll slip it in this bit.

Here's an example dialogue about how all this could fit together:

You: *'OK Mr X, just so I know I'm not missing anything important, my understanding is that you're naturally concerned that your wife hasn't been seen yet, and this is really worrying you as you're concerned that her condition may be unstable and you'd like an update on what's happened so far. Is this a fair summary of how you're feeling?'*

Actor: *'Yeah that sounds about right to me.'*

You: *'Is there anything else you'd like to discuss with me today?'*

Actor: *'Nope, you've got it all I reckon.'*

You: *'Fine, well how about we start with what has happened regarding your wife since she came to A&E, then we can talk about her current condition and discuss the plan for her care going forward? How does that sound?'*

Actor: *'Finally, this is all I've been after all bloody day.'*

You: *'Well I hope to be of some assistance in that case. Is there anything else you'd like to talk about whilst I'm here?'*

Actor: *'No, that should just about cover it.'*

Easy peasey eh? Now you're about half way through dealing with an angry patient and you've got a nice clear plan of how to finish things off.

25.2.4 Information giving

By now you should have found out what the patient wants to discuss, and why they are upset. If we reflect on a time when any one of us has been angry, we all know that when experiencing a strong emotion our ability to take in and remember information is impaired. Therefore it is essential to pair empathy to anger with an awareness of an impeded ability to take in information. Break down what you want to say into small chunks, and ensure you're not coming across as patronizing in doing so. Reinforce every statement you make with a reassuring fact, and whoever you are talking to will feel far more satisfied with the conversation. If you have a logical argument to why a person has found themselves in a situation, any residual anger should dissipate. Below is an example of how this could play out:

You: *'I understand the first concern you expressed was that your wife hadn't been seen by a doctor yet – is that correct?'*

Actor: *'Yeah, and I think it's a pretty shoddy state of affairs if I'm honest.'*

You: *'I can appreciate your concern; would you mind if I fill you in on what has happened so far today?'*

Actor: *'Be my guest.'*

You: *'Thank you. So when your wife came to A&E, she received a full assessment from a triage nurse, who took her bloods and arranged for her to have X-rays and other essential tests for us to optimize her care going forward.'*

Actor: *'Right.'*

You: *'I'm sure you can appreciate that here in A&E we all work as a close unit. I can wholly understand that it is concerning that she hasn't physically seen a doctor yet; however, I can tell you that the doctors in the department are aware of her and her clinical situation. Unfortunately, there are some people here who are more unwell than she is who have to take* *priority. This doesn't mean we aren't concerned about your wife's welfare, nor are we unaware of her current situation. She is on close observations and we shall assess her as soon as we can.'*

Actor: *'Yeah mate, I get that, I've seen some people here looking proper ill. It's just she's not well either you know? And it's really worrying me that she may not get better or that if she's not treated soon something serious will happen to her.'*

You: *'Of course it worries you, why don't we talk for a bit about your wife's current condition and the plan we have in place so far?'*

Actor: *'That would be great.'*

You: *'My understanding is your wife has come in with a chest infection. She is indeed poorly but her observations indicate that she is doing well at present. We need her blood test results and chest X-ray before we can really come up with a plan of how best to proceed. Once we have those then we can do our best as a team to get your wife feeling better as soon as possible. If we acted without these we may misdiagnose your wife and subsequently do her more harm than good.'*

Actor: *'Well I don't want that to happen!'*

You: *'Nor do we. Unfortunately these results can take a little while to come back. I'll make sure we keep an eye out for them to get your wife treated as soon as possible. I'm sorry but I have to get back to my other patients now; however, please don't think I'm forgetting about you or her. If you have any further concerns please ask a nurse to find me and we can talk further. Before I go is there anything I can get you? Tea? Coffee? Something to eat?'*

Actor: *'Well a cup of tea and a sandwich wouldn't go amiss.'*

You: *'No problem, I'll get someone to bring you some refreshments as soon as possible. Before I go is there anything else I can help you with?'*

Actor: *'Cheers doc. Sorry about before.'*

Let's take a moment to dissect the above hypothetical situation. It is important in these instances not to reflect too much on what was said, but instead the overall themes of conversation.

- The opening sentence offers both empathy and an indication that you're listening. The word "understand" allows you to express not only that you have been paying attention to their concerns, but also that you are reflecting upon it whilst your consultation is underway. By ending it with *'is this correct?'* it also makes you very personable to the person with whom you are talking, by offering some weakness. Coinciding with this, it allows the patient / relative, etc. to offer you further concerns / things they would like to discuss.
- Using phrases such as *'I can appreciate your concern'* yet again puts you on the same emotional plane as your consultee. Being able to show you can acknowledge somebody's strong emotion is a useful method of improving a negative situation by allowing them to explore it further.
- If you ask somebody for permission to explain a situation to them, it helps ensure you don't come across as arrogant or overbearing, further improving rapport with the patient / carer, etc.
- Be honest and avoid jargon! Let them know what you do and don't know, but more importantly let them know why you and your team have acted in a certain way. As previously discussed, anger is usually a secondary emotion to fear or confusion. By explaining a process to someone you can allay fear or confusion and subsequently decrease the amount of anger they may be feeling.

- Offer to go the extra mile – you could easily state that you'll leave them to their day and go back to your business. However, if you offer that "personal touch" such as stating a continuing active role in the healthcare of a patient or offering someone something to eat or drink, it proves that you care about the situation you are in and allows for a more positive experience for all concerned.

25.2.5 **Final thoughts**

Dealing with somebody expressing a strong emotion is always challenging, and can be quite intimidating. Hopefully, this chapter has been somewhat useful in giving you both a structure with which to address an angry person and some concepts to reflect upon whilst doing so. There are no hard and fast rules to this, however, and the only real way we can ever improve on our communication skills in tricky situations is to experience them first hand and reflect upon our own practices. We must learn from both our successes and failures in these situations to try to turn a negative experience into a positive one. Here are some parting words of wisdom for situations which prove more challenging than you would hope for:

- You can't please everyone! Don't get disheartened if you try your utmost to help somebody and they still remain angry. In these instances it is essential to keep your head, not be confrontational yourself and find yourself a quiet place to dust yourself off.
- Appreciate that everybody has their own agenda. As previously stated, try to work out why a patient is acting in a certain way. If you do your best to assess a situation, it will allow you to empathize with somebody far better and improve your rapport with them.
- Saying "sorry" is an essential tool. If you are honest, reasonable and apologetic, even the most dissatisfied person would find it hard to remain angry. Remember that saying "sorry" isn't an admission of guilt; it is an acceptance that somebody is in a regrettable situation. Incorporate this into your consultation by reflecting back their concerns.
  - *'I am sorry that you are upset with the wait.'*
  - *'I am sorry that you feel like the team has...'*
- Offering kind words can be just as therapeutic as the medical treatment you are offering.

> **Summary of key points (GET YOUR MARKS):**
>
> Establish rapport (clear introduction of who you are, what your role is and why you are there).
>
> Establish why the patient is angry: ask an open question and allow for the Golden Minute.
>
> Apologize: make the apology personal to what the patient is angry about.
>
> ICE: use this to get to the cause of their anger and then start to understand what you can do to help them.
>
> Address their issues in order: start with those issues which are easily resolved.
>
> Closing the consultation: Let the Calgary–Cambridge Model be your guide. Remember your key skills of summarizing and screening. Always leave the patient with a plan of care, even if it is that you need to speak with your colleagues. Thank the patient.

25.3 **Practice scenarios**

Don't worry too much about the medical aspect of the scenarios listed below. Instead, take this opportunity to explore the emotions of your role-play partner and try different methods of showing empathy to ascertain what works for you.

Ask your partner to come up with an "ulterior motive" – a hidden agenda making them angry, which this situation has made far worse.

1. You are working as an FY1 on the Acute Medical Unit. You have been asked to speak to Mr Smith (68), the husband of a 65-year-old woman who was discharged 2 days ago following admission for an infective exacerbation of COPD. Before discharge, Mrs Smith was medically fit to go home and was discharged with all relevant medications. Mrs Smith has returned to hospital with worsening breathing. Her husband is angry and he believes she was discharged too early.

2. You are working as an F2 in General Practice. Fiona Challoner has come to see you as she has had a dry cough for two days and is feeling generally unwell. You assess her and come to the conclusion she has a viral upper respiratory tract infection. You patiently explain to her that this is a viral infection and it will get better in a couple of weeks of its own accord. Miss Challoner takes umbrage to this, and sees this as you "fobbing her off".

3. A mother of a 14-year-old girl comes to see you because she knows her daughter had an appointment to see you two days ago and suspects you prescribed her the COCP. When you inform the mother that her daughter has the right to confidentiality and you cannot discuss this without her consent, the mother becomes angered, stating that her daughter is "just a child" and she has every right to know.

26

Communicating risk

RACHEL WAMBOLDT

> **Communicating Risk: Keys to Success**
>
> - Express risk in a way that is meaningful to the patient. Avoid percentages – use frequencies instead.
> - Avoid using descriptive terms such as "low risk" as the patient may have a different interpretation of what "low risk" means than you.
> - Visual aids can be helpful.
> - Remember the RISK mnemonic (*see box below*).

26.1 Essential skills to explaining risk

In order for a shared decision to be made between a healthcare provider and a patient, potential risk and benefits need to be communicated in a way that is easy for the patient to understand. To do this, the healthcare provider and patient need to engage in a two-way conversation, whereby the risk is communicated to the patient and the patient communicates back whether or not they accept the risk. Risk communication must always be patient-centred. This can be done using the following mnemonic:

> **Mnemonic: RISK**
> **R**elate relevant evidence
> **I**ndividualize the message, using a flexible approach
> **S**eek the patient's perspective and share the decision making process
> **C**heck the patient understands, monitor and review all decisions that are made.

Healthcare providers and patients like the use of verbal probabilities such as "likely" or "rare" to convey risk but these terms are easy to misinterpret as they rely on personal interpretation. It is often the emotions that primarily determine the risk rather than the actual facts. One person may think a risk of 1 in 100 is low risk, whereas another might think it is too high a risk to take. Interpretation is dependent on the context of its use and on the concerned person's experience. The difficulty with using percentages is that many people, including both the public and professionals, have difficulty interpreting them. Lay people often have an "all or nothing" perspective, interpreting risk as either high or low. In order to communicate effectively with the public, doctors need to express risk in a way that is meaningful to the recipient. At the end of the consultation, it is not how well you delivered the information but how well that patient has understood it.

26.1.1 The role of framing

The way in which risk is perceived by a patient may be influenced by how the communicator frames the information. By changing the frame in which the information is presented, the communicator can turn the presentation of a morbid risk (e.g. mortality rate – "loss framing") into a positive (e.g. survival data – "gain framing"). Positive framing is therefore more effective when trying to persuade a patient to undergo a risky or frightening procedure. A responsible healthcare provider will therefore counter the influence of framing by using a dual representation (e.g. describing mortality and survival data).

26.1.2 Communicating risk in the OSCE

- **Patient trust** – the patient needs to be convinced that the information that you are providing is accurate, objective and credible. Trust depends on multiple factors. The patient needs to believe that the doctor is competent, objective and empathetic to their decision. If the patient does not trust the informant, their perception of the information becomes distorted and perceived as biased.
  - *'I recently read a paper that showed....'*
  - *'The National Institute of Health and Care Excellence has guidelines that say...'*
- Remind the patient that all treatment will inevitably have some potential risk of harm. This helps to manage expectations and reassures the patient that the healthcare team will do their best, regardless of the treatment that is chosen.
- **Avoid using descriptive terms**, such as "low risk", as they reflect the communicator's perspective, which is usually quite different from the perspective of the patient.
- **Present risk in frequencies instead of percentages** – use 1 in 10 rather than 10%.
- **Use a common denominator** – to avoid confusion, continue to use one denominator so that the patient can make comparisons easily. For example, use 4 in 1000 and 50 in 1000 instead of 1 in 250 and 1 in 20.
- **Avoid using relative risk**. Instead use absolute numbers.
- **Link frequencies to scenarios the patient can relate to** (e.g. for a frequency of 1 in 100 000: *'If you took all the spectators at Wimbledon, only one of them would be at risk of ...'*). Alternatively, you can compare the information to an everyday risk, such as risk of stroke with atrial fibrillation compared to the risk of a car accident.
- **Use decision aids to express probability** – empirical studies suggest patients prefer crowd figures (see *Fig. 26.1*), simple bar charts and survival curves. Patient satisfaction has been shown to increase when a doctor has used a visual aid to improve patient understanding.
- When using **probability scales to calculate risk** (e.g. FRAX tool), involve the patient in the process of inputting risk factors so that they feel the results are more relevant to them.
- **Ensure that informed consent is actually "informed"**. This can be done by continually checking understanding and having the patient repeat back the information.
- Check the **patient's ICE** based on the information that you have provided them during the consultation. This helps to open up an open conversation with the patient and makes it safe for them to ask questions and clarify anything that they didn't understand. This can also help you tailor your responses to questions so that they are more relevant to the patient.

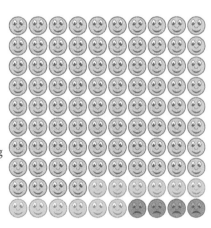

Figure 26.1 A crowd figure to express probability.

> **Key Knowledge: Definitions**
> **Absolute risk:** the risk of developing a disease over a certain time period.
> **Absolute risk reduction (ARR):** how much of the observed change is due to the treatment.
> **Relative risk (RR):** compares the risk between two groups of people (e.g. smokers vs. non-smokers).
> **Number needed to treat (NNT):** the number of patients that need to be treated in order to produce the target outcome in one patient; therefore, the smaller the NNT, the better the treatment. NNT= 1/ARR

26.1.3 Explaining research in the OSCE

Patients occasionally present asking for advice regarding medical information that they have read online, in the newspaper or in a magazine. It is important to have a good understanding of not only how to interpret research but also how to explain it in a way that the patient can understand and use to make clinical decisions. Explaining research is also a very common OSCE station.

1) Introduce yourself, your role and the reason for the consultation

2) Confirm the patient's name and age

3) Establish the reason for the consultation, allowing a Golden Minute for the patient to express their concerns.

4) Establish the patient's ICE regarding the information presented in the article and what they would like to get from the consultation.

5) Familiarize yourself with the material
- If the patient has brought in an article, inform them that you would like a couple of minutes to familiarize yourself with its contents. If not, ask them to describe the contents.
- *'Thank you for bringing in the article today. If you don't mind, I would just like to have a quick read of the article myself so that I can answer any questions that you might have.'*

6) Establish the patient's starting point
- *'What is your understanding of the information in the article?'* or
- *'What was your interpretation of the information in the article?'*

7) Establish how much information the patient would like to know about the article
- *'I'd like to know how much information you would like to know about the article. Would you like me to explain the terms and numbers in detail or simply summarize my understanding of the information and how it applies to you?'*

8) Set an agenda for the consultation using the RISK mnemonic above

9) Make it easy to understand

- After defining what various terms and numbers mean, it needs to be put in a way that they can understand. Metaphors are a great way of doing this but they need to be executed with caution because if used incorrectly they can lead to more confusion.

26.2 Rapid fire overview of research principles for OSCEs

26.2.1 Types of research studies

Case–control study: a study used to determine if a condition or disease is related to a certain exposure. As evidenced by the name, a group of people with the condition (cases) and a group of those without the condition (controls) are recruited and matched according to age, sex and other characteristics. Researchers then look retrospectively to compare the exposures between the cases and the controls.

Cohort study: a group of participants with certain characteristics are recruited and followed up over time (prospectively) to determine the incidence and mortality of a specific disease.

Randomized controlled trial (RCT): a clinical trial where a group of individuals are randomly assigned to intervention groups. Patients and researchers are unaware of what treatment they are receiving (double-blinding) and therefore difference between the treatment groups can be measured with biases being reduced. It is the gold standard for clinical trials.

26.2.2 Sensitivity and specificity

Sensitivity: a sensitive test helps to identify patients who actually have the disease (true positives). If a test has a sensitivity of 90% it will catch 90% of people who have the disease, but 10% will go undetected (false negatives). A highly sensitive test therefore helps to rule out disease if it is negative.

For example, the D-dimer test is highly sensitive. If a D-dimer is negative, you can be fairly certain that the patient does not have a pulmonary embolism.

- *'You install a burglar alarm in your house (the burglar alarm is the test). If your burglar alarm is very sensitive then you can be confident that there isn't a burglar in your home if it hasn't gone off. In other words, if your test is negative, you can be fairly confident that you do not have the disease.'*

Specificity: the ability of a test to identify those who do not have the disease (true negatives). It also refers to how positive you can be that you have the disease if the test is positive. If a test is highly specific and you test positive, you can be fairly certain that you have the disease.

For example, the D-dimer test is not very specific; therefore if it is positive you can't say for certain that it is due to a pulmonary embolism or whether it is due to another cause such as cancer or inflammation.

- *'If you have a burglar alarm that is highly specific and it starts to sound, you can be fairly confident that it is due to a burglar and not a cat or the wind.'*

26.2.3 Positive and negative predictive value

Positive predictive value: describes how likely you are to have the disease if the test is positive.

Negative predictive value: describes how likely you are to not have the disease if the test is negative.

The problem with these two principles is that they are highly influenced by the population that the test is used on and the prevalence of the disease.

26.2.4 Mean, median and mode

Mean: to calculate, all of the numbers are added together and then divided by the total number of values. This will give you the average.

Median: refers to the middle value. If you were to line up all of the given values from highest to lowest, the median would be the value that falls right in the middle.

Mode: the value that appears the most frequently.

26.2.5 Probability

Probability: a value between 0 and 1 that measures how likely it is for an event to occur. It is measured by the number of positive events divided by the total number of events. A positive event is defined as the phenomenon or desired event that you are researching (e.g. if you were researching the probability of developing lung cancer in smokers, the positive event would be lung cancer).

- *'A dice has 6 sides. To calculate probability, you divide 1 by the number of potential outcomes/events (sides of the dice). Therefore, 1 divided by 6 gives you a probability of 0.16 of the dice landing on the side that you want.'*

Odds: a value that measures how likely the desired event is to occur and is measured by the number of positive events ÷ the number of negative events.

- *'If you were to roll the dice again, the odds of it landing on a specific number are 1 in 5 or 20%.'*

Relative risk: used in cohort studies and RCTs to compare the risks between two groups, usually those exposed vs. those not exposed.

Odds ratio: used in case–control studies to compare the probability of an event occurring vs. an event not occurring.

***P* value**: used to determine if the results that were received from the study were due to chance rather than a true effect.

- If the *P* value is small (usually <0.05), there is enough evidence against the null hypothesis (no difference between the two test groups) to reject it. In other words, there is a less than 1 in 20 chance that the difference seen in the study could be due to chance; therefore we say that the results are significant.
- If the *P* value is large (>0.05) then there is not enough evidence to reject the null hypothesis; there is a greater than 1 in 20 chance that the results are due to chance, therefore the results are not significant.

Confidence interval (CIs): a range of values in which we can be 95% certain that the true mean lies.

- CIs are dependent on 1) variation within a sample (the greater the variation, the greater the CI) and 2) the size of the sample (the larger the sample, the smaller the CI).
- CIs can also be used to determine if the results of a study are significant. If the CI contains the value of "no effect", then the results are not significant. If the CI does not contain the value of "no effect" then the results are significant.

10) Summarize the findings of the study

11) Ask about their ICE

Determine the patient's opinion on the results of the research and how they believe it applies to them.

12) Discuss your opinion on how the results relate to the patient's condition

Come to a shared decision with the patient as to whether their plan on care needs to be altered.

13) Screen for any further questions or concerns

14) Thank the patient

> **Summary of key points (GET YOUR MARKS):**
>
> **Establish rapport:** clear introduction of who you are, what your role is and why you are there. Confirm patient's name and DOB and why they wish to speak to you.
>
> **Presenting complaint:** in this case it will most likely be a news article or research article which the patient has come across. Allow them the Golden Minute to summarize the article to you and explain why it is important to them.
>
> **Establish ICE:** do this early in this style of consultation as it will help you to frame the consultation and will allow you to know what details of the article to focus on for the patient and what particular questions they want answered.
>
> **Establish the patient's starting point and how much information they would like.**
>
> **Use the RISK mnemonic to set an agenda for the consultation.**
>
> **Explain the research findings to the patient.**
>
> **Re-examine ICE and understanding** of the research findings.
>
> **Close the consultation:** summarize everything that has been discussed and decisions which you have both come to. Check that there is nothing else the patient would like to discuss.

26.3 Practice scenarios

1. Johanna Beardy is a 23-year-old woman who smokes 15 cigarettes per day. She has recently had her first child and is thinking of giving up smoking. She knows that smoking can cause lung cancer but she is not aware of any other risks associated with smoking cigarettes. The GP has asked you to discuss Johanna's smoking habits and the risks associated with this lifestyle choice.

2. Sandy Beckles is a 17-year-old girl who is pregnant with her first child. During a GP appointment for a UTI she casually mentioned that she did not plan on vaccinating her infant when it is born. The GP has asked you to discuss the role of vaccinations in public health and the risks associated with not having her child vaccinated.

3. Leanne Tomlin is a 54-year-old post-menopausal woman who has come to the GP to discuss her risk of osteoporosis. Her mother had osteoporosis and suffered from a hip fracture which Leanne feels led to her death. She is worried that she is at risk for osteoporosis. She is sent for a bone mineral density (BMD) scan due to an initial FRAX score calculation of 7%. Her T score is −2.5 and on recalculation, her FRAX score is 33%. Explain the results of the bone mineral density scan using *Fig. 26.2* and what this means for Leanne's future management.

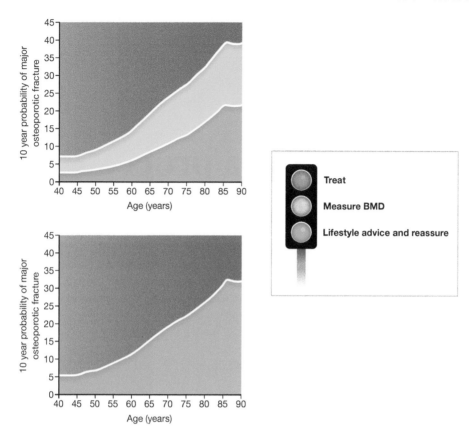

Figure 26.2 *Assessment and treatment thresholds without (top) or with (bottom) a BMD test. Reproduced from National Osteoporosis Guideline Group's* Guideline for the diagnosis and management of osteoporosis.

27

Consenting for a procedure

FLORENCE BECKETT

Consenting for a Procedure: Keys to Success

- Be aware of common procedures for which you may be asked to obtain consent.
- Know about common side-effects and complications including local complications, systemic complications and anaesthetic complications.
- Elicit the patient's ICE early in the consultation. You can then incorporate them into your explanations throughout.
- Have a clear structure in your head – DR ABCS.

27.1 Information gathering

Procedures and operations are commonplace within medicine and are carried out on a daily basis. We often become so used to doing them that it can be easy to forget these may be entirely new experiences to our patients. Taking a little time to clearly explain intended procedures to our patients not only allows for a more pleasant and patient-centred experience for both us and our patient but it is also good medical practice.

As the medical professional intending to carry out the procedure you are responsible for obtaining consent from the patient. You should only obtain consent for a procedure that you are competent to carry out. Consent can be implied, verbal or written. The type of consent required will vary on the type of intended procedure.

Arguably the most valuable component of your consultation is building good rapport with the patient. It allows you to get important questions in and gain valuable opening marks.

1) Introduce yourself and your role on the surgical or medical team

2) Consent and confidentiality

3) Confirm patient's name and DOB
Remember you may be talking to a parent who is there to discuss consenting a procedure for their child or an elderly relative.

4) Establish reason for consultation
- *'I understand you have come in today to talk about.... is that right?'*
- Remember you will often already know the reason for the consultations so asking why the patient has come in for these scenarios may make you appear slightly uninformed.

- Establish the sequence of events leading up to today's consultation including previous tests, surgeries, procedures, etc. Use open questions here, e.g. *'Can you tell me a little bit about what has happened so far?'*

5) Specific history taking / ICE

- This is a good opportunity to ascertain the patient's ICE.
- **What do they know already?** *'What do you know about the procedure?'*
- **What are they worried about?** *'Is there anything that is worrying you about having the procedure?'*
- **What do they want to know?** *'What were you expecting to find out about today?'*

6) General history taking

Often you may get points for just ticking the box for this. There may even be some gem of hidden information that helps give a basis to the rest of the consultation. This should only take about 1–2 minutes tops!

Past medical history: *'Do you suffer from any other health conditions?'*

Past surgical history: *'Have you ever had surgery before, and if so what was this for?'*

Drug history including allergies: *'Are you currently taking any medications? Any over-the-counter medications? Do you have any allergies?'*

Family history: *'Does anything run in your family? Has anyone in your family experienced any complications during surgery?'* (think malignant hyperthermia)

Social history: *'Do you smoke?'* – quantify if they do. *'Do you drink alcohol?'* – again quantify if they do. Illicit drug use is relevant in case they are at risk for withdrawal symptoms or over- or under-sedation / analgesia. *'Do you have anyone at home with you?'* It may also be appropriate to ask if they have anyone to pick them up after the procedure, especially if it is a day procedure.

27.2 Information giving and shared decision making

The following is an outline of common scenarios that may come up in consenting for a procedure scenarios.

Important guidelines to follow:
- Careful use of language, ensuring you avoid medical jargon
- The 3 S's: Signpost, Signal, Summarize
- Chunk and check
- Draw simple diagrams
- Offer a follow-up session and written information
- If in doubt summarize using information brought out from your 'ICE' discussions, to see if these have been resolved / addressed.

Remember: you are being tested on ability to consent for a procedure but make sure you are aware that you should only be consenting for procedures that you are skilled enough to do and competent therefore to consent for.

27.2.1 DR ABCS

> Mnemonic: **DR ABCS**
> **D**etails (outlines the process before, during and after the procedure)
> **R**isks
> **A**lternatives (although logistically fits better after B and C)
> **B**enefits
> **C**onsequences
> **S**afetynetting

Details
- **What happens before the procedure?**
  - Where and when to arrive? Nil by mouth (NBM)? Full bladder? Medications the night before/morning prior to procedure? Clothing to wear?
- **What will happen during the procedure?**
  - Who will be present/carry out the procedure? Use of analgesia or sedation? Basic description of the procedure? Length of procedure?
- **What will happen after the procedure?**
  - What is the recovery time? When can they return to work? How long before they can drive? How and when will they receive the results?

Risks
Common or serious side-effects/risks:
- **Immediate** e.g. bleeding, pain, damage to local structures
- **Short-term** e.g. infection, DVT
- **Long-term** e.g. recurrence of problem, need to repeat procedure or alternative.

It is also important to discuss anaesthetic risks although the anesthesiologist will likely discuss these in more detail (e.g. nausea/vomiting, sore throat, damage to teeth, allergy to the anaesthetic, cardiorespiratory collapse).

Benefits
Overlapping benefits between procedures include:
- Quicker and more accurate diagnosis, or alternatively reassurance
- Gold standard treatment
- Relief of symptoms
- Improved quality of life.

Consequences of not having the procedure
Overlapping consequences include:
- Delay in diagnosis
- Delay in potential treatment required after diagnosis
- Increased risk of complications whilst waiting for procedure.

Alternatives
- Including different imaging modalities and less invasive techniques.

Safetynetting
- Discuss the normal recovery timeline
- Alert them to warning signs of complications and when to seek help.

27.2.2 **Example procedures**

Table 27.1 Abdominal ultrasound

D	Pre	• Arrive at pre-appointed time, date and place • +/– required to arrive with a full bladder • +/– NBM for 6 hours pre-USS
	During	• Abdomen uncovered, lying on couch • Cold jelly on abdomen and US probe placed on the skin to look at soft tissue layers underneath • Invisible sound waves; pain free; pressure only
	Post	No recovery time; back to normal activities straight after
R	Risks	Failure to visualize some structures due to e.g. body weight, gas in the bowel
B	Benefits	No radiation; non-invasive; good for soft tissue structures
C	Consequences of not	• Delay in diagnosis • More invasive imaging or increased radiation doses
A	Alternatives	Blood tests; alternative imaging modalities
S	Safetynetting	Not curative, therefore symptoms likely to continue

Table 27.2 Appendicectomy

D	Pre	• NBM when decision for surgery • IV fluids, analgesia +/– antibiotics prior to surgery
	During	• Carried out in operating theatre under general anaesthetic; keyhole surgery for most people, usually 3 incisions • Procedure usually lasts under an hour • Possibility of having to change to open surgery if complications arise
	Post	Monitoring post-op, generally home within 48 hours
R	Risks	• Infection, bleeding, damage to local structures (in particular reproductive organs) and adhesions • Increased chance of hernia in future • Risk associated with the general anaesthetic
B	Benefits	Treatment of appendicitis
C	Consequences of not	Failure of treatment; worsening infection (sepsis) and pain; unlikely resolution of symptoms
A	Alternatives	Antibiotics and expectant management – but this would not be encouraged
S	Safetynetting	Normal to have some discomfort for a few days Warn about: • Fever or infection at wound site post-op • Signs and symptoms of DVT and PE • Reproductive and adhesion complications in future

Table 27.3 Lumbar puncture

D	Pre	Blood test: especially clotting CT head: to rule out raised intracranial pressure (high pressure inside your skull)
	During	• Either on left-hand side with knee drawn on to chest or sitting hunched forward • Doctor will use sterile gloves, gowns and drapes • Your back is cleaned with e.g. iodine; appropriate space located and local anaesthetic injected into site • Small amount of spinal fluid removed
	Post	• You will have to lie flat for a few hours afterwards; continue simple analgesia such as paracetamol • Some results within a few hours, others may take up to a week
R	Risks	• Discomfort inserting the needle and adjusting it into position • Pain or pins and needles in back or legs • Infection, bleeding, post lumbar puncture headache
B	Benefits	Diagnostic accuracy; confirmation of clinical suspicion e.g. subarachnoid haemorrhage
C	Consequences of not	Delay in diagnosis; delay in starting treatment
A	Alternatives	Blood tests, imaging of brain or spinal column, clinical examination
S	Safetynetting	• May have slight discomfort at puncture site for a few hours • Warn about: persistent headache, weakness in lower limbs, signs or symptoms of meningism (neck stiffness, intolerance to bright lights, headache)

Table 27.4 Urethral catheterization

D	Pre	No preparation generally required
	During	• Lying down, bottom clothing removed and covered with a modesty sheet. Genitalia cleaned with sterile water • Catheter inserted up urethra into bladder; this may be slightly uncomfortable but we will use anaesthetic jelly before insertion
	Post	Catheter either removed after sample obtained or kept in for a period of time
R	Risks	Infection; trauma to urethra and bladder; bleeding.
B	Benefits	Relief from obstruction; obtaining urine sample
C	Consequences of not	• Continued obstruction, bladder or kidney damage • Stagnant urine, increased risk of infection
A	Alternatives	Trans-abdominal aspiration or catheterization
S	Safetynetting	• May feel slightly uncomfortable but shouldn't be painful • May feel the urge to pass urine despite drainage • Warn about: failed trial without catheter; symptoms of UTI

Summary of key points (GET YOUR MARKS):

Use appropriate language throughout that the patient will understand. Avoid medical jargon!

Use your important communication skills: signpost, signal and summarize; and chunk and check.

Ask whether a picture would help the patient; for example, this could show where the incisions would be made if it was a surgical procedure or how a TURP biopsy would be performed.

Elicit and incorporate the patient's ICE throughout.

ALWAYS REMEMBER DR ABCS:

- Details (outlines the process before, during and after the procedure)
- Risks
- Alternatives (although logistically fits better after B and C)
- Benefits
- Consequences
- Safetynetting

Allow the opportunity to ask questions.

27.3 Practice scenarios

1. Jason Andrew is a 33-year-old man pre-consented for a renal biopsy, following a recent admission for renal failure. He has arrived for his listed biopsy today and has a few questions, especially regarding the risks associated with the procedure. He would also like to know what happens after the procedure and how quickly he can be picked up. He would also like to know how quickly he can return to playing weekend rugby.

2. Betty Graham is a 68-year-old lady who has been admitted with a right-sided pleural effusion. She is clinically stable and is planned to have a routine ultrasound guided chest drain. She has questions about how this has occurred and no one has explained what has caused 'water on the lung'. She also wants to know whether this could be cancer as she overheard a medical student saying it.

3. Edward Hopkins is a 72-year-old gentleman who has been listed for a routine TURP following a year or so of prostatic symptoms. He has read about side-effects including difficulties with ejaculation and would like to discuss this and other possible side-effects. He is also worried about the spinal anaesthetic and having to have a catheter afterwards.

4. Michael Jones is a 58 year old gentleman with a 60 pack-year history and a recent mass found on CT chest. MDT outcome is to carry out a bronchoscopy. He has a few questions about the procedure, he is nervous about the risk and wants to know if there is an alternative procedure he could have done.

5. James Henderson is a 35-year-old sales manager with iron deficiency anaemia. He is generally fit and well and there is no obvious cause for blood loss. His GP has referred him for routine work-up investigations. He attends clinic and the consultant advises a colonoscopy. He has a few questions for you especially about why the colonoscopy is suggested. He wants to know if he could have a scan instead.

6. Amanda Johnson is a 45-year-old lady currently pregnant with her second child. She has been offered investigations to screen for Down syndrome including amniocentesis. She would like to discuss this and other screening options available to her, particularly in relation to associated risks of the procedures.

7. Gisela Sanchez is a 22-year-old student recently admitted with her first episode of uncomplicated biliary colic. She is attending clinic to discuss with the consultant about having a routine laparoscopic cholecystectomy. Your consultant asks you to discuss the options available to her first and answer her questions, particularly in relation to the chance of recurrence of symptoms.

8. Nazneen Begum is a 28-year-old graphic designer who has come to discuss genetic screening for the BRCA gene with you. Her mother has recently been diagnosed with breast cancer and had a double mastectomy; she tested positive for the BRCA gene. She would like to discuss with you the pros and cons of having the screening test carried out, as well as what a positive test may mean for her.

28

Talking to colleagues

LOUISE PATTERSON

28.1 Communication over the telephone

What an examiner needs to know in this particular OSCE station is that you are able to communicate key information in an organized and coherent way. In order to score highly you must identify what in the patient's story is relevant, adjust to whom you need to relay this information to and then come to a reasonable joint decision or end point. The likely scenario will be a patient who has become unwell, whom you have assessed; you now need some senior advice on their management.

The recommended way to provide the appropriate information over the phone is through the use of SBAR and this is increasingly used by all medical professionals across all fields of healthcare. SBAR provides a more standardized communication platform that maximizes patient safety, so any mark scheme will be based around the following:

Situation	<ul><li>Hello</li><li>Am I speaking with the... *Medical registrar*?</li><li>I am... *William Bosh, a colorectal surgery FY2*</li><li>The patient I am calling about is... *Penelope Pitstop – her hospital number is 1111222 and she is on B ward*</li><li>The reason I am calling is... *I am concerned that she is having a pulmonary embolism*</li></ul>
Background	<ul><li>The patient was admitted... *for an open elective Hartmann's procedure for sigmoid carcinoma three days ago*</li><li>During this admission / PMH... *she was well post-operatively; her only past medical history is hypertension and diet-controlled type 2 DM*</li><li>This has changed... *two hours ago she suddenly dropped her oxygen saturations to 80% on air and became breathless*</li></ul>

Assessment	• I therefore think the problem is… *that she has a pulmonary embolism*
	• OR if you are not sure…
	• *I am not sure what the problem is but I am concerned the patient is deteriorating or that there is something potentially serious going on and I am worried*
	• On examination… *she appears breathless, is tachycardic, on auscultation her chest is clear, abdomen is soft non-tender and the wound is clean and dry, and she has no evidence of proximal DVT*
	• I have… *given her high flow oxygen, completed an ECG, which shows sinus tachycardia, and done an ABG, which shows hypoxia on 100% oxygen. I have also ordered an urgent portable chest X-ray. Nursing staff have repeated her observations; BP is stable at 130/80, pulse is 110, respiratory rate is 25, saturations are 90% on 100% O$_2$ and she is apyrexial*
Recommendation	• Would you be able to come and see the patient?
	• Is there any investigation you think might be helpful that I can do in the meantime?
	• Is there anything I should be doing to further manage this patient before you are able to come?
	• May I just repeat the plan back to you so that I can check I haven't missed anything? *You would like me to order a CT pulmonary angiogram urgently, give treatment dose low molecular weight heparin and you will come and see the patient in approximately 20 minutes*
	• Are you happy for me to document our conversation and your name in the notes?
	• Thank you. *My bleep is 0007 and I am Dr Bosh, if you should need to contact me.*

Sometimes an extra R is added on to SBAR; this second R stands for **"read-back"** or you may have heard of it being referred to as **"check-back"**. Here you may ask your colleague who is receiving the information to repeat back the key points they have understood from the conversation, in order to ensure the information has been effectively and correctly communicated.

Remember these key points:
- Take the time to write down the important points for what you want to say.
  - This will prevent too much waffle or going off at a tangent.
  - Try to ensure it is clear to the person listening what you want them to do, be it giving advice or reviewing a patient.
- Talk at a speed that is clear and appropriate.
  - If you know you're one to mumble or rush…. PRACTISE, PRACTISE, PRACTISE.
- Be polite and listen carefully when needed, otherwise you may miss something important.
- Avoid having to hand through any notes, observation charts or appropriate imaging reports as this will only waste your time in the exam.
- Write down any instruction received.
  - Sometimes in the heat of the moment you will even forget your name, so don't forget any important instructions you may need to act on.
- Document all conversations.
  - More applicable to work than OSCE but important to mention that you will document the conversation in the notes!

> **OSCE TIP**: Practise with a friend; get them to call you from another room and role-play scenarios. Use the above SBAR checklist to make sure the important points are covered and then give constructive feedback to each other.

28.2 Communicating in writing

28.2.1 Patient notes

An OSCE station requiring you to write an entry in the notes should be an easy station to pick up points. The examiner will want you to make notes in a format that is easy to read and contains all the relevant information. Your notes not only communicate to colleagues your management plan, but they are also important written proof that events have happened.

After hospital placement you may already feel confident at writing in the notes but if not don't worry and try the SOAP mnemonic:

Subjective	• Symptoms • History of presenting complaint • *'Reports central chest pain, radiating to back'* Keep it brief, keep it relevant
Objective	• Observations: *'Appears breathless'* • Bedside observations (temperature / pulse / respiration) • Physical examination findings • Investigation results
Assessment	• The chief diagnosis • Further differential diagnoses Always good to consider a few diagnoses or list the patient's current problems
Plan	• Stepwise management plan • Estimated discharge date Number the plan, be as concise and clear as possible, write legibly and don't use jargon

Remember these key points to pick up easy marks:
- Use BLACK ink ONLY.
- Appropriately date and time each entry (24 hour clock).
- Number pages.
- Make sure there are **three** identifiable patient details on all pages, back and front:
  - Name, DOB and hospital number, for example.
- Identify the type of entry:
  - Identify the consultant in charge, the doctor leading the ward round and any other relevant members of the team.
- Always leave a contact extension or bleep number.
- Sign and initial at the end of every entry.
- Write legibly:
  - If you can't read your own writing, then how will the examiner be able to?
- Don't use too many acronyms / abbreviations:
  - They often mean different things in different specialties.
- Make any corrections with a single strike through.

OSCE TIP: Practise jotting down your own notes down in your notebook whilst on ward rounds (remember to keep all patient details confidential!). Try to test yourself to see if you can keep up with the fast pace.

A typical page in a patient's medical notes is shown in *Fig. 28.1*.

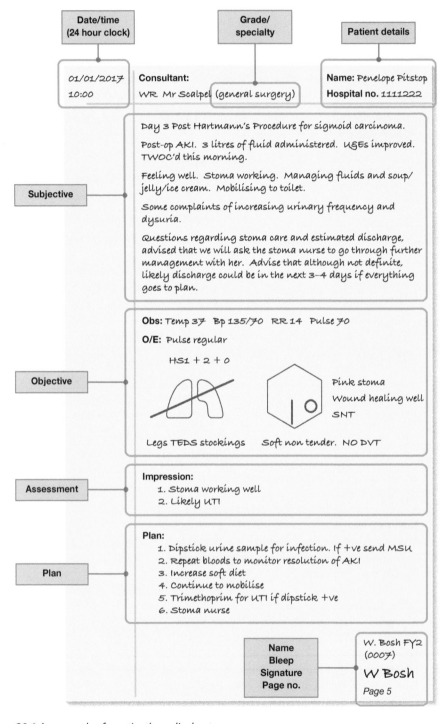

Figure 28.1 An example of a patient's medical notes.

28.2.2 Discharge letters

A potential station that may arise is the handwritten discharge summary. In the workplace discharge summaries are likely to be electronic, but the same principles will apply to any discharge, as they are the link between secondary and primary care. They cover everything from diagnosis to management, complications and follow-up. The information included must be accurate and succinct as it directly links to the quality of care that patients receive (see *Fig. 28.2*).

In the exam, you are likely to be provided with a template to complete. It usually won't be just a blank piece of paper, but it's worthwhile remembering the following points anyway.

Points to include:
- Admission type
  - Elective / emergency
- Primary diagnosis
- Summary of care received
  - Management
  - Relevant investigations
- Follow-up with primary and secondary care
  - Important co-morbidities
- Medication on discharge
  - Changes to medication and reasoning
- Allergies (new or old)
- Appropriate contact details for the doctor completing discharge.

> **Summary of key points (GET YOUR MARKS):**
> - Check patient details!
> - Try to avoid abbreviations unless they are standardized.
> - Be clear and concise.
> - Remember the GP and the patient can access this document.
> - Use black ink.
> - Write legibly.

Patient Name: Penelope Pitstop	Date of Admission: 02/12/2016
Hospital/NHS Number: 456 3456 756	Date of Discharge: 09/12/2016
D.O.B: 08/09/1940	GP Name and Address: Dr Tophat. Magic
Consultant: Mr Marvellous	Medical Practice, London

Admission

Elective

Define route of admission: Elective, Emergency or GP

Main Condition

Hartmann's Procedure for sigmoid cancer

Give the definitive diagnosis or reason for admission.

Care Summary

Admitted for elective Hartmann's Procedure for Sigmoid carcinoma. Post operatively complicated Acute Kidney Injury 1 secondary to dehydration, this resolved with fluid resuscitation. Stoma working well by Day 3 and Mrs Pitstop confident with self-stoma care. Treated for a UTI just prior to discharge with Trimethoprim for 3/7. Discharged to home once inflammatory markers stabilised, AKI resolved, eating, drinking and mobilising around ward.

This is where to include a story of admission. Keep it brief and concise. 1) PMC 2) Relevant investigations 3) Working diagnosis 4) Management 5) Follow up plans.

Special Investigations/Scans

Contrast CT Abdomen

Any extensive investigation or CT/USS/MRI/Colonoscopy/OGD with relevant or important findings.

Follow up and notes for GP

Please monitor U&Es in 1 week for continued resolution of AKI. Please restart Ramipril for hypertension if kidney function remains stable.

Outpatient appointment with Mr Marvellous in 3 months time.

Any outpatient scans, follow up clinic appointments. Any monitoring or results the GP may need to chase or check.

Past Medical History

Hypertension, Non insulin dependent type 2 Diabetes – Diet controlled

Discharge Destination

Own home

Important for a patient with a stay at a rehabilitation ward or if increased package of care.

TTO

Medication	Dose	Frequency	Indication	Duration
Oramorph	5mg	4 hourly	Pain	PRN – short term
Ramipril	1.25mg		HTN	Hold until repeat U&Es
Trimethoprim	200mg	BD	UTI	Stop 10/12/2016

Allergies NKDA

Completed by Dr William Bosh FY2 (Bleep 0007)

Figure 28.2 Sample discharge letter.

28.3 **Practice scenarios**

1. Charlie Dingle is a 90-year-old man who was admitted with severe community-acquired pneumonia. He is generally quite fit for 90 years, usually on warfarin for his AF and some other blood pressure medications. He also wears a buprenorphine patch due to his OA pain. He had been recovering well on the ward following 48 hours of intravenous antibiotics and was stepped down to oral antibiotics 2 days ago.

   The nurse has called you to see him because he had a fall about an hour ago. It was not witnessed by medical staff, but Mr Dingle seems to think he hit his head. When you arrive to examine him his GCS (Glasgow Coma Scale) score is E2V4M6 and he has a small bruise forming on his occiput. He is moving all four limbs, and pupils are equal and reactive to light. You ask the nursing staff to start neuro observations every hour (the first set are stable); you look up the head injury guidelines and check his last INR (international normalized ratio), which was 3.7. Because he has had a drop in GCS alongside warfarin use, you are concerned that Mr Dingle has had a brain haemorrhage. You book a CT scan and immediately call the radiology registrar to expedite your scan.

   Use SBAR to call the radiologist to stress the urgency of this CT scan.

2. Edna Frog is an unfit, obese 50-year-old lady. Her past medical history includes chronic back pain, hypertension, grommets and gallstones. She was admitted after bouts of right upper quadrant pain and fevers. A diagnosis of cholecystitis was made and she was started on IV antibiotics and a low-fat diet. She complains to you that she is having some chest pain – central and crushing when she is lying in bed. She also says there is some tingling in her left hand. Observations are stable apart from mild tachycardia of 110. You organize the relevant bloods and have a glance at her ECG. The ECG has very obvious ST elevation in anterior leads. You call the cardiologist immediately to discuss further management; you know you need to give aspirin and clopidogrel, but want to double-check your management plan and see when they are able to come and review the patient.

   Use SBAR to call the cardiologist, pick out what is relevant and think about what information you need or want from them.

References

1. Hargie, O. (2006) *The Handbook of Communication Skills*. 3rd ed. Taylor & Francis.
2. Asnani, M.R. (2009) Patient–physician communication. *West Indian Medical Journal*, **58(4)**: 357–61.
3. Kurtz, S.M., Silverman, J.D. and Draper, J. (2005) *Teaching and Learning Communication Skills in Medicine*. 2nd ed. Radcliffe Publishing.
4. Silverman, J.D., Kurtz, S.M. and Draper, J. (2013) *Skills for Communicating with Patients*. 3rd ed. Radcliffe Publishing.
5. Kurtz, S., Silverman, J., Benson, J. and Draper, J. (2003) Marrying Content and Process in Clinical Method Teaching: enhancing the Calgary–Cambridge Guides. *Academic Medicine*, **78(8)**: 802–9.

Index

abdominal pain, 129–30, 139–40, 141, 164–5
abuse, 246, 247–8
acne vulgaris, 192
acute kidney injury (AKI), 148–51
adrenal, 196–7
agenda setting, 9, 18
akinesia, 61–2
alcohol, 14, 39–41
allergies, 232
amenorrhoea, 172
angina, 101–2
anti-diuretic hormone, 198
anxiety, 28, 33–4, 46
asthma, 112
atopic eczema, 191
atrial fibrillation, 102

back pain, 73–4
benign prostatic hyperplasia, 158
bipolar disorder, 37, 46–7
blackouts, *see* syncope
bladder cancer, 160–1
breast-feeding, 236
breast lump, 176–7

CAGE questionnaire, 40
Calgary–Cambridge Model, 7–9
capacity, 205–7
cataracts, 89
chest pain, 92–3, 107–8
chlamydia, 180
chorea, 63
chronic obstructive pulmonary disease (COPD),
    112–13
chronic rhinosinusitis, 125
cirrhosis, 143
clozapine, 52
cognitive impairment, 210–11
collateral history, 208–9
compliance, 233–4, 235
contraceptive history, 173–6, 180–3
cough, 107

delirium, 209–10, 211
dementia, 211, 216–17
depression, 28, 32–3, 48, 211
diabetes mellitus, 199, 202
dialysis, 157–8
diarrhoea, 136–7, 140
diet, 15
diplopia, 86
discharge letter, 289–90
driving, 217
drug misuse, 41–2
DVLA, *see* driving
dysmenorrhoea, 172
dyspareunia, 175
dyspnoea, *see* shortness of breath

dystonia, 63
dysuria, 152–3

ears, 117–19
eating disorders, 42–3
electroconvulsive therapy (ECT), 53
empathy, 8
endoscopy, 144–5
epilepsy, 60–1
exercise, 15, 100

falls, 212
family history, 13
fearful child, 224–5
fever, 169
flank pain, 153–4
flashing lights, 85
floaters, 85
forensic history, 31
fractures, 74, 215
framing, 272
Fraser Guidelines, 224
functional assessment, 213–14

gestational diabetes, 180
glaucoma, 89
growth hormone, 197

haematemesis, 130–2, 139, 140
haematochezia, 135–6, 140, 141
haematuria, 154, 160–1
haemoptysis, 109
hallucinations, 35–6
headache, 56, 67, 165
hearing loss, 117–18
hepatic impairment, 237
hyperkinesia, *see* movement disorders
hypokinesia, *see* movement disorders

ideas, concerns and expectations (ICE), 12, 265–6
illicit drugs, 234–5
immunization, 227–8
infant, 222
infertility, 170
inflammatory bowel disease (IBD), 144
information giving, 17–20
inhalers, 113
insight, 28, 36
intermenstrual bleeding, 173
intermittent claudication, 97
irritable eyes, 86
itching, 186

jaundice, 132–4, 139, 140
joint pain, 70
joint swelling, 72–3

kidney failure, 157–8

language barrier, 241
lithium, 50–1
loss of consciousness, 59–60
lower urinary tract symptoms (LUTS), 152

medication history, 13, 231–8
menopause, 172–3
menorrhagia, 171
menstruation, 170–1
methotrexate, 81
migraine, 67
motivational interviewing, 43–5
movement disorders, 61–3
myocardial infarction, 101–2
myoclonus, 63

nasal discharge, 120
nasal obstruction, 120
negative symptoms, 36
neglect, 248
newborn, 222
normalizing, 8
nose, 119–20

objective structured clinical exam (OSCE), 1
obsessive–compulsive disorder, 37–8, 48
oedema, 97, 167–8
otalgia, 118
otitis media, 125
otorrhoea, 118

palpitations, 94
parathyroid gland, 196
past medical history, 12
past surgical history, 12
peak flow monitoring, 114
peripheral arterial disease, 102–3
personal history, 30
pituitary gland, 195
placental abruption, 179
positive symptoms, 35
postural instability, 62
pre-eclampsia, 179
premorbid personality, 31
pre-school age, 222–3
primary school age, 223
probability, 275
prolactin, 198
prostate cancer, 158
psoriasis, 192
psychosexual history, 31
psychosis, 28, 34–6

rash, 186
red eye, 84

renal impairment, 237
renal stones, 159
research, 273–6
rheumatoid arthritis, 79–81
rigidity, 61
risk, 271–3
risk assessment, 36
role play, 2–3

safeguarding, 245–53
SBAR, 285–6
schizophrenia, 45
SCOFF questionnaire, 42
seizures, see epilepsy
sensory impairment, 207
sex hormones, 198
sexual history, 173–6
shared decision making, 20–2
shortness of breath, 94–5, 106–7, 167
signposting, 9
social history, 13
SOCRATES, 11, 70; see also inside front cover
SPIKES protocol, 256–60
spirituality, 15
sputum, 108–9
steroids, 193
stiffness, 72
stroke, 64
substance misuse, 39–42
suicide risk, 38–9
summarizing, 9
syncope, 59–60, 95–7
systems review, 23–6

tanning, 187
teenager, 223–4
telephone consultation, 285–7
throat, 120–1
thyroid gland, 195–6, 202–3
tics, 63
tinnitus, 118–19
tonsillitis, 126
tremor, 61, 62, 63

urinary incontinence, 154–5, 159–60

vaginal bleeding, 164
vaginal discharge, 175
vertigo, 119
visual loss, 85
vomiting, 137–8, 140, 141, 165

weight loss, 134–5
wheeze, 108
writing notes, 287–8